STREET ATLAS
Durham

Contents

PHILIP'S

First colour edition published 1996 by

Ordnance Survey
Romsey Road
Maybush
Southampton SO16 4GU

and

George Philip Ltd.
an imprint of Reed Books
Michelin House, 81 Fulham Road, London SW3 6RB
and Auckland, Melbourne, Singapore and Toronto

ISBN 0-540-06365-7 (Philip's, hardback)
ISBN 0-540-06366-5 (Philip's, wire-o)

ISBN 0-319-00849-5 (Ordnance Survey, hardback)
ISBN 0-319-00850-9 (Ordnance Survey, wire-o)

Printed and bound in Spain by Cayfosa

Key to map symbols

Motorway	British Rail station
Primary Routes (Dual carriageway and single)	Private railway station
A Roads (Dual carriageway and single)	Bus, coach station
B Roads (Dual carriageway and single)	Ambulance station
C Roads (Dual carriageway and single)	Coastguard station
Minor Roads	Fire station
Roads under construction	Police station
County boundaries	Casualty entrance to hospital
All Railways	Churches, Place of worship
Track or private road	Hospital
Gate or obstruction to traffic (restrictions may not apply at all times or to all vehicles)	Information Centre
All paths, bridleways, BOAT's, RUPP's, dismantled railways, etc.	Parking

> The representation in this atlas of a road, track or path is no evidence of the existence of a right of way

	Post Office
	Public Convenience
174 Adjoining page indicator	Important buildings, schools, colleges, universities and hospitals

Acad	**Academy**	Mon	**Monument**	River Soar — Water Name
Cemy	**Cemetery**	Mus	**Museum**	
C Ctr	**Civic Centre**	Obsy	**Observatory**	Stream
CH	**Club House**	Pal	**Royal Palace**	
Coll	**College**	PH	**Public House**	River or canal (minor and major)
Ex H	**Exhibition Hall**	Resr	**Reservoir**	
Ind Est	**Industrial Estate**	Ret Pk	**Retail Park**	Water Fill
Inst	**Institute**	Sch	**School**	
Ct	**Law Court**	Sh Ctr	**Shopping Centre**	Tidal Water
L Ctr	**Leisure Centre**	Sta	**Station**	
LC	**Level Crossing**	TH	**Town Hall/House**	Woods
Liby	**Library**	Trad Est	**Trading Estate**	
Mkt	**Market**	Univ	**University**	Houses
Meml	**Memorial**	YH	**Youth Hostel**	

0	¼	½	¾	1 mile
0	250 m	500 m	750 m	1 Kilometre

The scale of the maps is 5.52 cm to 1 km (3½ inches to 1 mile)

The small numbers around the edges of the maps identify the 1 kilometre National Grid lines

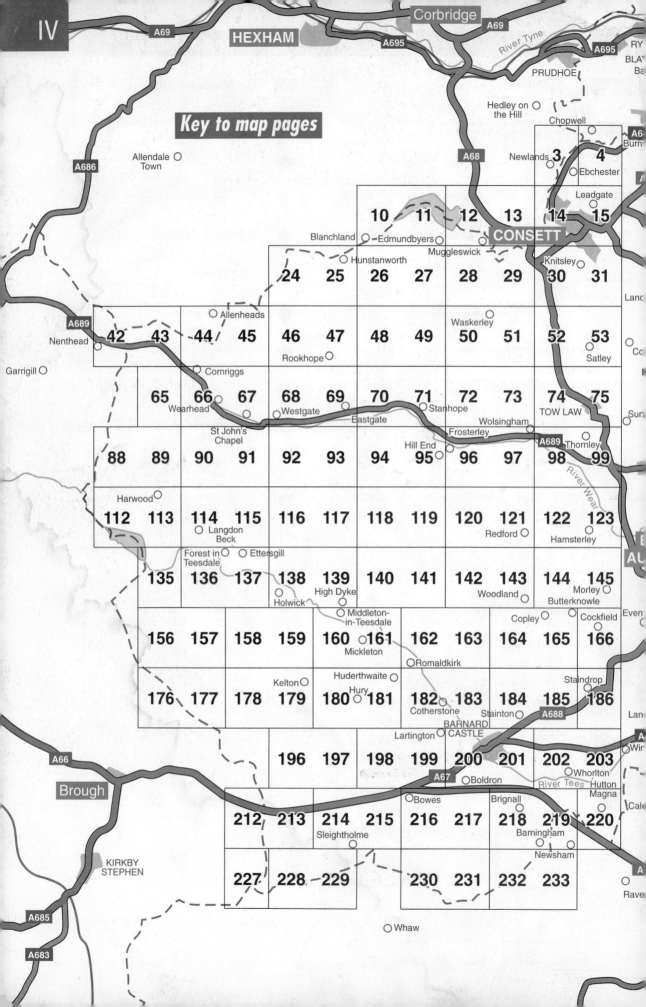

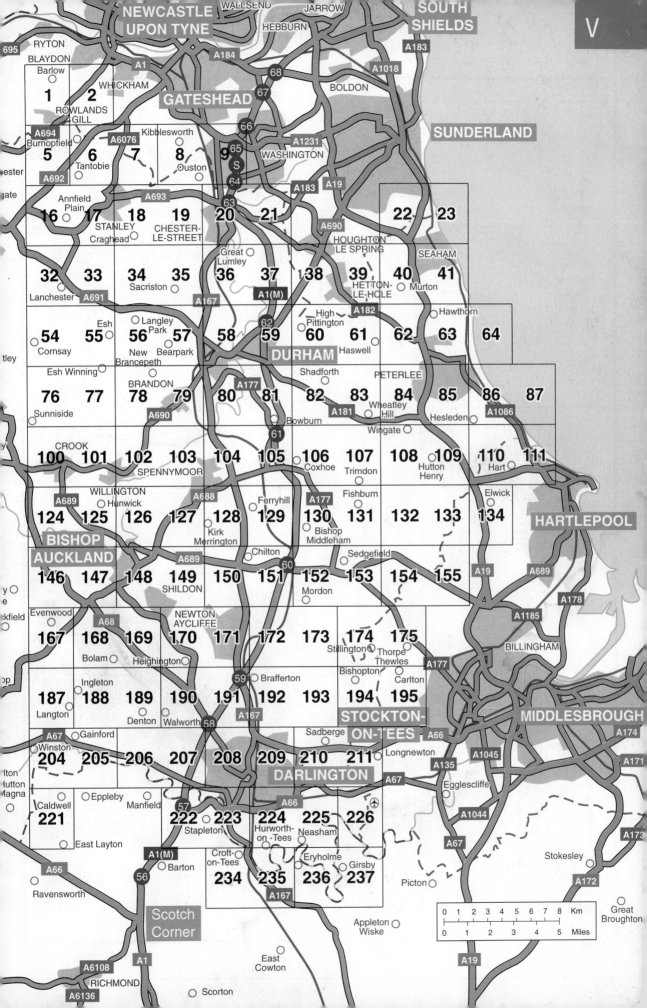

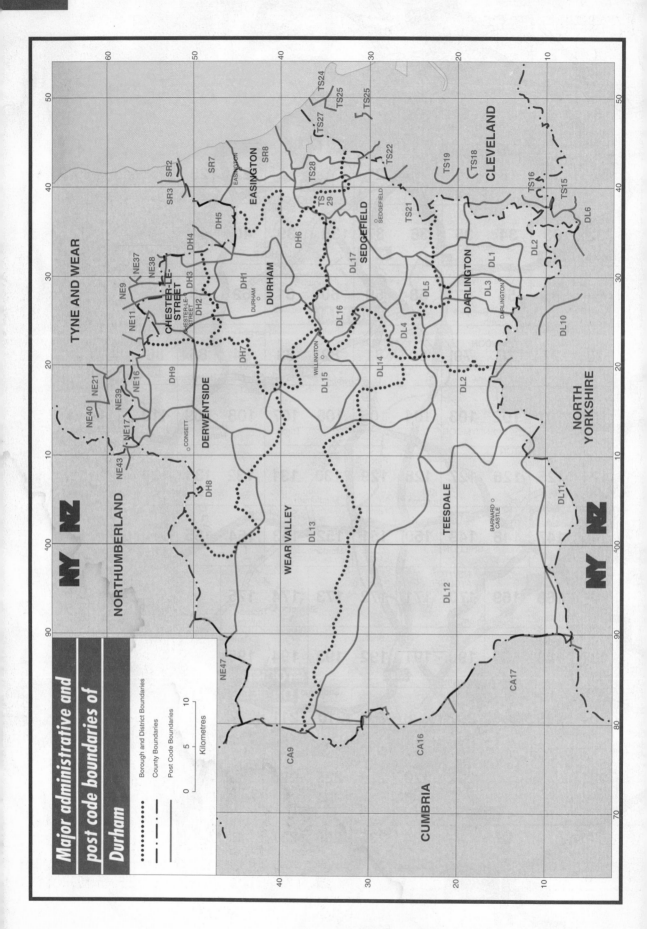

Major administrative and post code boundaries of *Durham*

Borough and District Boundaries

County Boundaries

Post Code Boundaries

Kilometres

0   5   10

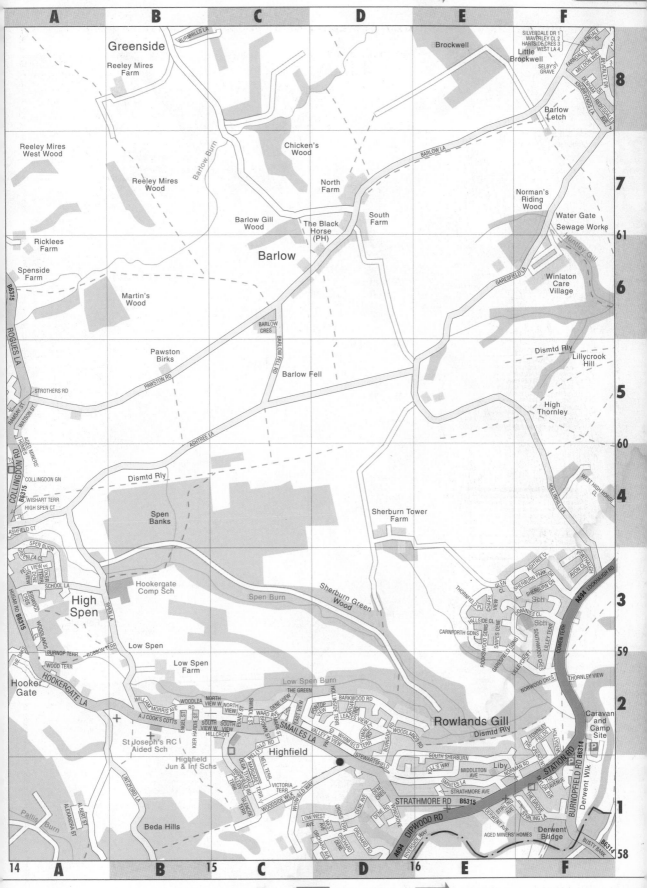

A B C D E F

8

7

61

6

5

60

4

3

59

2

1

58

Greenside

Reeley Mires Farm

BURNHILLS LA

Brockwell

Little Brockwell

SILVERDALE DR 1
WAVERLEY CL 2
HARTSIDE CRES 3
WEST LA 4

FARNDALE
GLENDALE CL
BEVERLEY DR

SELBY'S GRAVE

MELDON WAY

DENHAM DR
REDESDALE
KINGSDENNIS LA

Reeley Mires West Wood

Barlow Burn

Chicken's Wood

Barlow Letch

BARLOW LA

Reeley Mires Wood

North Farm

Norman's Riding Wood

Water Gate Sewage Works

Ricklees Farm

Barlow Gill Wood

South Farm

The Black Horse (PH)

GARESFIELD LA

Huntley Gill

Winlaton Care Village

B6315

ROGUES LA

Spenside Farm

Barlow

Martin's Wood

BARLOW CRES

BARLOW FELL RD

Dismtd Rly

Lillycrook Hill

Pawston Birks

PAWSTON RD

Barlow Fell

High Thornley

STROTHERS RD

RAMSAY ST
WATSON ST

ASHTREE LA

WEST HIGH HORSE CL

COLLINGDON RD

AGED MINERS HOMES

Dismtd Rly

HOLLINHILL LA

Sherburn Tower Farm

COLLINGDON GN
WISHART TERR
HIGH SPEN CT
ASHFIELD CT

Spen Banks

SPEN BURN
GREENLEA CL
FELL VIEW
STOKOE TERR
DENE
SCHOOL LA
ELMWOOD CRES

Hookergate Comp Sch

Sherburn Green Wood

ASHTREE CL
SHERBURN PARK
PONTHAUGH
AVON CL
THORNFIELD PL
GLEN
CHAPEL VIEW
SHERBURN GN
DOMNIES CT
Sch

High Spen

SPEN LA

Spen Burn

HILLSIDE CL
SNIPES DENE
Sch
GARESFIELD GDNS
LILLEY CROFT
BOWER TERR

A694 LOCKHAUGH RD

WOODLANDS
HILLAR RD
B6315

Low Spen

CARNFORTH GDNS

ROOKSWOOD GDNS
SOUTHWOOD CRES
SOUTHWOOD GDNS

BURNOP TERR
ROBSON TERR

Low Spen Farm

Thornley View

NORWOOD CRES

WOOD TERR

HOOKERGATE LA

Hooker Gate

Low Spen Burn

THE GREEN

Rowlands Gill

Dismtd Rly

Caravan and Camp Site

WILLIAM MORRIS AVE
WOODLEA
NORTH VIEW W
NORTH VIEW
A J COOK'S COTTS
ENGEL ST
DENE VIEW
WARD AVE
BROWNS ST
SWINDLE ST
PONTOP VIEW
BARKWOOD RD
HOLLINSIDE TERR
LEAZES VIEW
WOODLANDS RD

STATION RD

BURNOPFIELD RD B6314

Derwent Wlk

KIER HARDIE ST
SOUTH VIEW W
SOUTH VIEW
HILLCROFT
VALLEY VIEW
EAST VIEW
SMAILES LA
PARK VIEW
WHINFIELD TERR
BURNSIDE

THE FIELDS

TOWNLEY
HOLLYSIDE
THE CRESCENT

St Joseph's RC Aided Sch

Highfield Jun & Inf Schs

Highfield

STEWARTSFIELD

SOUTH SHERBURN
KELLS WAY

Liby

THE AVENUE

Libby

MIDDLETON AVE
NORMAN RD
THE GROVE

ALBERT ST
LINTZFORD LA

VICTORIA TERR
DELGA TERR
MARGARET TERR
GLENCOE TERR
WOODSIDE WLK

WHINFIELD WAY

SMAILES LA

STRATHMORE AVE

STRATHMORE RD B6315

STIRLING AVE
STIRLING LA

DERWENT WAY

ALEXANDRA ST
Pallis Burn

Beda Hills

LOW WEST AVE
CROSS TERR
DENE AVE
ORCHARD AVE
DENE RD
INGROVE
ORCHARD RD

A694 DIPWOOD RD

AGED MINERS' HOMES

Derwent Bridge

BUSTY BANK
B6314

RIVERSIDE WAY

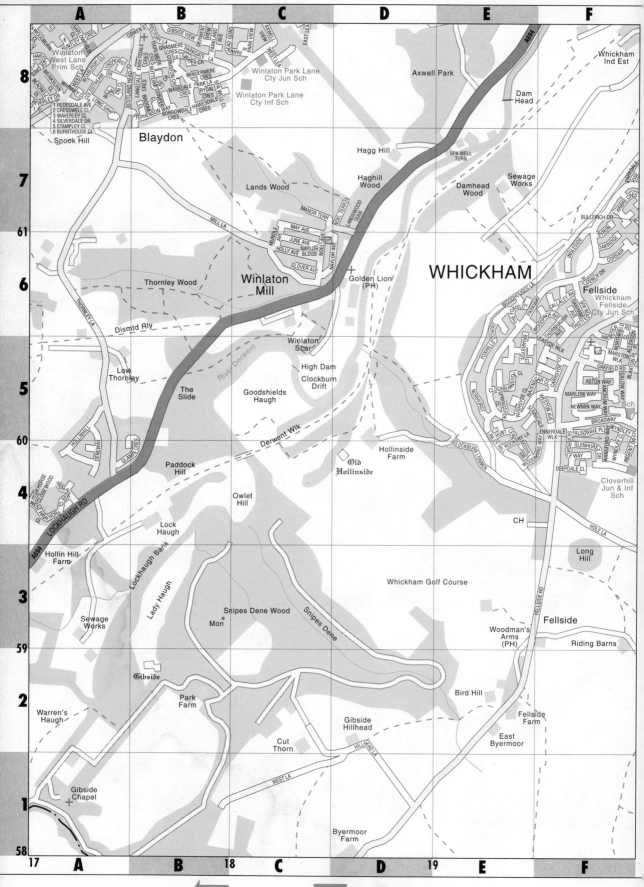

A   **B**   **C**   **D**   **E**   **F**

8

Winlaton
West Lane
Prim Sch

1 REDESDALE AVE
2 CRESSWELL CL
3 WAVERLEY CL
4 SILVERDALE DR
5 STAMPLEY CL
6 BURNTHOUSE CL

Winlaton Park Lane
Cty Jun Sch

Winlaton Park Lane
Cty Inf Sch

Axwell Park

Dam
Head

Whickham
Ind Est

Snook Hill

Blaydon

7

Lands Wood

Hagg Hill

Haghill
Wood

SPA WELL
TURN

Damhead
Wood

Sewage
Works

BULLFINCH DR

61

MILL LA

MAY AVE

JUNE AVE

HOLLY AVE

CLOVER AVE

NAYLOR BLDGS

6

Thornley Wood

Winlaton
Mill

Golden Lion
(PH)

WHICKHAM

Fellside

Whickham
Fellside
Cty Jun Sch

THORNLEY LA

Dismtd Rly

Winlaton
Scar

High Dam

Clockburn
Drift

River Derwent

5

Low
Thornley

The
Slide

Goodshields
Haugh

Derwent Wlk

60

HOLLINHILL

DENEWAY

GLAMIS CRES

Paddock
Hill

Hollinside
Farm

Old
Hollinside

CLOCKBURN LONNEN

Cloverhill
Jun & Inf
Sch

4

High Horse
Close Wood

WEST HIGH HORSE

LOCKHAUGH RD

Owlet
Hill

CH

HOLE LA

FELLSIDE RD

Long
Hill

A694

Hollin Hill
Farm

Lock
Haugh

3

Sewage
Works

Lockhaugh Bank

Lady Haugh

Snipes Dene Wood

Mon

Snipes Dene

Whickham Golf Course

Woodman's
Arms
(PH)

Fellside

Riding Barns

59

Gibside

Park
Farm

Bird Hill

Fellside
Farm

2

Warren's
Haugh

Gibside
Hillhead

East
Byermoor

Cut
Thorn

HILL HEAD LA

1

Gibside
Chapel

WEST LA

Byermoor
Farm

58

17   **A**   **B**   18   **C**   **D**   19   **E**   **F**

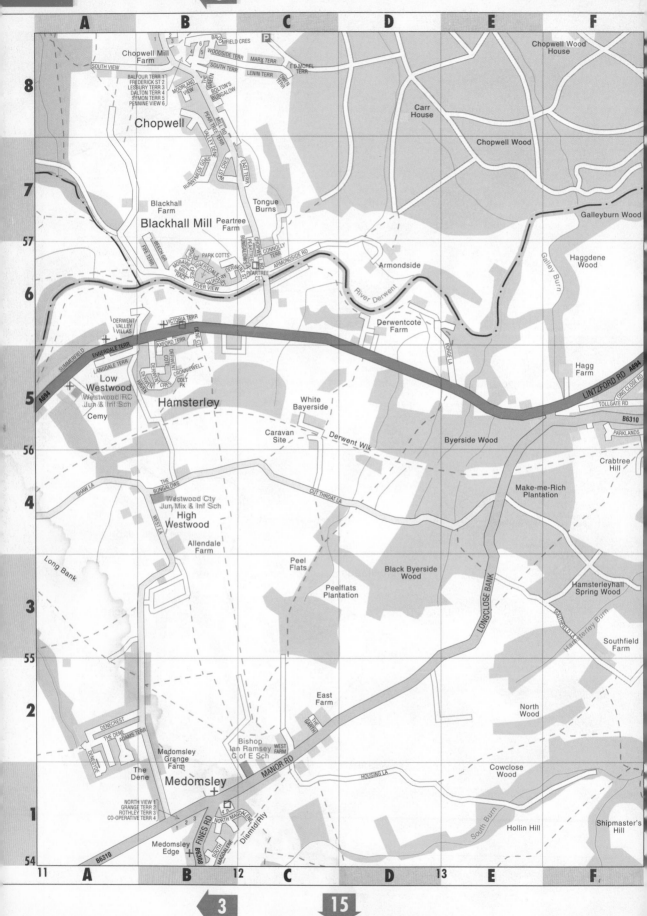

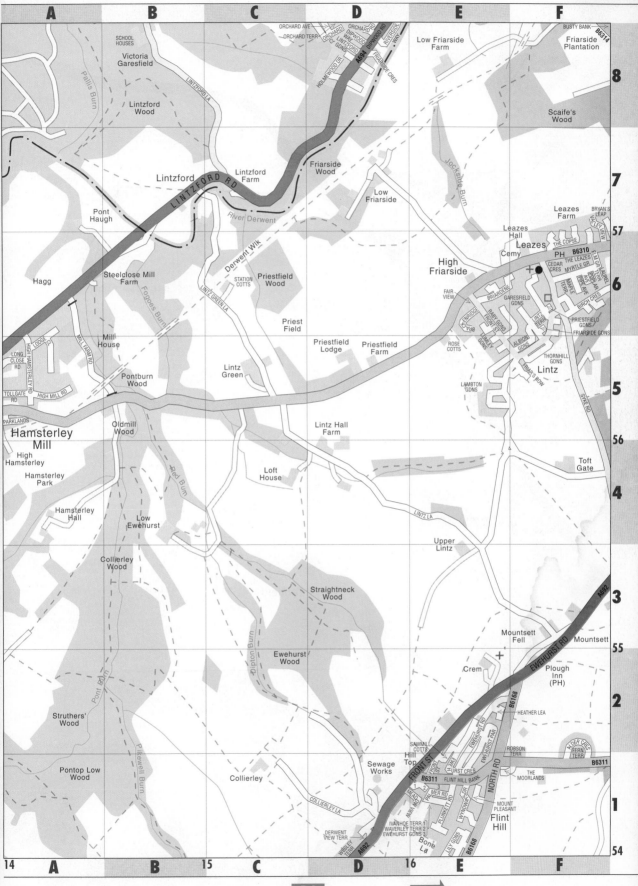

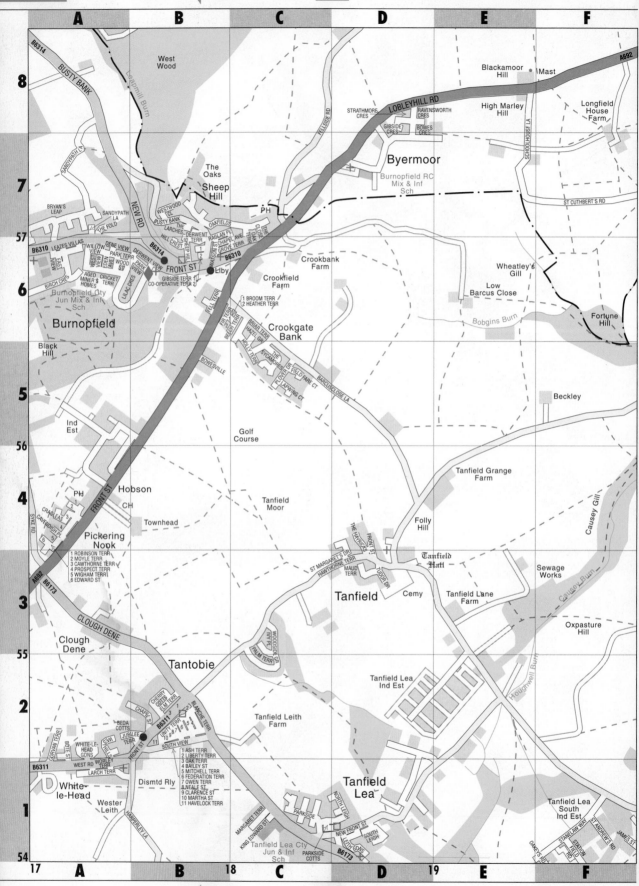

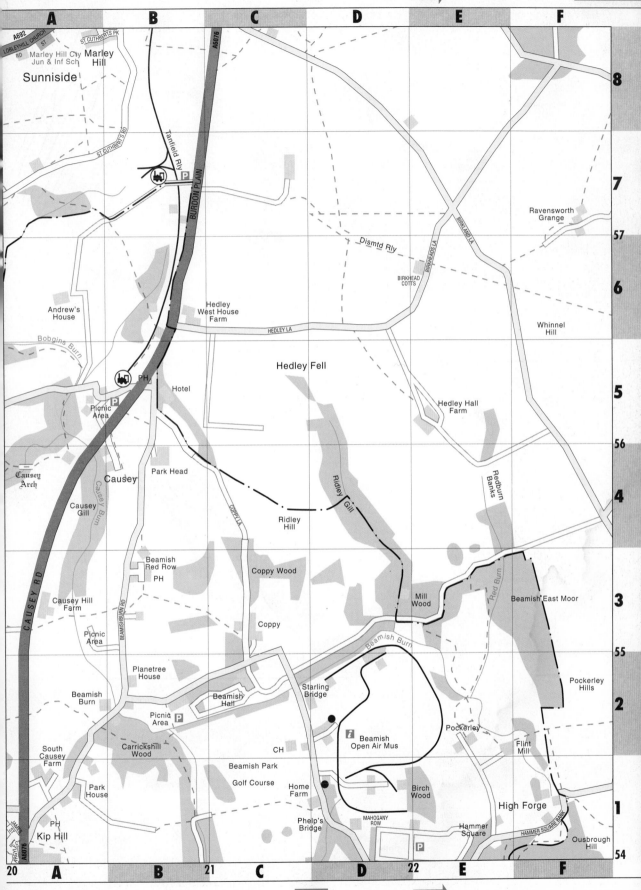

A B C D E F

8

7

57

6

Ravensworth Grange

Whinnel Hill

5

56

4

Beamish East Moor

3

55

Pockerley Hills

2

1

54

A B C D E F

A692
LOBLEYHILL CHURCH
RD
ST CUTHBERTS PK
Marley Hill Cty
Jun & Inf Sch
Marley Hill
Sunniside
ST CUTHBERT'S RD
Tanfield Rly
BURDON PLAIN
A6076
Dismtd Rly
BIRKLAND LA
BIRKHEADS LA
BIRKHEAD COTTS
Andrew's House
Hedley West House Farm
HEDLEY LA
Hedley Fell
Bobgins Burn
PH
Hotel
Hedley Hall Farm
Picnic Area
Causey Arch
Causey
Park Head
Causey Gill
Causey Burn
COPPY LA
Ridley Gill
Ridley Hill
Redburn Banks
Causey Hill Farm
Beamish Red Row
PH
Coppy Wood
Mill Wood
Red Burn
Picnic Area
Coppy
CAUSEY RD
BEAMISHBURN RD
Planetree House
Beamish Burn
Starling Bridge
Beamish Burn
Pockerley
Beamish Hall
Picnic Area
Flint Mill
South Causey Farm
Carrickshill Wood
CH
Beamish Open Air Mus
Beamish Park Golf Course
Home Farm
Birch Wood
High Forge
A6076
PH
Kip Hill
Park House
Phelp's Bridge
MAHOGANY ROW
Hammer Square
HAMMER SQUARE BANK
Ousbrough Hill

20 A 21 C 22 E F

A · B · C · D · E · F

8

Old Ravensworth Farm

Chapel Banks

Beldy

Meadowgate

Lamesley Bridge

South Farm

Longacre Wood

Hotel

Coltspool Bridge

Tyne Marshalling Yards

THE BUNGALOWS

Moor Mill Farm

7

Briar Dene

Mitcheson's Gill

Strandy Burn

Coltspool Burn

River Team

57

Kibblesworth East Farm

1 THE WOODLANDS
2 WOODLANDS CT
3 BARRACK TERR

6

High Hills

Kibblesworth West Farm

THE CRESCENT 1
CORONATION TERR 2

PROSPECT TERR

Liby

Sch

MOORMILL LA

GREENFORD

Sch

Kibblesworth

Clarty La

Sewage Works

5

Kibblesworth Grange

Brick Works

Urpeth Bridge

56

Cooper House

White House

4

RIDING LA

Urpeth Wood

Low Urpeth

Kibblesworth Common

Riding Farm

Cooper Wood

River Team

Team Valley

Walter's Wood

Ouston

3

West Banks

55

Pockerley Bldgs

Target Wood

Urpeth

CORNSAY 1
PRIMROSE GDNS 2
CALLANDER 3
CANNOCK 4

2

Greenburn Howl

Ouston Cty Jun Sch

Bog Hill

Money Hills

P

1

Urpeth Forge

Urpeth North Farm

Mire Dubs

St Benet's RC Jun Mix & Inf Sch

Martin Scar

Mount Escob

High Urpeth

54

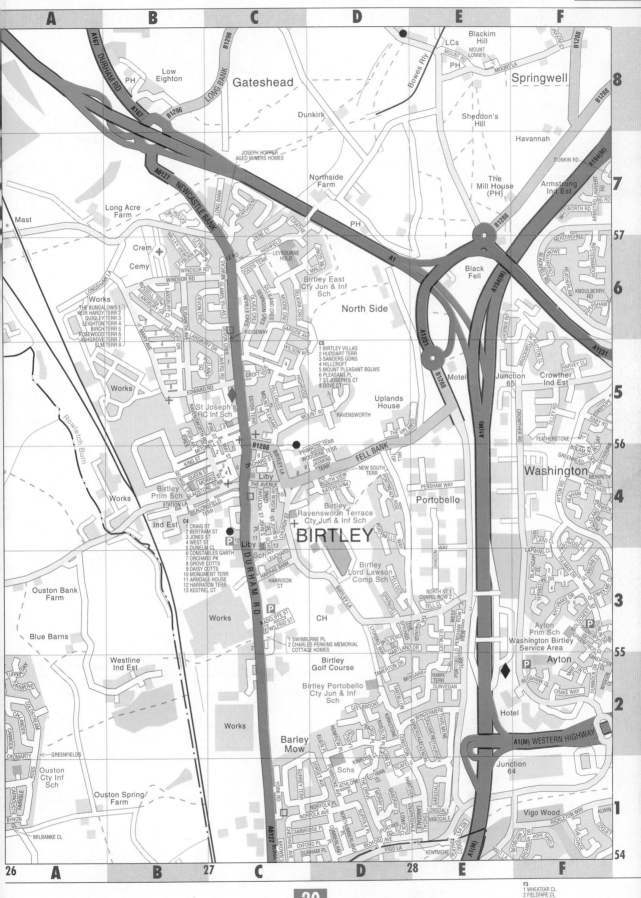

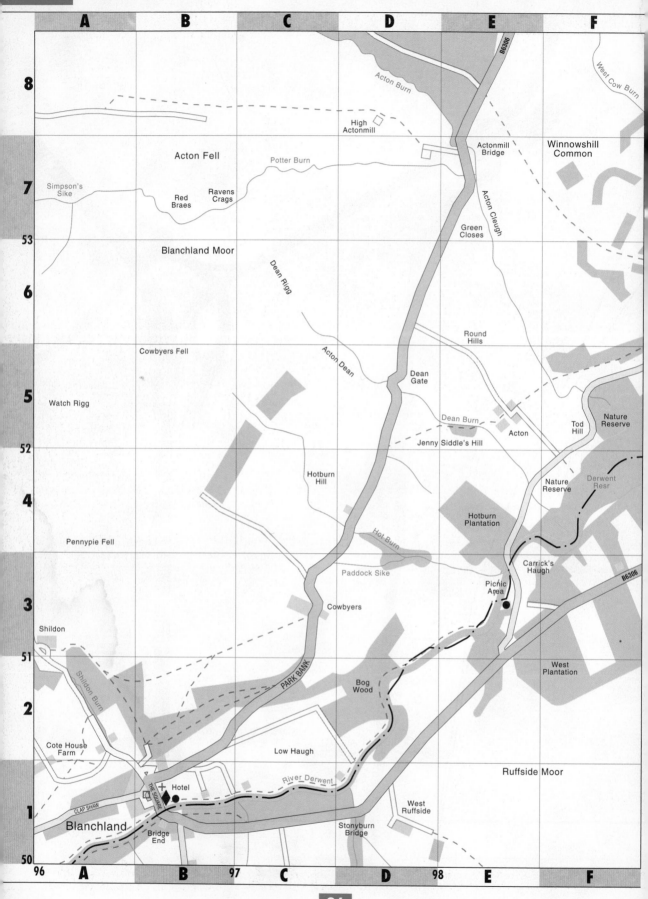

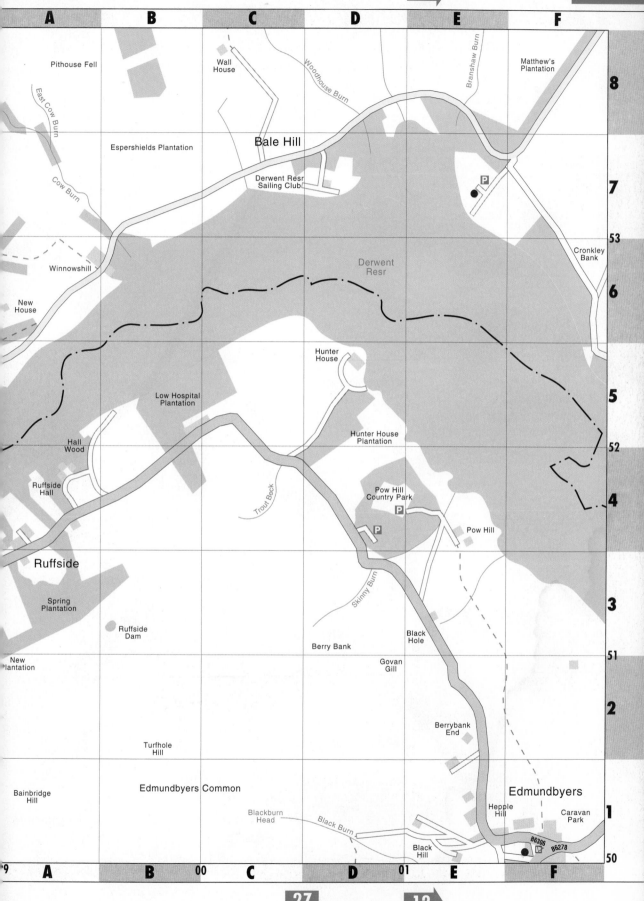

Pithouse Fell

East Cow Burn

Espershields Plantation

Wall House

Woodhouse Burn

Bale Hill

Branshaw Burn

Matthew's Plantation

8

Cow Burn

Derwent Resr Sailing Club

P

7

Winnowshill

Derwent Resr

53

Cronkley Bank

New House

6

Low Hospital Plantation

Hunter House

Hall Wood

Hunter House Plantation

5

Ruffside Hall

Trout Beck

52

Pow Hill Country Park

P

Pow Hill

4

Ruffside

P

Spring Plantation

Ruffside Dam

Berry Bank

Skinny Burn

Black Hole

3

New Plantation

Govan Gill

51

Turfhole Hill

Berrybank End

2

Bainbridge Hill

Edmundbyers Common

Edmundbyers

Blackburn Head

Black Burn

Hepple Hill

Caravan Park

1

Black Hill

B6306

B6278

50

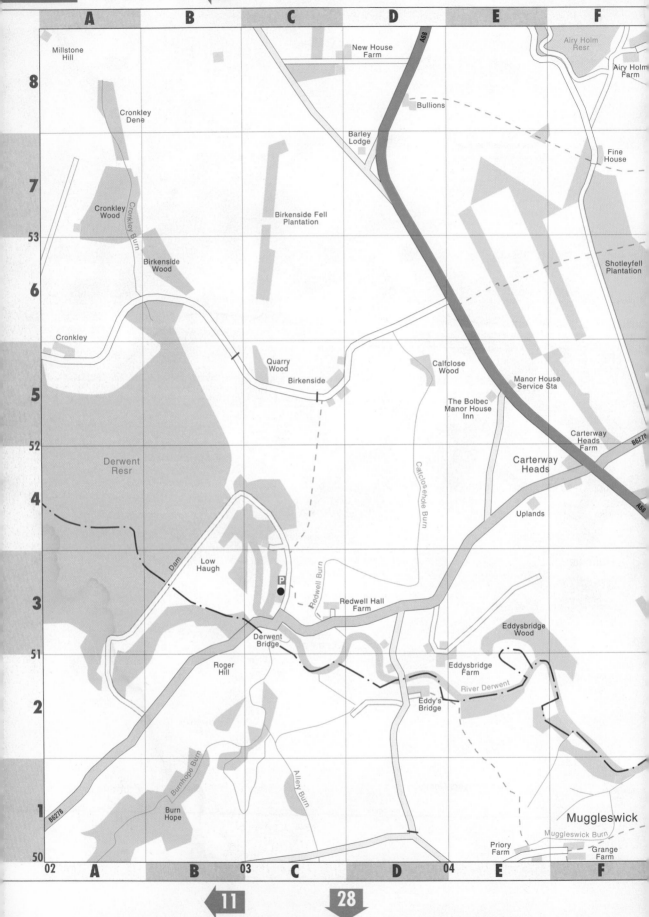

D4	F2	F3	10 PROSPECT ST	20 HARTINGTON ST
1 TEMPLAR ST	1 JOHN STREET SQ	1 JAMESON ST	11 GARDEN CL	21 HERBERT ST
2 HAWTHORN ST	2 ANN ST	2 AVONDALE RD	12 GARDEN PL	
3 ST OSWIN'S PL	3 SEYMOUR ST	3 HUTCHINSON AVE	13 CLARENDON ST	F4
4 HAWTHORN COTTS	4 ROSEBERY TERR	4 BEVERLEY GDNS	14 STANLEY ST	1 STRATFORD GDNS
	5 KELVIN GDNS	5 BEVERLEY TERR	15 STANLEY GDNS	2 BEACONSFIELD ST
	6 UNSWORTH ST	6 BARR HILLS	16 PALM ST	3 MORLEY GDNS
	7 UNSWORTH GDNS	7 BELLE VUE GDNS	17 LIVINGSTONE ST	4 BALFOUR ST
		8 CLEADON ST	18 MAPLE ST	
		9 PROSPECT PL	19 SHERBURN VILLAS	

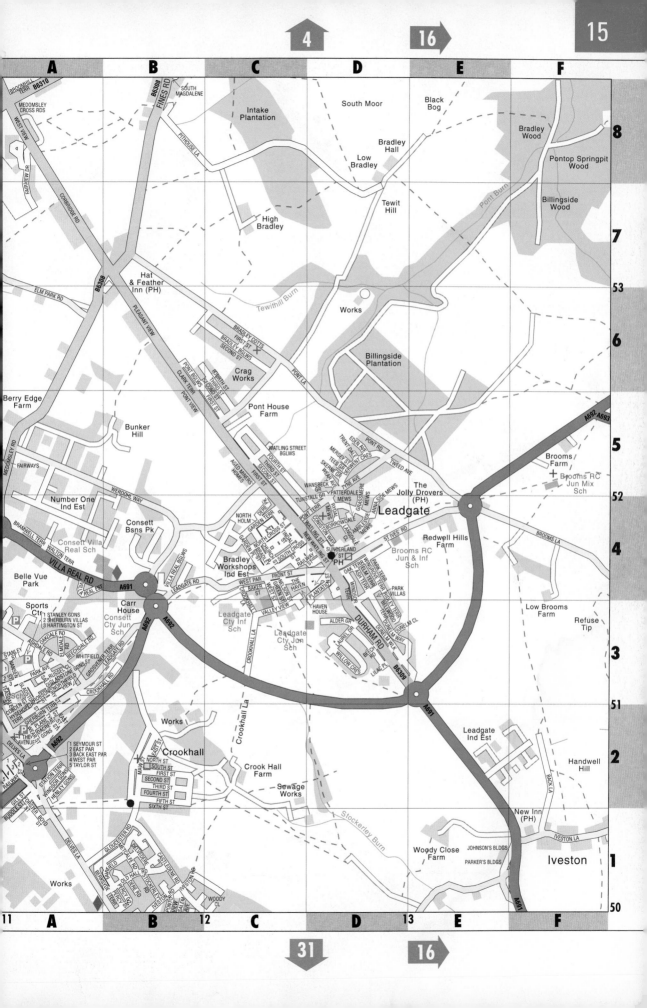

A B C D E F

8

Pontop
Springpit
Wood

Pontop Hall

Pikewell Burn

A692

BOWLES SOUTH MEADOWS

Dipton

DELIGHT ROW

CO-OPERATIVE BLDGS 1
CO-OPERATIVE TERR W 2
Collierley Cty
Jun & Inf Sch

FRONT ST

NINIAN TERR

ST JOHN'S ST

ST EDMUND'S TERR

TENNYSON GDNS

DELIGHT BANK

MURRAY TERR

COLERIDGE ST

GEORGE ST

WORDSWORTH GDNS

DELIGHT CT

CATCHWELL RD

EAST VIEW

CO-OPERATIVE TERR E

Simpson's
Hill

Flint
Hill

LILY GDNS

B6168

LILY BGLWS

POPLAR
GR

Dipton RC
Jun & Inf Sch

BRADLEY CLOSE DR

UNITY TERR

BRADLEY TERR

Harelaw
Ind Est

BUSHBLADES LA

Low
Windways
Farm

Bush
Blades

7

SWINBURNE TERR

JAMES ST

PIKE'S

PONTOP'S DE

PARK VILLAS

WOODLANDS TERR

FARRELL'S AVE

SUNNY TERR

BEECH GR

Cemy

FONDLYSET LA

Stob
House

NORTH RD

HARELAW GDNS

Hare Law

53

Pontop

HEDLEY TERR

DOUGLAS TERR

Pontop Pike

Masts

TV and WT
Sta

Pontop Pike
Farm

Pontop Fell

PONTOP PIKE LA

Cemy

CARRMYERS

Hare Law
Sch

Harelaw

Carrmyers
Farm

6

A692

HARPER

CENTURY TERR

KINKELL

TOLLGATE BGLWS

BEVERLEY

ASHILL

TALLOW

ST

GREEN LA

FIGERLEY GDNS

TERR

LANGDON

HEATHFIELD GDNS

PRINCE'S ST

KING ST

BETHANY GDNS

RYDE TERR

BETHANY TERR 1
SANDRINGHAM DR 2
RIDING HILL RD 3
RYDE TERRACE BGLWS 4

West Kyo

5

A693

East
Castle

STONYHEAP LA

Newhouse Burn

Catchgate

LUMSDEN TERR 1
PINE TERR 2
MAPLE TERR 3
HILDA ST 4
PERCY AVE 5
TROWSDALE ST 6
LILAC TERR 7
ASH TERR 8
OLD BLACKETT ST 9
NEW BLACKETT ST 10
BACK VICTORIA TERR 11

ANNUM TERR

ELM TERR

SWAN ST

BEECH TERR

VICTORIA TERR

10

LIBRARY

YORK ST

KYO RD

HEXHAM

GSOR DR

MANOR

LOW CHURCH ST

FINES PK

RYDE TERR

52

Catchgate Cty
Jun & Inf Schs

Annfield
House

Loud
Hill

BLACKETT ST

ANNFIELD PL

DAWOOD

ALLENDA

Annfield
Plain

Lib't

ANTLIFF TERR 1
BOURNE TERR 2
OAKWOOD
CT

QUEENS TER

DUNN ST

PONTOP
CT

GREENFIELD TERR

Greencroft
Comp Sch

STAINDROP
TERR

NEW FRONT ST

RAILWAY GDNS

FRONT ST

HARTSIDE
COTTS

B6168

STATION

4

BROOMS LA

Loud
Hill

LOUD TERR

DERWENT TERR

FAIRVIEW

Greencroft

SNOWDON TERR

WEST RD

CLAVERING
PL

NORTHGATE

S

51

A693

Stony
Heap

Copwell House
Farm

Refuse Tip

HANGINGSTONE LA

Hanging
Stone

DISMTD RLY

LARWOOD CT

THE AVENUE

THE VILLAS

LOUD VIEW

WESTWAY

PONTOP TERR

CHURSIDE TERR

GRAMPIAN

CREFELL

Annfield Plain
Cty Inf Sch

1 SKIDDAW CT
2 HELVELLYN CT
3 CHEDDAR CT
4 CRAGSIDE CT
5 CHEVIOT CT

ST AIDAN'S
CRES

DODD TERR

P

3

Sunnyside

Newhouse Burn

STONYHEAP LA

Boxers'
Hill

1 GREENCROFT TERR
2 MOOR VIEW TERR

Greencroft
Ind Pk

2

Bank Foot
Farm

LUNDS LA

Durham
Hill

GORECOCK LA

Greencroft
Ind Est

Park
Head

TOWER RD

Caravan
Site

1

Bank Top
Farm

WESTOW LA

Durhamhill
Wood

Moorside

TOWER BANK

50

14 A B 15 C D 16 E F

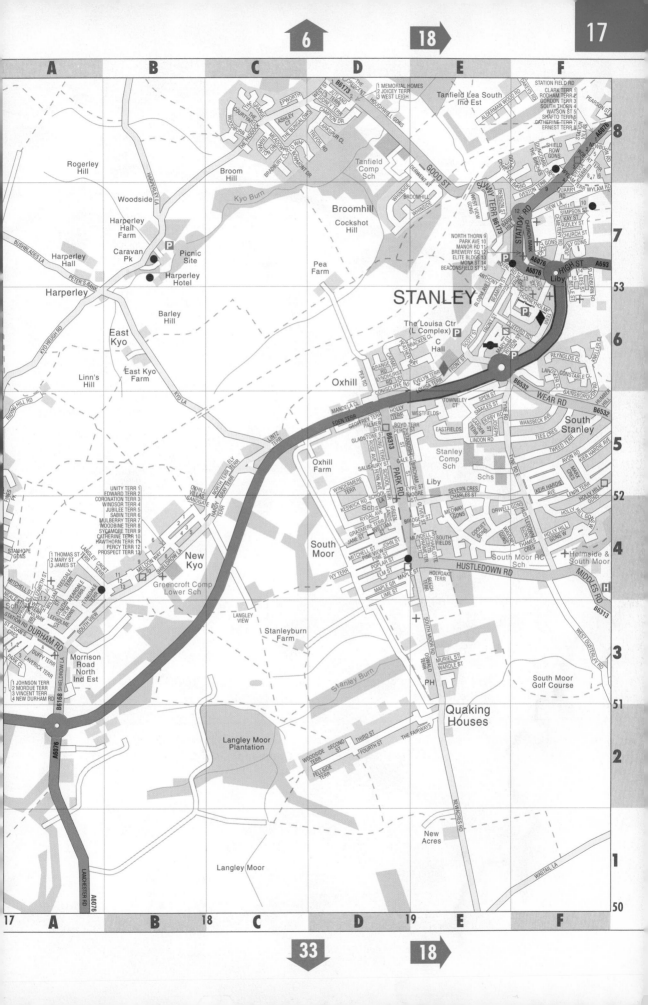

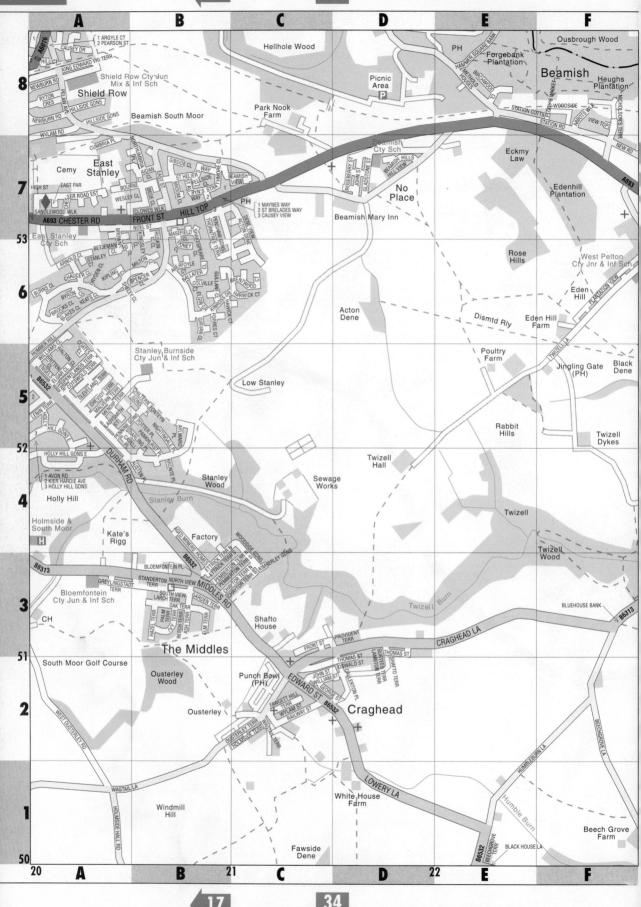

C2
1 REAY CT
2 GIBBS CT
3 PENTLAND CT
4 LAWSON CT
5 RIDDELL CT

A B C D E F

8

Penshaw

HARGILL DR
SETTING STONES
VIGO LA
SWINHOPE
ROCKHOPE
LINBURN WAY
ALDERWOOD
RICKLETON WAY
WEST WARD
SOUTH CRES
WEST CRES
ST GEORGE'S EST
BONEMILL LA
WEST AVE
EAST AVE
NEW RD
THE GENERAL'S WOOD
VIGO LA
WASHINGTON HIGHWAY
BIDDICK LA
Fatfield Prim Sch
WEST BRIDGE ST
ST STEPHENS CL
BRANDON
DALE
STATION RD
BEATRICE TERR
SANDWELL DR
WINSTON GN
BISHOPDALE
LAMBTON TERR
GLADSTONE TERR
The General's Wood
Picnic Area
Chartershaugh Bridge
WASHINGTON HIGHWAY
Penshaw Park

North Belt

7

Biddick Gill Wood

A102
53

Virginia Water
Three Acre Clump
HARRATON TERR
River Wear
Shepherd's Gill
Biddick Hall

6

Lambton Park
New Bridge
Lambton Castle
Sheep Hill
THE AVENUE
Biddick Woods

Lamb Bridge
Scorer's Wood
BLACK DR
FENCE RD
Bowes House
Shiney Row

Kennel Field
The Grange
The Paddocks
Bowes House Farm
WEARDALE WAY
GAINSBOROUGH CRES
BURNDEN GR
PADDOCK CL
GOLF COURSE

5

Kennel Pond
Wapping Bridge
A183
BRIAR LEA
BOWES LEA
BRIAR CL
BRIAR LEA

52

White House
SOUTH BELT
Estate Houses
PARK VIEW

4

A1052
HOUGHTON GATE
County Show Ground (Agricultural)
CHESTER RD
Bournmoor Cty Jun & Inf Sch
Burnside

3

FORGE LA
ST BARNABAS
CASTLEREAGH
THE MEADOWS
BEUMARIS
MERE
VIOLET TERR
LILAC CRES
HIGH ARLINGTON CL
CARNATION AVE
MEDWYN CL
ALVIN CT
ASTER TERR
MARGOD CL
PRIMROSE CL
LAMBOURNE CL
AGED MINERS HOMES NORTH
MEADOW GRANGE
New Lambton

Lumley Forge Bridge
PH
PRIMROSE HILL
ELLESMERE
Bournmoor
Primrose Hill
Lumley Park Burn
Weardale Way
WILL TERR
CALTON CT
PANFIELD TERR
LANGTON TERR

51

Lumley Park Wood
The Manor House
PH
Brecon Hill
FORGE LA

2

Castle Dene
ROPERY LA
LUMLEY NEW RD
A1(M)
SCORERS LA
B1284
NEY ST
SCHOOL
HIGH ROW
FINCHALE
Fence Houses
Woodlea Cty Jun & Inf Sch
HENRY ST
SOUTH CRES
Co-operative TERR
WOODLANDS
MORTON
WOODLAND GRANGE
RAVENSWORTH RD
AVENUE VIVIAN
STATION TERR

BACK LA
AGED MINERS' HOMES
TINKLER TERR
Lumley Thicks
Woodstone Village
MAPLEWOOD ST
OAK ST
BRIAR RD
PINEWOOD ST
ATWOOD
BRIARWOOD
ELM WOOD RD
GILL CRESCENT N
GILL CRESCENT S
MORTON GRANGE TERR
STATION AVE N
LG
A1052

1

WOODSTONE TERR
Woodstone Farm House
EWE HILL TERRACE W
EWE HILL TERR
STATION AVE S
EWE HILL COTTS

50

A B 30 C D 31 E F

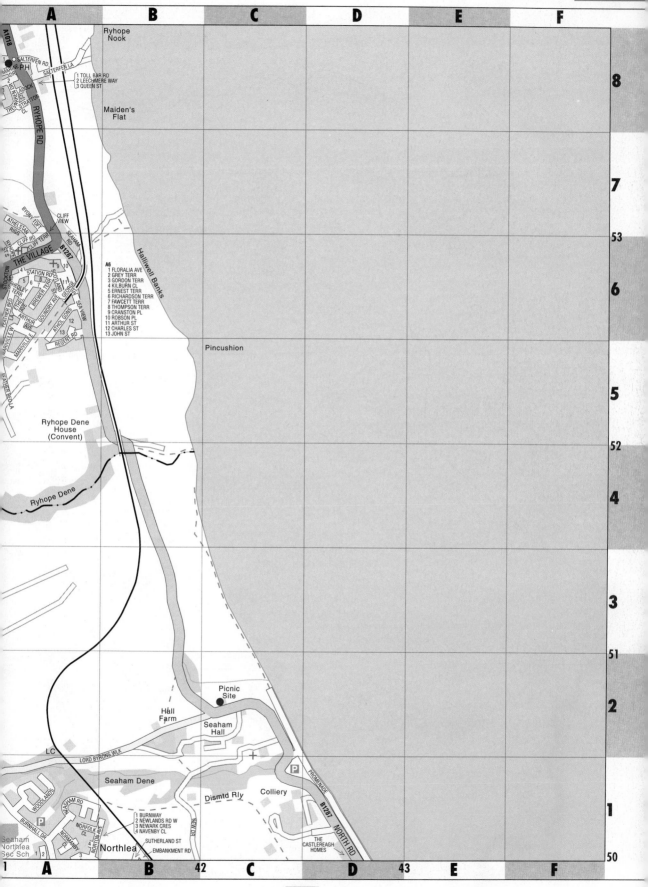

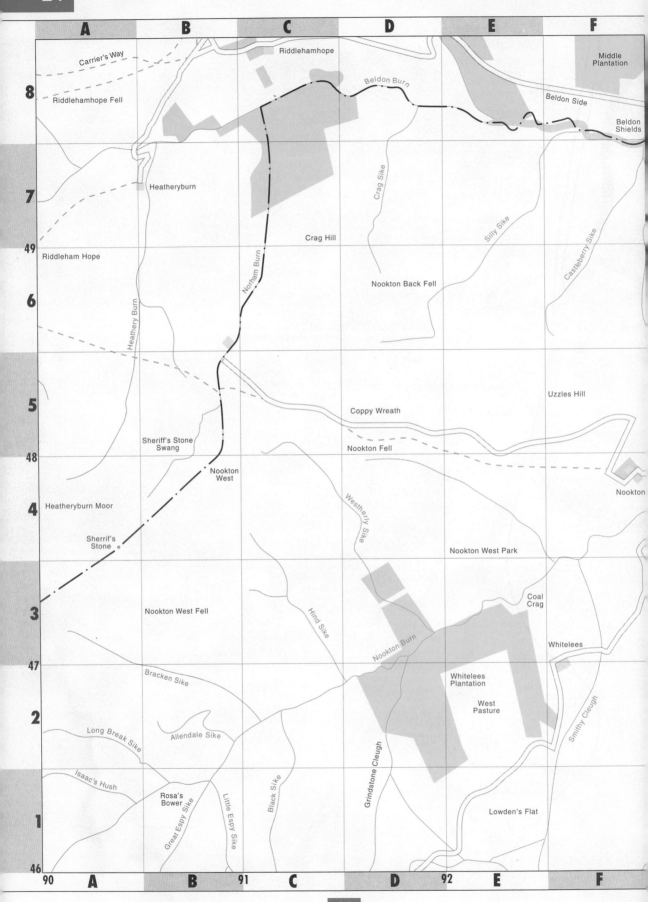

Carrier's Way

Riddlehamhope

Beldon Burn

Middle
Plantation

Beldon Side

8

Riddlehamhope Fell

Beldon
Shields

7

Heatheryburn

Crag Sike

Silly Sike

49

Riddleham Hope

Crag Hill

Castleberry Sike

Norham Burn

Nookton Back Fell

6

Heathery Burn

Uzzles Hill

5

Coppy Wreath

Sheriff's Stone
Swang

Nookton Fell

48

Nookton
West

Nookton

4

Heatheryburn Moor

Westherly Sike

Nookton West Park

Sherrif's
Stone

Coal
Crag

3

Nookton West Fell

Hind Sike

Whitelees

Nookton Burn

47

Bracken Sike

Whitelees
Plantation

Smithy Cleugh

West
Pasture

2

Long Break Sike

Allendale Sike

Grindstone Cleugh

Isaac's Hush

Rosa's
Bower

Great Espy Sike

Little Espy Sike

Black Sike

Lowden's Flat

1

46

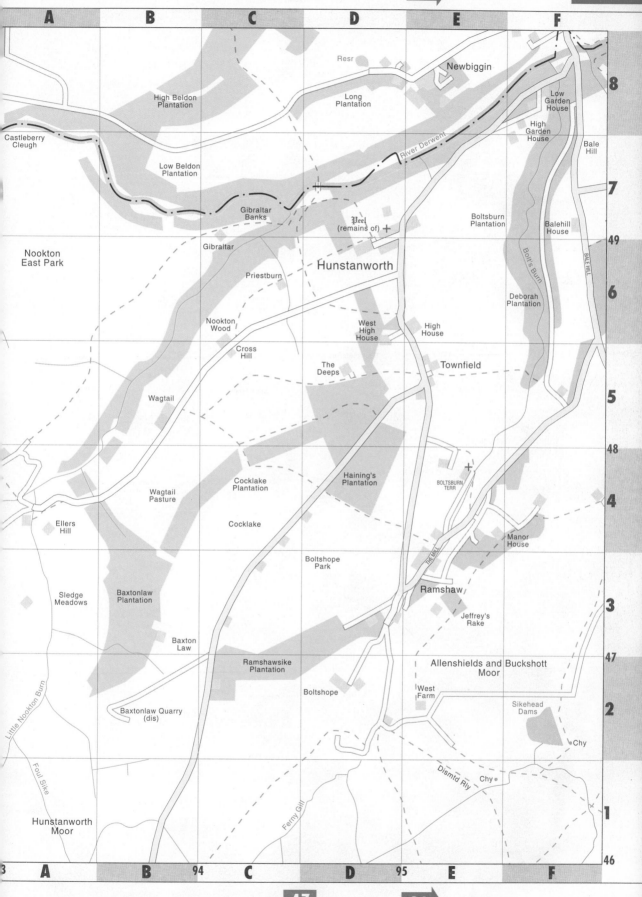

A B C D E F

Newbiggin

Low Garden House

High Garden House

Bale Hill

Castleberry Cleugh

High Beldon Plantation

Long Plantation

River Derwent

Boltsburn Plantation

Balehill House

BALE HILL

Low Beldon Plantation

Gibraltar Banks

Peel (remains of)

Bolt's Burn

Nookton East Park

Gibraltar

Hunstanworth

Deborah Plantation

Priestburn

West High House

High House

Nookton Wood

Cross Hill

The Deeps

Townfield

Wagtail

Haining's Plantation

BOLTSBURN TERR

Cocklake Plantation

Ellers Hill

Wagtail Pasture

Cocklake

Boltshope Park

Manor House

Sledge Meadows

Baxtonlaw Plantation

Ramshaw

Little Nookton Burn

Baxton Law

Jeffrey's Rake

Allenshields and Buckshott Moor

Ramshawsike Plantation

West Farm

Sikehead Dams

Boltshope

Chy

Baxtonlaw Quarry (dis)

Foul Sike

Dismtd Rly

Chy

Ferny Gill

Hunstanworth Moor

A   B   C   D   E   F

8

River Derwent

Rope
Barn

Buckshott
Farm

Stony Burn

Allensshields

Horden Sike

Near Haw Burn

Bock Sike

Stonyburn
Head

West Sike

7

Allenshields

49

Balehill
Plantation

Buckshott
Park

Pedamsoak

6

Buckshott Fell

Pedamsoak Sike

Pedam's
Oak

5

Taylor's
Shaft
(dis)

Chop Hardy

Abbey
Weathers

48

Edmondbyers
Common

4

Belmount

Sunnyside

Burnhope Burn

Beaufie Sike

Burn Hope

3

Sandyford

47

Near
Sandyford

The
Middles

Haygarth's
Flat

Eudon Burn

2

Far
Sandyford

Canal Hill

1

Black Hill

Burnhope
Dam

46

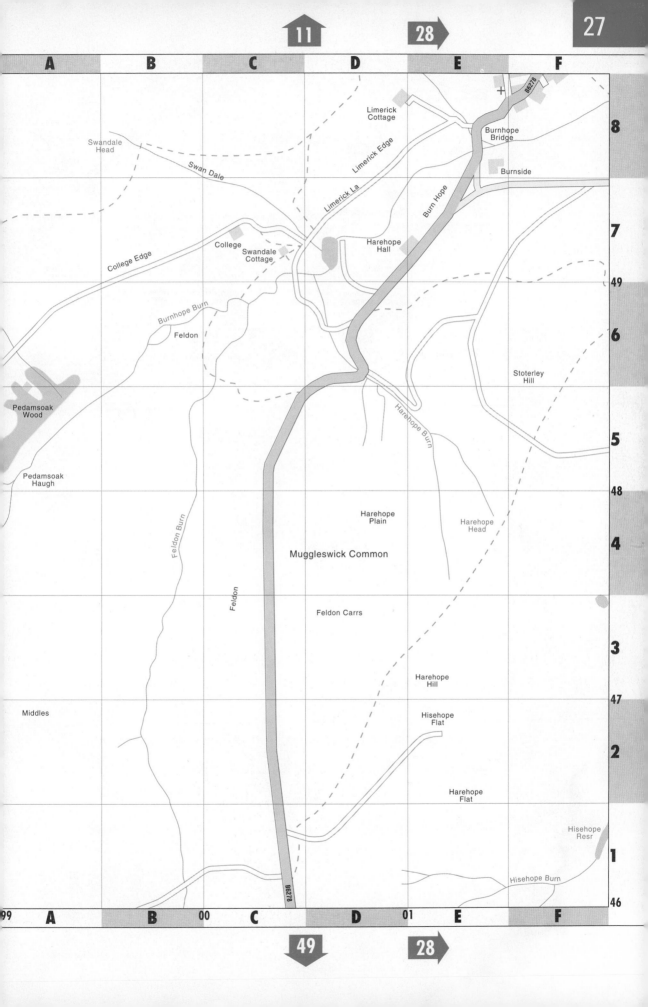

A   B   C   D   E   F

8

7

49

6

5

48

4

47

3

2

1

46

Limerick
Cottage

Burnhope
Bridge

Burnside

B6278

Swandale
Head

Swan Dale

Limerick Edge

Limerick La

Burn Hope

College Edge

College

Swandale
Cottage

Harehope
Hall

Burnhope Burn

Feldon

Pedamsoak
Wood

Feldon Burn

Pedamsoak
Haugh

Harehope Burn

Stoterley
Hill

Harehope
Plain

Harehope
Head

Mugglewick Common

Feldon

Feldon Carrs

Harehope
Hill

Middles

Hisehope
Flat

Harehope
Flat

Hisehope
Resr

B6278

Hisehope Burn

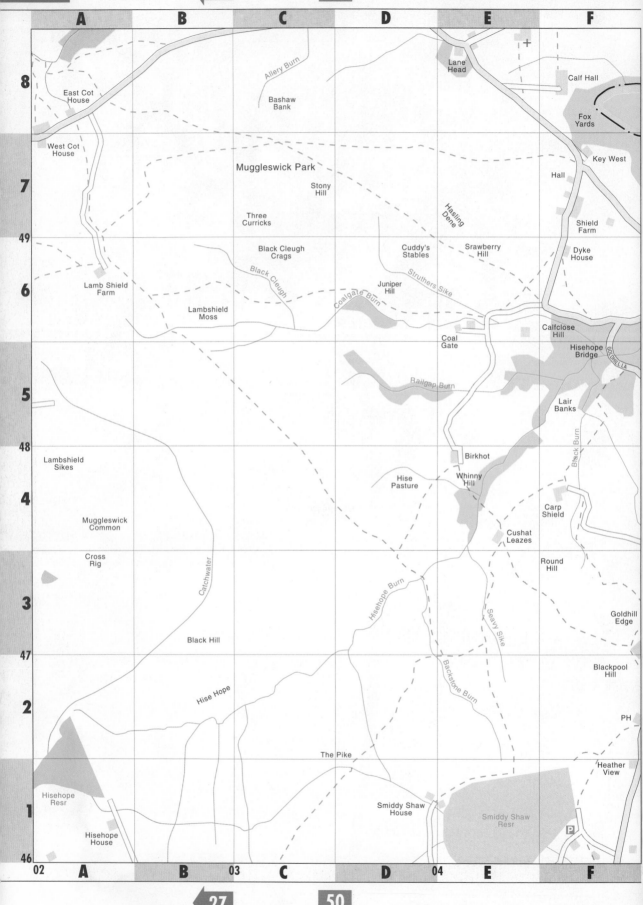

8

East Cot
House

West Cot
House

Allery Burn

Bashaw
Bank

Lane
Head

Calf Hall

Fox
Yards

Key West

7

Muggleswick Park

Stony
Hill

Three
Curricks

Hall

Hasling
Dene

Shield
Farm

49

Black Cleugh
Crags

Cuddy's
Stables

Srawberry
Hill

Dyke
House

6

Lamb Shield
Farm

Black Cleugh

Lambshield
Moss

Coalgate Burn

Juniper
Hill

Struthers Sike

Coal
Gate

Calfclose
Hill

Hisehope
Bridge

GOLDHILL LA

5

Railgap Burn

Lair
Banks

48

Lambshield
Sikes

Birkhot

Whinny
Hill

Black Burn

4

Muggleswick
Common

Hise
Pasture

Cushat
Leazes

Carp
Shield

Round
Hill

Cross
Rig

Catchwater

Hisehope Burn

Seavy Sike

Goldhill
Edge

3

Black Hill

47

Backstone Burn

Blackpool
Hill

2

Hise Hope

PH

The Pike

Heather
View

1

Hisehope
Resr

Smiddy Shaw
House

Smiddy Shaw
Resr

P

Hisehope
House

46

02

A

B

03

C

D

04

E

F

A B C D E F

8

River Derwent

Ravens' Crag

Bog
Wood

Wharnley
Burn

Crooked
Oak

Snape
Wood

Wharnley Burn
Bridge

Bessy's
Bank

7

Fox
Hill

River Derwent

East
Crag

Derwent
Grange

Wharnley
Hill

49

Graham's
Flat

West
Crag

Combfield
House

Birks
Wood

Castleside Cty
Jun & Inf Sch

Castleside

6

Spring
Hill

Comb
Bridges

Dean Howl
Farm

MOORLAND
VIEW

Hisehope Burn

Dene Howl

Cemy

Watergate

5

Leazes

Spring
Well

Healeyfield

Horsley
Hope

Healeyfield

48

Muggleswick Common

Cockshot
Banks

Charlton Howl

4

Goldhill

Middle
Horsleyhope

Fell
Close

Waskerley Way

Dismtd Rly

3

High
Horsleyhope

Low
Horsleyhope

Honey Hill
Treatment
Works

Middles
End

47

The Bent

Greenside

Whitehall Moss

2

Green Hill

Mown
Meadows

North Horsleyhope Burn

South Horsleyhope Burn

Dismtd Rly

Crow Cleugh Sike

Redhouse Sike

Hart Burn

1

Lindisfarne

46

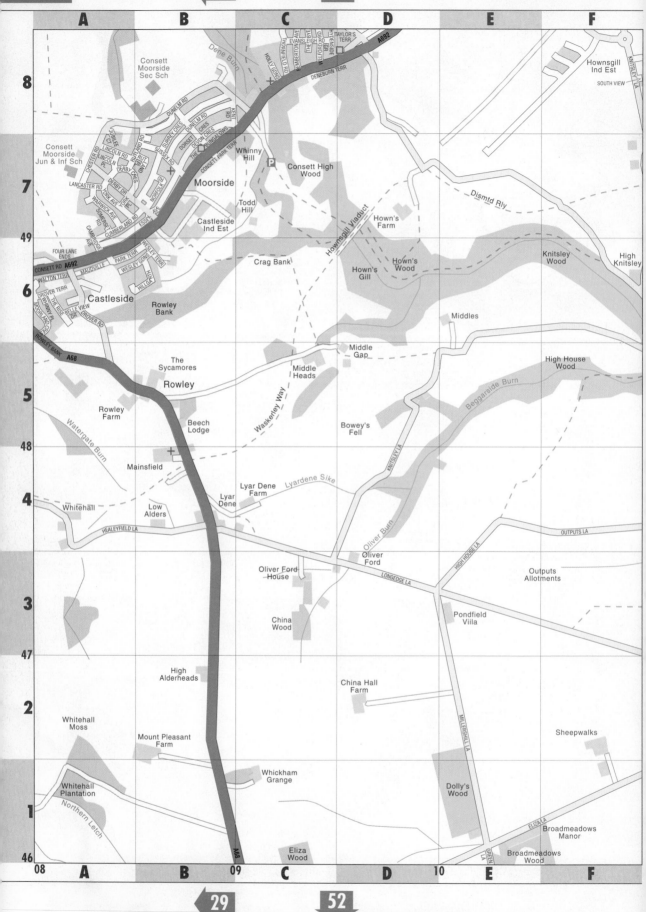

A B C D E F

8

7

49

6

5

48

4

47

2

1

46

Works

Percy Gdns

Delves Lane Cty
Jun Mix & Inf Schs

Knitsley La

Delves

Caribbees
Plantation

Stockerley
Ridge

High
Woodside

Low Castle
Dene

High Castle
Dene Farm

Castle
Hill

Black
Wood

Woodside Bank

Stockerley Burn

A691

A691

Little
Greencroft

Stockerley La

Stockerley
Bridge

Knitsley

Low
Farm

Dismtd Rly

Back
Gill

Backgill Burn

Valley
View

Butsfield La

East Knitsley
Grange

West Knitsley
Grange

Sewage
Works

Hurbuck
Cotts

Hurbuck

Beggarside Burn

Knitsley Burn

Dam
Wood

Knitsley
Bridge

Knitsley
Mill

Sunnyside
Farm

Smallhope Burn

Humberhill La

Dyke
Nook

Outputs La

Woodlands Park

Barley
Hill

Dunleyford
House

Newbiggin La

New House
Farm

Woodlands
Hall

David's
Town

Woodlands
Park Farm

Eliza La

Longedge La

Windy Hill

Humber
House

Red
House

Knitsley La

Redhouses
Bridge

Rippon Burn

Sawmill
Wood

Humberhill La

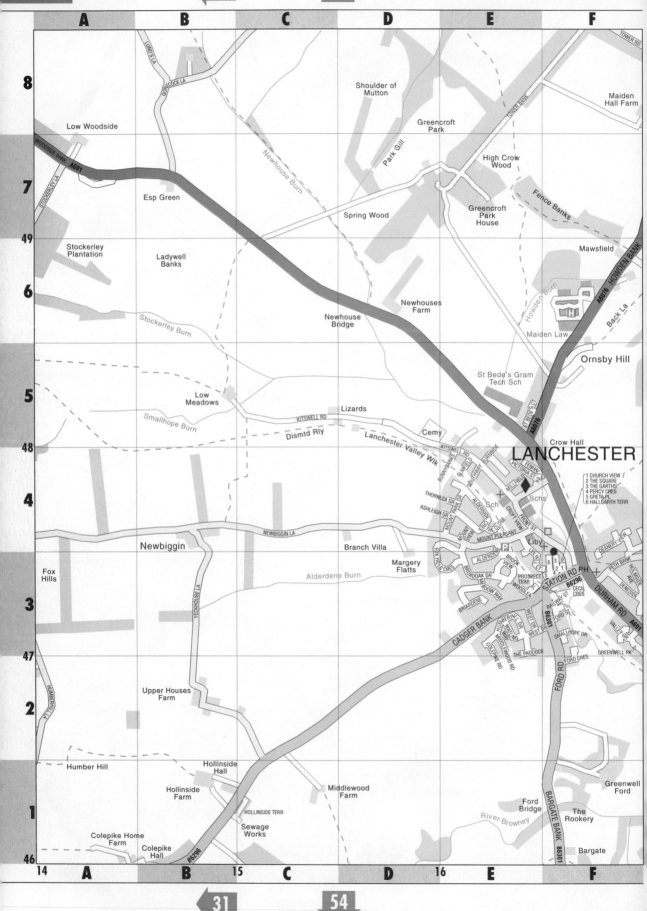

A B C D E F

8

Low Woodside

Shoulder of Mutton

Greencroft Park

Maiden Hall Farm

7

GORCOCK LA

LUND'S LA

WOODSIDE BANK

A691

STOCKERLEY LA

Esp Green

Park Gill

Newhouse Burn

High Crow Wood

TOWER BANK

Fence Banks

TOWER RD

49

Stockerley Plantation

Ladywell Banks

Spring Wood

Greencroft Park House

Mawsfield

HOWDEN BANK

A6076

6

Stockerley Burn

Newhouse Bridge

Newhouses Farm

Howden Burn

Maiden Law

H

A6076

Back La

Ornsby Hill

5

Low Meadows

Smallhope Burn

KITSWELL RD

Lizards

Lanchester Valley Wlk

Cemy

St Bede's Gram Tech Sch

ST BEDE'S CLT

Crow Hall

48

Dismtd Rly

KITSWELL RD

SUNNYBANKS

ELMFIELD

SOUTHFIELD

BURNSIDE

VICTORIA ST

FENHALL

LANCHESTER

1 CHURCH VIEW
2 THE SQUARE
3 THE GARTHS
4 PERCY CRES
5 GRETA PL
6 HALLGARTH TERR

4

THORNLEA GR DR

ASHLEIGH GR

MOUNT PARK DR

ALDERSIDE

MOUNT VIEW

STKD PK CLOSE

CROFT VIEW

FRONT ST

MILLFIELD RD

Schs

Sch

MOUNT PLEASANT

Liby

P

1
6
5
3
4
2

STATION RD PH

DEANERY VIEW

PETH BANK

MANOR AVE

DEMESIDE

NEWBIGGIN LA

Newbiggin

Branch Villa

Margery Flatts

FOX HILL'S CRES

BROADOAK DR

BRIARDENE

ALDERDENE

BROOK VIEW

PROSPECT TERR

WOODLEA

CECIL CT

RAILWAY ST

B6296

CECIL CRES

B6296

DURHAM RD

A691

3

Fox Hills

Alderdene Burn

MEADOW WAY

BRIARDENE

CADGER BANK

HUMBERHILL DR

WEST DR

MIDDLEWOOD RD

WEST ST

FORD ST

B6301

Smallhope Dr

THE PADDOCK

VALLEY GR

Greenwell Pk

47

COLEPIKE RD

FORD CRES

FORD RD

2

HUMBERHILL LA

Upper Houses Farm

YECKHOUSE LA

BARGATE BANK

Humber Hill

Hollinside Hall

Middlewood Farm

Ford Bridge

Greenwell Ford

1

Hollinside Farm

HOLLINSIDE TERR

Sewage Works

River Browney

The Rookery

B6301

46

Colepike Home Farm

Colepike Hall

B6296

Bargate

14 A B 15 C D 16 E F

A   B   C   D   E   F

Three Horse Shoes (PH)
Maiden Law Farm
Maiden Law
Maiden Hall Farm
Chapman's Well Farm
Howden Bank
Howden Burn
TOWER RD
A6076
LANCHESTER RD
THE CRESCENT

NEWACRES RD
WAGTAIL LA
Newacres Plantation
Morrowedge Plantation
Morrow Edge
Wheatley Hill
Burnhope Flatts Farm
Little Holmside
GREEN LA

Tait's House
Opencast Workings
EDGE LA

8
7
49
6

Spring Gardens
Black Wood
Moor Leazes

PH
Liby
PARKSIDE
HOLMSIDE LA
VALE VIEW
CO-OPERATIVE TERR
THE AVENUE
Ibbetson's Sike
Fellside Plantation

PAVILION TERR
WHITEHOUSE TERR
WEST TERR
LANGLEY TERR
SOUTH VIEW
THE VILLAS
LANGLEY AVE
THE GROVE
WHITEHOUSE AVE
HILL CREST
THE PLEASANT VIEW
CABLE MOUNT
THE HAUGH
PLEASANT TERR
BIRKSIDE
HOLLY VILLA
Burnhope Cty Jun & Inf Sch
White House
Burnhope
Standagainstall Plantation

5
48
4

Peth House
DEANERY VIEW
PETH BANK
PETH LA
Black Wood
Path Burn
Burnhope Television Sta
Mast
BEECH GR
Recn Gd
GREENWOOD AVE
FAIR VIEW
LONG EDGE
LANGLEY LA

Dowfit Hill
Foxcover Wood

3
47

BURNHOPESIDE AVE
PETHSIDE AVE
DENESIDE
MANOR GRANGE
DURHAM RD
GREENWELL PK
MANOR CT
Warriors Bridge
Manor House
High Burnhopeside Plantation
High Burnhopeside
Manor House Bridge
Lanchester Valley Wlk
Sewage Works
Waters' Meeting
Lanchester Valley
River Browney
Browney Bridge
Malton
OFFICIAL TERR
P
Burnhopeside Cottages
Burnhopeside Hall
Burnhopeside Farm
Langley West House
Long Plantation
A691

2
1
46

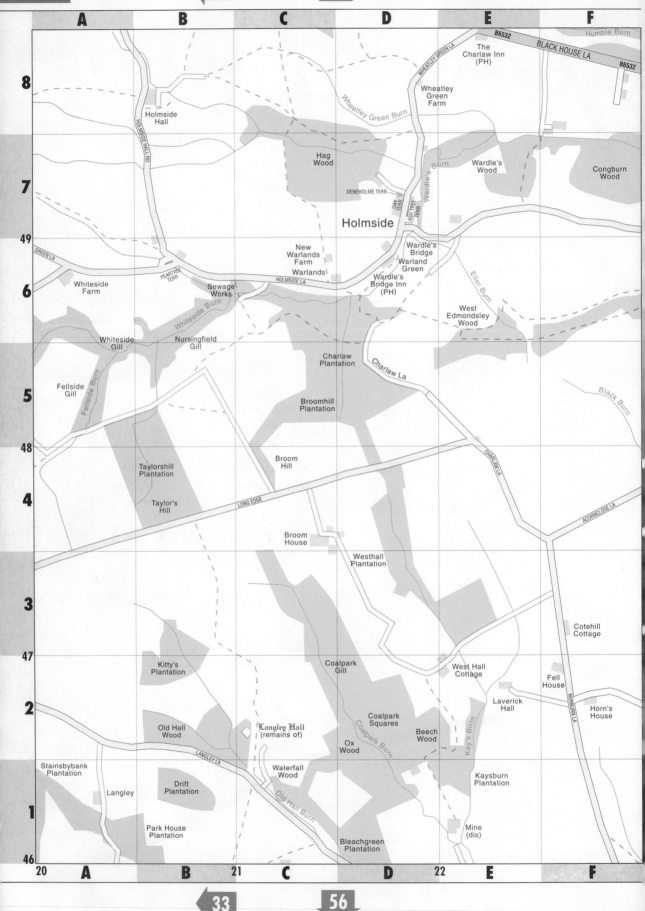

A B C D E F

8

7

49

6

5

48

4

3

47

2

1

46

20 A B 21 C D 22 E F

Humble Burn

B6532 BLACK HOUSE LA B6532

WHEATLEY GREEN LA

The Charlaw Inn (PH)

Holmside Hall

HOLMSIDE HALL RD

Wheatley Green Burn

Wheatley Green Farm

Hag Wood

Wardle's Burn

Wardle's Wood

Congburn Wood

DENEHOLME TERR

OAK TERR

ASH TREE TERR

Holmside

Eller Burn

GREEN LA

New Warlands Farm

Wardle's Bridge

Warland Green

Warlands

PEARTREE TERR

Sewage Works

HOLMSIDE LA

Wardle's Bridge Inn (PH)

West Edmondsley Wood

Whiteside Farm

Whiteside Gill

Whiteside Burn

Nursingfield Gill

Charlaw Plantation

Charlaw La

Black Burn

Fellside Gill

Fellside Burn

Broomhill Plantation

Taylorshill Plantation

Broom Hill

Taylor's Hill

LONG EDGE

Charlaw La

ACORNCLOSE LA

Broom House

Westhall Plantation

Cotehill Cottage

Kitty's Plantation

Coalpark Gill

West Hall Cottage

Fell House

NORBURN LA

Langley Hall (remains of)

Old Hall Wood

LANGLEY LA

Waterfall Wood

Coalpark Squares

Coalpark Burn

Ox Wood

Beech Wood

Kay's Burn

Laverick Hall

Horn's House

Stainsbybank Plantation

Langley

Drift Plantation

Old Hall Burn

Kaysburn Plantation

Park House Plantation

Bleachgreen Plantation

Mine (dis)

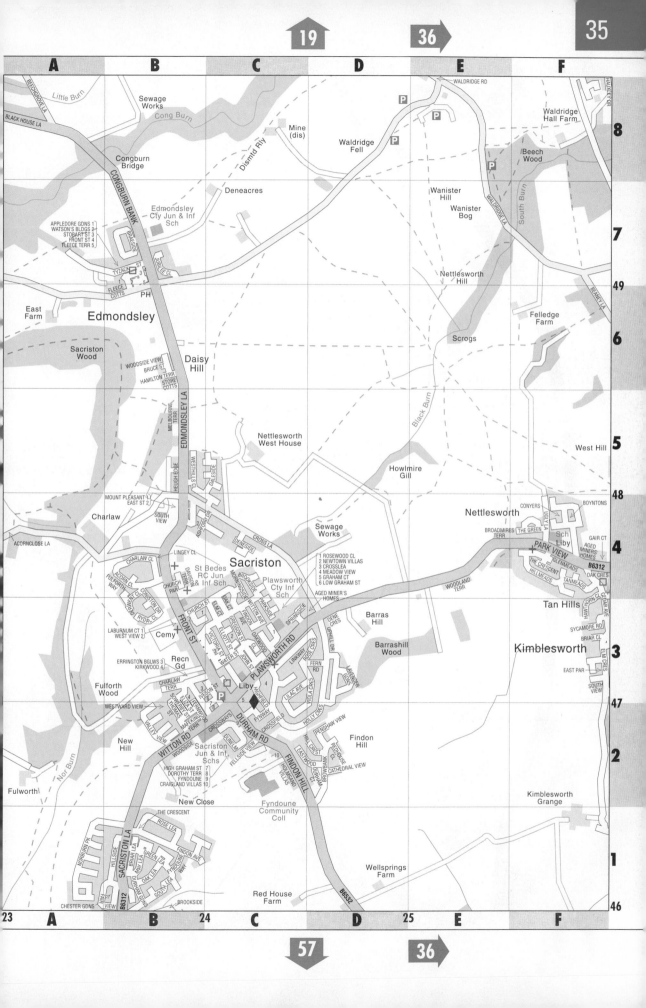

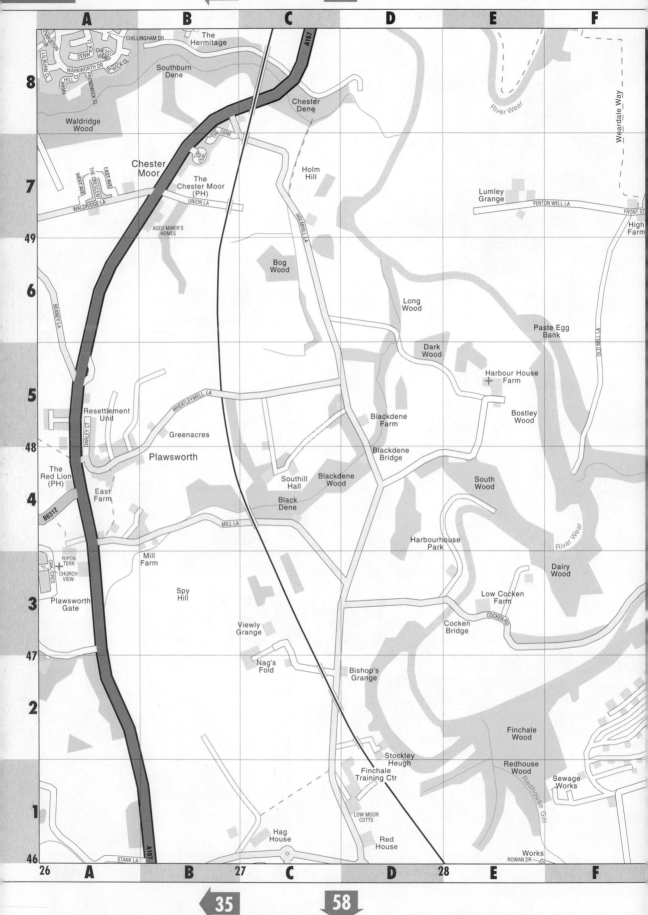

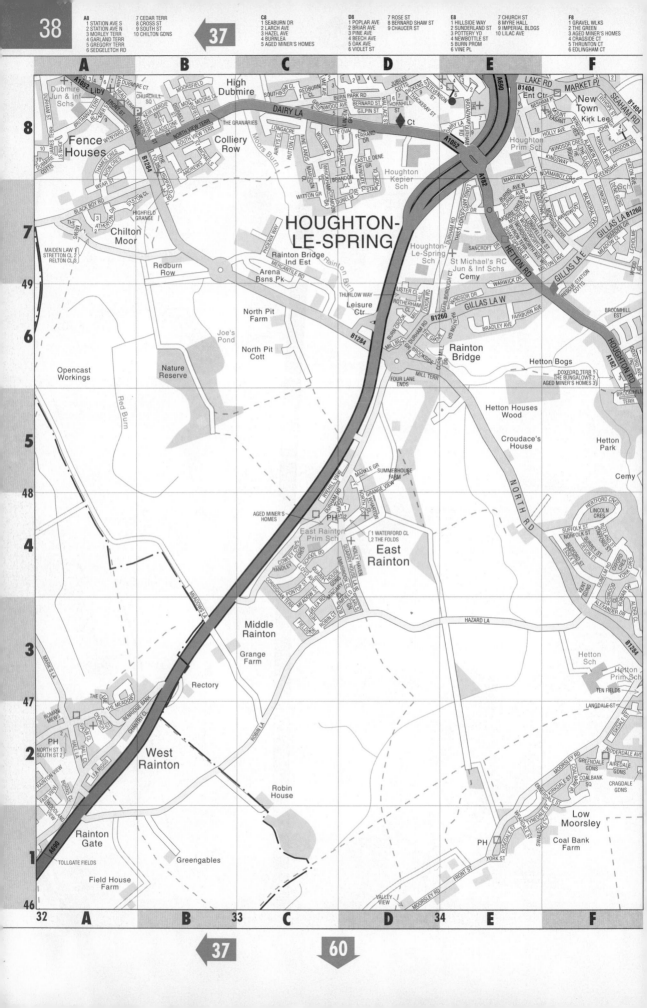

SEAHAM

Dalton-le-Dale

Parkside

Dawdon

Cold
Hesledon

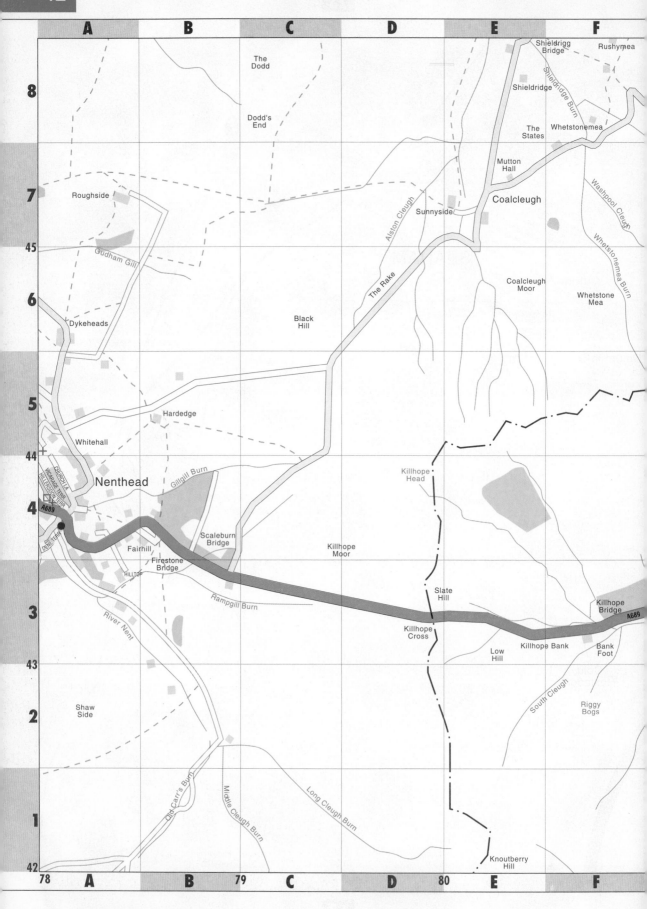

The Dodd

Dodd's End

Roughside

Gudham Gill

Dykeheads

Black Hill

Hardedge

Whitehall

Nenthead

Gillgill Burn

Fairhill

Firestone Bridge

HILLTOP

Scaleburn Bridge

Rampgill Burn

River Nent

Shaw Side

Old Carr's Burn

Middle Cleugh Burn

Long Cleugh Burn

Shieldrigg Bridge

Rushymea

Shieldridge

Shieldridge Burn

The States

Whetstonemea

Mutton Hall

Coalcleugh

Sunnyside

Alston Cleugh

The Rake

Coalcleugh Moor

Washpool Cleugh

Whetstone Mea

Whetstonemea Burn

Killhope Head

Killhope Moor

Killhope Cross

Slate Hill

Low Hill

Killhope Bank

Killhope Bridge

Bank Foot

South Cleugh

Riggy Bogs

Knoutberry Hill

A689

CHURCH LA

VICARAGE TERR

HILLERSDON TERR

OGLE TERR

78 79 80
42 43 44 45

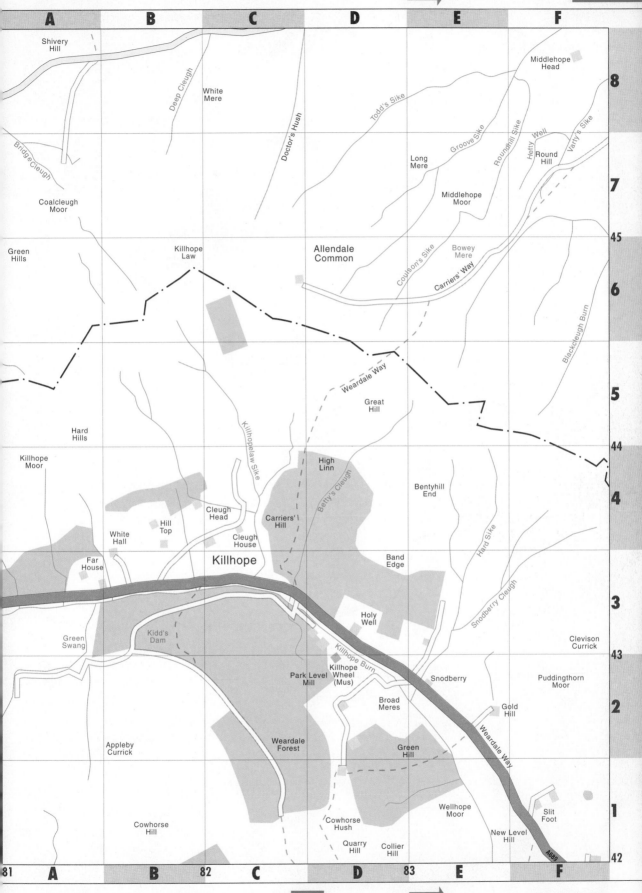

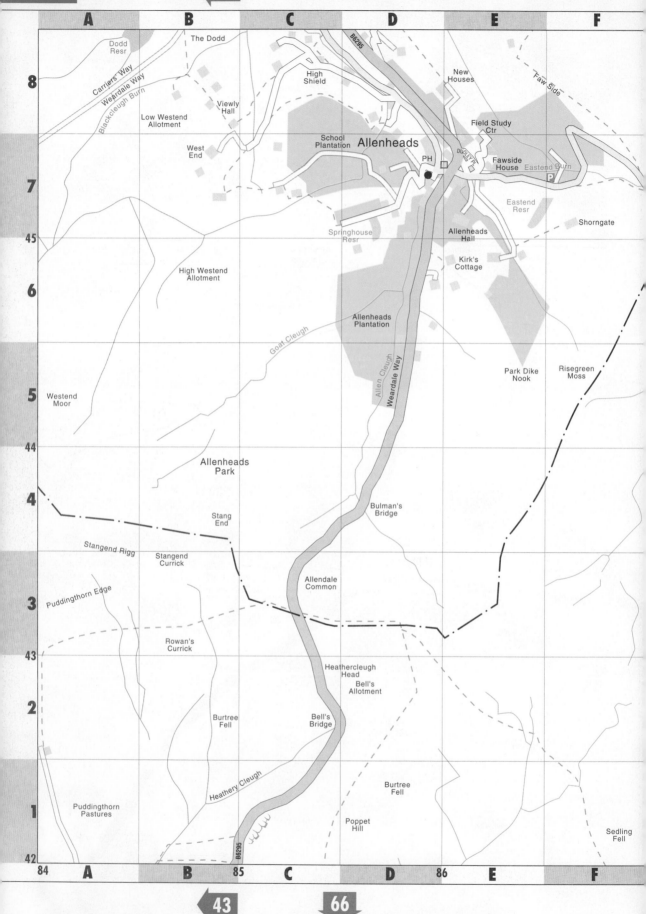

A B C D E F

8

Dodd
Resr

The Dodd

Carriers' Way

Weardale Way

Blackcleugh Burn

High
Shield

B6295

New
Houses

Faw Side

Low Westend
Allotment

Viewly
Hall

Field Study
Ctr

West
End

School
Plantation

Allenheads

PH

DURLEY PL

Fawside
House

Eastend Burn

P

7

Eastend
Resr

45

Springhouse
Resr

Allenheads
Hall

Shorngate

High Westend
Allotment

Kirk's
Cottage

6

Goat Cleugh

Allenheads
Plantation

Park Dike
Nook

Risegreen
Moss

5

Westend
Moor

Allen Cleugh

Weardale Way

44

Allenheads
Park

4

Stang
End

Bulman's
Bridge

Stangend Rigg

Stangend
Currick

Allendale
Common

3

Puddingthorn Edge

Rowan's
Currick

43

Heathercleugh
Head

Bell's
Allotment

2

Burtree
Fell

Bell's
Bridge

Burtree
Fell

1

Heathery Cleugh

Puddingthorn
Pastures

Poppet
Hill

Sedling
Fell

B6295

42

84 A 85 B C 86 D E F

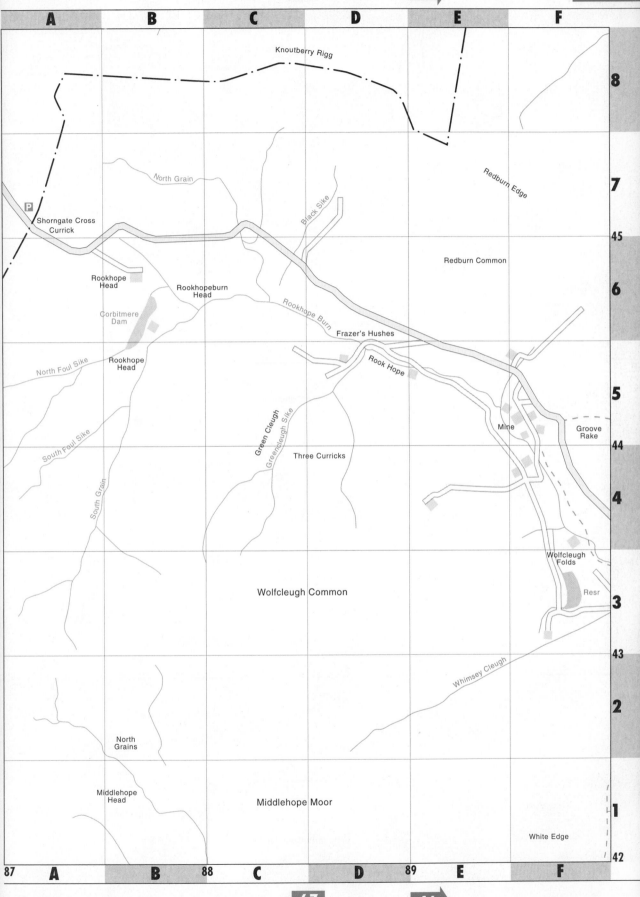

A **B** **C** **D** **E** **F**

8

North Grain

South Grain

Grindstone Cleugh

Brokenbank Sike

Shooting Cabin

Hackford's Hush

7

Hackford's Dam

Black Hags

45

6

Dry Rigg

Redburn Common

5

44

Groove Rake

Snow Wreaths

Rookhope Chimney (course of)

4

Hawk Hill

Hawk Sike

Red Burn

Redburn

Thorny Slit

Bield Hill

Bank Foot

3

Mine (dis)

Rispey Sike

Rushy Hole

Redburn Mine

Wolf Cleugh

43

Rispey Mill

Lintzgarth

2

Wolf Cleugh Common

Rookhope Burn

Lintzgarth House

Wolf Cleugh

Shafts (dis)

Scar Sike

Lintzgarth Bield

1

Lintzgarth Plantation

Lintzgarth Common

42

90 **A** **B** 91 **C** **D** 92 **E** **F**

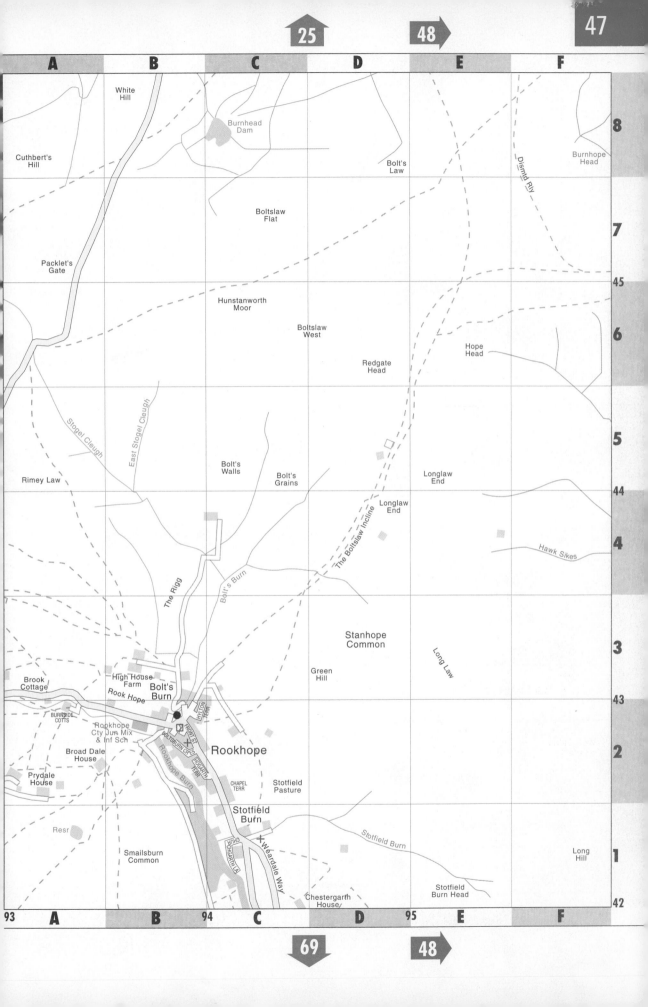

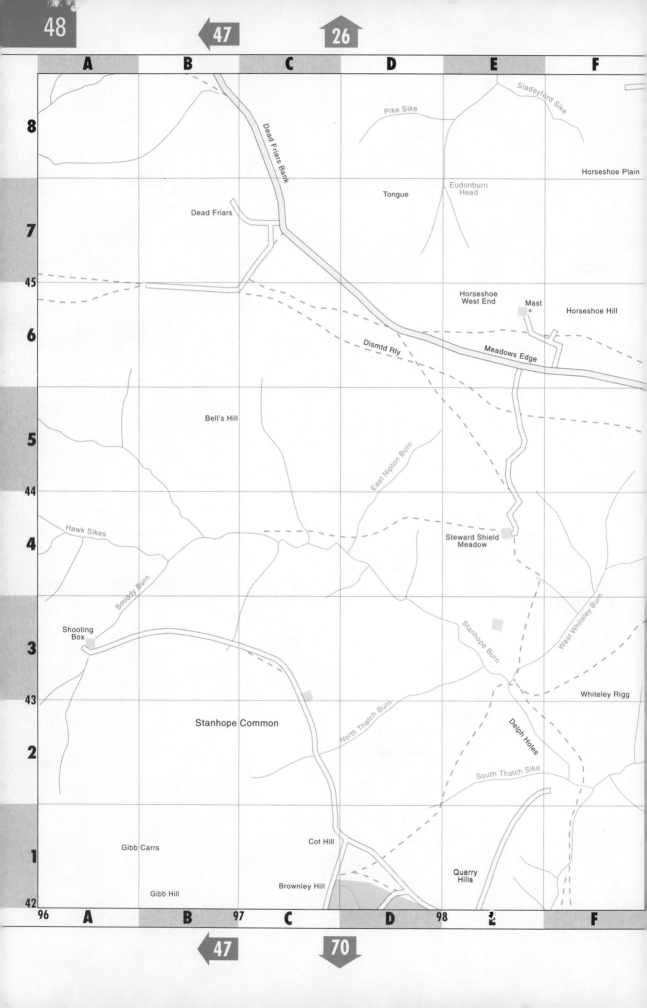

47
26

A B C D E F

Sladeyford Sike

Pike Sike

8

Dead Friars Bank

Horseshoe Plain

Tongue

Eudonburn Head

Dead Friars

7

45

Horseshoe West End

Mast

Horseshoe Hill

6

Dismtd Rly

Meadows Edge

Bell's Hill

5

East Nipton Burn

44

Hawk Sikes

4

Steward Shield Meadow

Smiddy Burn

Stanhope Burn

West Whiteley Burn

Shooting Box

3

43

Whiteley Rigg

North Thatch Burn

Stanhope Common

Delph Holes

2

South Thatch Sike

1

Gibb Carrs

Cot Hill

Quarry Hills

Gibb Hill

Brownley Hill

42

96 A B 97 C D 98 2 F

47
70

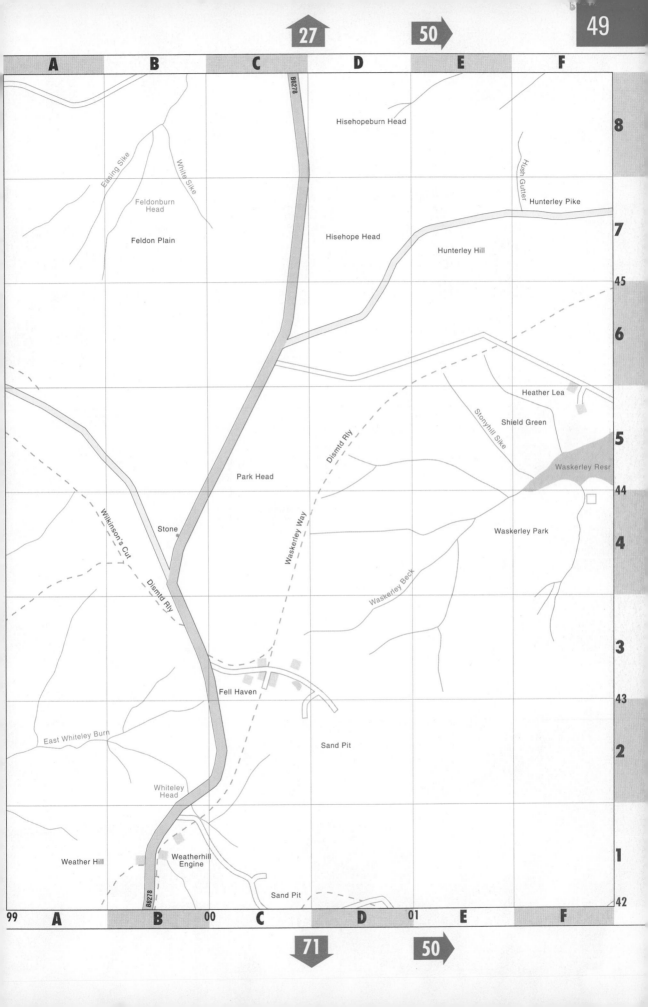

A B C D E F

8

Hisehopeburn Head

Easing Sike

White Sike

Feldonburn Head

Hush Gutter

Hunterley Pike 7

Feldon Plain

Hisehope Head

Hunterley Hill

45

6

B6278

Heather Lea

Stonyhill Sike

Shield Green

Dismtd Rly

5

Park Head

Waskerley Resr

Waskerley Way

44

Wilkinson's Cut

Waskerley Park 4

Stone

Dismtd Rly

Waskerley Beck

3

Fell Haven

43

East Whiteley Burn

Sand Pit 2

Whiteley Head

1

Weather Hill

Weatherhill Engine

B6278

Sand Pit

42

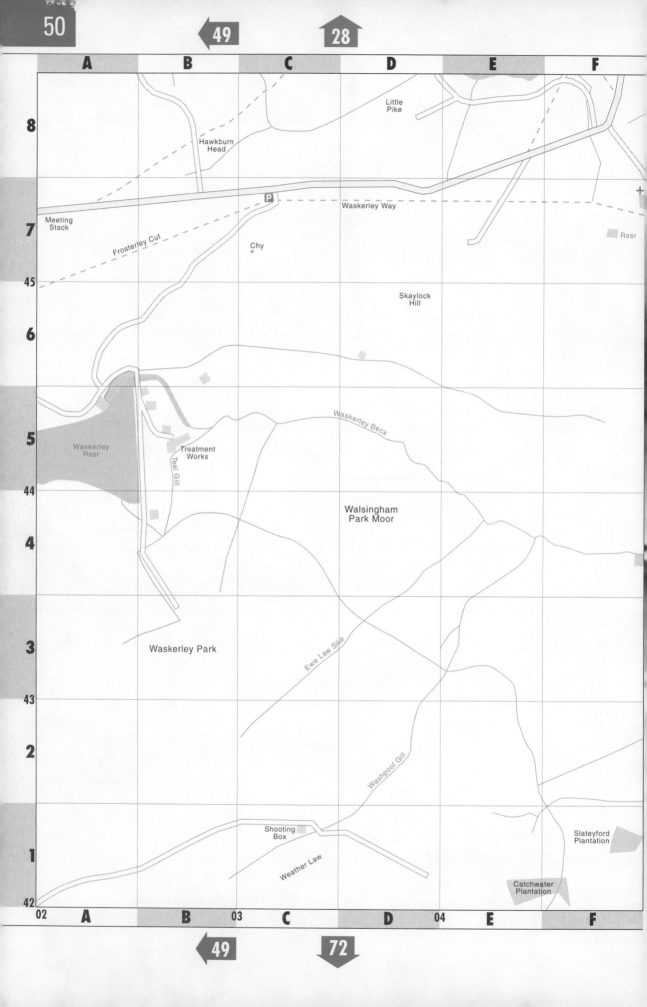

A B C D E F

8

Little
Pike

Hawkburn
Head

P

Waskerley Way

Meeting
Stack

7

Frosterley Cut

Chy

Resr

45

Skaylock
Hill

6

Waskerley Beck

Waskerley
Resr

Treatment
Works

Teel Gill

5

44

Walsingham
Park Moor

4

Waskerley Park

3

Ewe Law Syke

43

2

Washpool Gill

Slateyford
Plantation

Shooting
Box

1

Weather Law

Catchwater
Plantation

42

02 A B 03 C D 04 E F

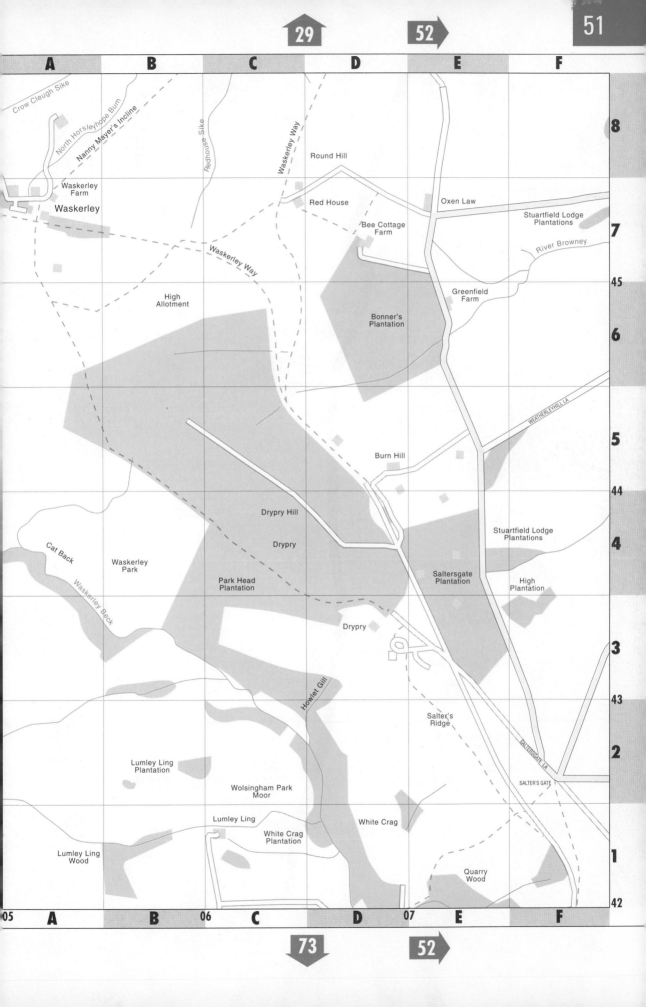

A B C D E F

8

North
Plantation

Eliza
Farm

Broadmeadows

Northern Letch

Southern Letch

ELIZA LA

GREEN LA

Stuartfield Lodge
Plantations

Black Burn

7

BUTSFIELD LA

45

Stuartfield
Lodge

WEATHERLEYHILL LA

WEST LA

North
Farm

East
Farm

West
Butsfield

Weatherley
Hill

Stuartfield
Bridge

West
Bank

6

River Browney

Butsfield
Burn

South
Plantation

Sawmill
Bridge

Byerleyhouse
Wood

Woodburn
Plantations

Denehouse
Bridge

Wood Burn

BYERLEYHOUSE LA

Abbey Burn

5

Woodburn

GREEN LA

Byerleyhouse
Bridge

Byerley
House

44

Springwell
House

Dene
House

Butsfield
Abbey

Springwell
Farm

4

Hermitage
Bridge

Dead Burn

Field
House

Quick Burn

3

Chimney •

Quickburn
Grange

Meadowfield
Farm

43

Low
Hermitage

High
Hermitage

2

Wheatley
Grange

Droverhouse
Plantation

DROVERHOUSE LA

Bedlam
Wood

Drover
House

Adelphi
Plantations

Adelphi

1

42

08 A B 09 C D 10 E F

A68

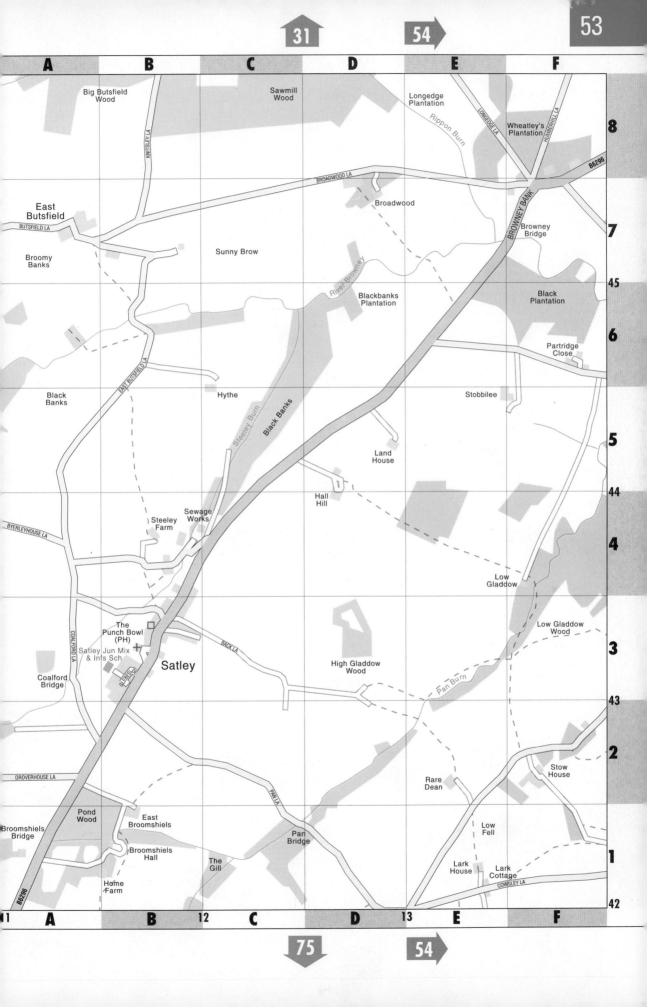

A B C D E F

8

Big Butsfield Wood

Sawmill Wood

Longedge Plantation

Rippon Burn

Wheatley's Plantation

BROADWOOD LA

KNITSLEY LA

LONGEDGE LA

HUMBERHILL LA

B6296

East Butsfield

Broadwood

BUTSFIELD LA

Browney Bridge

7

Broomy Banks

Sunny Brow

45

River Browney

Blackbanks Plantation

Black Plantation

EAST BUTSFIELD LA

6

Partridge Close

Black Banks

Hythe

Black Banks

Steeley Burn

Stobbilee

5

Land House

44

Hall Hill

BYERLEYHOUSE LA

Sewage Works

Steeley Farm

4

Low Gladdow

Low Gladdow Wood

COALFORD LA

The Punch Bowl (PH)

Satley Jun Mix & Infs Sch

BACK LA

High Gladdow Wood

Pan Burn

3

Satley

GLEBESIDE

Coalford Bridge

43

Stow House

2

DROVERHOUSE LA

PAN LA

Rare Dean

Broomshiels Bridge

Pond Wood

East Broomshiels

Pan Bridge

Low Fell

B6296

Broomshiels Hall

The Gill

Lark House

Lark Cottage

1

Home Farm

COWSLEY LA

42

A 11 B 12 C D 13 E F

A B C D E F

8

B6296

Black House Farm

Throstle Nest

Greenwell Farm

B6301

Colepike Mill

Lead Hill

BARGATE BANK

7

Triangle Plantation

HOLEHOUSE LA

Hole House

River Browney

Bleach Green

Square House

45

Partridgeclose Mill Bridge

Ragpathside Plantation

HAMSTEELS LA

Squarehouse Cotts

6

Ragpath Side

Lowmill Bridge

RAGPATH LA

5

Lowmill Wood

CORNSAY LA

Click-Em-Inn Farm

44

Clickemin Hill

B6301

4

Grange Farm

Cornsay

East Ravensbush Wood

Cornsay House

Black Horse Inn (PH)

North Ravensbush Wood

3

POST OFFICE ROW

South Farm

43

Low Row

2

Greenacres

Lane Foot

Hedleyhope Burn

1

Lodge House Farm

COWSLEY LA

Bell's House

The Firtree (PH)

HEDLEYHILL LA

NESLEY LA

B6301

42

Cowsley

B6301

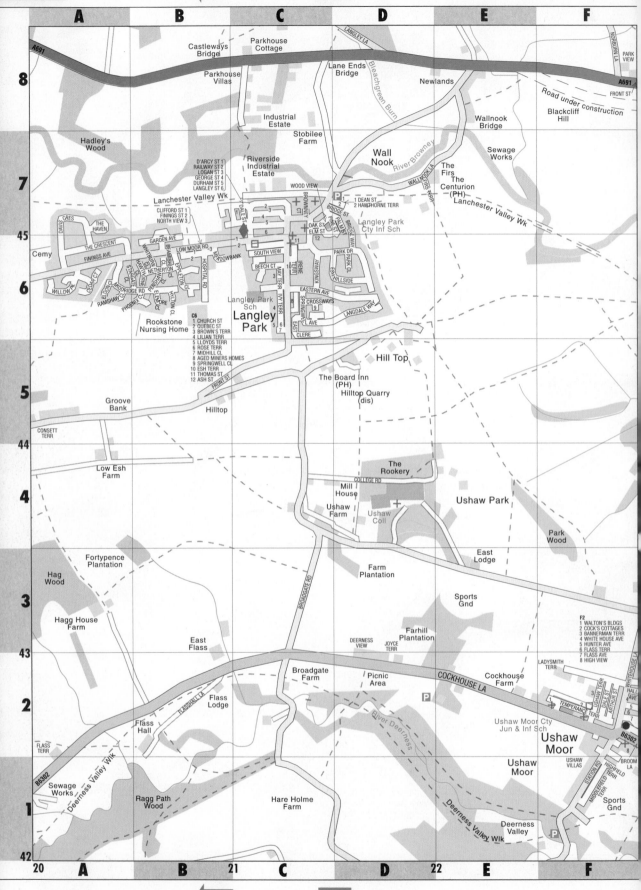

8

7

45

6

5

44

4

3

43

2

1

42

A691

Castleways Bridge
Parkhouse Cottage
Parkhouse Villas

Langley La

Lane Ends Bridge

Newlands

Bleachgreen Burn

Park View
NORBURN LA

A691
FRONT ST

Road under construction

Blackcliff Hill

Wallnook Bridge

Hadley's Wood

Industrial Estate

Stobilee Farm

Wall Nook

River Browney

Sewage Works

The Firs
The Centurion (PH)

Lanchester Valley Wk

D'ARCY ST 1
RAILWAY ST 2
LOGAN ST 3
GEORGE ST 4
DURHAM ST 5
LANGLEY ST 6

Riverside Industrial Estate

WOOD VIEW

WALLNOOK LA

Lanchester Valley Wk

CLIFFORD ST 1
FININGS ST 2
NORTH VIEW 3

BROWNEY CT

BRIDGE ST
BRIDGE WAY

1 DEAN ST
2 HAWTHORNE TERR

DAVIS CRES
THE HAVEN

THE CRESCENT

GARDEN AVE

LOW MOOR RD

HOSPITAL RD

MEADOWBANK

OAK ST
ELM ST
PALMS

PARK DR

Langley Park Cty Inf Sch

Cemy
FININGS AVE

WHITBURN CL
HARTHORNE CL
BEAMISH CL
APPLETON CL

SOUTH VIEW

BEECH CT

MAY TERR
IVY TERR
IRENE TERR

PARK PL
PARK CL

Hillside

WILLOW WK
CEDAR CT
ELDON CL
CLARTRIDGE RD
RAMSHAW CL
STARGATE
PHOENIX
PARKSIDE CL
ELMORE CL
HYLTON CL

NETHERTON CL

EASTERN AVE
CROSSWAYS

AYKNSWAY
ESH HILLSIDE

Rookstone Nursing Home

C6
1 CHURCH ST
2 QUEBEC ST
3 BROWN'S TERR
4 LILIAN TERR
5 LLOYDS TERR
6 ROSE TERR
7 MIDHILL CL
8 AGED MINERS HOMES
9 SPRINGWELL CL
10 ESH TERR
11 THOMAS ST
12 ASH ST

Langley Park Sch

Langley Park

SPRINGWELL

L AVE
CLERE

LANGDALE WAY

Hill Top

The Board Inn (PH)

Hilltop Quarry (dis)

FRONT ST

Groove Bank

Hilltop

CONSETT TERR

Low Esh Farm

The Rookery

COLLEGE RD

Mill House

Ushaw Farm

Ushaw Coll

Ushaw Park

East Lodge

Park Wood

Fortypence Plantation

Hag Wood

Hagg House Farm

East Flass

Farm Plantation

Sports Gnd

F2
1 WALTON'S BLDGS
2 COCK'S COTTAGES
3 BANNERMAN TERR
4 WHITE HOUSE AVE
5 HUNTER AVE
6 FLASS TERR
7 FLASS AVE
8 HIGH VIEW

Farhill Plantation

DEERNESS VIEW
JOYCE TERR

LADYSMITH TERR

WHITEHOUSE LA

Broadgate Farm

Picnic Area

COCKHOUSE LA

Cockhouse Farm

USHAW TERR
DALE ST
ARTHUR ST
HALL AVE

BROADGATE RD

FLASSHALL LA

Flass Lodge

River Deerness

TEMPERANCE TERR

Ushaw Moor Cty Jun & Inf Sch

B6302

Flass Hall

FLASS TERR

B6302

Sewage Works

Deerness Valley Wk

Ragg Path Wood

Hare Holme Farm

Deerness Valley Wk

Deerness Valley

Ushaw Moor

Ushaw Villas

STATION RD
HIGHFIELD TERR
MIDDLEFIELD TERR
BROOM LA

Sports Gnd

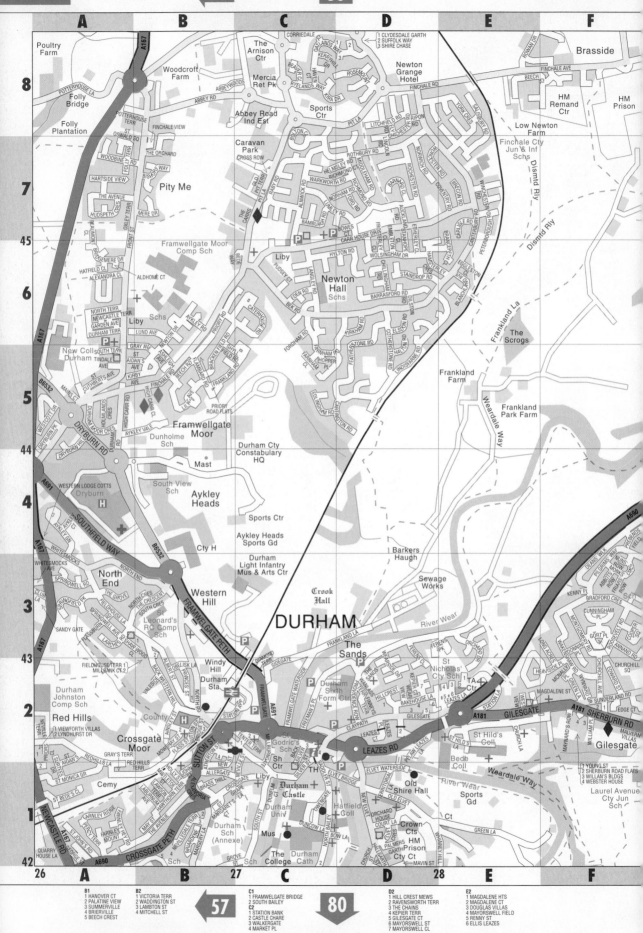

B1
1 HANOVER CT
2 PALATINE VIEW
3 SUMMERVILLE
4 BRIERVILLE
5 BEECH CREST

B2
1 VICTORIA TERR
2 WADDINGTON ST
3 LAMBTON ST
4 MITCHELL ST

C1
1 FRAMWELGATE BRIDGE
2 SOUTH BAILEY
C2
1 STATION BANK
2 CASTLE CHARE
3 WALKERGATE
4 MARKET PL

D2
1 HILL CREST MEWS
2 RAVENSWORTH TERR
3 THE CHAINS
4 KEPIER TERR
5 GILESGATE CT
6 MAYORSWELL ST
7 MAYORSWELL CL

E2
1 MAGDALENE HTS
2 MAGDALENE CT
3 DOUGLAS VILLAS
4 MAYORSWELL FIELD
5 RENNY ST
6 ELLIS LEAZES

A   B   C   D   E   F

8   Pitfield House
    Homer Hill Farm
    High Moorsley
    High Moorsley Farm
    VALLEY VIEW

7   PITTINGTON RD
    MOORSLEY RD
    Cobbler's Hill
    Quarryhouse Wood

45 STATION RD
    CORONATION CRES
    Pittington Hill
    Hillside Farm
    ELEMORE LA

6   PITTINGTON LA
    PH
    FRONT ST   HIGH ST
    Low Pittington
    1 WELLINGTON ST
    2 HILLSIDE GROVE
    3 GRAHAM TERR
    4 HALLGARTH VIEW

5   LADY'S PIECE LA
    PRIORS GRANGE
    ELEMORE ST   LAWRENCE RD
    ST JOHN'S ST   ST LAWRENCE
    GLEN'S FLATS   NORMAN TERR   NEWBY LA
    HALLGARTH LA
    Pittington Cty Jun & Inf Sch
    High Pittington
    Willow Garth
    The Moor
    Horseshoe Wood

44 SOUTH END
    MANOR VIEW   COALFORD LA
    CHURCH VALE   Sewage Works
    Coldwell Burn

4   Hallgarth Farm
    Hallgarth
    Hallgarth Manor (Hotel)
    MOOR COTTAGES
    White's Wood
    Littletown
    Dog Kennel Bank
    Hastings House

3   Pittington Bridge
    Coalford Beck
    Stand Bridge
    Littletown Farm
    Littletown House
    CROSS ST
    PLANTATION AVE
    Duke of York (PH)
    LITTLETOWN LA

43

2   FORSTER AVE
    Sherburn Cty Jun & Inf Sch
    PARK HOUSE GDNS
    MITFORD DR
    COOKSHOLD LA
    Cook's Hold Farm
    Saw Mill
    Black Banks

1   B1283
    GEORGE ST
    NELSON TERR
    HALL GDNS
    MELDON AVE
    KINNOCK CL   HALLGARTH
    ALSTON WLK   VILLAS
    WHALTON CL
    Broadview Villas
    Sherburn
    Sherburn Hill
    WEST VIEW
    BANNERMAN TERR
    WESLEY TERR
    LOCAL AVE
    KELL CRES
    NORTH VIEW
    SOUTH VIEW
    JUBILEE CRES
    EAST VIEW
    Sherburn Hill Cty Mix Inf Sch
    THE CROFT
    High House Farm
    FRONT ST
    PINDERS WAY
    1 CO-OPERATIVE VILLAS
    2 BRIGHTON TERR
    3 DURHAM LA

42 MILL LA
    PEART CL
    CHAPEL CT
    NEW ST
    SOUTH ST
    FRONT ST
    Aged Miners Homes
    PH
    B1283

32   A   B   33   C   D   34   E   F

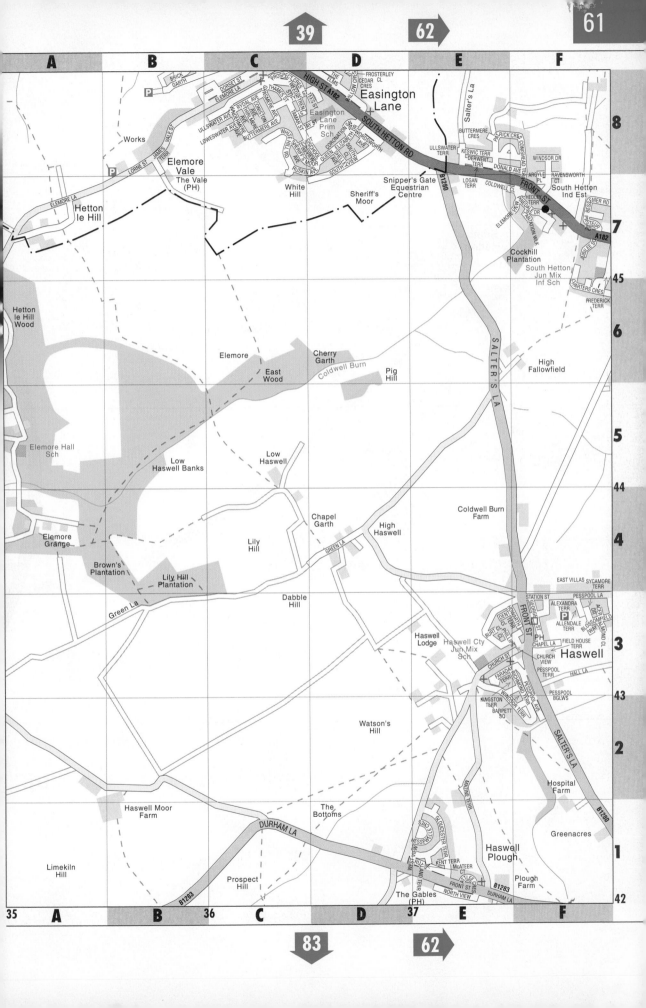

South Hetton Ind Est
BESSEMER RD
Liby
1 FREDERICK TERR
2 ROSE COTTS
3 FALLOWFIELD TERR
PH
A182 FRONT ST
CHARTERS CRES
Low Fallowfield

South Hetton
CORONATION SQ
HAWTHORN COTTS
GRASMERE TERR
WINDERMERE RD
GREENCROFT
PARKLANDS GR
THE BUNGALOWS
WELFARE CRES
JAMESON TERR
BEVIN SQ
FIELD ST
PALMER ST
HAWTHORN CRES
OAKWOOD
FORSTER CRES
MATTHEWS CRES
VICARAGE CL
GREGSON TERR
Carr's Farm

WEST LA
Coop Hill
Coop House Wood
Great Coop House Farm
Round Hill
Hallfield

Milestone Hill
North Hill
West Moor House Farm
Duncombe Moor
Milestone House

Holy Cross Farm
Dismtd Rly
Pesspool LA
Junction House Farm

A182 HALL WALKS
B1283
A19

Cove Holes
Chestnut DR
Rymer's Moor
Low Ling Close
Bridge Hills

Pesspool Hall
HALL LA
Mawson's Hill
Cow Close Farm
Holmlea
Calf Close Farm
Loaning Burn
Kippering Banks
DURHAM LA

High Ling Close

Pesspool Wood
B1200
Haswell to Hart Countryside Walkway
Pesspool Dene
Moor House Farm
Mast

Tuthill House
SALTER'S LA
B1283
Tuthill Bridge
Sandy Carrs
DURHAM LA
Westmoor Farm
North West Ind Est
KITCHING RD
HACKWORTH CL
MILL RD

East Batter Law Farm
Little Coop House Farm
West Batter Law Farm

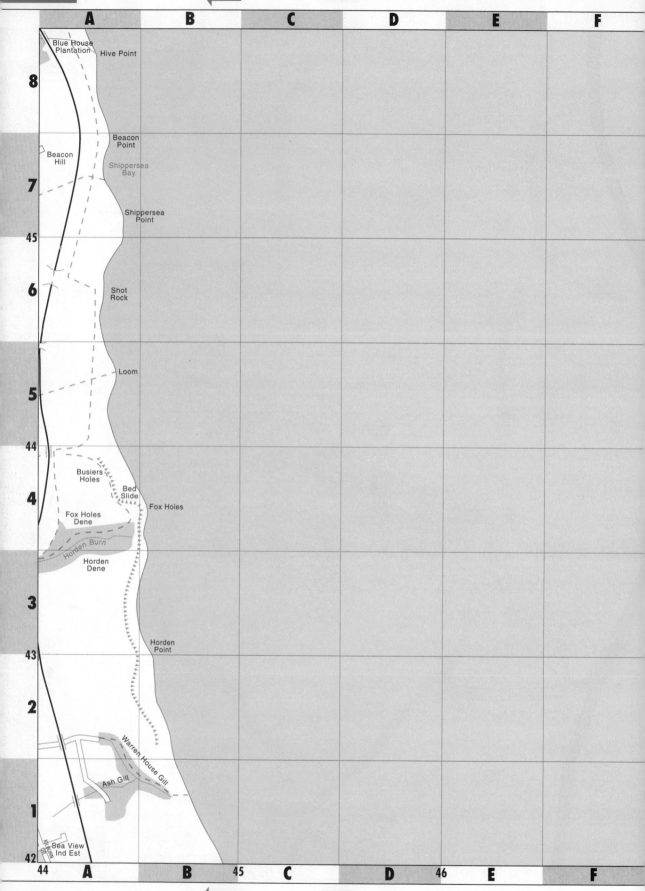

A B C D E F

8

Blue House
Plantation
Hive Point

Beacon
Point

Beacon
Hill

Shippersea
Bay

7

Shippersea
Point

45

Shot
Rock

6

Loom

5

44

Busiers
Holes

Bed
Slide
Fox Holes

4

Fox Holes
Dene

Horden Burn

Horden
Dene

3

Horden
Point

43

2

Warren House Gill

Ash Gill

1

Sea View
Ind Est

42

44 A B 45 C D 46 E F

A   B   C   D   E   F

8

A689

Benty Brow

Weardale
Forest

Carrick's
Hags

High
Byre

Killhopeburn
Bridge

Wellhope

Trodden
Ground

Far Green
Hill

Weardale Way

Killhope Burn

Bram Sike

Blakeley
Field

Black
Brocks

Five Sike

Wellhope Burn

Whitestone
House

Bowmans Well

Wellhope
Pastures

7

41

Wellhope
Fold

Cow
Hill

Well Hope

White
Spots

Lamb's
Hill

Wellhope
Green

Moss
Moor

6

Copt
Hill

5

The
Malakoff

Plover
Hill

Black Cleugh

40

Burnhope
Moor

Cleugh
Head

Scurraberry

Green Laws

4

Fox Pits

Featherstone's
Allotment

Poppet
Hill

Black
Hill

Poppet Well

Rowantree Sike

The
Bands

Burnhope
Pastures

3

39

Burnhope Burn

Burnhope
Resr

Burn
Hope

2

Milburn's Hush

Crooked Sike

Langtae Burn

Smith's Hush

Green Sike

Blackhill
End

1

Langtae
Moss

The
Quicksands

38

81   A   B   82   C   D   83   E   F

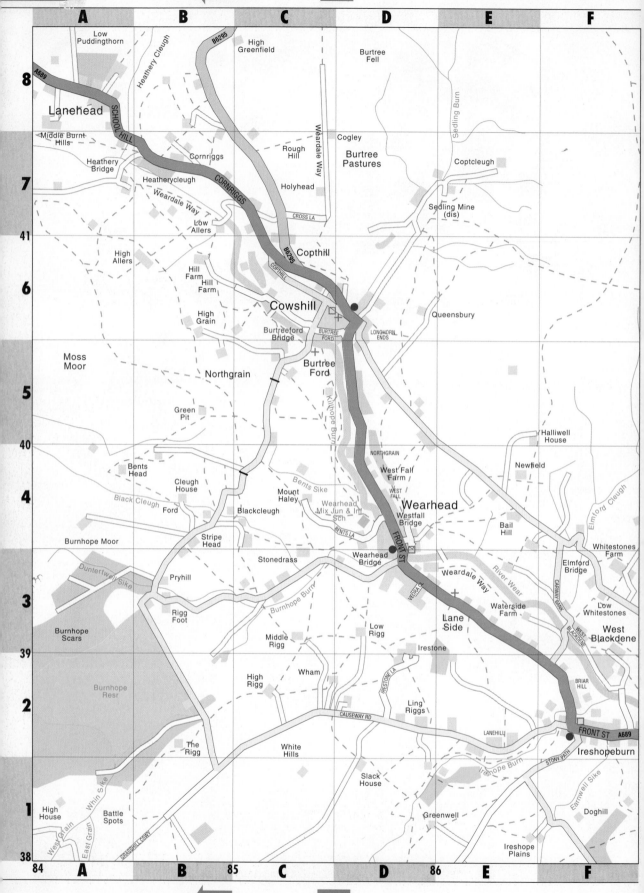

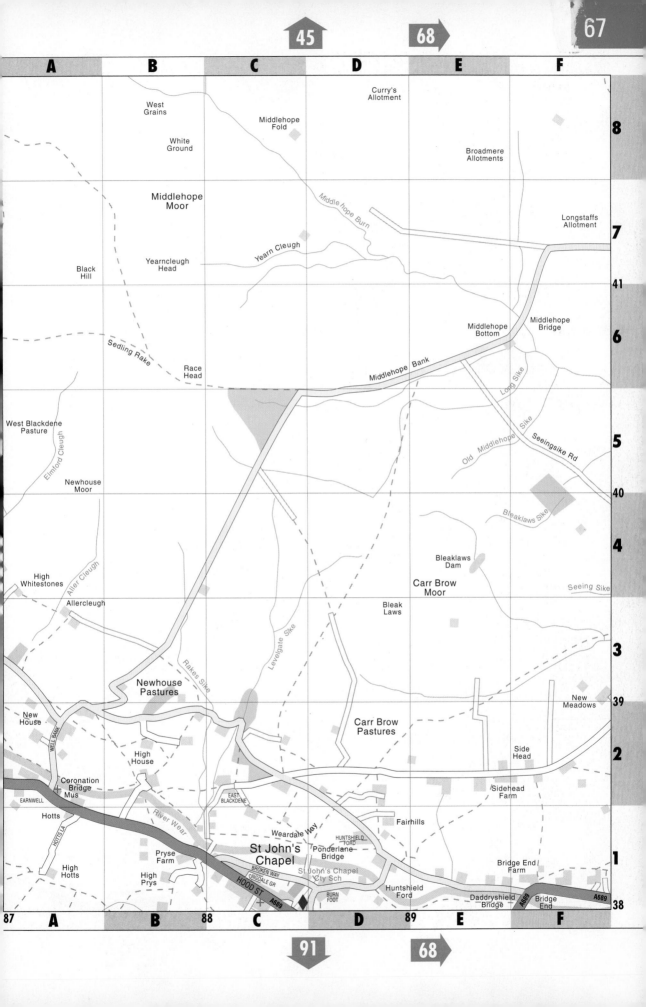

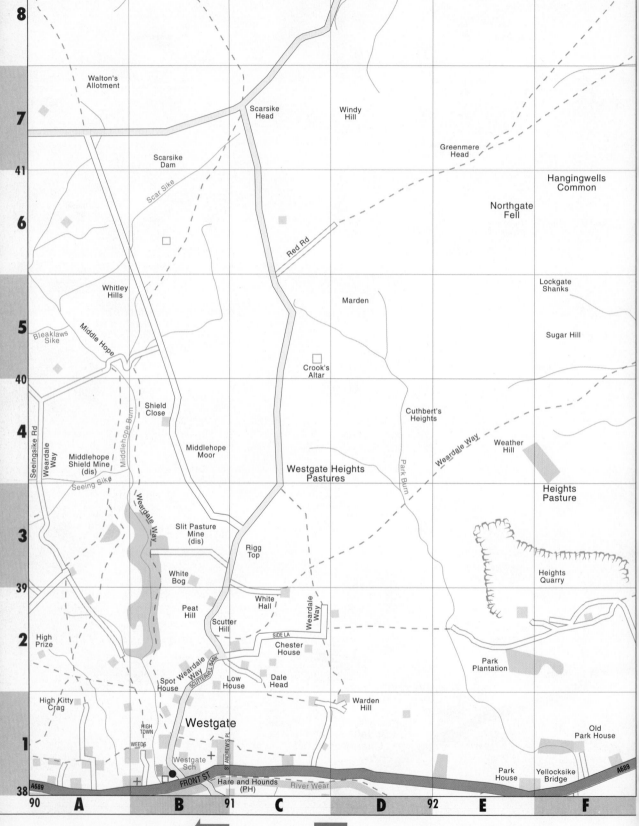

A **B** **C** **D** **E** **F**

8

7

41

6

5

40

4

3

39

2

1

38

Lintzgarth Common

Walton's Allotment

Scarsike Head

Windy Hill

Greenmere Head

Scarsike Dam

Hangingwells Common

Northgate Fell

Scar Sike

Red Rd

Whitley Hills

Lockgate Shanks

Middle Hope

Marden

Bleaklaws Sike

Sugar Hill

Shield Close

Crook's Altar

Cuthbert's Heights

Weardale Way

Weather Hill

Seeingsike Rd

Weardale Way

Middlehope Burn

Middlehope Shield Mine (dis)

Middlehope Moor

Westgate Heights Pastures

Park Burn

Heights Pasture

Seeing Sike

Weardale Way

Slit Pasture Mine (dis)

Rigg Top

Heights Quarry

White Bog

White Hall

Peat Hill

Weardale Way

Scutter Hill

High Prize

SIDE LA

Chester House

Park Plantation

Spot House

Weardale Way

SCUTTERHILL BANK

Low House

Dale Head

High Kitty Crag

Warden Hill

Old Park House

HIGH TOWN

Westgate

ST ANDREW'S PL

WEEDS

Westgate Sch

Park House

Yellocksike Bridge

A689

FRONT ST

Hare and Hounds (PH)

River Wear

A689

90 **A** **B** 91 **C** **D** 92 **E** **F**

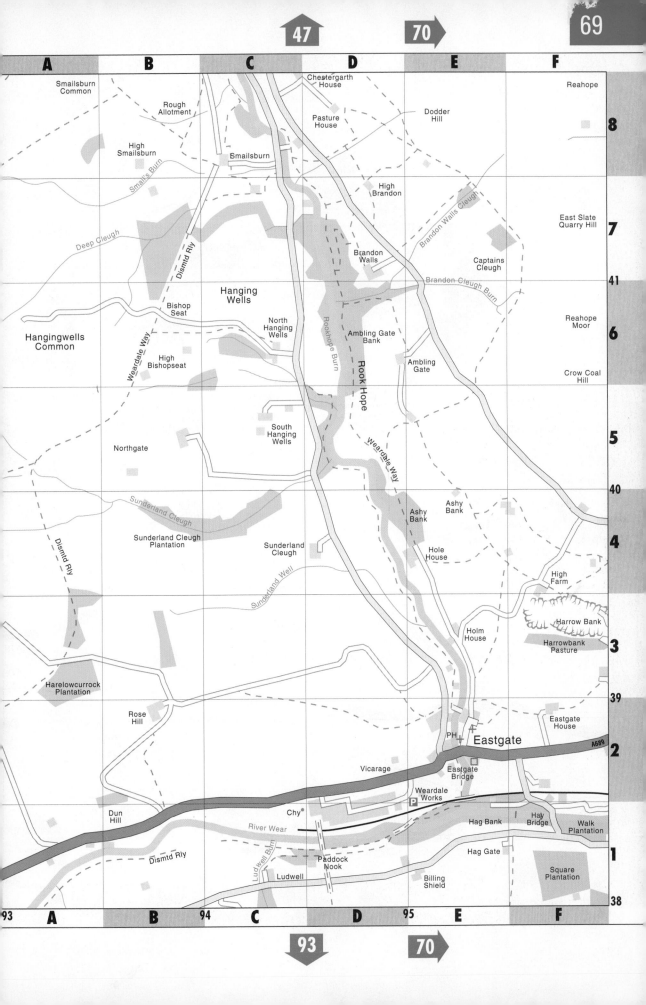

A B C D E F

8

Shank Sike

Hope House

High House

Park Plantation

Longwell Sike

7

Deep Sike

Reahope Burn

Park Shops

Clint's Plantation

Shield Hurst

41

Isaac Sike

Reahope Moor

Stoneby Sike

Fiddle Plantation

Noah's Ark

Stanhope Burn

West Pasture

6

Pease Mires

Stanhope Common

5

Hungry Hill

Mount Pleasant

Spring Plantation

Keeper's Lodge

Widley Field

Black Hill

40

Bewdley Plain

Belle Vue

4

Bewdley

Green Head Cottage

Allerton Burn

Allerton Wood

Stanhope Hall

Spain's Field

West Bewdley

Green Head

Greenfoot Caravan Site

Kell's Bank

Thrush Nest

Guy's Close

Stanhope Bridge

Horn Hall

A689

B6278

H

3

Brock Bank

Sweet Wells

Golden Lands

B6278

39

Hare Law

Weardale Way

East Softley Plantation

B6278

Howl John

Horsley Burn Wood

River Wear

Snow Field

West Softley Plantation

2

A689

White House Farm

Horsley Burn Farm

Aller Gill House

Crutch Bank

Walk Plantation

Aller Gill Cottage

1

Horsley Hall

Horsley Burn

B6278

Hag Top

38

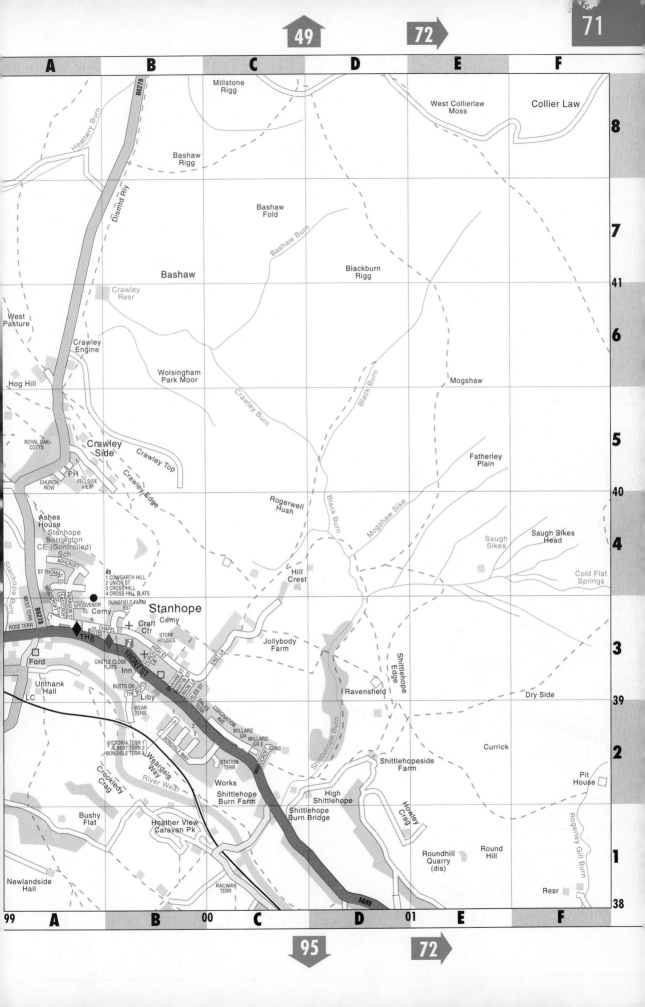

8

Millstone
Rigg

West Collierlaw
Moss

Collier Law

Bashaw
Rigg

7

Bashaw
Fold

Bashaw Burn

41

Bashaw

Blackburn
Rigg

Crawley
Resr

Black Burn

Mogshaw

6

West
Pasture

Crawley
Engine

Hog Hill

Wolsingham
Park Moor

Crawley Burn

Fatherley
Plain

5

Royal Oak
Cotts

Crawley
Side

Crawley Top

PH

CHURCH
ROW

FELLSIDE
VIEW

Crawley Edge

40

Rogerwell
Hush

Mogshaw Sike

Saugh Sikes
Head

Ashes
House

Stanhope
Barrington
CE (Controlled)
Sch

ASHCROFT

ST THOMAS
CL

A3

Black Burn

Saugh
Sikes

Saugh Sikes
Head

Cold Flat
Springs

4

A3
1 COWGARTH HILL
2 UNION ST
3 CROSS HILL
4 CROSS HILL FLATS

Hill
Crest

WESTCROFT

B2278

GROSVENOR
CL

DUNSFIELD FARM
EST

Stanhope

Cemy

ROSE TERR

WEST TERR

St Thomas CL

Craft
Ctr

Chapel St

STONE
HOUSES

Jollybody
Farm

Shittlehope
Edge

3

Ford

TH
PH

CASTLE CLOSE
FLATS

FRONT ST

Inn

HIGH ST

CHURCH LA

EAST LA

Ravensfield

Dry Side

39

Unthank
Hall

LC

BUTTS GR

THE BUTTS

Liby

WEAR
TERR

BARHAM ST

MARTIN ST

DALES ST

DALES DRV

CORONATION AVE

WILLARD
GR

WILLARD
GR E

Shittlehope Burn

Currick

2

VICTORIA TERR 1
ALBERT TERR 2
BONDISLE TERR 3

BONDISLE WAY

1
2
3

STATION
TERR

WILLARD
GDNS

WESTCROFT

Shittlehopeside
Farm

Howley
Crag

Pit
House

Crookledy
Crag

Weardale
Way

River Wear

Works

Shittlehope
Burn Farm

High
Shittlehope

Shittlehope
Burn Bridge

1

Bushy
Flat

Heather View
Caravan Pk

Roundhill
Quarry
(dis)

Round
Hill

Rogerley Gill Burn

Resr

Newlandside
Hall

RAILWAY
TERR

A68

38

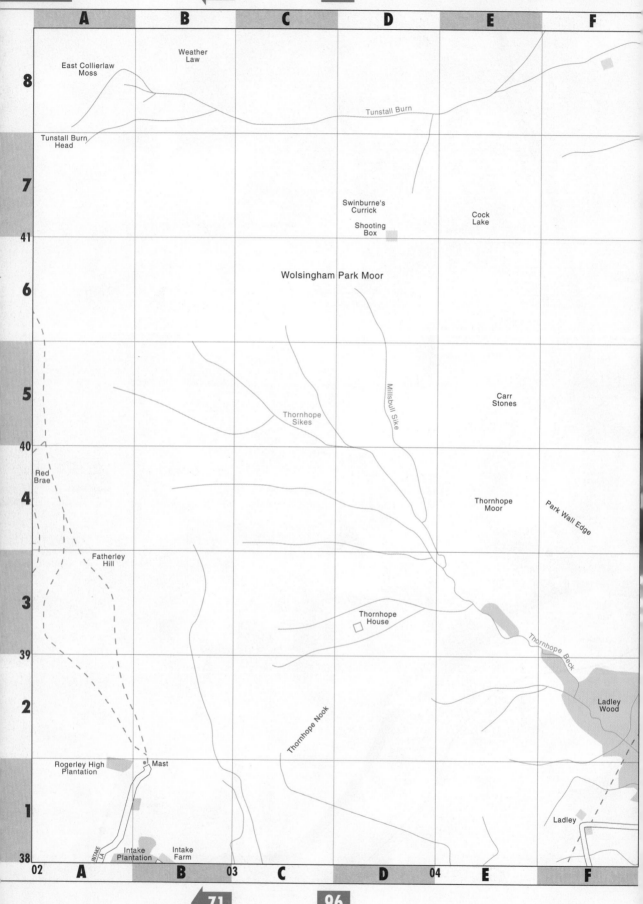

East Collierlaw
Moss

Weather
Law

Tunstall Burn
Head

Tunstall Burn

8

7

41

Swinburne's
Currick

Shooting
Box

Cock
Lake

6

Wolsingham Park Moor

Thornhope
Sikes

Millsbull Sike

Carr
Stones

5

40

Red
Brae

Thornhope
Moor

Park Wall Edge

4

Fatherley
Hill

Thornhope Beck

3

Thornhope
House

39

Ladley
Wood

2

Thornhope Nook

Rogerley High
Plantation

Mast

1

Ladley

38

INTAKE LA

Intake
Plantation

Intake
Farm

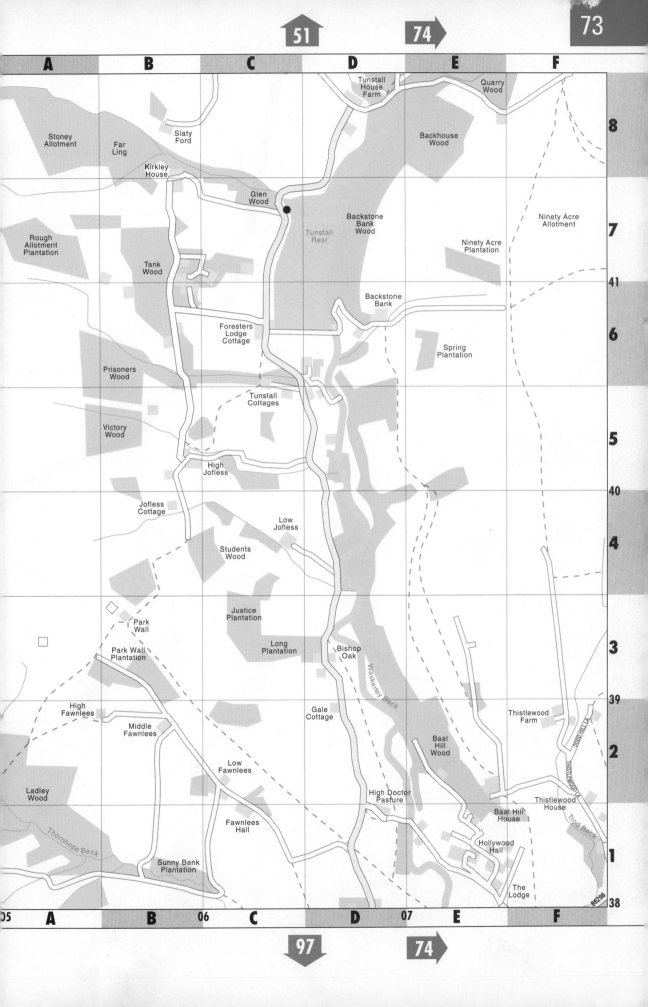

A B C D E F

8

Wharndean
Wood

Springwell
Cottage
Farm

7

Dismtd Rly

41

Greenfield
Cottage

6

Sand Edge

Low
Houselop

High House
Farm

Wolsingham
North Moor

High
Houselop

High
Stoop

5

The Brown
Horse
(PH)

Middle
Houselop

Ward's End
Cottages

40

Armond Carr
Works

4

Redmires

Houselop Beck

Viewly
Hill

3

Dodd
Hill

Richmond
Farm

39

Castle
Hills

Armond
Carr

Houselop
Bridge

2

Sandy
Carr

Houselope
Grange

Redgate
Grange

Houselopbridge
House

Mount
Pleasant

Grey's
Well

1

Redgate
Farm

Redgate
Head

New
Row

REDGATE BANK

Redgate
Hall

B6297

38

LOW REDGATE BANK

08 A B 09 C D 10 E F

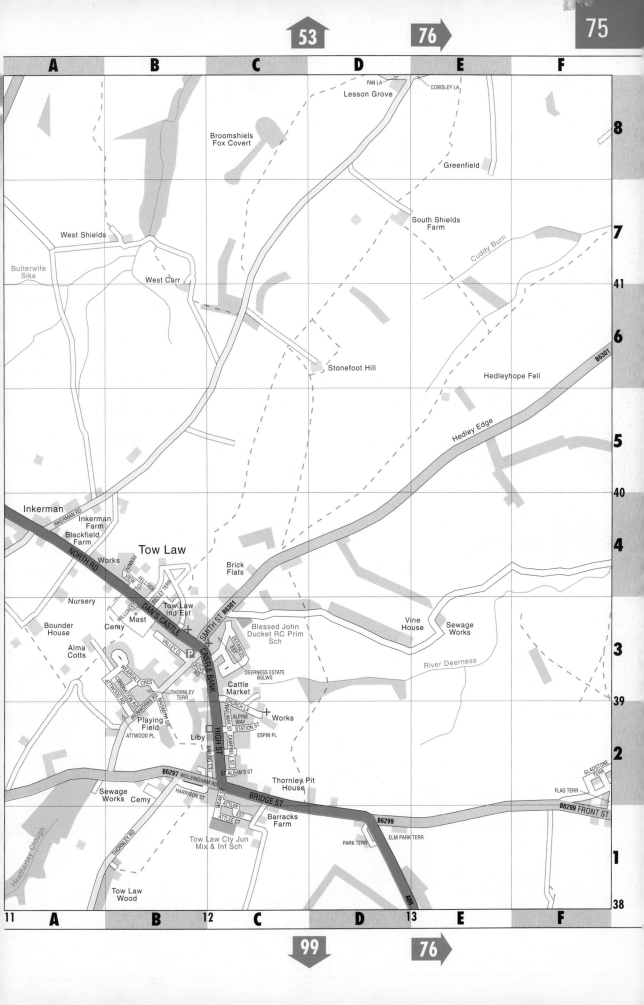

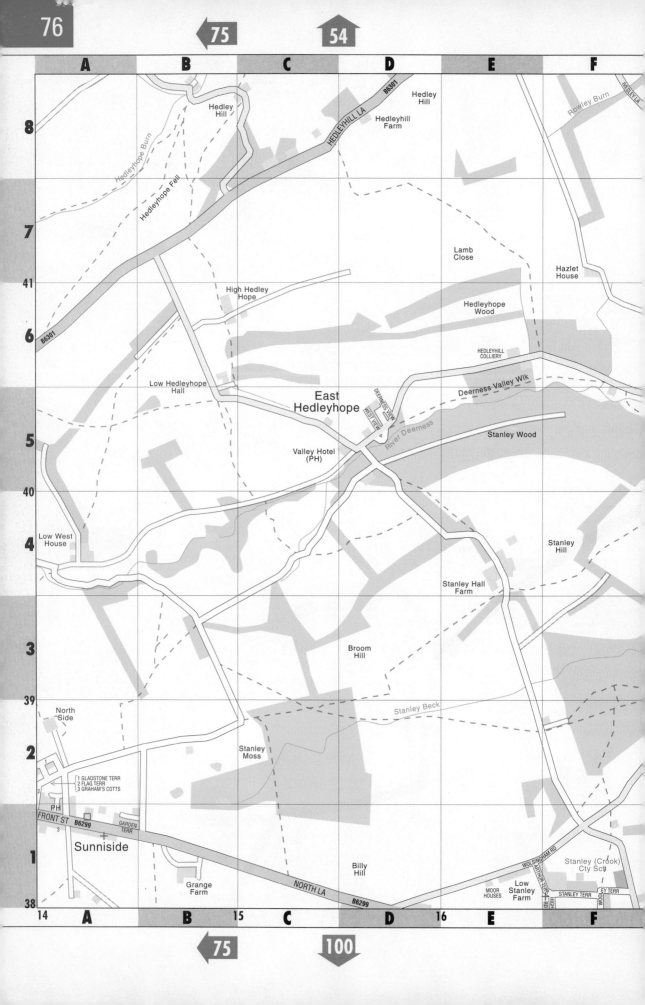

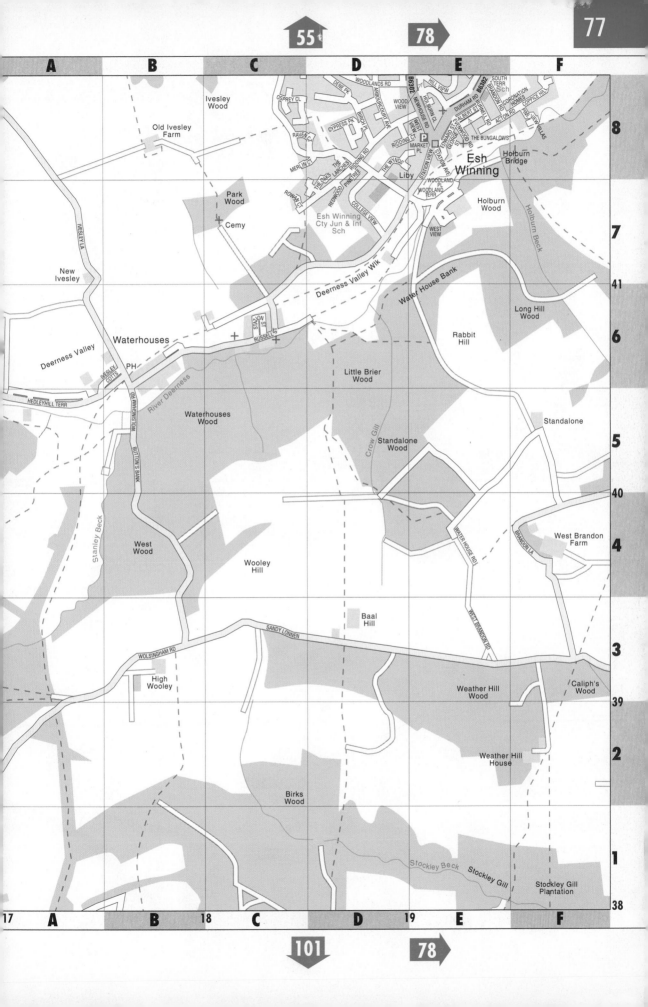

A   B   C   D   E   F

8

7

41

6

5

40

4

3

39

2

1

38

Ivesley Wood

Old Ivesley Farm

IVESLEY LA

New Ivesley

Deerness Valley

HEDLEYHILL TERR

Park Wood

Cemy

Waterhouses

IVESLEY COTTS

PH

WOLSINGHAM RD

BUTTON'S BANK

Stanley Beck

Waterhouses Wood

West Wood

River Deerness

OSPREY CL

DENE PK

WOODLANDS RD

ARBOURCOURT AVE

WOOD VIEW

HILL VIEW

B6302

SOUTH TERR

CORONATION HOMES

BRANDON RD

COPPICE HILL

THE VILLAS

ACTON RD

DURHAM RD

BURNELL RD

ALBERT ST

GEORGE ST

EDWARD ST

DENNOOD RD

STATION VIEW

MERLIN CT

THE OAKS

THE LARCHES

REDWOOD

PINE TREE

RIDDING RD

WEST

RIDDING CT

THE WYNDS

CYPRESS PK

BIRCH PL

RAVEN CT

ROWAN CT

RIDDING CT

COLLEGE VIEW

Esh Winning Cty Jun & Inf Sch

MARKET PL

STATION RD

Libry

WEST VIEW

WOODLAND PL

WOODLAND TERR

WEST VIEW

Esh Winning

The Bungalows

Holburn Bridge

Holburn Wood

HOLBURN BECK

Holburn Wood

Deerness Valley Wlk

Water House Bank

41

Long Hill Wood

Rabbit Hill

Little Brier Wood

Crow Gill

Standalone Wood

Standalone

BRANDON LA

West Brandon Farm

Wooley Hill

WATER HOUSE RD

Sandy Lonnen

Baal Hill

WEST BRANDON RD

Weather Hill Wood

Caliph's Wood

Wolsingham Rd

High Wooley

Weather Hill House

Birks Wood

Stockley Beck

Stockley Gill

Stockley Gill Plantation

A B C D E F

8

Biggin Farm

Park Lodge

Redburn Wood

Eshwood Hall

Red Burn

Esh Wood

New Brancepeth

WOODBINE TERR
PROSPECT PL
BEWLEY TERR 1
BENVILLE TERR 2
HAWTHORN TERR 3
THE BUNGALOWS
Deerness Valley
River Deerness
ROCK TERR
EDWARD TERR
PROSPECT TERR
CO-OPERATIVE TERR
WALTONS TERR
BRAUNESPATH EST
FAIRFALLS TERR
TUSCAN CL
New Brancepeth Cty Jun & Inf Sch
DORIC RD
ROWLEY CL
PRINGLE PL
PRINGLE GR
PRINGLE CL
Pringle House

41

7

Hill House

6

Long Hill Wood

Stob House

5

North Wood

PIT LA

Cemy

BRANDON LA

Pithouse East Plantation

40

4

East Brandon Wood

Pithouse Plantation

CHERRY PK 1
LABURNAM PK 2
MAPLE CL
BRANCEPETH VIEW
SCRIPTON GILL RD
FOREST
ASHBROOK CL

3

Rabbit Hill Plantation

Bowser's Gill

Morley Farm

MORLEY LA

Scripton Gill

BEECHCROFT AVE 3
CAMBERLEY DR 4

39

South Brandon Farm

Caliph's Gill

Brawn's Den

WOLSINGHAM RD

Quarry Hill

Quarryhill Cottages

Littlewhite Farm

2

Tunstall Burn

Brandon-Bishop Auckland Walk

A690

1

Stockley Beck

Stockley Gill Wood

Goodwell Farm

P

1 WILLIAM RUSSELL HOMES
2 FOXES ROW

THE OLD FORGE
THE CLOSE
GOODWELL LEA

A690

DURHAM RD

38

20 A B 21 C 22 D E F

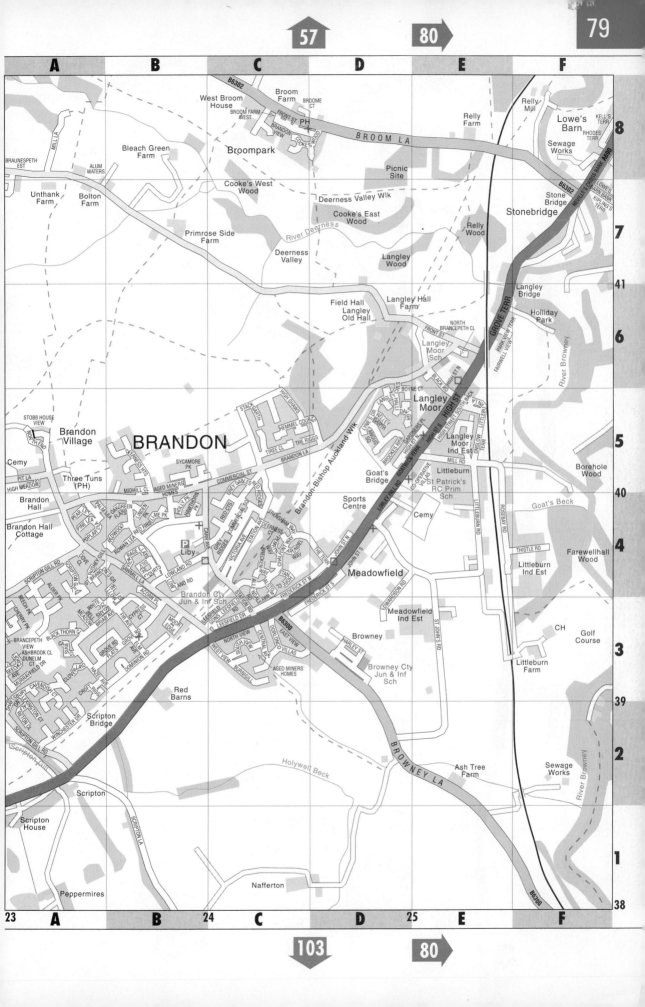

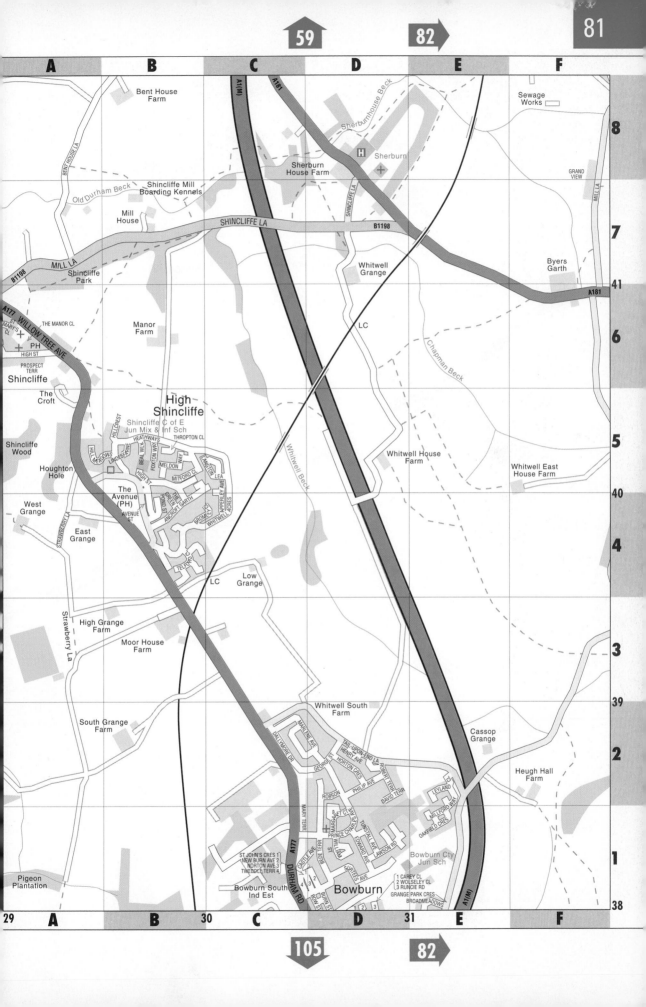

81
60

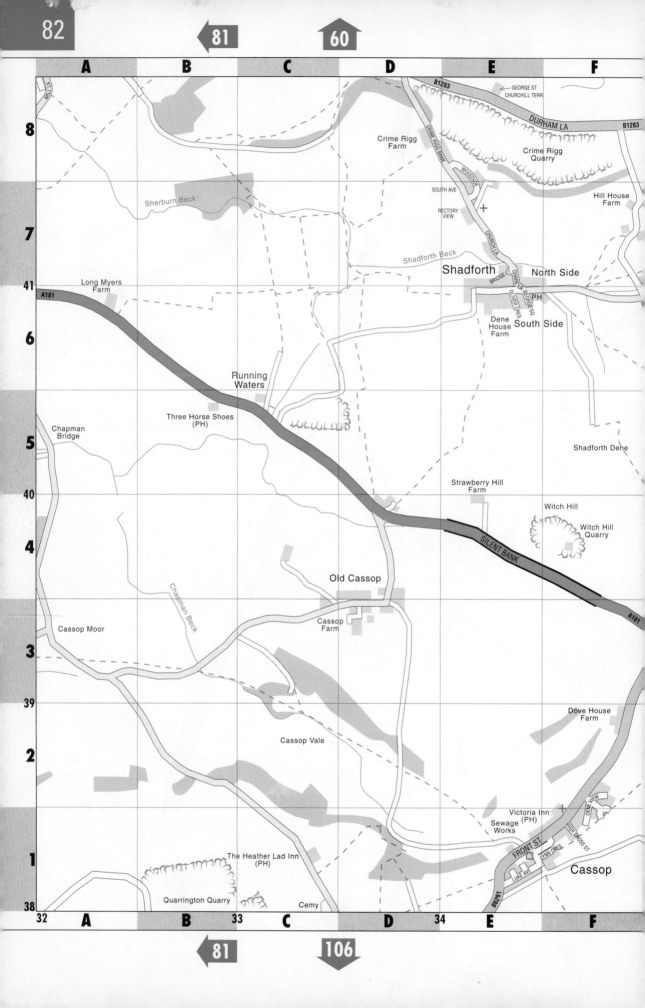

B1283
DURHAM LA
B1200
B1283
Pemberton Arms
(PH)
North Moor
Farm
Haswell
Moor
Recn
Gd
Landing Strip

8

Thorpe
Moor

MILL HILL
DAVY DR
PEASEC

Harehill
Moor
Shotton RC
Jun Mix & Inf Sch
Fleming Hotel
(PH)
1 CROSSFIELD CRES
2 MARCIA AVE
3 CHURCH VIEW
4 GRANGE TERR
Shotton Colliery
Cty Jun Sch
Shotton
Colliery
Cty Inf
Sch
5 FARM COTTS
6 THE TERRACE
Shotton Colliery
Ind Est

7

North West
Ind Est
COOK WAY
BURDON DR

Wapping Burn

Fleming
Field
FLEMING
CT
Flemingfield
Farm
STATION RD
BELVEDERE GDNS
WEST GARTH GR
ATKINSON GR
HAWHILL RD
WINFIELD RD
Co-OPERATIVE TERR 7
BEVAN GROVE 8
JUBILEE
PL
ARDEN ST
FRONT ST
ROSE COTTS
SHOTTON RD

41

WHITEHOUSE
CRES
DOXFORD DR
BRINDLEY RD

6

Liby
HASWELL GR
WEST GARTH
TEE TERR
LILAC TERR
HAZEL TERR
LABURNUM TERR
HAWTHORNE TERR
DUNELM
PL
COWLEY ST
WINDSOR PL
EDEN
VIEW
DENE CRES
South West
Ind Est
WHITEHOUSE WAY

HAMILTON
CT
FRIARS
GR
ALLCOTE GR
GEORGE
ST
KING ST
EAST GN
DENE TERR
BRACKENHILL
Council
Bldgs
WHITWORTH RD
BRACKEN HILL

VICTORIA ST
MILBANK TERR
MILTON GR
DENE AVE
BRACKEN HILL

Bracken Hill

Shotton
Colliery
SWAN'S TERR
MOORE TERR
SHOTTON LA

Brackenhill
Farm No 1
Bracken Hill
Farm

BYRON TERR
Brackenhill

5

CARLYLE CRES
BRIDGE RD
BGLWS
BRIDGE RD
BRUCE GLASIER TERR
GROVE CT
1 WILLIAM MORRIS TERR
2 KIER HARDIE TERR
Gore Burn
Calfpasture
Dene

High Crow's
House
DIXON EST
1 COOK
TERR

40

DIXON ESTATE
BGLWS
Swan
Castle
Farm
Haswell to Hart
Countryside Walkway
Edder
Acres

Edderacres Dene

Low Crow's
House
Haswell
Plantation
Thornley Station
Ind Est

4

Wapping Burn

LYNN TERR
B1279
Round
Hill

Green
Hills
Thornley Crossings
Picnic Area
SHOTTON BANK

WATSONS CL
GREENWOOD CL
DODDS CL
OFFICE ST
Edderacres Burn

3

PATTON WLK
CHURCH
ST
WEARDALE PK

39

Edderacres
Plantation

2

Warden
Lodge
Burn
Plantation
Nanny's
Plantation
Green Hills
Moor
Winning
Plantation

A19

New
Winning

Foxhole
Wood
TRUSCATE LA
A181
TAYLOR GR
DURHAM RD
WINGROVE
CL
GREEN
HILLS
ES
Wellfield
1 2 3
WELLFIELD RD N
WELLFIELD RD
WELLFIELD RD S
A181

1

MOORE SQ 1
LAING SQ 2
SALTER'S LA 3
KING'S RD
CORONATION
TERR
DODDS TERR
DOBSON
TERR
WALTON
ST
NORTH RD
B1200
FOUR WAYS
GRANBY
CT
GRANBY
TERR
BURDON CRES
Wellfield
A J Dawson
Sec Sch
1 RAILWAY COTTS
2 WELLFIELD TERR
3 HIGH WINNING COTTS
Catchgate
Farm

38

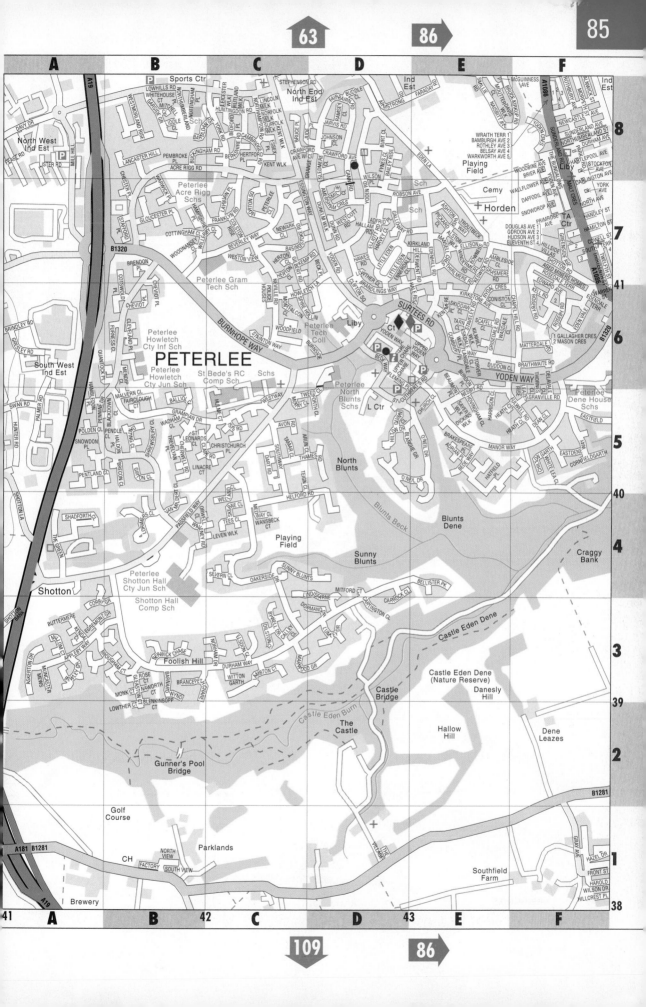

A B C D E F

8

Horden
Whitesides Gill
Kilburn Dr
Blackhills Gill
Blackhills Farm
LC

7
Sea View Gdns
Simpson St
7th
Helm St
Park View
Lathorpe
First St
John Wilson Cl
South East View
Allot Gdns
Horden Cotsford Cty Jun Sch

A7
1 EAST VIEW
2 WEST VIEW
3 GRANT ST
4 EMERSON CT
5 CLAXTON ST
6 NINTH ST
7 TENTH ST
8 ELEVENTH ST
9 EDWARD CAIN CT

South Terr
Tees St
Schs
Eighth St
Dene St
Third St

41
Warren St
Blackhills Terr
Park Terr
Sixth St
Fifth St
Beach
Paradise St
Windsor Terr
GR 2
Cotsford La
Acacia Ave
Cedar St
Bay Ave
Cherry St
Alder Rd
11 10

B6
1 BRAEMAR TERR
2 GLANTON TERR
3 ADAM ST
4 EVE ST
5 ALMOND TERR
6 AZALEA AVE
7 ASPEN AVE
8 MARLBROUGH CRES
9 BLACKTHORNE AVE
10 LANGTHORNE AVE
11 SANDRINGHAM CRES

6
B1320
Yoden Way
Dene Terr
A1086
Hawthorne Cres
Burnhope Ave
Cresswell
Ash Cres
Elm Terr
Murray St
COAST RD
Dene Bank Ave
Woodland Ave
Rosetown Ave
Cotsford Park Est
Dene Villas
Yohden Hall Comp Sch
Sch
Reynolds Ct
Macbeth Wlk
Dixon Pl
Staton Cotts
Limekiln Gill
Hartlepool Point

A6
1 ROGERS CL
2 CORONATION AVE
3 COTSFORD CRES
4 BEECH TERR

Peterlee Dene House Sec Sch
Horden Dene View Special Sch
Dene Mouth

EASTFIELD
Thorntree Gill
Castle Eden Burn

5
Priest's Gill
Wordsworth Ave
Tennyson Ave
Shakespeare Ave
Milton Ave
Kipling Ave
Shaftesbury Rd
Coleridge Ave
Chaucer Ave
Allot Gdns

40
Scotchman's Gill
Ash Gill
Burns Ave
Snowdon Ave
Shaftesbury Ave
Mackworth Rd
Blackhall Colliery Ind Est

4
Fulwell Plantation
Hardwick Dene
SHAFTESBURY CRES
Eleventh St
Tenth St
Ninth St
Eighth St
Seventh St
Sixth St
Fifth St
East St
Third St
Second St
First St
Blue House Gill
Welfare Cres
West St Cl
West St
School Ave
Park Ave
Aspatria Ave
Corby Cl
Oak Rd
Gill Rd

3
Hardwick Hall Farm
Hardwick Hall Manor Hotel
Blackhall Colliery
North St
Hesleden Rd
Rees Cl
Stuart Cl
Kenber Dr
Primrose Ct
Bluebell Cl
Daffodil Cl
Keading
Liby
Blackhall RC Sch
B1281
Aged Miners Homes
Thornton Terr
Coronation Ave
Hepscott Ave
Old Gdns
Hanthorne Ave
Lime Ave
Sycamore Ave
Proctor Ave
Beech Terr
Yohden Hall Comp Sch
Allot Gdns

39
HESLEDEN RD
COAST RD
Cemy
Maureen Ave
Meadow Ave
Glenholm Terr
Elizabeth St
Lilac Ave

2
B1281
Mickle Hill
Blackhall Rocks
Station Rd
Bglws
Station Rd
A1086
Broad Rd
Railway Cotts
Pattison Gdns
Princess Cl
Ocean View
Sea View
Ocean Cres
Ocean View
Marine Cres
Hart Cres
Weddle Ave
Lilac Ave
Belford Cl

1
Hazel Gr
Front St
Myra Ave
Church St
Weems' Farm
Hesleden Cty Sch
High Hesleden Farm
Ship Inn (PH)
The Bungalows
Mickle Hill Rd
South Black Halls Farm
Attlee Ave
Pattison Cres 1
Warnbrook Cres 2

1 HAROLD WILSON DR
2 HILLCREST PL

38
Station Rd
Eden Cotts
Hesleden
East Terr
Dene View
High Hesleden

44 A B 45 C D 46 E F

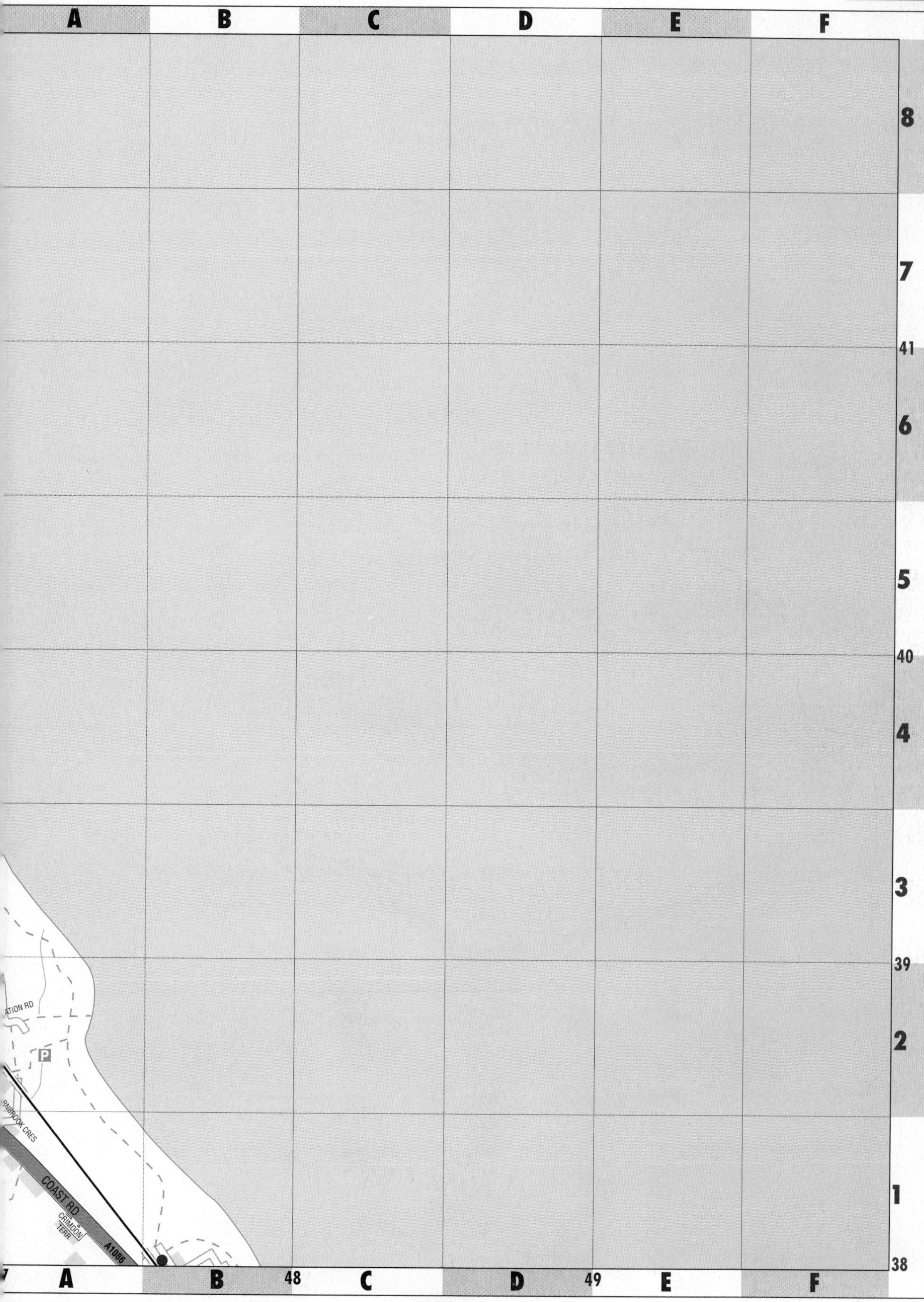

A | B | C | D | E | F

8

7

41

6

5

40

4

3

39

2

1

38

STATION RD

P

RHYBROOK CRES

COAST RD

CRIMSON TERR

A1088

A | B | 48 | C | D | 49 | E | F

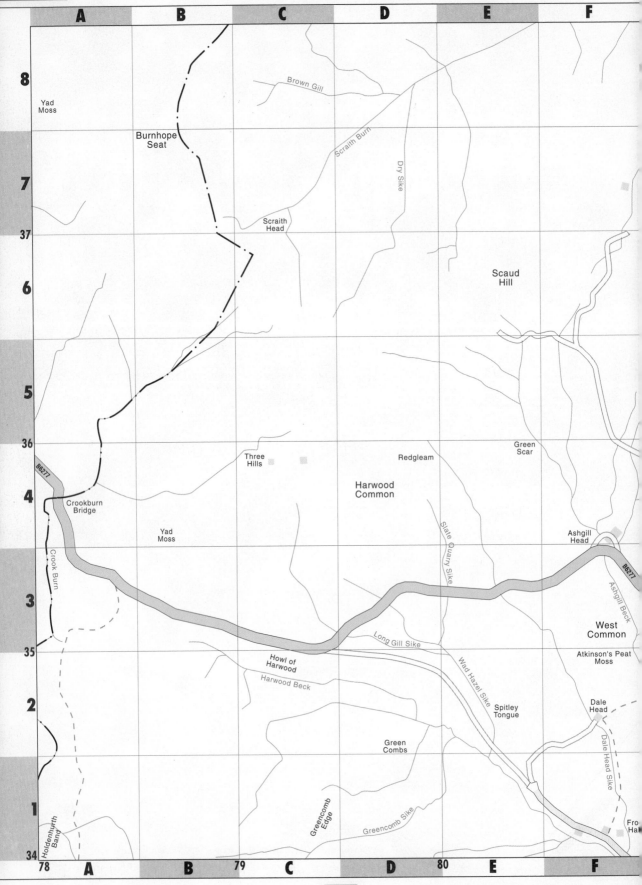

Yad
Moss

Brown Gill

Burnhope
Seat

Scraith Burn

Dry Sike

Scraith
Head

Scaud
Hill

B6277

Green
Scar

Three
Hills

Redgleam

Harwood
Common

Crookburn
Bridge

Yad
Moss

Slate Quarry Sike

Ashgill
Head

Ashgill Beck

Crook Burn

B6277

West
Common

Long Gill Sike

Atkinson's Peat
Moss

Howl of
Harwood

Harwood Beck

Wad Hazel Sike

Spitley
Tongue

Dale
Head

Green
Combs

Dale Head Sike

Greencomb
Edge

Greencomb Sike

Fro
Ha

Holdenhurth
Band

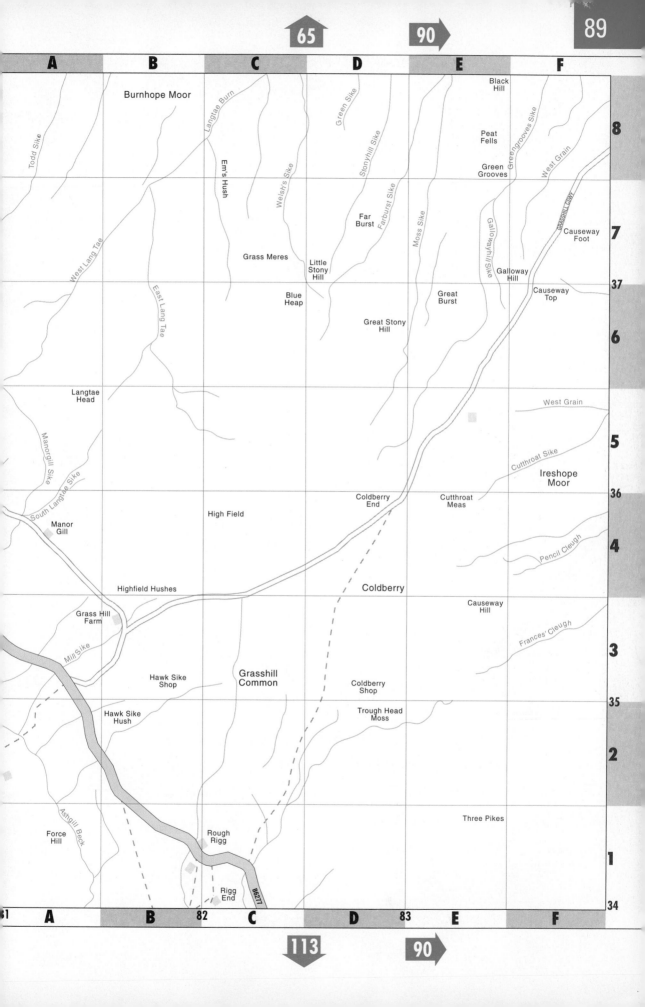

A   B   C   D   E   F

Burnhope Moor

Black Hill

Todd Sike

Langtae Burn

Green Sike

Peat Fells

Greengrooves Sike

West Grain

8

Em's Hush

Welsh's Sike

Stonyhill Sike

Green Grooves

GRASSHILL CSWY

Farburst Sike

Far Burst

Moss Sike

Gallowayhill Sike

Causeway Foot

7

West Lang Tae

Grass Meres

Little Stony Hill

Galloway Hill

37

East Lang Tae

Blue Heap

Great Burst

Causeway Top

Great Stony Hill

6

Langtae Head

West Grain

Manorgill Sike

Cutthroat Sike

Ireshope Moor

5

South Langtae Sike

High Field

Coldberry End

Cutthroat Meas

36

Manor Gill

Pencil Cleugh

4

Highfield Hushes

Coldberry

Causeway Hill

Grass Hill Farm

Frances' Cleugh

Mill Sike

3

Hawk Sike Shop

Grasshill Common

Coldberry Shop

35

Hawk Sike Hush

Trough Head Moss

2

Ashgill Beck

Three Pikes

Force Hill

Rough Rigg

1

Rigg End

B6277

34

A B C D E F

8

Greenwell
Crags

GRASSHILL SWY

The
Hags

Peatcleugh Sike

Ires
Hope

Ireshope
Plains

Hawkwell
Head

Black
Rigg

Wham
Pasture

Ireshope Burn

Groove Heads Sike

Rowantree
Plantation

7

37

Gravel Edge

Broad Sike

The
Burst

6

Clints
Crags

West Grain

Ireshope
Moor

Cormick's Currock
Rigg

Grooves Cleugh

Deep Cleugh

5

Harthope
Moor

Jenny Meggy's Sike

Nein
Head

Peat
Rigg

36

Bulls
Head

Noon
Hill

Birk Sike

4

Long Sike

3

Langdon
Common

Harthope
Head

35

Langdon
Head

Langdon
Head
Shop

2

Three
Comb

West Beck

Langdon Beck

1

Westbeck
Hush

34

84

A

85

B

C

86

D

E

F

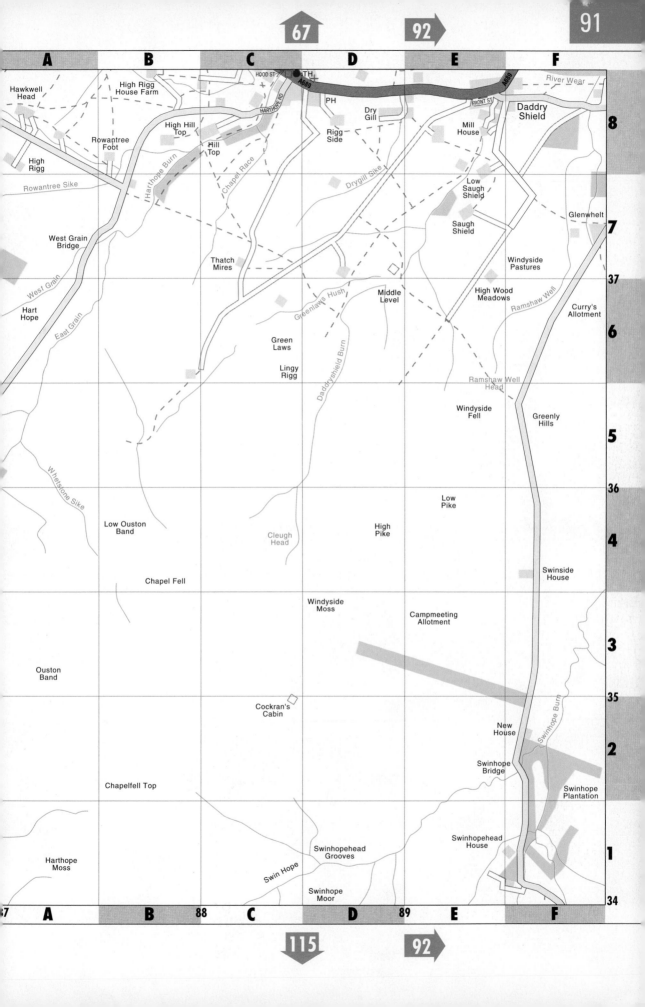

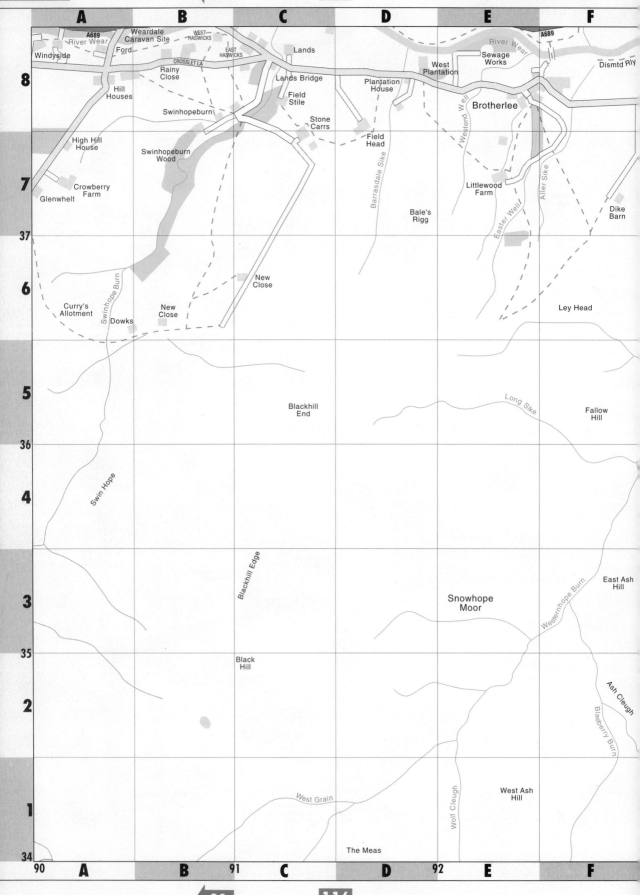

Windyside
River Wear
A689
Weardale Caravan Site
Ford
WEST HASWICKS
CROSSLET LA
EAST HASWICKS
Lands
Lands Bridge
West Plantation
Sewage Works
River Wear
A689
Dismtd Rly
Rainy Close
Hill Houses
Field Stile
Plantation House
Brotherlee
Westend Well
Swinhopeburn
Stone Carrs
Field Head
High Hill House
Swinhopeburn Wood
Littlewood Farm
Crowberry Farm
Glenwhelt
Barrasdale Sike
Bale's Rigg
Easter Well
Aller Sike
Dike Barn
Swinhope Burn
New Close
Ley Head
Curry's Allotment
Dowks
New Close
Blackhill End
Long Sike
Fallow Hill
Swin Hope
Blackhill Edge
Snowhope Moor
East Ash Hill
Westernhope Burn
Black Hill
Ash Cleugh
Blaeberry Burn
West Grain
Wolf Cleugh
West Ash Hill
The Meas

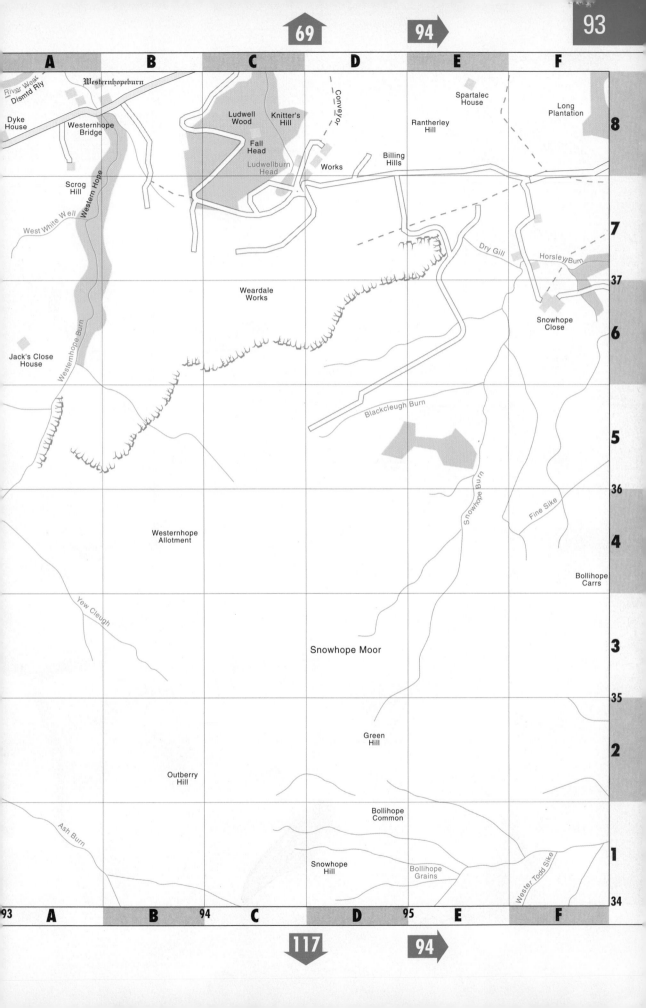

69
94

A B C D E F

Westernhopeburn
River Weat
Dismtd Rly
Dyke
House
Westernhope
Bridge
Scrog
Hill
West White Well
Western Hope
Ludwell
Wood
Knitter's
Hill
Fall
Head
Ludwellburn
Head
Works
Conveyor
Billing
Hills
Rantherley
Hill
Spartalec
House
Long
Plantation

8

Weardale
Works
Dry Gill
Horsley Burn
Snowhope
Close

7

37

Jack's Close
House
Westernhope Burn
Blackcleugh Burn
Snowhope Burn
Fine Sike
Bollihope
Carrs

6

5

36

Westernhope
Allotment

4

Yew Cleugh
Snowhope Moor

3

35

Green
Hill

2

Outberry
Hill
Bollihope
Common
Ash Burn
Snowhope
Hill
Bollihope
Grains
Wester Todd Sike

1

34

117
94

A　　　B　　　C　　　D　　　E　　　F

8

Horsley High
Cottage

Birkshaw

Newlandside Quarry
(Limestone)

Newlandside

B6278

Horsley Head

West
Newlandside

High
House

Shield
Ash

Moor
House

7

Horsley Burn

Easter
House

Snape
Gate

37

Cowburn
Head

6

Round
Hill

Brackenbridge Sike

Snapegate
Plantation

Brackenbridge
Moss

Fine Sike

Scot
Hill

5

Turfhill
End

36

Jopla Grains

Turf
Hill

4

Bridget
Hill

Stony
Hill

Jopla Sike

Carrs
Top

Rotten Holes

3

Bollihope
Carrs

Howl Slack

35

Washpool
Crags

P

2

Black Sike

Bollihope Burn

Bolli Hope

Bollihope Common

1

Smithy Burn

B6278

34

96　　A　　　B　　97　　C　　　D　　98　　E　　　F

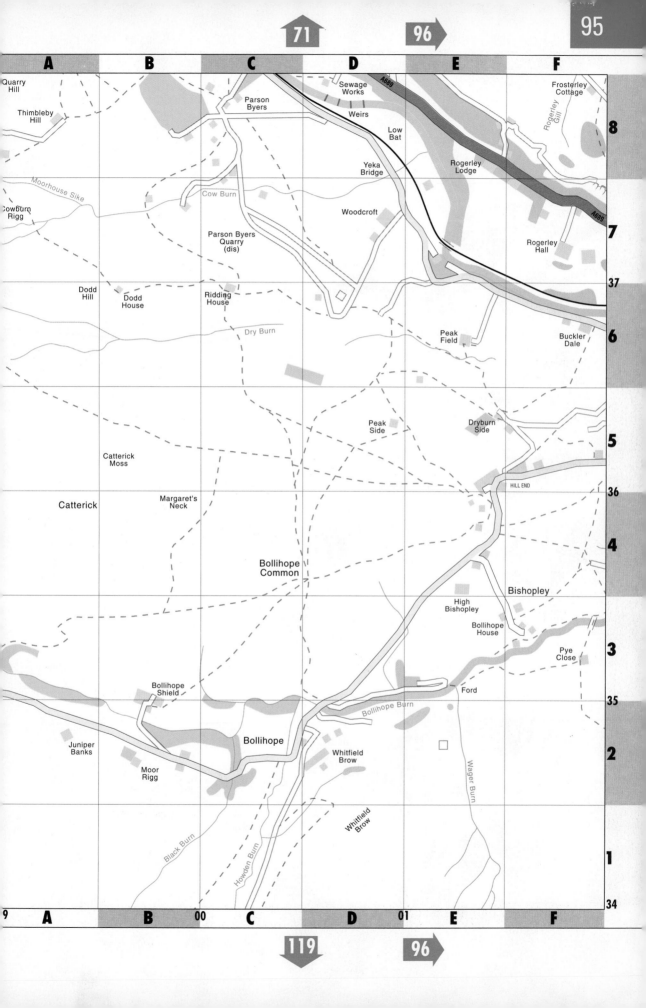

A B C D E F

Quarry Hill

Thimbleby Hill

8

Moorhouse Sike

Cow Burn

Cowburn Rigg

Parson Byers

Sewage Works

Weirs

Low Bat

Yeka Bridge

Woodcroft

A689

Frosterley Cottage

Rogerley Gill

Rogerley Lodge

7

Parson Byers Quarry (dis)

Rogerley Hall

A689

37

Dodd Hill

Dodd House

Ridding House

Dry Burn

Peak Field

Buckler Dale

6

Catterick Moss

Peak Side

Dryburn Side

5

Catterick

Margaret's Neck

HILL END

36

Bollihope Common

Bishopley

4

High Bishopley

Bollihope House

Pye Close

3

Bollihope Shield

Ford

35

Juniper Banks

Bollihope

Whitfield Brow

Bollihope Burn

Wager Burn

2

Moor Rigg

Black Burn

Howden Burn

Whitfield Brow

1

34

95 72

A B C D E F

8

Wiserley
Hill

High
Barn

Willow Green Burn

Newlands
Hall

7

A689

WESTFIELD

KIRK
RISE

Willow Green Gill

West
Newlands

Willow
Green

37

PH

STOCKLEY CRES

STOCKLEY GR

CROMER LEA

FRONT ST

Frosterley
Bridge

MELLBUT'S
BANK

WEAR VIEW

HOLMEFIELD

CROFT
TERR

GLEBE VIEW

WESTERN
HILL

TOLL
LA

THE
BATS

River Wear

LC

Sewage
Works

A689

Green Bank

6

Frosterley

Broadwood

The Eilands
Caravan Pk

LC

Landieu

Bridge End

Frosterley
South Cty
Sch

BELLE
VUE

East
Bridge End

Works

5

Miln House
Farm

Wise Eel
Bridge

36

Low Bishopley

Bollihope Burn

WHITE
KIRKLEY

West
Biggins

East
Biggins

4

Harehope Gill

North
Rigg

Harehope Burn

3

Fine
House

Harehope

East Biggins
Cottage

Harvey
Hill

35

Fine Gill

Fine Burn

Folly
Plantation

2

Weardale Way

Allotment
Plantations

1

Allotment
House

34

02 A B 03 C D 04 E F

101 78

A B C D E F

8

Fern Cottage

Stockley Fell Plantation

Stockley Fell Reservoir

Stockley

Brancepeth

Brancepeth Bridge

Brancepeth Castle

CH

Park Lodge

GOODWELL LEA

FOXES ROW

THE VILLAGE

A690

Works

STOCKLEY LA

Stockley Bridge

Stockley Beck

Brancepeth Beck

7

NEW ROW

Hundred Acre Plantation

Tripsy Bank

STOCKLEY GR

Brancepeth Castle Golf Course

37

WOOD VIEW

INSTITUTE ST

REED AVE

Park House Gill

WHITWORTH LA

6

MULLIN CI

ACORN

SHOP ROW

Oakenshaw

Ox Close Cottage

Ox Close Farm

Page Bank Lodge

Park House

Brandon-Bishop Auckland Wlk

5

Holland Hall

PARK VIEW

Page Bank East

Lingey Close

36

BRANCEPETH TERR

PARK ST

Works

Page Bank Wood

Page Bank Beck

4

BOURNE WAY

VICTORIA

BOYNE'S

RUSSELL PL

Allot Gdns

RAILWAY DR

RUTLAND DR

WARWICK PL

BEDFORD PL

ESSEX PL

Factory

Cemy

Tile Sheds Plantation

Tilery Cottage

Old House Beck

3

ROSEDALE TERR

DUNELM AVE

DEVON DR

DORSET DR

ROSEMEAD AVE

RECTORY

PRIORY GDNS

VICARAGE

MANOR RD

QUEENS

GDNS

CHURCH VIEW

SYCAMORE GR

LABURNUM GDNS

CEDAR

ASH DR

1 RUSSELL'S YD
2 WESLEY ST
3 NORTHUMBERLAND AVE
4 WESTMORLAND PL
5 SURREY PL
6 ST STEPHEN'S CL

35

COMMERCIAL ST

A690

SAINBRIDGE AVE

EDEN TERR

LOW WILLINGTON

OAK AVE

BIRCH DR

Lowfield

SALISBURY ST

DELL SIDE

RIVER VIEW

STONY BANK

2

HALL LANE EAST

Willington C of E Jun & Inf Sch

Willington Old Hall

The Park

Sewage Works

1 NORTH TERR
2 JUBILEE TERR
3 HALL TERR
4 MINERS' HOMES
5 SNOWDEN TERR
6 PARK TERR

Weardale Way

River Wear

Lowfield Farm

Sewage Works

WEAR RD

The Strait

Old Hall

Hall Farm

Nancy's Wood

Picnic Area

Wright's Wood

Byers Green

1

Jubilee Bridge

COBEY'S CARR LA

LONG LA

Cobey's Carr

Whinney Bank

Todhills

Byers Green Cty Jun & Inf Sch

WEAR LODGE

SHAFTO ST

INSTITUTE ST

NORTH ST

Marquis of Granby (PH)

ROBINSON TERR

GREENFIELD ST

GHENT ST

VINE ST

34

20 A 21 B C 22 D E F

101 126

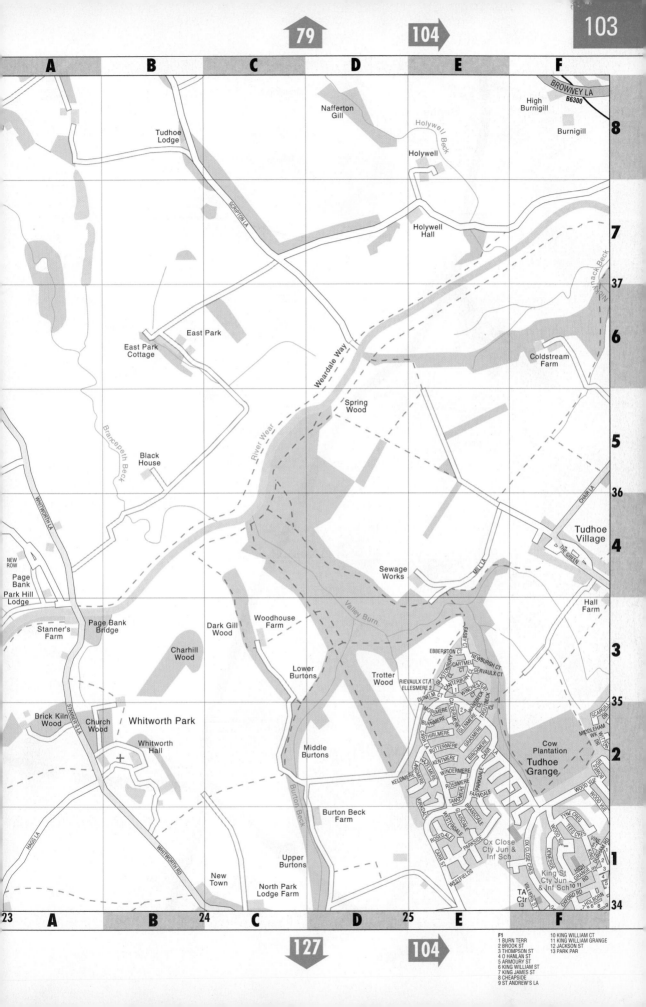

BROWNEY LA
B6300

High Burnigill

Burnigill

Nafferton Gill

Holywell Beck

Holywell

Tudhoe Lodge

SCRIPTON LA

Holywell Hall

8

7

37

6

East Park

East Park Cottage

Weardale Way

Coldstream Farm

Spring Wood

River Wear

Brancepeth Beck

Black House

5

36

MILL LA

CHAIR LA

Tudhoe Village

THE GREEN

4

WHITWORTH LA

NEW ROW

Page Bank
Park Hill Lodge

Stanner's Farm

Page Bank Bridge

Charhill Wood

STANNER'S LA

Dark Gill Wood

Woodhouse Farm

Sewage Works

Valley Burn

Hall Farm

Trotter Wood

Lower Burtons

EBBERSTON CT
NEWBURGH CT
CARTMEL CT
GLASTONBURY CT
GERVAULX CT
CANTERBURY CT
RIEVAULX CT 1
ELLESMERE 2
WINCHESTER CT
DUNELM CT
CALDERMERE
TROUTBECK CL
MOSSMERE
GLENMERE
GRASMERE
BUTTERMERE
CHAIR LA
THIRLMERE
BIRCHMERE
CARR LA
BUTTERMERE
WINDERMERE
KENTMERE
ROSSMERE
KELDMERE
TAMMERE
PARKDALE
FARNDALE
LANGDALE
HAZELMERE
WESTERDALE
GLASSDALE
BEANSDALE
RAVENSDALE
KIRKDALE
ROSEDALE
PARKSIDE
CARRS ST
WESTFIELDS

SCARGILL DR
MIDDLEHAM WY
DR
WITTON DR

Cow Plantation

Tudhoe Grange

WOOD VUE
WOOD VUE

TYNE CRES
TEES CRES
VINE CRES
WEAR CRES
DENESIDE
DURHAM RD
HIGH GRANGE RD
KING ST
OXFORD RD
HOLBORN
VILLIERS ST
JACKSON ST

Ox Close Cty Jun & Inf Sch

King St Cty Jun & Inf Sch

TA Ctr 13

3

35

2

Brick Kiln Wood

Church Wood

Whitworth Park

Whitworth Hall

Middle Burtons

BURTON BECK

Burton Beck Farm

HASE LA

WHITWORTH RD

New Town

Upper Burtons

North Park Lodge Farm

1

34

F1
1 BURN TERR
2 BROOK ST
3 THOMPSON ST
4 O HANLAN ST
5 ARMOURY ST
6 KING WILLIAM ST
7 KING JAMES ST
8 CHEAPSIDE
9 ST ANDREW'S LA
10 KING WILLIAM CT
11 KING WILLIAM GRANGE
12 JACKSON ST
13 PARK PAR

103
80

A B C D E F

8

River Browney
B6300
B6300
BROWNEY LA
Sunderland Bridge Way
Croxdale Bridge
Sunderland Bridge
The Mill House
Croxdale Hall
Square Plantation
High Croxdale
Annie's Wood
Weardale Way
River Wear
Works
Croxdale Viaduct
South Park
Croxdale Beck
Tursdale Wood

7

Johnson Terr
CROSS
ROGERSON CL
WINDSOR TERR
QUEEN'S GARTH
ROGERSON TERR
WATSIDE
FOSTER TERR
HETT LA
B6288

37

Coldstream Wood
WOOD VIEW
SALVIN ST
FRONT ST
VALLEY VIEW
FRONT ST E
PH
Blagden Beck
Cemy
NORTH ST
High Grange Farm
THE GREEN
EAST ST
Hett

6

Croxdale
Nickynack Beck
Nickynack Bridge
Cemy
Hett Village Inn (PH)
SOUTH VIEW
WEST ST
SOUTH GN
GROVE CT
LEEMAN'S LA
Falls Farm

5

Shieldfield House
CHAR LA
The Loggins
Loggins Wood
Coldstream House

36

Tudhoe Colliery Jun & Inf Sch

4

ATTWOOD TERR
FRONT ST
Tudhoe Ind Est
Tudhoe Colliery
The Coach & Horses (PH)
Lower Butcher Race
Hett Moor

3

THE GREEN
TUDHOE LA
ELM CL
OVAL
Tudhoe
MARY'S CR
CHARLES RD
ST DAVID'S CL
YORK VILLAS
Mount Huley Farm

35

SCARBILL DR
STENHOUSE
BARNARD
NORTH LA
THE CLOSE
DURHAM RD
YORK HILL CRES
TWEED RD
YORK HILL RD
WOLSEY RD
YORK HILL RD
Enterprise City
Sedgefield Enterprise Ctr
East Farm
Hill View
A688

2

Tudhoe Grange Comp Sch
Tudhoe St Charles's RC Sch
MIDDLEHAM WLK
WITTON DR
BOWES GR
BARWICK ST
LUMLEY CT
GILBERT ST
Tudhoe Park Villas
Five Lane Ends
SPENNYMOOR
Cemy
NORTH RD
WESTMORLAND CL
NEVILLE CL
MEADOWFIELD AVE
BUTCHERS RACE
Green Lane Ind Est
ENTERPRISE WAY
The Thinford (PH)
Thinford
THINFORD LA

1

WOOD VIEW
LOW GRANGE
HARTLEY TERR
SOUTH TERR
GERARD ST
BRYAN ST
DERWENT TERR
Spennymoor North Road Cty Jun Mix Sch
THE GARTH
MOUNT PLEASANT VIEW
MOUNT PLEASANT CL
Mount Pleasant
TUDHOE MOOR
NORTH RD
THE SPINNEY
GREEN LA

34

MARMADUKE ST
BARNFIELD RD
ST ANDREW'S LA
ST ANDREW'S CL
Bessemer Park Sch
RICHMOND FIELDS
WORKS RD
ELSWATER RD
KESWICK CL
B6288
UPPER CHURCH ST
HALF MOON LA
SPENNYMOOR LA
GRANGER ST
MOUNT PLEASANT
MOOR BROOM
PH
A688
A688
A167

26 A 27 B C 27 D 28 E F

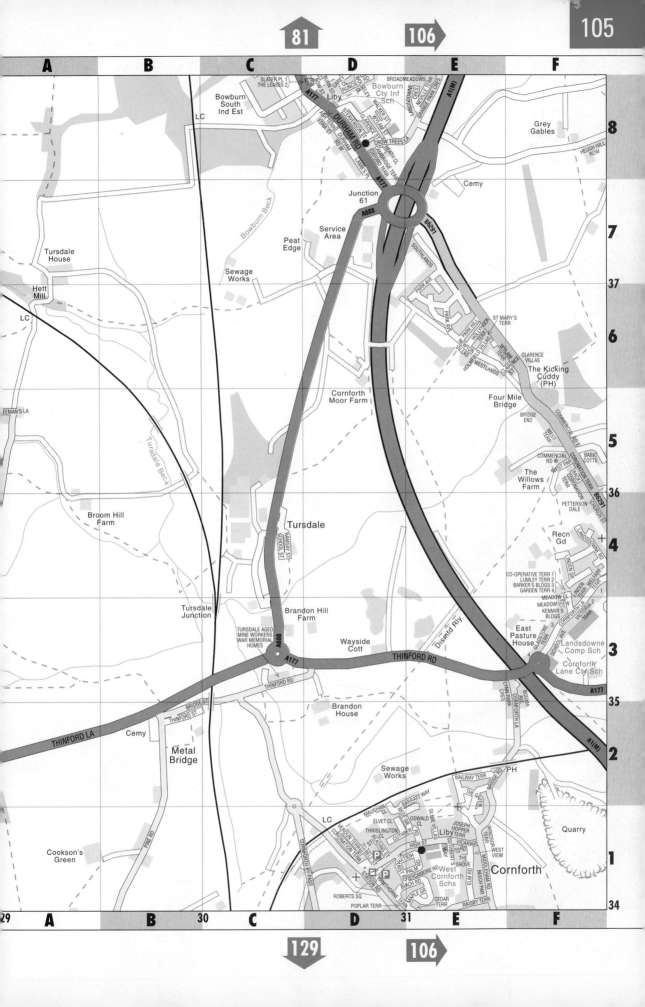

105
82

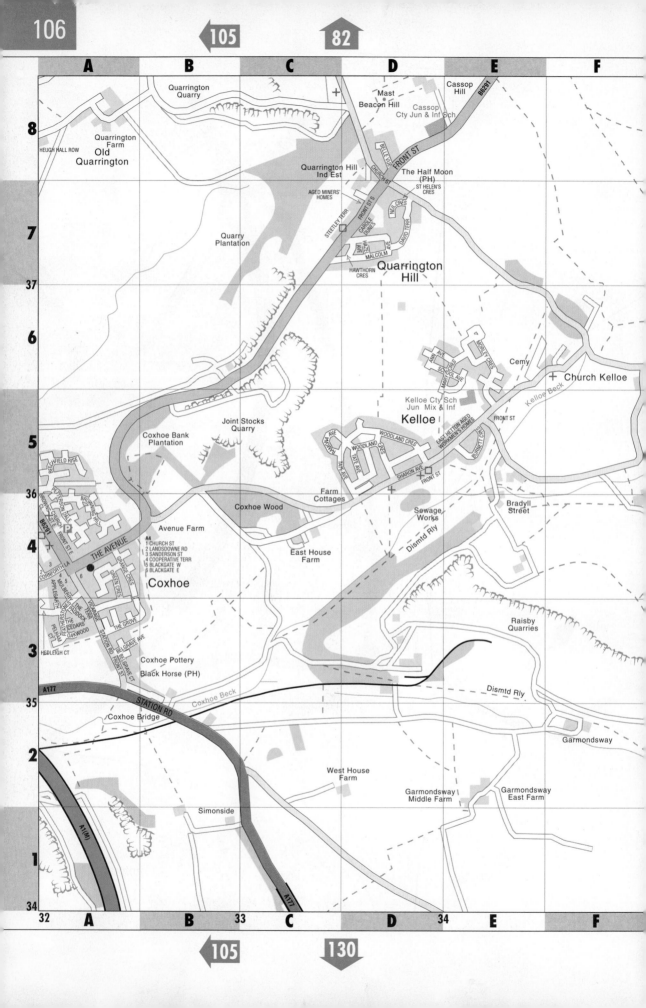

105
130

A   B   C   D   E   F

8

Nature Reserve

Old Wingate
Marley Banks

The Bottoms

7

Carr House

The Banks
Kelloe Law

37

Kelloe Plantation

GREEN LA

Wingate Lodge

Cemy
West Moor Farm

Deaf Hill Farm

Kelloe Hall
Town Kelloe

Kelloe Law Plantation

6

Wingate House
WINGATE RD 1
ST AIDAN'S TERR 2
Deaf Hill Prim Sch

CORONATION TERR
DEAF HILL TERR
STATION RD
TOBIN ST

Kelloe Hill
Southern Law

PROSPECT PL 1
FRONT ST 2
GROSVENOR TERR 3
VICTORIA TERR 4
FARFIELD TERR 5

5

WINDSOR ST
Dismtd Rly
LUKE ST
RODWELL ST
GEORGE ST   3
5   4
LAUREL CRES
NORTH MOOR AVE

36

Works
ROSE ST
GALBRAITH TERR
1 GOOD AVE
2 LONSDALE AVE
3 ALNWICK AVE
4 BERWICK CT
5 REDESDALE CT

4

SALTER'S LA
CO-OPERATIVE TERR
BERRY AVE
PEEL AVE
ROTHBURY
KIELDER DR
HARWOOD CT
5   4
3
Recn Gd

Trimdon Grange

ST ALBAN'S
SOUTH VIEW
1   2
NORTHSIDE
Cemy

GRANGE TERR
KIELDER DR
2
NORTHSIDE TERR
SUNNYSIDE TERR
3
HOMESIDE AVE
BEECH GR

BALMORAL TERR 1
EAST VIEW 2
TAYLOR AVE 3
ROPER'S TERR 4

Trimdon Grange Cty Inf Sch

1 DOWN TERR
2 HOPPER TERR

Mast

3

East Grange

North Side

Cleveland Gorse
HORSE CLOSE LA

35

Kelloe Bank

River Skerne
Parkwood

2

Watch Bank
HORSE CLOSE LA

Greenside Farm

SKERNE AVE
1
Trimdon
Sewage Works

Mast
BURN OVAL
2
HALL FARM CT
ST CUTHBERT'S CRES
3
FRONT ST N
FRONT ST N
VICARAGE DR
CORONATION TERR

1

BROADWAY AVE
FRONT ST S
FRONT ST N
FRONT ST S
Cemy

WEST LA
CLEVELAND AVE 1
TEES VIEW 2
BANK TOP TERR 3
WEST GR 4
DUNELM RD
LILAC GR
MAIN RD
CHURCH RD
MYRTLE GR
BOYNE VIEW
SWAINBY RD
1 LANDRETH GR
2 SPRINGWELL AVE
HURWORTH BURN RD

34

B1278

B1278

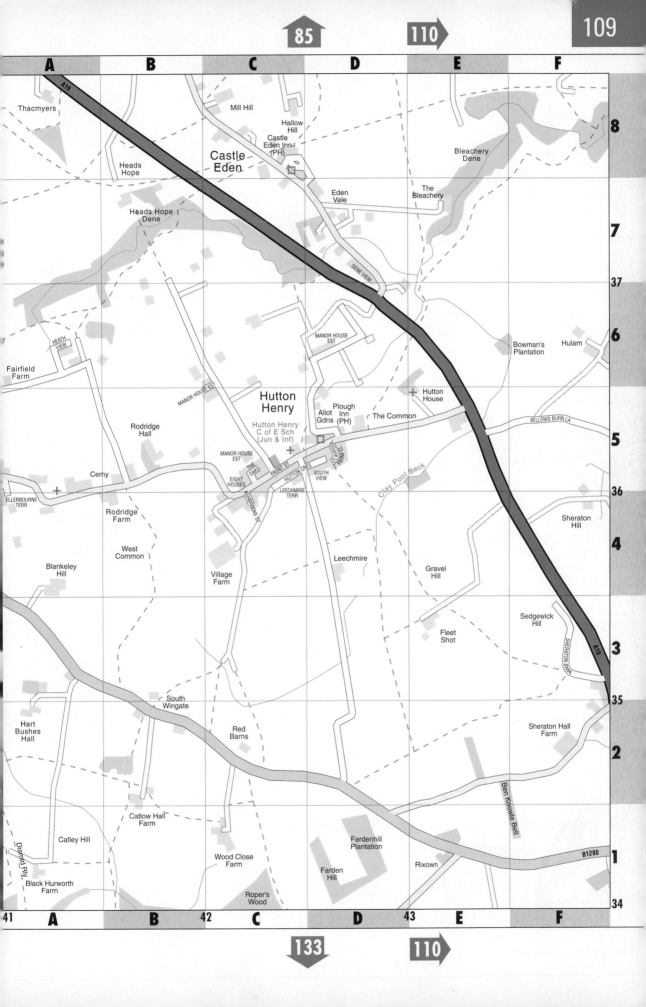

A　B　C　D　E　F

8

7

37

6

5

36

4

3

35

2

1

34

41　A　B　42　C　D　43　E　F

Thacmyers

A19

Mill Hill

Hallow
Hill

Castle
Eden Inn
(PH)

Castle
Eden

Heads
Hope

Bleachery
Dene

Eden
Vale

The
Bleachery

Heads Hope
Dene

DENE VIEW

HEATH
VIEW

MANOR HOUSE EST

Fairfield
Farm

Bowman's
Plantation

Hulam

Rodridge
Hall

Hutton
Henry

Hutton Henry
C of E Sch
(Jun & Inf)

Allot
Gdns

Plough
Inn
(PH)

Hutton
House

The Common

BELLOWS BURN LA

MANOR HOUSE
EST

Cerny

MANOR HOUSE
EST

THE
OAKS

FRONT ST

HUTTON CRES

SOUTH
VIEW

TO MIRY LA

Clay Pool Beck

Sheraton
Hill

ELLERBOURNE
TERR

EIGHT
HOUSES

LEECHMIRE
TERR

ASHBROOKE DT

Rodridge
Farm

West
Common

Leechmire

Gravel
Hill

Sedgewick
Hill

SHERATON BANK

A19

Blankeley
Hill

Village
Farm

Fleet
Shot

Sheraton Hall
Farm

South
Wingate

Hart
Bushes
Hall

Red
Barns

Ben Knowle Belt

Catlow Hall
Farm

Fardenhill
Plantation

Rixown

B1280

Catley Hill

Disd Rly

Wood Close
Farm

Farden
Hill

Black Hurworth
Farm

Roper's
Wood

A **B** **C** **D** **E** **F**

8

Hesleden Dene

West Plantation

Dismtd Rly

Tweddle Black Halls

Benridge Farm

7

Battersley Plantation

Low Hesleden Farm

Monk Hesleden

Hesleden Dene

Hesleden Hall

37

Battersley Hill

Nesbitt Dene

Silver Hill Plantation

6

Hulam

Porrit's Close Plantation

Nesbitt Hall

Thorpe Bulmer Dene

Porrit's Close Hill

5

BELLOWS BURN LA

Bellows Burn

36

Thorpe Bulmer

Short Cake Hill

Sheraton Hill

4

3

Sheraton

Sheraton Farm

BUTTS LA

BURN'S CL

North Hart Farm

Hart

Hart Village Prim Sch

MAGDALE NS

35

Fox Hill

PALACE ROW 1
CLEVECOAT WLK 2
WHITE HART CT 3

SOUTH VIEW

ST JAMES GR

BUCKINGHAM AVE

HOLYROOD CRES

FRONT ST

2

Hart Moor Farm

NINE ACRES

Glebe Farm

A179

East Grange Farm

A19

1

A179

B1280

Whelly Hill

34

Mast Whangdon Hill

A19

Whelly Hill Farm

High Volts Farm

44 **A** 45 **B** **C** **D** 46 **E** **F**

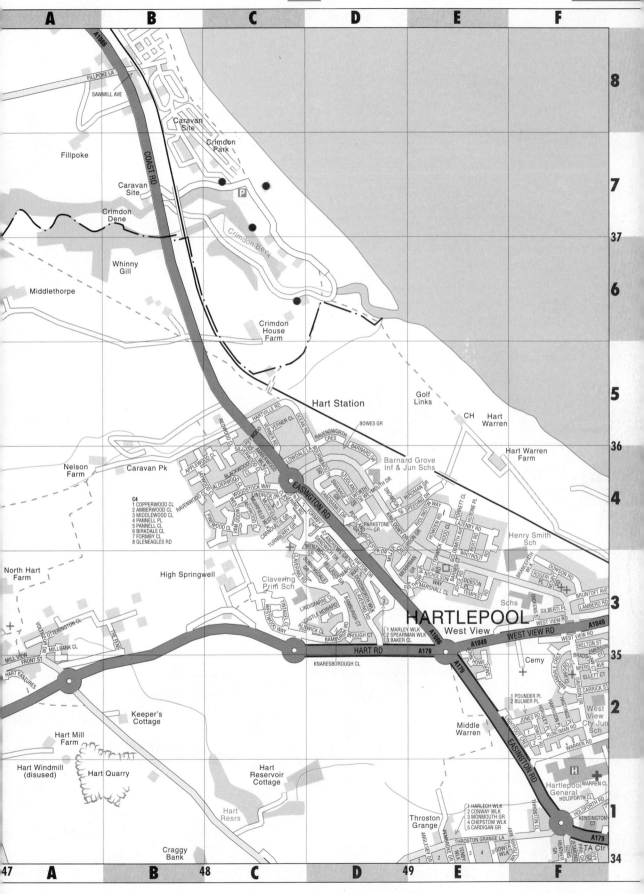

A B C D E F

8
7
37
6
5
36
4
3
35
2
1
34

Fillpoke
SAWMILL AVE
FILLPOKE LA
A1086
Caravan Site
Crimdon Park
Crimdon Beck
Caravan Site
Crimdon Dene
COAST RD
Whinny Gill
Middlethorpe
Crimdon House Farm
Hart Station
Golf Links
BOWES GR
CH
Hart Warren
Hart Warren Farm
Nelson Farm
Caravan Pk
Barnard Grove Inf & Jun Schs
HARTVILLE RD
RENWOOD RD
TURNER RD
OCEAN RD
RAVENSWORTH CRES
BARNARD GR
LOWDALE LA
BOURNEMOUTH DR
SWINTON GR
STOUGHTON GR
LUDWORTH GR
PORTLAND GR
WETMOUTH GR
SNOWDON RD
HIRDMAN GR
SPEEDING DR
RIDLINGTON WAY
HOWDEN RD
LAZENBY RD
PORRETT CL
HITHONE RD
Henry Smith Sch
C4
1 COPPERWOOD CL
2 AMBERWOOD CL
3 MIDDLEWOOD CL
4 PANNELL PL
5 PANNELL CL
6 BIRKDALE CL
7 FORMBY CL
8 GLENEAGLES RD
APPLEWOOD CL
SILVERWOOD CL
AMBERWOOD
BLACKWOOD
ALDERWOOD
LAWWOOD CL
RAVENWOOD CL
WOODSTOCK WAY
KESTWOOD CL
ASHWOOD GR
MURFIELD RD
MUIRFIELD RD
INDRICK DR
CARNOUSTIE GR
TURNBERRY GR
PINEWOOD CL
EASINGTON RD
CLAVERING RD
FORMBY
ST ANDREWS GR
SANDWICH GR
WENTWORTH GR
BELASYSE GR
PARKSTONE GR
ROLLINGTON WAY
RAFTON DR
MILL LA
MILBURY CRES
MERRIMAN
FULTHORPE
NICHOLSON WAY
GOLDSMITH AVE
GOLDSMITH CT
BARNES
DOBSON CL
TEMPEST
WHITROUT
BRANCEPATH
ROGERS RD
DOWSON RD
DICKENS RD
GILBERTI PL
Schs
BRUNTOFT AVE
LAMBERD RD
High Springwell
Clavering Prim Sch
LINDISFARNE GR
TINTAGEL GR
WESTWOOD WAY
CLAVERING GR
SUNNINGDALE
CASTLE HOWARD
ALNWICK CL
WOODSWORTH WLK
BAMBURGH CT
CLAVERING RD
BAMBURGH CT
BOROUGH CT
1 MARLEY WLK
2 SPEARMAN WLK
3 BAKER CL
HARTLEPOOL
West View
A1096
A1049
WEST VIEW RD
WEST VIEW RD
SKELTON ST
BRADSHAW ST
EMERSON
MIERS CL
ELLETT CT
AVE
CARRICK ST
North Hart Farm
VOLTIGEUR DR
OTTERINGTON CL
THE FENS
MILLBANK CL
MILL VIEW
FRONT ST
Hart Pastures
HART RD
A179
KNARESBOROUGH CL
HOWE GDNS
Cemy
1 POUNDER PL
2 BULMER PL
HARRISON GR
JONES GDNS
HORSLEY PL
JOWITT RD
HASTINGS PL
RUNCIMAN RD
WARREN RD
DAVISON DR
West View Cty Jun Sch
EASINGTON RD
Keeper's Cottage
Middle Warren
Hart Mill Farm
Hart Windmill (disused)
Hart Quarry
Hart Reservoir Cottage
Hart Resrs
Craggy Bank
Throston Grange
1 HARLECH WLK
2 CONWAY WLK
3 MONMOUTH GR
4 CHEPSTOW WLK
5 CARDIGAN GR
THROSTON GRANGE LA
ANGLESEY GR
PEMBROKE GR
TENBY
GOWER WLK
A179
Hartlepool General
HOLDFORTH CL
WARREN CL
H
KENSINGTON CT
HEATHER GR
PINE GR
TA Ctr

47 A B 48 C D 49 E F 34

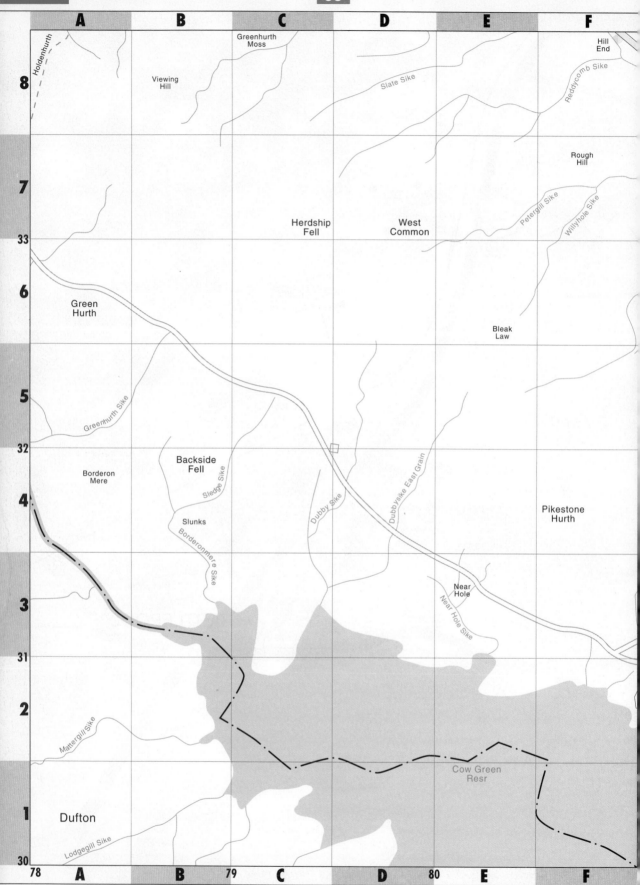

| | A | B | C | D | E | F |

8 Holdenhurth

Greenhurth
Moss

Viewing
Hill

Slate Sike

Hill
End

Reddycomb Sike

7

Rough
Hill

Herdship
Fell

West
Common

Petergill Sike

Willyhole Sike

33

6 Green
Hurth

Bleak
Law

Greenhurth Sike

5

32

Borderon
Mere

Backside
Fell

Sledge Sike

Dubby Sike

Dubbysike East Grain

Pikestone
Hurth

4

Slunks

Borderonmere Sike

3

Near
Hole

Near Hole Sike

31

2

Matergill Sike

Cow Green
Resr

1 Dufton

Lodgegill Sike

30

| 78 | A | | B | 79 | C | | D | 80 | E | | F |

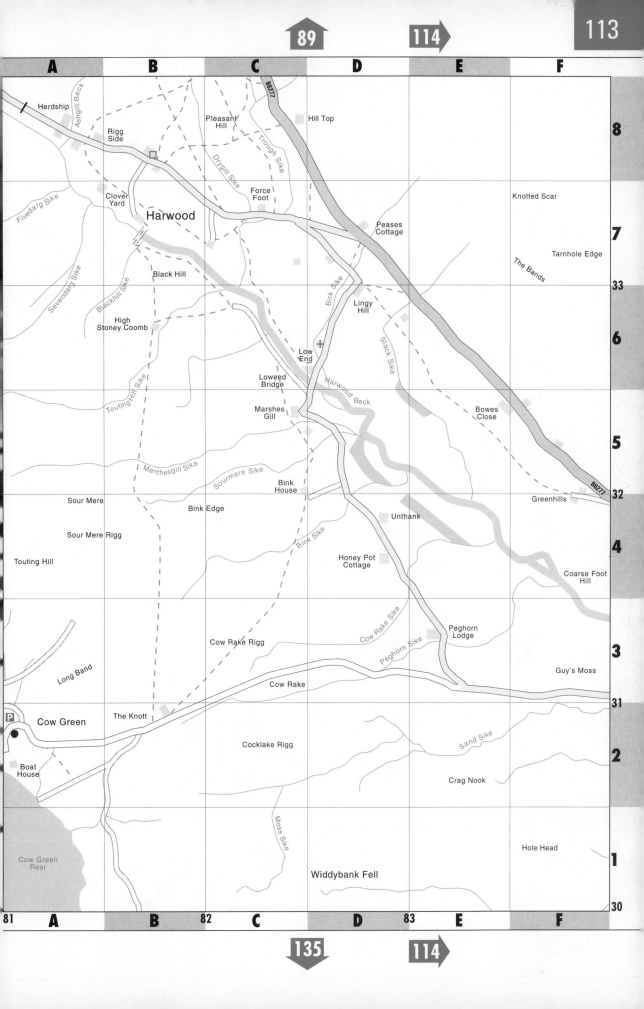

A B C D E F

Herdship

Ashgill Beck

Rigg Side

Pleasant Hill

Hill Top

Knotted Scar

B6277

Drygill Sike

Trough Sike

Clover Yard

Force Foot

Harwood

Peases Cottage

Tarnhole Edge

The Bands

Fivedarg Sike

Black Hill

Birk Sike

Lingy Hill

Sevendarg Sike

Blackhill Sike

High Stoney Coomb

Low End

Slack Sike

Touting Hill Sike

Lowend Bridge

Harwood Beck

Marshes Gill

Bowes Close

Marchesgill Sike

Sourmere Sike

Bink House

Greenhills

B6277

Sour Mere

Bink Edge

Unthank

Sour Mere Rigg

Bink Sike

Honey Pot Cottage

Coarse Foot Hill

Touting Hill

Cow Rake Sike

Peghorn Lodge

Long Band

Cow Rake Rigg

Peghorn Sike

Guy's Moss

Cow Green

The Knott

Cow Rake

Cocklake Rigg

Sand Sike

Crag Nook

Boat House

Cow Green Resr

Moss Sike

Widdybank Fell

Hole Head

8
7
33
6
5
32
4
3
31
2
1
30

113

90

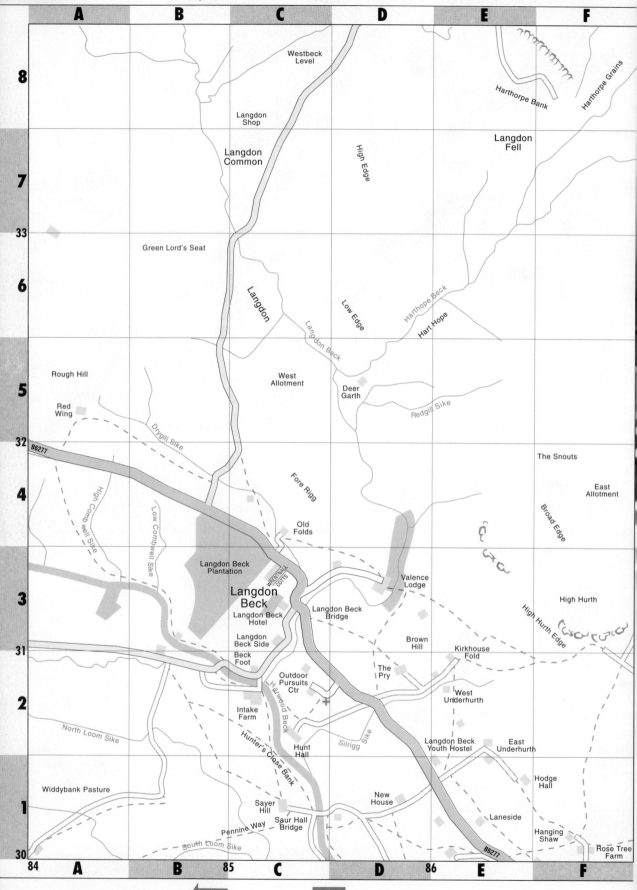

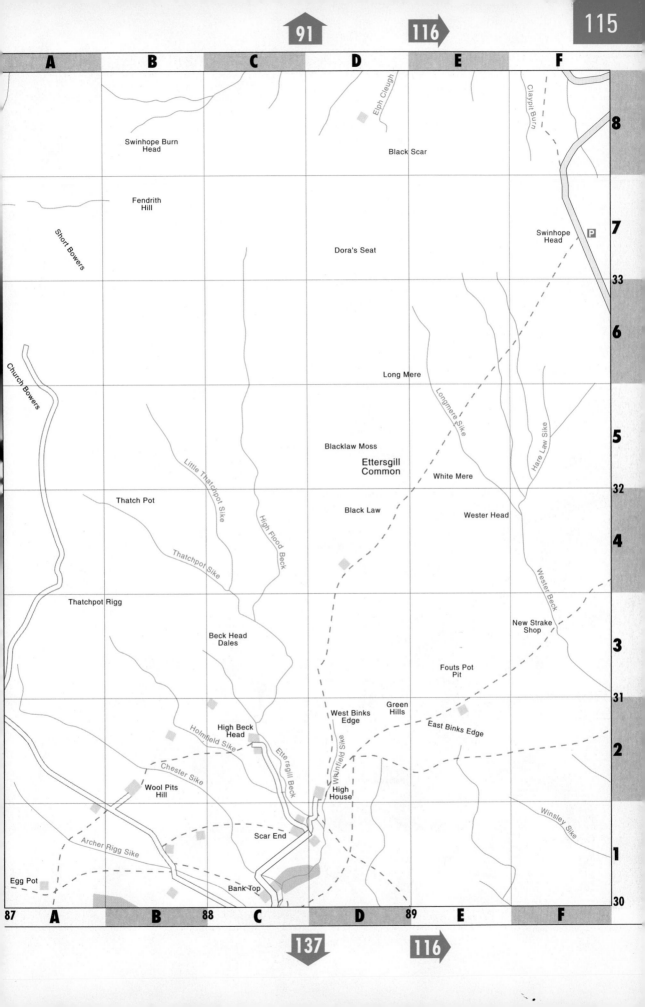

A B C D E F

8
7
33
6
5
32
4
3
31
2
1
30

Elph Cleugh

Claypit Burn

Swinhope Burn Head

Black Scar

Fendrith Hill

Short Bowers

Swinhope Head

P

Dora's Seat

Church Bowers

Long Mere

Longmere Sike

Hare Law Sike

Blacklaw Moss

Ettersgill Common

White Mere

Little Thatchpot Sike

Thatch Pot

High Flood Beck

Black Law

Wester Head

Thatchpot Sike

Wester Beck

Thatchpot Rigg

New Strake Shop

Beck Head Dales

Fouts Pot Pit

West Binks Edge

Green Hills

East Binks Edge

High Beck Head

Holmfield Sike

Ettersgill Beck

Whinfield Sike

Chester Sike

Wool Pits Hill

High House

Winsley Sike

Archer Rigg Sike

Scar End

Egg Pot

Bank Top

115
92

A   **B**   **C**   **D**   **E**   **F**

8

West Grain

Green Sike

Westernhope Moor

Wolf Cleugh

Hawk Crag

Wolfcleugh Head

7

Blaeberry Burn

33

Blaeberry Grains

Blaeberry Cleugh

6

Black Hill

Broperygill Sike

5

Three Folds Sike

32

Pike Law

Flushie Mere

Broadley Hill

Rowantreegill Sike

4

Newbiggin Common

James's Hill

Carr Crags

3

Green Fell

Ford

Flushiemere House

31

Flushiemere Beck

2

Wester Beck

Bales Allotment

Bleagill Sike

Weather Beds

Bales Hush

Bleagill Allotment

Goreemoss Sike

1

Watson's Bridge

Blea Gill

Winsley Sike

Lingy Rigg

30

90   **A**   **B**   91   **C**   **D**   92   **E**   **F**

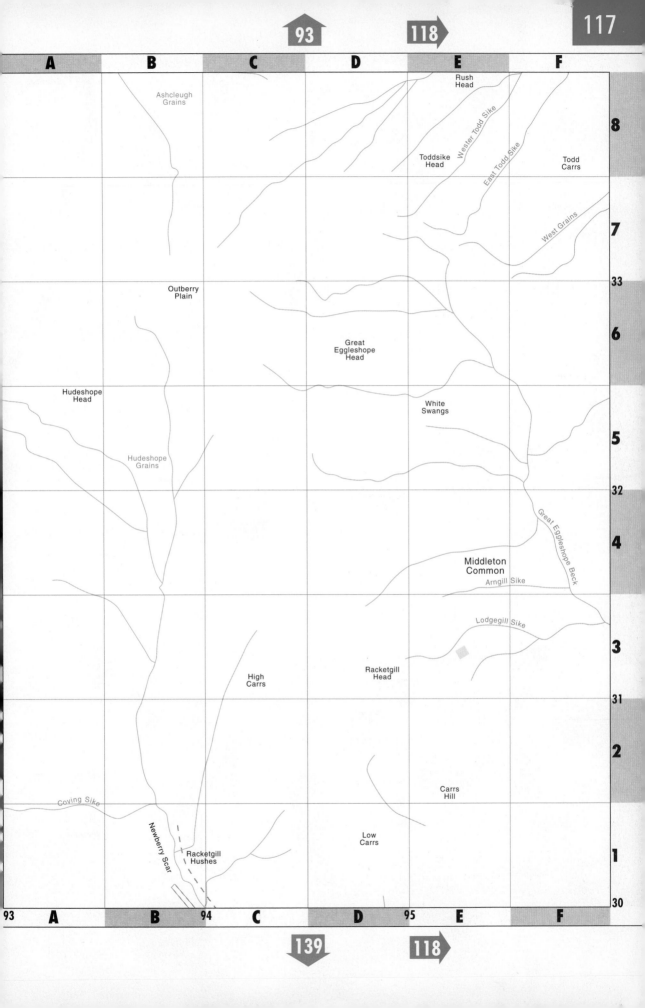

A B C D E F

8

7

33

6

5

32

4

3

31

2

1

30

Ashcleugh
Grains

Rush
Head

Toddsike
Head

Wester Todd Sike

East Todd Sike

Todd
Carrs

West Grains

Outberry
Plain

Great
Eggleshope
Head

Hudeshope
Head

White
Swangs

Hudeshope
Grains

Great Eggleshope Beck

Middleton
Common

Arngill Sike

Lodgegill Sike

High
Carrs

Racketgill
Head

Carrs
Hill

Coving Sike

Newberry Scar

Racketgill
Hushes

Low
Carrs

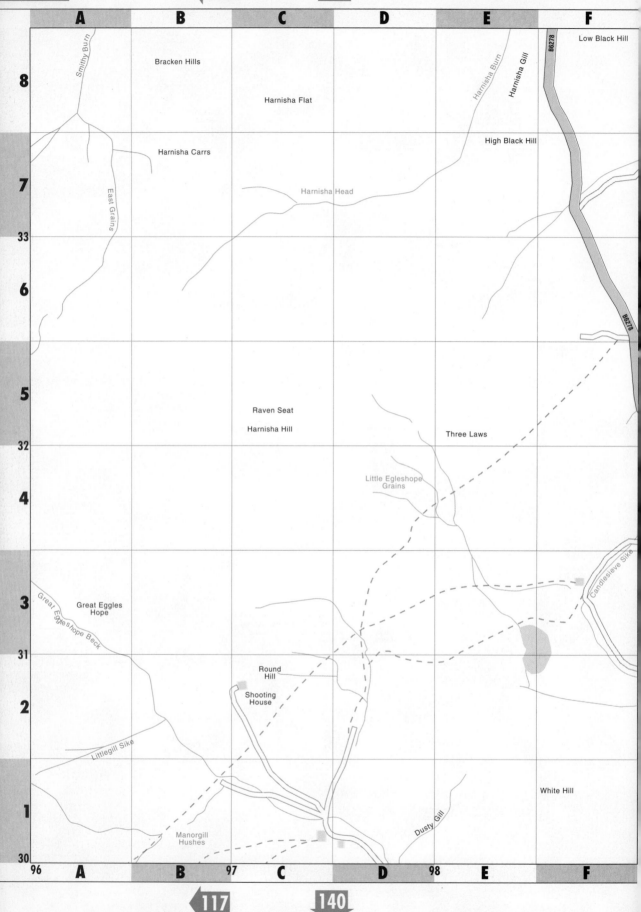

A B C D E F

8

7

33

6

5

32

4

3

31

2

1

30

96 A B 97 C D 98 E F

Smithy Burn

Bracken Hills

Harnisha Flat

Harnisha Carrs

East Grains

Harnisha Head

Harnisha Burn

Harnisha Gill

B6278

Low Black Hill

High Black Hill

B6278

Raven Seat

Harnisha Hill

Three Laws

Little Egleshope Grains

Candlesieve Sike

Great Eggles Hope

Great Egleshope Beck

Round Hill

Shooting House

Littlegill Sike

Manorgill Hushes

Dusty Gill

White Hill

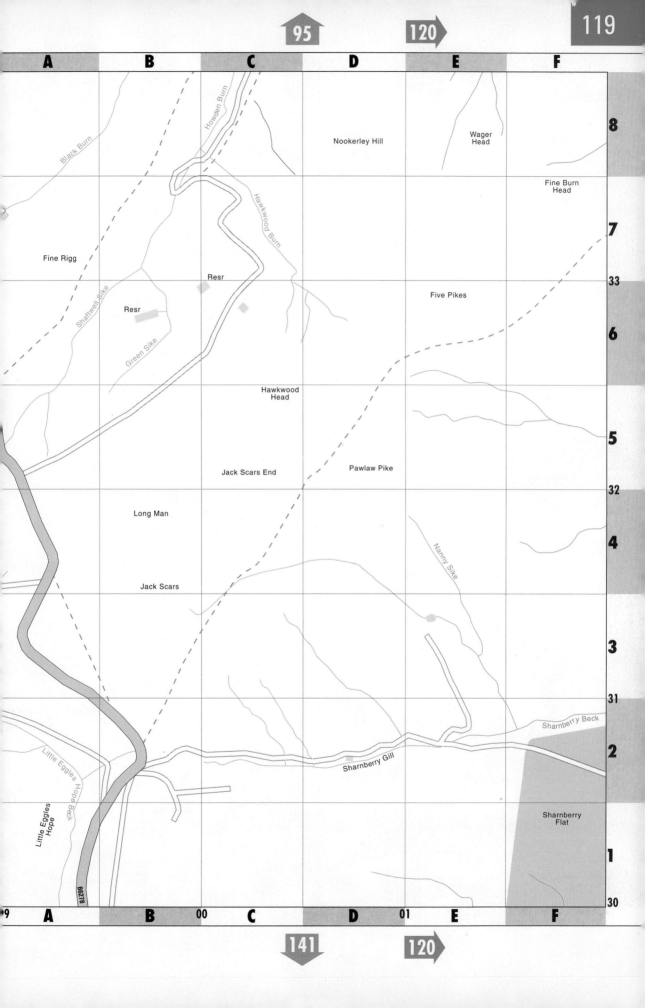

95
120

A **B** **C** **D** **E** **F**

8

Nookerley Hill

Wager
Head

Fine Burn
Head

Black Burn

Howden Burn

7

Hawkwood Burn

Fine Rigg

Resr

33

Five Pikes

Shaftwell Sike

Resr

6

Green Sike

Hawkwood
Head

5

Jack Scars End

Pawlaw Pike

32

Long Man

Nanny Sike

4

Jack Scars

3

31

Sharnberry Beck

Little Eggles Hope Beck

2

Sharnberry Gill

Little Eggles
Hope

Sharnberry
Flat

1

B6278

30

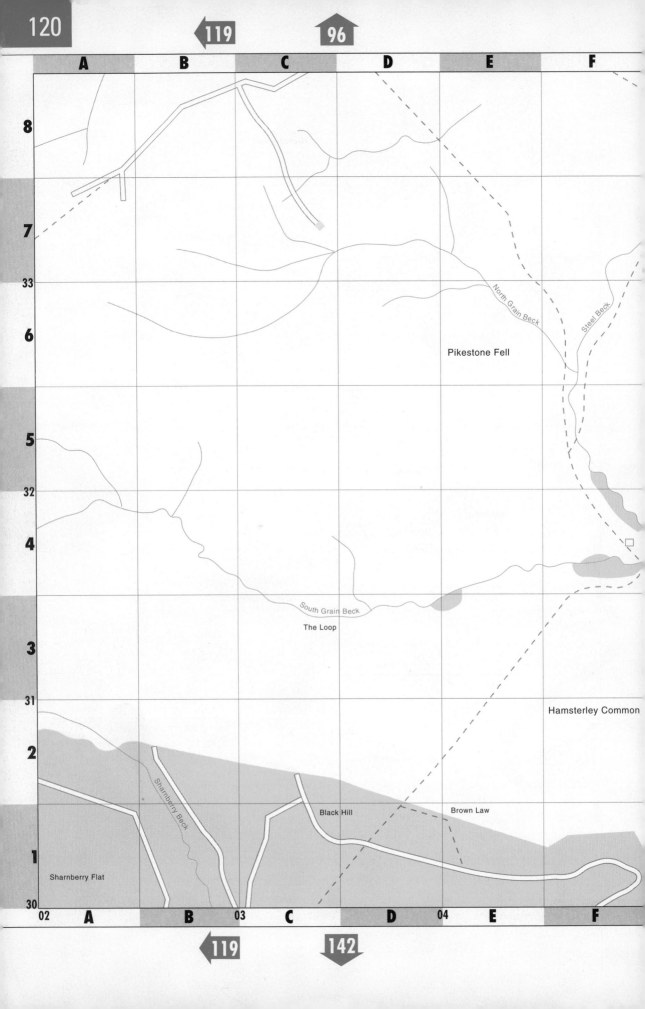

A B C D E F

8
7
33
6
5
32
4
3
31
2
1
30

Beech Wood

St John's Hall

Blackburn Wood

Drift Wood

Tank Wood

Ruddy Carr

Blackburn Lodge

Doctor's Gate

Cabin Hill

Cliff Sike Beck

Cliff Sike Gill

Hawke Sike

Meeting of the Grains

Ford

Ayhope Beck

Potato Hill

North Plantation

North Crag Wood

Middle Redford

Bedburn Beck

Crossfield Plantation

Paddy's Plantation

Eudenbeck

Nest Plantation

Frog Wood

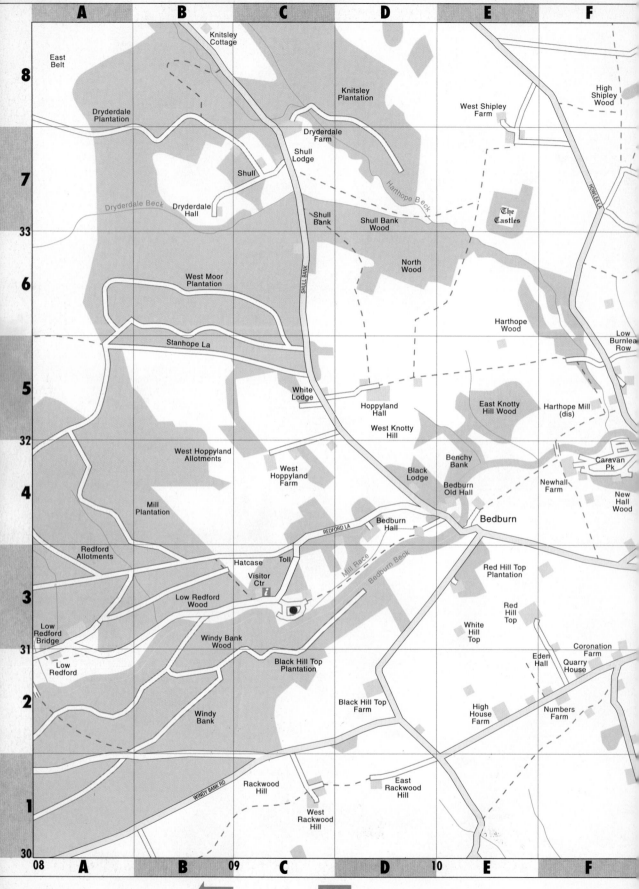

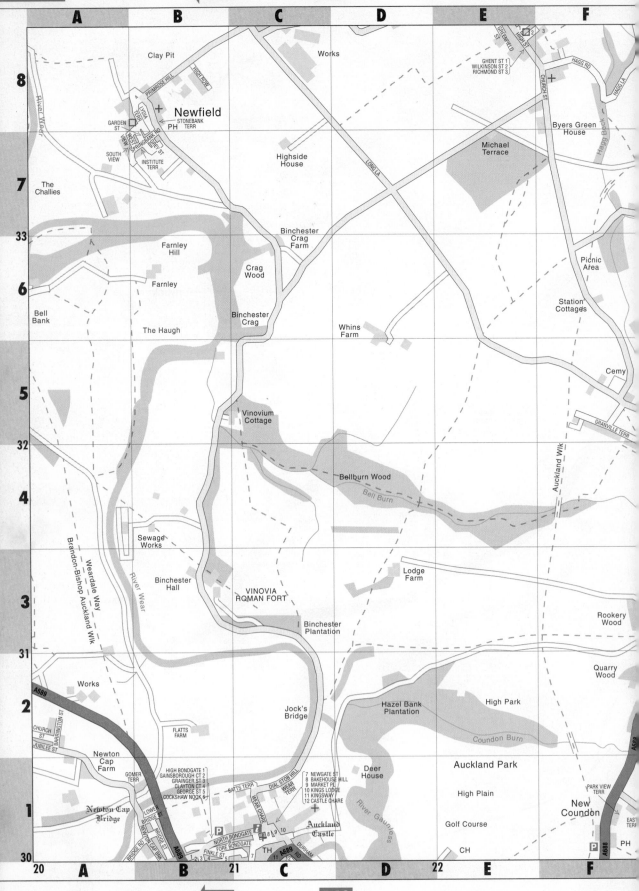

St Andrew's La
Gilling La
Catherine St
Kenmir
Linden Av
Fairview Ct
Raby Way
Richmond Fields
Half Moon La
Pearson St
Merrington View
A688
A688
Coulson St
B6288
Front St

P

Low
Spennymoor

Skibbereen

Red Hall
Farm

Merrington
Lane

1 MORPETH CL
2 BAMBURGH PAR
3 BYLAND TOWERS
4 FOUNTAINS MEADOW
5 LANGLEY DR

6 ST ANDREW'S LA
7 UPPER CHURCH ST
8 FENWICK ST
9 GRAINGER ST

8

Merrington Lane
Ind Est

Sewage
Works

7

33

MANOR CT 14
CHESNUT AVE 15
WILLOW RD 16

10 WEST ST
11 PARKER TERR
12 KENSINGTON GDNS
13 GLEBE HOUSES

Mary
Lands

Dean & Chapter
Ind Est

Saddler
St

Durham Rd

TH
North
Market St
Church
Rd
Oswald Pl
Church La
The Garth

Liby

Oaklea

High Hill
House

Low Hill
House

12 13

6

Vyners Cl

Ferryhill Windmill
(dis)

Brunel St
Faraday St
Watt St
Beaumont St
Newton St
Newcomen St
Davy St
Serpas St
B6287
Main St
Eamont Rd
Duncan Rd
Bowness Gr
Derwent
Windermere Rd
Ullswater Rd
Rydal Rd
Darlington Rd
Coniston Rd

Dean
Bank

Fox
Covert

Mast

The
Joseph Patterson
Cres

The
William Keers
Cres

Allot
Gdns

Paxton St
Stephenson St
Kelvin St
Bessemer St
Rennie St
Napier Ct
Ramsey Dr
Cavendish Ct
Hackworth St
Meats St
Blandford Rd
Owen St
Parsons Ct
Compton Cl

Grasmere Rd
Thirlmere Rd

1 THE VILLAS
2 WESTCOTT TERR
3 LIGHTFOOT TERR
4 HAIG TERR
5 HACKWORTH ST
6 BARRINGTON TERR
7 ST CUTHBERT'S TERR
8 DEAN COURT GRANGE
9 HOLYOAKE ST

Allot
Gdns

Dean Rd

South Side
(DEAN RD)

5

Ferryhill
Comp Sch

Ridgeside
Ridgeside

North
Close

32

North Close Rd

Merrington Rd

East
Roughlea

Bridge House
Farm

4

1 COULTON TERR
2 BEDE PL
3 ROCKCLIFFE TERR
4 HOPKINSON PL
5 FRONT ST
6 MISSION PL
7 RICHARDSON PL
8 CHAPEL ST

B6288

West Roughlea
Farm

Bridge House Est

St John's
Ct

B6287

Church Cl
Hallgarth
Mer
Beckwith's La
Kirkstone Cl
South View
Ringtons

Kirk
Merrington

West Cl

3

PH

Blue Houses

Kirk Merrington
Cty Jun Mix &
Inf Sch

9 RAMSHAW TERR
10 CORONATION TERR
11 JOWSEY PL

31

Chilton
Ind Est

2

Blue
House

Windlestone La

Merrington
Grange

Dene Bridge

Dene
Villas

Avenue 3
Avenue 1
Avenue 4
Avenue 2
Dene Bridge Row
Chilton Way

Cemy

1

Blue House
Farm

West Chilton Terr

West Chilton
Farm

A167

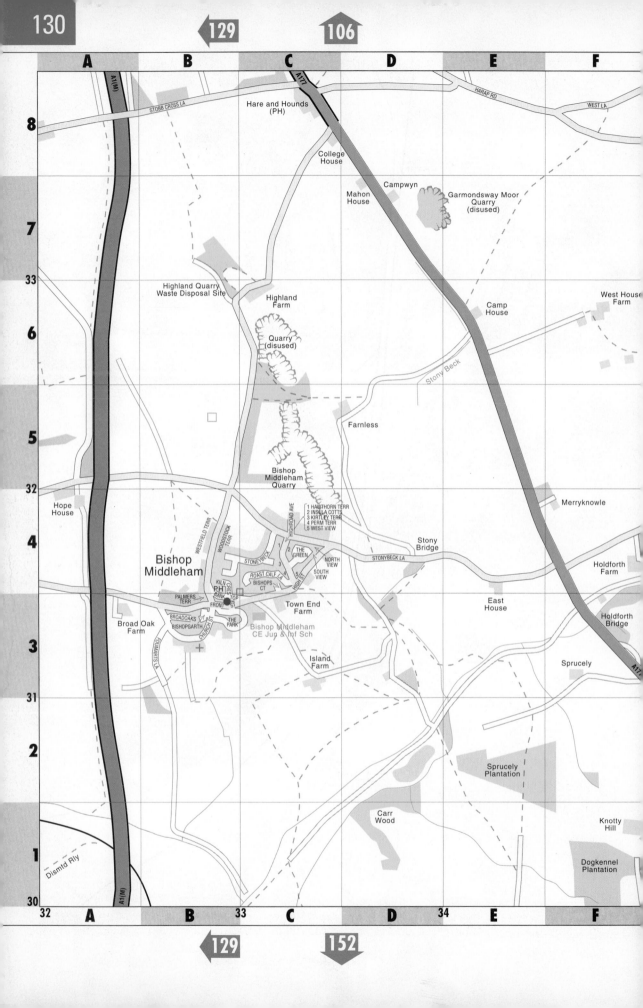

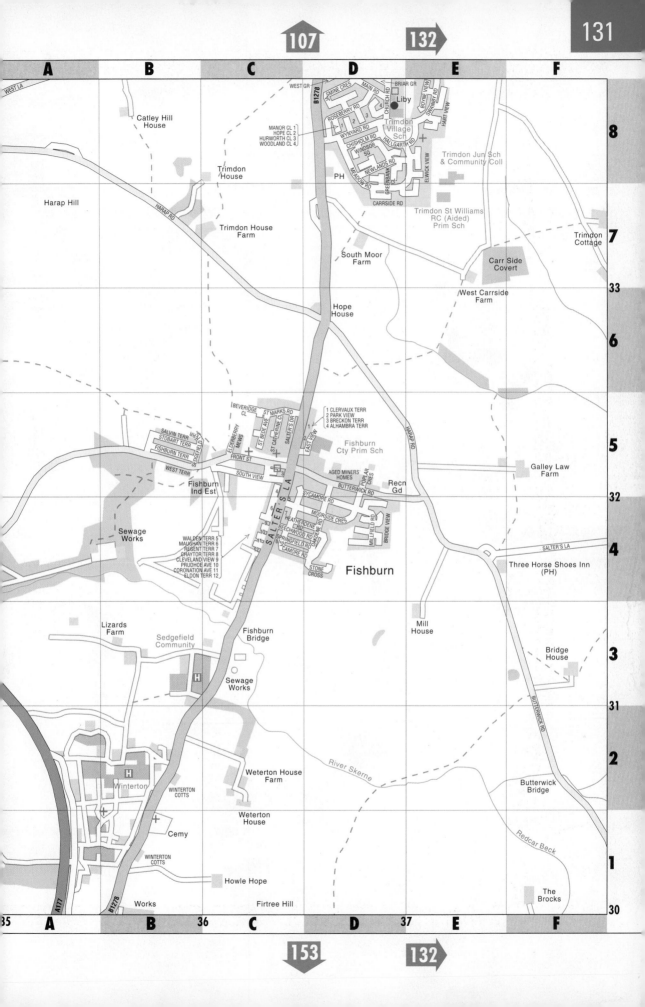

WEST LA

Catley Hill House

WEST GR

B1278

JASMINE CRES
ROSEBERRY RD
MAIN RD
BRIAR GR
BOYNE VIEW
SWAINBY RD
HART VIEW

CHURCH RD

Liby

MANOR CL 1
HOPE CL 2
HURWORTH CL 3
WOODLAND CL 4

WYNYARD RD

Trimdon Village Sch

Trimdon Jun Sch & Community Coll

Trimdon House

CHISHOLM RD

WINDSOR SQ

HALLGARTH RD

ELWICK VIEW

Harap Hill

HARAP RD

Trimdon House Farm

MEADOW RD

NEWLANDS RD

GREENBANK CL

PH

CARRSIDE RD

Trimdon St Williams RC (Aided) Prim Sch

Trimdon Cottage

South Moor Farm

Carr Side Covert

West Carrside Farm

Hope House

BEVERIDGE CL

ST MARKS RD

ST BEDE AVE

ST CATHERINE CL

SALTER'S DR

EAST VIEW

1 CLERVAUX TERR
2 PARK VIEW
3 BRECKON TERR
4 ALHAMBRA TERR

Fishburn Cty Prim Sch

HARAP RD

SALVIN TERR

STOBART TERR

FISHBURN TERR

SEDGEFIELD TERR

ELDERBERRY MEWS

FRONT ST

Galley Law Farm

WEST TERR

SOUTH VIEW

AGED MINERS' HOMES

POPLAR CRES

Recn Gd

Fishburn Ind Est

SYCAMORE RD

BUTTERWICK RD

MOORSIDE CRES

MILLFIELD RD

BRIDGE VIEW

Sewage Works

WALDEN TERR 5
MAUGHAN TERR 6
REGENT TERR 7
CHAYTOR TERR 8
CLEVELAND VIEW 9
PRUDHOE AVE 10
CORONATION AVE 11
ELDON TERR 12

SALTER'S LA

HEATHERDENE RD

BEECHWOOD RD

SPRINGFIELD RD

OAKDENE RD

SYCAMORE RD

SALTER'S LA

Three Horse Shoes Inn (PH)

STONE CROSS

Fishburn

Mill House

Bridge House

Lizards Farm

Sedgefield Community

Fishburn Bridge

H

Sewage Works

BUTTERWICK RD

Weterton House Farm

River Skerne

Butterwick Bridge

H

Winterton

WINTERTON COTTS

Weterton House

Cemy

Redcar Beck

WINTERTON COTTS

A177

B1278

Howle Hope

Firtree Hill

The Brocks

Works

35 36 37 8 7 33 6 5 32 4 3 31 2 1 30

A **B** **C** **D** **E** **F**

8

Dropswell
Farm

Beanley
Carr

Redding's
Hill

Stob
Hill

Hurworth Burn
Resr

Trimdon East
House

HURWORTH BURN RD

7

Hurworth
Burn

East Carr
Side

West Holling
Carr

Hurworth
Burn
Farm

33

Sunnyside

East Holling
Carr

Murton Blue
House

6

Humble Knowle
Plantation

5

Humble Knowle
Farm

River Skerne

West Murton
Blue House

32

SALTER'S LA

4

Butterwick
Moor

Whin
Houses

3

31

Butterwick
Plantation

2

Whin Houses
Belt

BUTTERWICK RD

1

Butterwick
House

30

38 **A** **B** **39** **C** **D** **40** **E** **F**

109
134

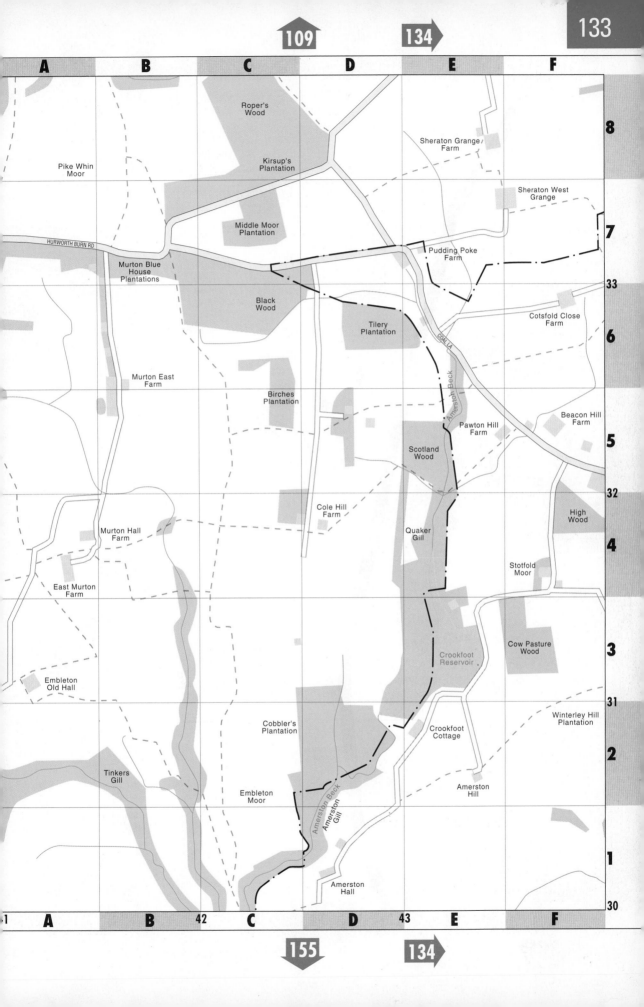

155
134

A B C D E F

8

Roper's
Wood

Sheraton Grange
Farm

Pike Whin
Moor

Kirsup's
Plantation

Sheraton West
Grange

7

Middle Moor
Plantation

HURWORTH BURN RD

Murton Blue
House
Plantations

Pudding Poke
Farm

33

Black
Wood

Cotsfold Close
Farm

Tilery
Plantation

6

ODALLA

Murton East
Farm

Amerston Beck

Birches
Plantation

Beacon Hill
Farm

Pawton Hill
Farm

5

Scotland
Wood

Cole Hill
Farm

32

High
Wood

Murton Hall
Farm

Quaker
Gill

4

Stotfold
Moor

East Murton
Farm

Cow Pasture
Wood

3

Crookfoot
Reservoir

Embleton
Old Hall

31

Winterley Hill
Plantation

Cobbler's
Plantation

Crookfoot
Cottage

2

Tinkers
Gill

Amerston Beck

Amerston
Hill

Embleton
Moor

Amerston Gill

1

Amerston
Hall

30

1 A B 42 C D 43 E F

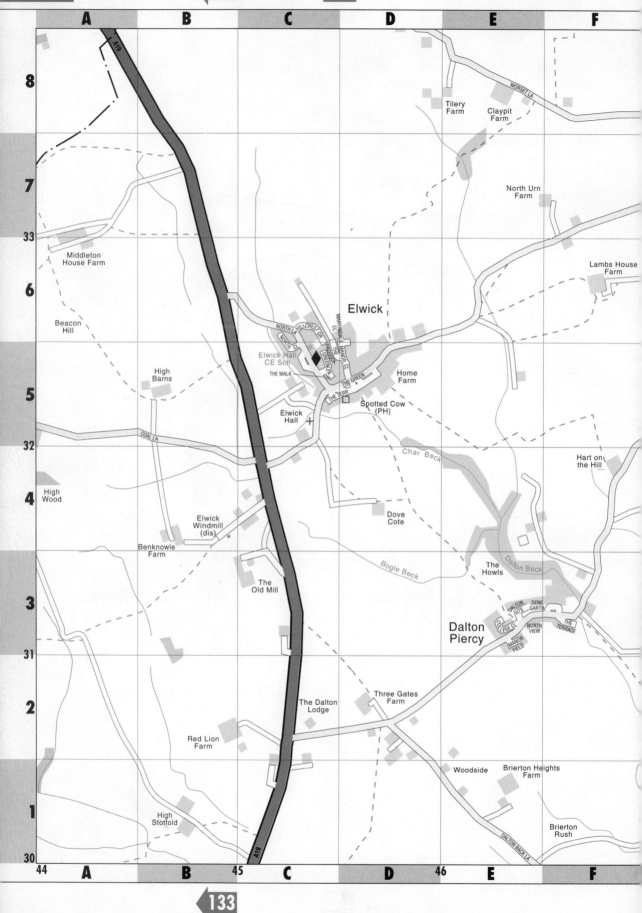

A B C D E F

8

7

33

6 Elwick

5

32

4

3 Dalton Piercy

31

2

1

30
44 A 45 B C 45 D 46 E F

Middleton House Farm

Beacon Hill

High Barns

Elwick Hall CE Sch

Elwick Hall

THE WALK

NORTH LA
NORTH CL
HILLCREST GR
MARTINDALE
MANOR CL
THE PADDOCK
THE GREEN LA
THE GREEN
THE TERR

Home Farm

Spotted Cow (PH)

Char Beck

High Wood

Elwick Windmill (dis)

Benknowle Farm

The Old Mill

COAL LA

Dove Cote

Bogle Beck

The Howls

Dalton Beck

Hart on the Hill

Tilery Farm

Claypit Farm

WORSET LA

North Urn Farm

Lambs House Farm

DALTON CL
GSE CL
DALTON HTS
DENE GARTH
NORTH VIEW
MANOR FIELD
THE TERRACE

The Dalton Lodge

Red Lion Farm

High Stotfold

A19

Three Gates Farm

Woodside

Brierton Heights Farm

Brierton Rush

DALTON BACK LA

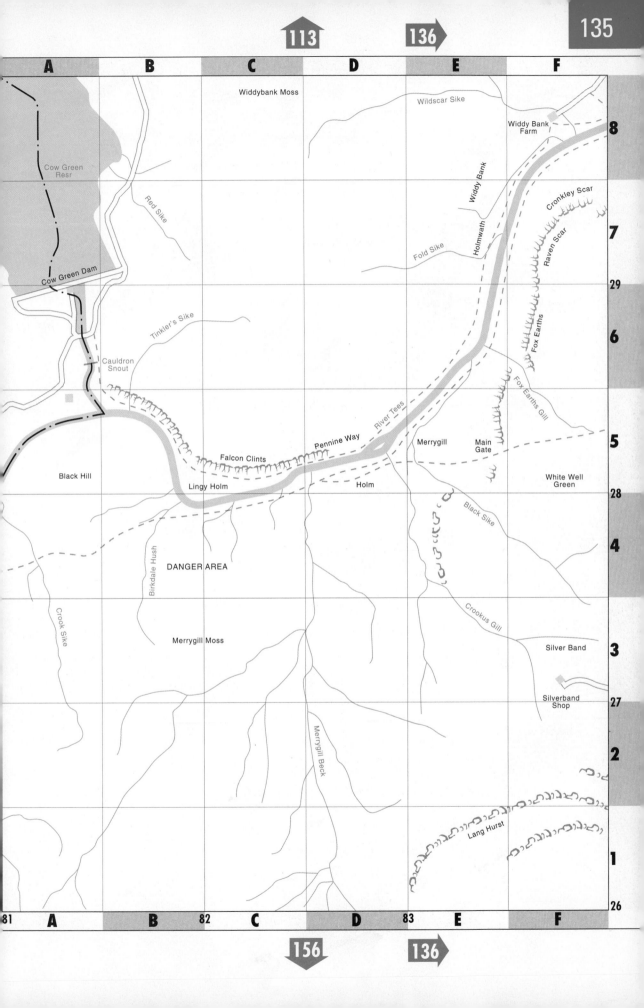

A **B** **C** **D** **E** **F**

Pennine Way

8

The Looms

Knott Hill

Harwood Beck

Haugh Hill

Wheysike House

B6277

Forest of Teesdale Cty Jun Mix & Inf Sch

The Dale

River Tees

Cronkley Scar

Green Hill

High House

Forest-in -Teesdale

Wat Garth

7

Green Hill Scar

Cronkley Pasture

Hill End

29

Skue Trods

Tarn Rigg

Cronkley

6

Tarn Dub

Pennine Way

Thistle Green

Bracken Rigg

5

Birk Rigg

Fell Dike Sike

28

White Force

Caw Bank

Skyer Beck

Black Ark

4

Noon Hill Side

Black Sike

Cronkley Fell

Noon Hill

White Rigg

3

Noon Hill Moss

27

DANGER AREA

Dry Beck

2

High Hurst

Blea Beck

Crake Sike

1

Howden Moss

26

84 **A** 85 **B** **C** 86 **D** **E** **F**

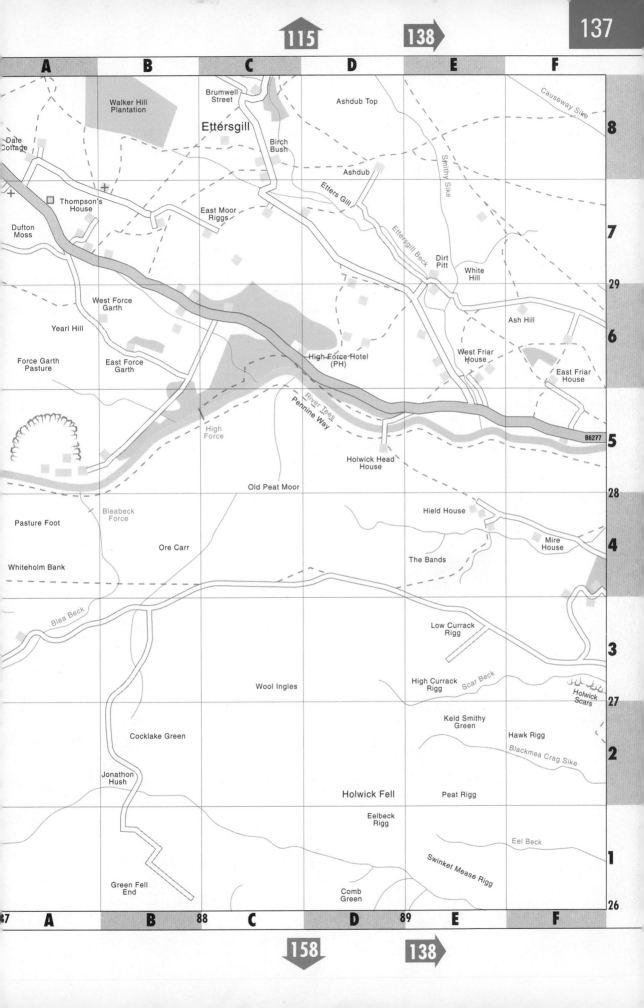

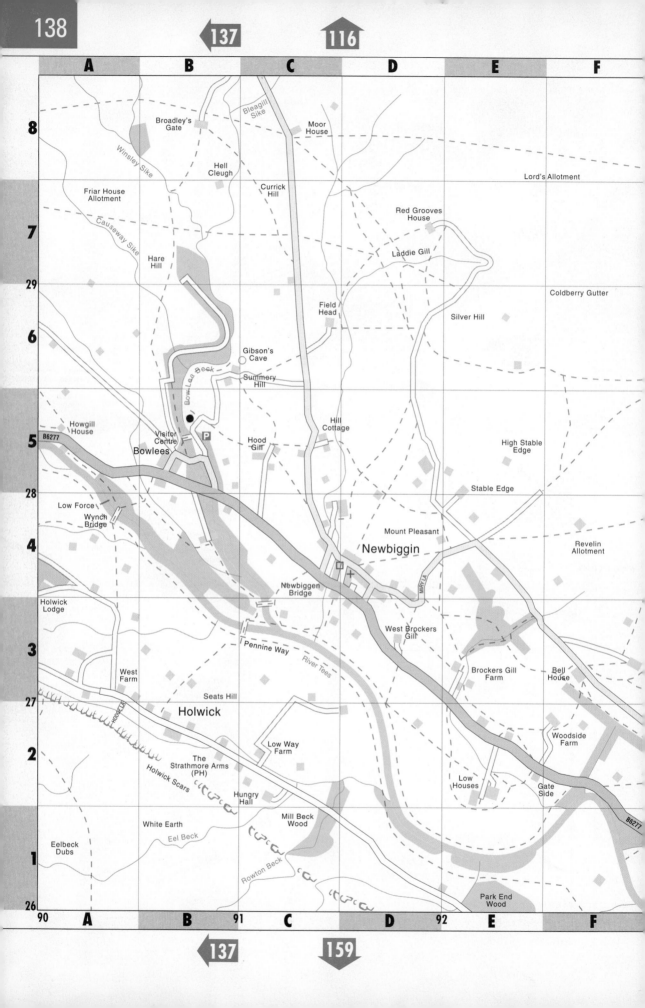

A B C D E F

8

Broadley's
Gate

Bleagill
Sike

Moor
House

Lord's Allotment

Hell
Cleugh

Winsley Sike

Currick
Hill

Friar House
Allotment

Red Grooves
House

7

Causeway Sike

Laddie Gill

Hare
Hill

Coldberry Gutter

29

Field
Head

Silver Hill

6

Gibson's
Cave

Bow Lea Beck

Summery
Hill

Hill
Cottage

High Stable
Edge

Howgill
House

Visitor
Centre

Hood
Gill

5

B6277

P

Bowlees

Stable Edge

28

Low Force

Wynch
Bridge

Mount Pleasant

Revelin
Allotment

4

Newbiggin

Newbiggen
Bridge

MIRY LA.

Holwick
Lodge

West Brockers
Gill

Pennine Way

River Tees

Brockers Gill
Farm

Bell
House

3

West
Farm

Seats Hill

27

Holwick

Woodside
Farm

Low Way
Farm

The
Strathmore Arms
(PH)

2

LANE HEAD

Holwick Scars

Hungry
Hall

Low
Houses

Gate
Side

Mill Beck
Wood

B6277

White Earth

Eel Beck

Eelbeck
Dubs

Rowton Beck

Park End
Wood

26

1

90   A   91   B   C   91   D   92   E   F

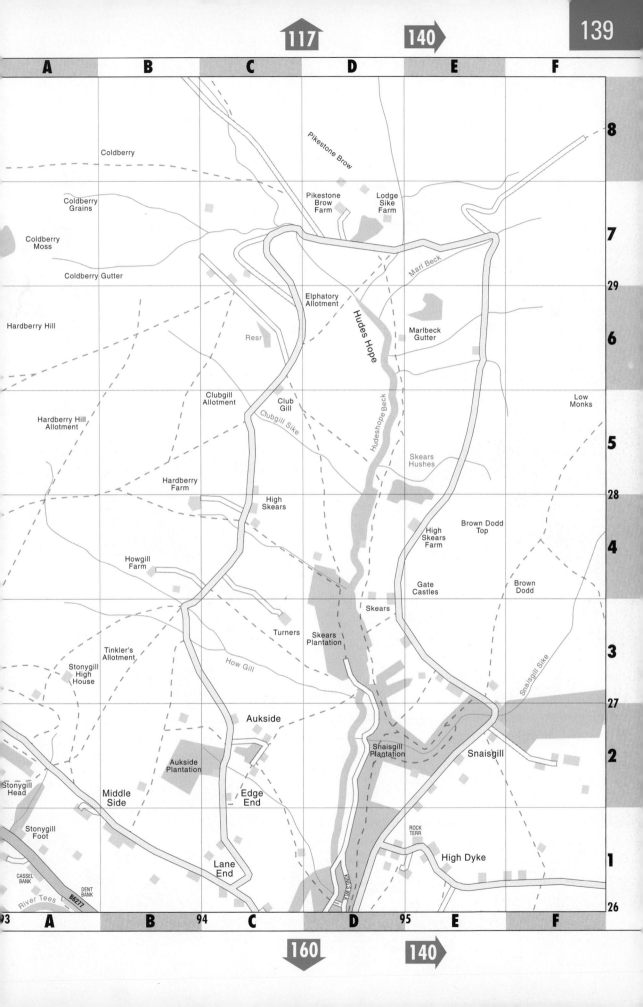

A   B   C   D   E   F

8

Coldberry

Pikestone Brow

Coldberry
Grains

Pikestone
Brow
Farm

Lodge
Sike
Farm

7

Coldberry
Moss

Marl Beck

29

Coldberry Gutter

Elphatory
Allotment

Hardberry Hill

Hudes Hope

Marlbeck
Gutter

6

Resr

Low
Monks

Clubgill
Allotment

Club
Gill

Hardberry Hill
Allotment

Clubgill Sike

Hudeshope Beck

Skears
Hushes

5

28

Hardberry
Farm

High
Skears

Brown Dodd
Top

High
Skears
Farm

4

Howgill
Farm

Gate
Castles

Brown
Dodd

Skears

Turners

Skears
Plantation

Snaisgill Sike

3

Tinkler's
Allotment

How Gill

Stonygill
High
House

27

Aukside

Snaisgill
Plantation

Snaisgill

2

Aukside
Plantation

Stonygill
Head

Middle
Side

Edge
End

Rock
Terr

High Dyke

Stonygill
Foot

1

Lane
End

CASSEL
BANK

DENT
BANK

KING'S WALK

River Tees

B6277

26

93   A   B   94   C   D   95   E   F

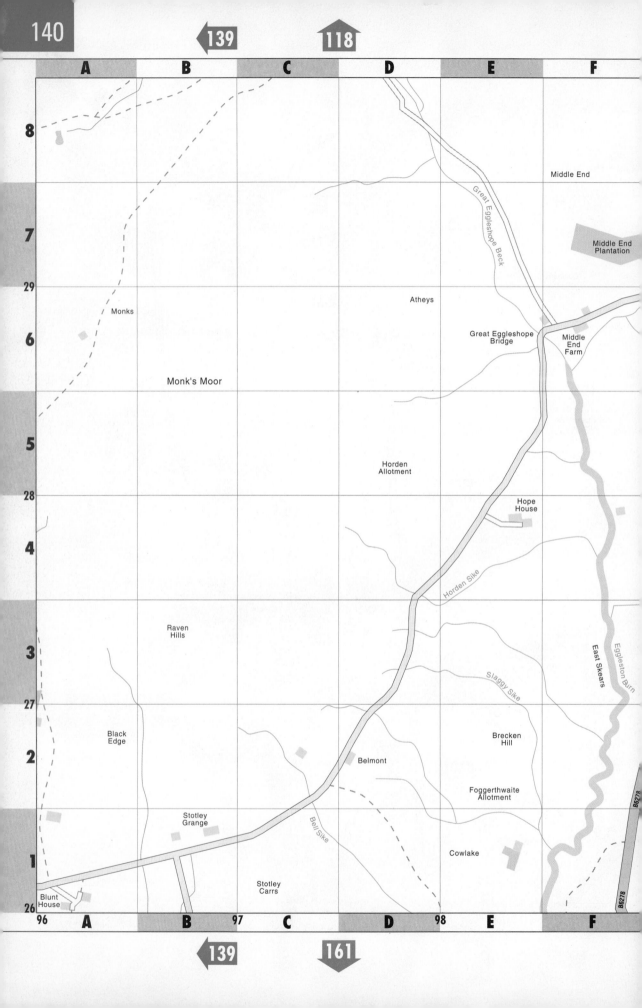

A | B | C | D | E | F

8

Middle End

7

Middle End
Plantation

29

Atheys

Great Eggleshope Beck

6

Monks

Great Eggleshope
Bridge

Middle
End
Farm

Monk's Moor

Horden
Allotment

5

Hope
House

28

4

Horden Sike

East Skears

Eggleston Burn

Raven
Hills

3

Slaggy Sike

27

Black
Edge

Brecken
Hill

2

Belmont

Foggerthwaite
Allotment

B6278

Stotley
Grange

Bel Sike

Cowlake

1

Stotley
Carrs

Blunt
House

26

96 | A | 97 | C | D | 98 | E | F

119
142

A B C D E F

8

7

29

6

5

28

4

3

27

2

1

26

B6278

Little Eggles Hope

Little Egglehope Beck

Islington
Hill

Robin
Weathers

Brown
Dodd

Millstone Rigg

Eggleston Common

Ever Rigg

Cloudlam Beck

Cloudlam
Rake

Neighbour
Moor
Head

Morton
Shield

Trinity Rigg

Morton Shield Beck

Foller Gill

Quarter Burn

Slate Ledge

Knotts
lantation

Knotts
Allotment

9 A B 00 C D 01 E F

162
142

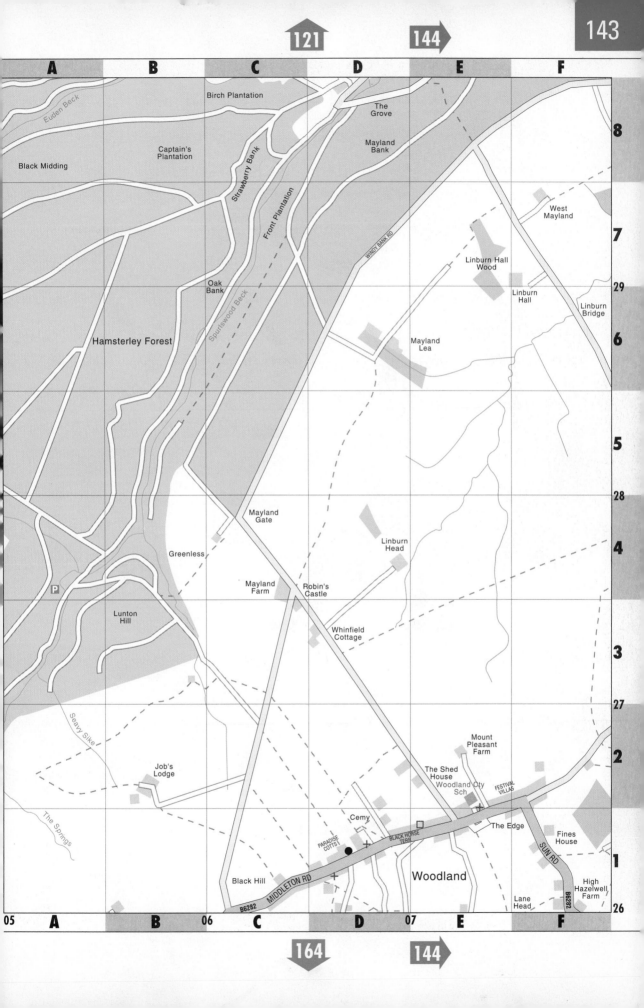

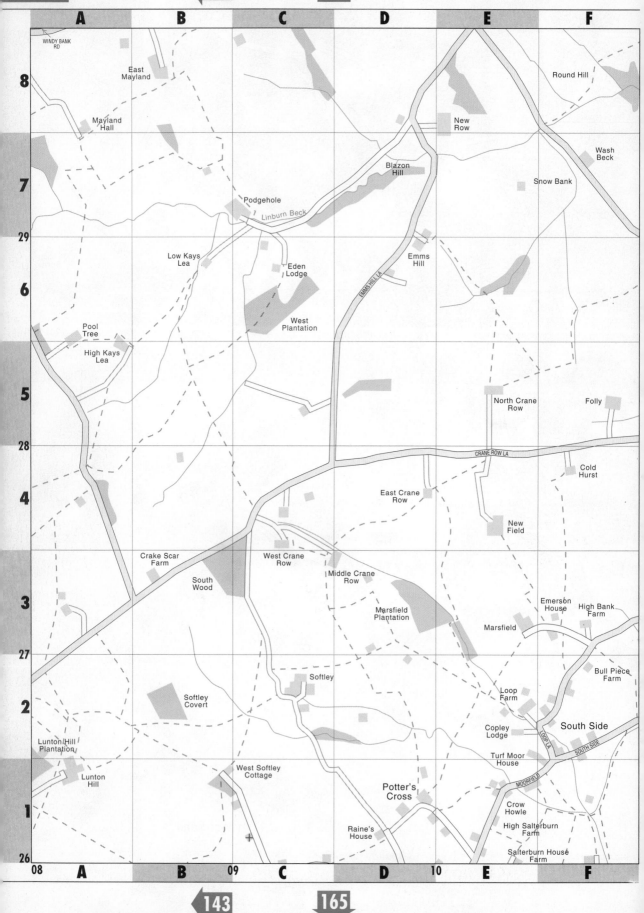

WINDY BANK RD

East Mayland

Mayland Hall

Round Hill

New Row

Blazon Hill

Wash Beck

Podgehole

Linburn Beck

Snow Bank

Low Kays Lea

Emms Hill

Eden Lodge

EMMS HILL LA

Pool Tree

West Plantation

High Kays Lea

North Crane Row

Folly

CRANE ROW LA

Cold Hurst

East Crane Row

New Field

Crake Scar Farm

South Wood

West Crane Row

Middle Crane Row

Emerson House

High Bank Farm

Marsfield Plantation

Marsfield

Bull Piece Farm

Softley

Loop Farm

Softley Covert

Copley Lodge

South Side

LOOP LA

SOUTH SIDE

Turf Moor House

Lunton Hill Plantation

West Softley Cottage

MOORFIELD

Lunton Hill

Potter's Cross

Crow Howle

High Salterburn Farm

Raine's House

Salterburn House Farm

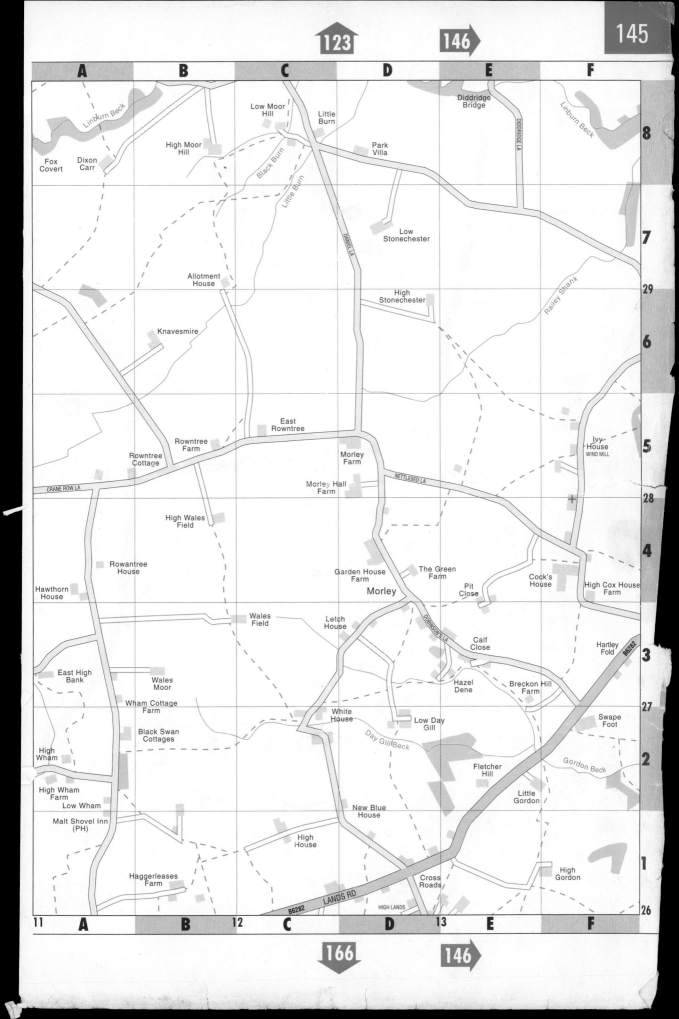

A B C D E F

8
7
29
6
5
28
4
3
27
2
1
26

Linburn Beck
Fox Covert
Dixon Carr
High Moor Hill
Low Moor Hill
Little Burn
Black Burn
Little Burn
Diddridge Bridge
Linburn Beck
DIDDRIDGE LA
Park Villa
Low Stonechester
DANIEL LA
Railey Shank
Allotment House
High Stonechester
Knavesmire
East Rowntree
Rowntree Farm
Rowntree Cottage
Morley Farm
NETTLEBED LA
Ivy House
WIND MILL
Morley Hall Farm
CRANE ROW LA
High Wales Field
Rowantree House
Hawthorn House
Garden House Farm
The Green Farm
Morley
Pit Close
Cock's House
High Cox House Farm
Wales Field
Letch House
Calf Close
Hartley Fold
B6282
East High Bank
Wales Moor
DOBINSON'S LA
Hazel Dene
Breckon Hill Farm
Wham Cottage Farm
White House
Low Day Gill
Swape Foot
Black Swan Cottages
Day Gill Beck
Gordon Beck
High Wham
Fletcher Hill
High Wham Farm
Low Wham
New Blue House
Little Gordon
Malt Shovel Inn (PH)
High House
High Gordon
Haggerleases Farm
Cross Roads
LANDS RD
B6282
HIGH LANDS

11 12 13

A B C D E F

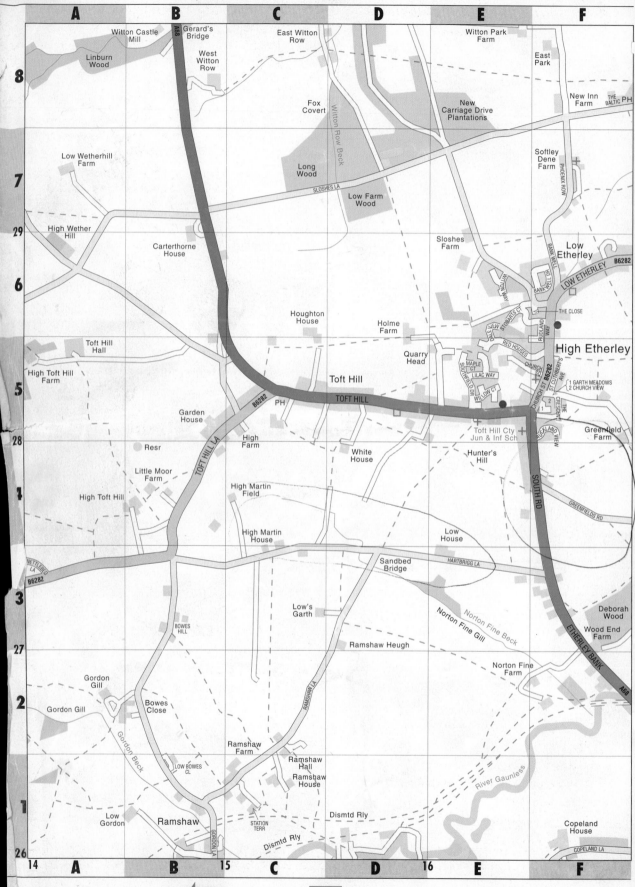

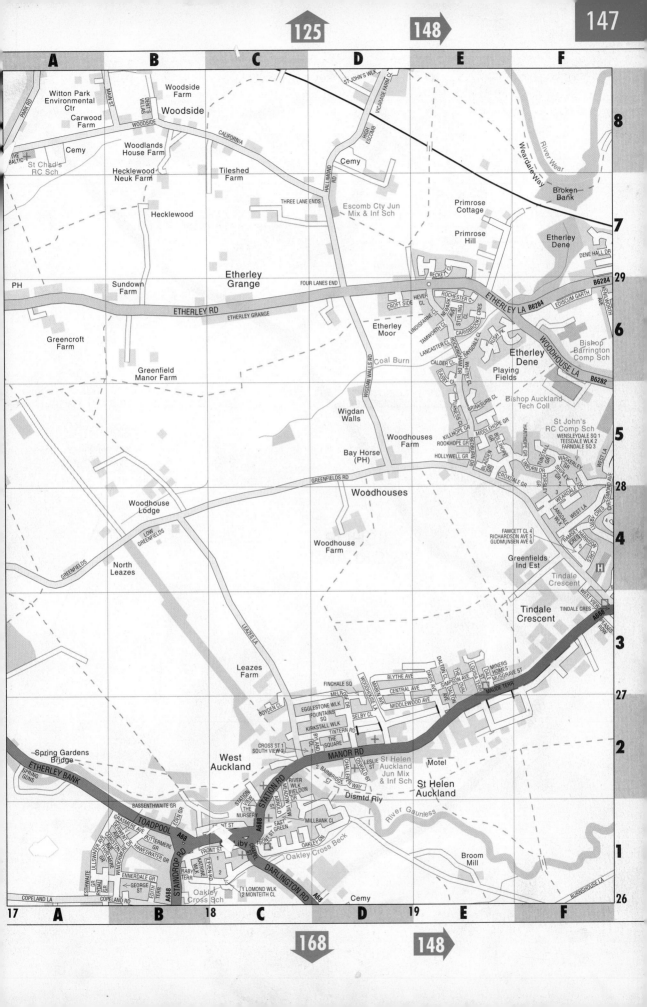

125
148

A B C D E F

8

7

29

6

5

28

4

3

27

2

1

26

168
148

Witton Park Environmental Ctr
Carwood Farm
Woodside Farm
Woodside
Woodlands House Farm
St Chad's RC Sch
THE BALTIC
Cemy
PARK RD
MAIN ST
DERE'S VILLAS
WOODSIDE
CALIFORNIA
St John's Wlk
VICARAGE FARM CL
HIGH ESCOMB
Cemy
Escomb Cty Jun Mix & Inf Sch
HALLIMOND RD
Primrose Cottage
Primrose Hill
Etherley Dene
DENE HALL DR
Weardale Way
River Wear
Broken Bank

Hecklewood Neuk Farm
Hecklewood
Tileshed Farm
THREE LANE ENDS
FOUR LANES END
Etherley Grange
Sundown Farm
PH
ETHERLEY RD
ETHERLEY GRANGE
Etherley Moor
CROFT SIDE
HEVER CL
BECKET CL
ROCHESTER CL
NEWPORT CL
ST HILDS CL
CARISBROOK CRES
ETHERLEY LA
B6284
B6284
EDISCUM GARTH
KENILWORTH AVE

Greencroft Farm
Greenfield Manor Farm
WIGDAN WALLS RD
Coal Burn
Wigdan Walls
Woodhouses Farm
LINDISFARNE CL
TAMWORTH CL
LANCASTER CL
CALDER CL
WHITBY CL
EASBY CL
BATSDALE CL
BRINKBURN CL
HUSH PK
Etherley Dene
Playing Fields
Bishop Auckland Tech Coll
WOODHOUSE LA
B6282
Bishop Barrington Comp Sch

Bay Horse (PH)
Woodhouses
GREENFIELDS RD
Woodhouse Lodge
LOW GREENFIELDS
KILLHOPE GR
ROOKHOPE GR
HOLLYWELL GR
MIDDLEHOPE GR
BOLTHOPE GR
BURNHOPE GR
BEDBURN GR
BLAGDEN GR
CROXDALE GR
ST John's RC Comp Sch
WENSLEYDALE SQ 1
TEESDALE WLK 2
FARNDALE SQ 3
HARTHOPE GR
WASKERLEY GR
INSTALL GR
HORSLEY GR
SUERLEY
UNBURN DR
WEST LA
WEARDALE DR

North Leazes
GREENFIELDS
Woodhouse Farm
FAWCETT CL 4
RICHARDSON AVE 5
GUDMUNSEN AVE 6
LANSDALE WLK
WEST LA
RAMSEY CRES
HARRISON CRES
BIBBY CRES
CHESMOND AVE
Greenfields Ind Est
Tindale Crescent
H

Leazes Farm
LEAZES LA
Tindale Crescent
TINDALE CRES
A686
PEASES ROW
WEST VIEW

Spring Gardens Bridge
ETHERLEY BANK
SPRING GDNS
West Auckland
FINCHALE SQ
MELROSE DR
EGGLESTONE WLK
FOUNTAINS SQ
KIRKSTALL WLK
TINTERN RD
BOYDEN CL
CROSS ST 1
SOUTH VIEW 2
BLYTHE AVE
CENTRAL AVE
MIDDLEWOOD AVE
WOODHOUSE LA
MABRA AVE
DAVIS AVE
DALTON CL
DALTON ST
SIMPSON ST
THREE TUNS
LOUISA ST
DALE TERR
MINERS HOMES
MUSGRAVE ST
MAUDE TERR

Bassenthwaite GR
TOADPOOL
A68
STATION RD
SELBY CL
THE SQUARE
MANOR RD
BVLAND
STATION VIEW
THE NURSERY
RIVER WLK
MEADOW VIEW
FIELDON
EAST GREEN
BAMBRIDGE CT
CHALLENGER WAY
TISWELL ST
LESLIE ST
St Helen Auckland Jun Mix & Inf Sch
ST HELEN ST
Motel
St Helen Auckland

GRASMERE AVE
BUTTERMERE
ULLSWATER AVE
DERWENT DR
CONISTON GR
HAWESWATER AVE
WINDERMERE
ENNERDALE GR
ESTHWAITE GR
COPELAND LA
GEORGE ST
EDITH TERR
FRONT ST
RABY TERR
KATRINE WLK
COPELAND RD
DARLINGTON RD
A68
Oakley Cross Sch
1 LOMOND WLK
2 MONTEITH CL
Oakley Cross Beck
Millbank CL
OAKLEY GN
Liby
Dismtd Rly
River Gauntless
Broom Mill
Cemy
BURNSHOUSE LA
A688

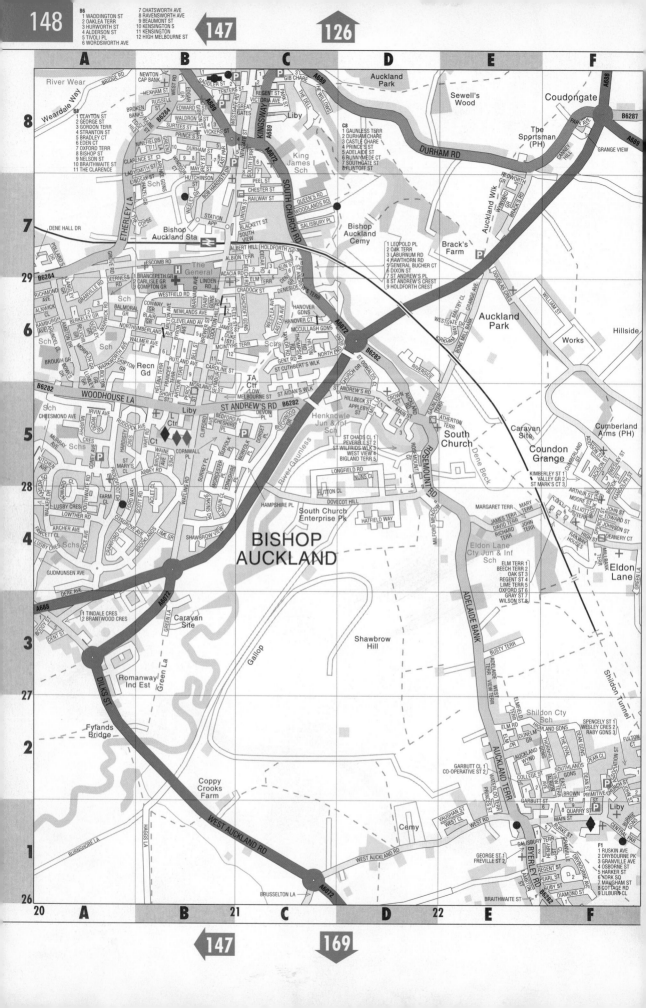

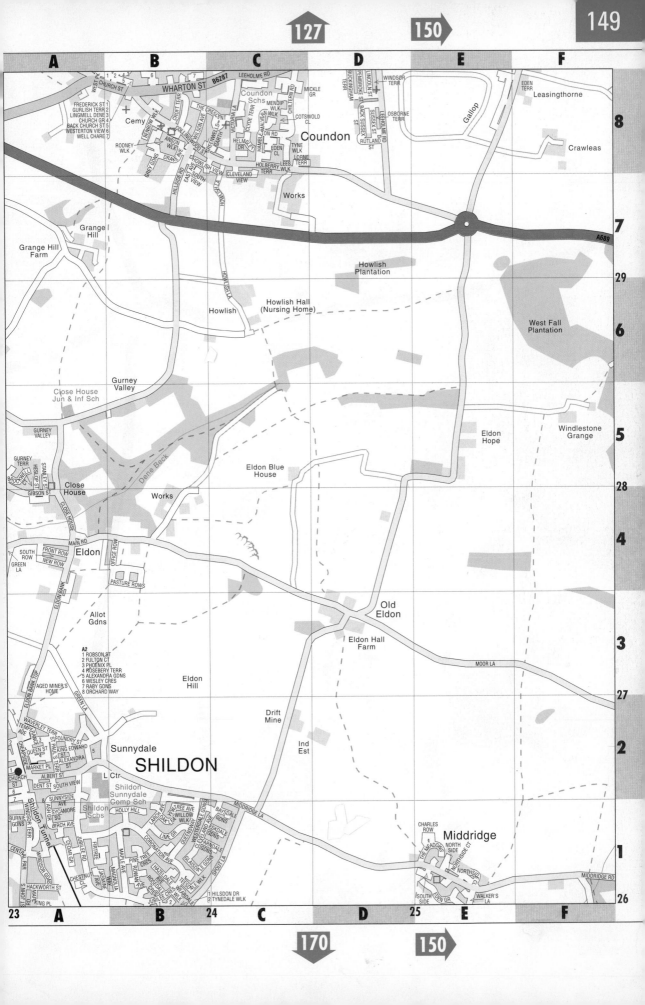

149
128

A B C D E F

8

Paddock
Plantation

Merrington Mill
Farm

Mill
Wood

DENE TERR 1
OSWALD TERR 2
NORMAN TERR 3
VICTORIA TERR 4
RABY TERR 5

1 WEST CHILTON TERR
WORDSWORTH RD
KEATS RD
BYRON RD
TENNYSON RD
DALE ST
EDEN TERR A167

PEARL CL
CRAG
SIDE

ASH GR
FORD TERR
ROSEWOOD

COL CRES
BURNS RD

Sch
DIAMOND CL
CRYSTAL CL
THE
GOLDEN
GR
RUBY AVE
OPAL CL
EMERALD GR
ADE WLK

THE POPLARS

BEECH AVE

THE CRESCENT
HUNTER
TERR
BEVERLEY GDNS
THE PENTLANDS
SOUTH DOWNS

Chilton

MENDIP
GN

Turkey Hill
Plantation

Millwood
Farm

CHARLOTTE TERR
DURHAM RD

Chilton City
Jun Sch

THE COTSWA

7

Nursery
Garden

Well
Plantation

Mill
Plantation

WOODHAM
VIEW
NEW SOUTH VIEW
SHELLEY TERR
THE SOUTH VIEW
GROVE
BROOKLYN
RD
LYNDHURST RD

MEADOWDALE

A689

Clare
Lodge

Windlestone

29

Mill
Cottages

Rushyford
Farm

6

Windlestone
Farm

Eden
Arms
Hotel

Rushyford Beck
A689

Windlestone Hall
Residential Sch

ROOKERY GDNS

Rushyford

The
Avenue

Lower
Pond

Windlestone
Park

Middle
Pond

Stephenson's
Plantation

Woodham
Lodge

Lowfield
Farm

5

High
Pond

The Breaks

28

Home
Farm

Middridge Lane
Plantation

Carrsides
Wood

Park
House

Woodham North
Plantation

CARRSIDES LA

4

MIDDRIDGE RD

Stotforth Hill
Farm

The
Larches

Old
Wood

Golf
Course

ST ANDREWS CL
ANDREWS
CT

CH

Eldon Moor
Plantation

Ropemoor

ACLE
MEADOWS

RYDER CT

Woodham
Village

Woodham

3

27

Eldon Moor
Cottage

Rope Moor
Plantation

ACLE BURN

Agnew
Plantation

THE GRANGE

HIGH GN

LON GN

SCALINGDALE
THE SPINNEY

YARROW GR
CAMPION
CT

WOODLAND WAY
WATTS AVE
THE PADDOCK
THE CROFT

L Ctr

Woodham
Bridge

2

Eldon Moor
House

MOOR LA

BLAKISTON CL
HASLEWOOD RD

BURNHILL WAY

CARWARDINE
CL

WOODHAM LA

THE BRIDLE

SORREL
CT

CLOVER
CT
DUDLEY CT
DICKINSON
CRES

ELIZABETHS
ST

HAREBELL
MEADOWS

YARROW CT

SANDOWN DR
OAKS
VILLAGE CT

FALLOW
CT

FAWN CL

THE BEECHERS
GR

HICKSTEAD RISE

STAG LA
RABY GR
BARNARD
CT

KENILWORTH

STONELEIGH

1 CHILLINGHAM GR
2 BRANCEPETH CL

Cobbler's Hall
Plantation

GREENFIELD WAY

BLUEBELL WAY

BURN LA

FENHALL GN 1
ELEMORE PL 2
PHOENIX PL 3
BROCKWELL CL 4
OSBERT PL 5

CALLERTON
RISE

HUTTON
PL

WELL HOUSE PL

DEERNESS

KIMBLESWORTH

TARGELD PL

WOODHAM WAY

EGERTON CT

KIRKHAM CL

BEAUMONT CL

THE
BALLARAT

STARGATE CL

FARNHAM CL

BROOK
CL
ALNWICK
GR

FAWN CL
HELMSLEY
CT

BADMINTON

LOWTHER TERR
BURGHLEY WAY

STONLEY
STOCK
CL

GRANGE
CT

WOODHAM BURN

WOODHAM WAY

1

26

CLAXTON
CT
ELWICK AVE

MIDDRIDGE RD

RUSSELL CT

ALVERTON
CT

IDA
PL

KINGS
DR

AGNEW WAY

WELL HOUSE PL

GUTHRUM
PL

MORRISON CL

ALFRID
PL

CHILTON CL

BRANTFORD CT

LAYTON CT

GRINDON CL

WHITTON CL

MILLGATE CT

A167

26 A B 27 C D 28 E F

A B C D E F

8
7
29
6
5
28
4
3
27
2
1
26

1 CRAGSIDE
2 EMERALD WLK

ALDWIN CL
GRANVILLE CL
SKIRLAW CL
ALINGTON CL
KIRKHAM CL
VILLIERS CL

JADE WLK
PAL AVE
CORDINGTON RD
SOUTH DOWNS
HAMBLETON WAY

3 GRAMPIAN WAY
4 PENNINE WAY
5 MALVERN

Kay's
Hill

ALBERT ST
ARTHUR ST
PROSPECT TERR

6 THE COTSWOLDS
7 SOUTH VIEW
8 LYNDHURST RD
9 BROOKLYN RD

Standalone

Sewage
Works

Chilton
Grange

Dismtd Rly

Lark
Hill

Thrundle

GIPSY LA

Nunstainton
East

Depot

A1(M)

Borehole
Plantation

Nunstainton
Grange
Cottages

Nunstainton
Grange

Junction 60

Nunstainton
Carrs

Low
Farm

High
Farm

A689

Bradbury

Pityme
Wood

Rushyford Beck

CARRSIDES LA

Carrsides

Carrsides
Carrs

Nunstainton Grange
Carrs

River Skerne

Bradbury
Carrs

Bradbury
Plantation

Little
Isle

Great
Isle

Woodham Burn

The Isle

Swan Carr
Farm

A1(M)

Low
Copelaw

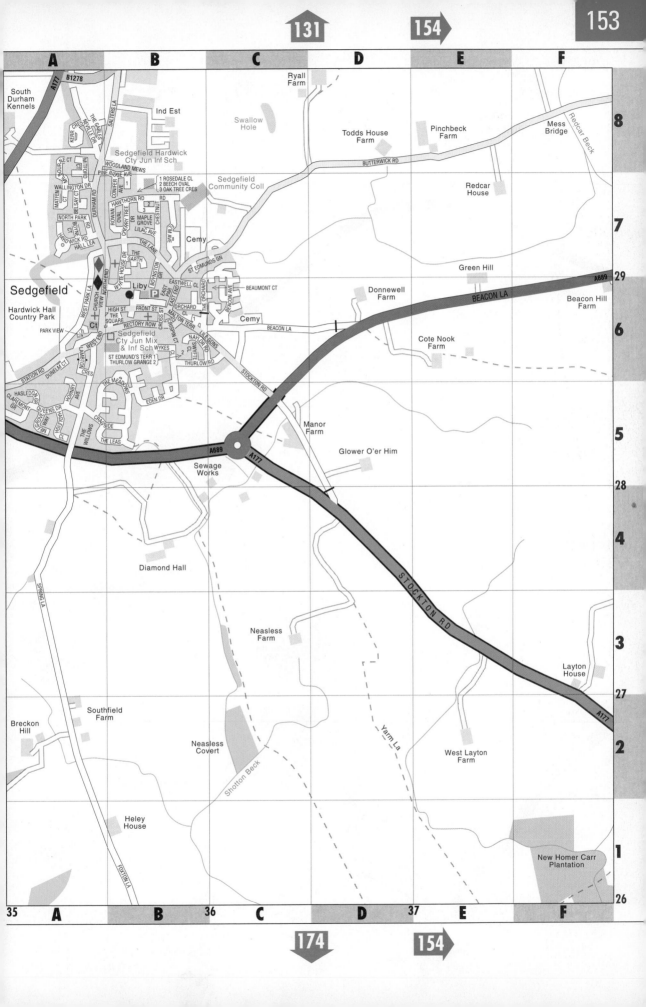

A **B** **C** **D** **E** **F**

8

Butterwick
West Farm

East
Farm

Ten-o'-Clock
Farm

Whin Houses
Belt

Green Lane
Cottages

South Farm

BUTTERWICK RD

Butterwick

Waterloo
Plantation

Lumpley's
Covert

7

BEACON LA

Beacon
Farm

Old Acres
Lodge Farm

Oldacres
Bridge

High
Swainston

29 A689

Beacon Hill
Farm

HARTLEPOOL RD

Newlands

6

Old Acres
Hall Farm

Tilery
Cottage

P

Picnic
Site

Middle
Swainston
Plantation

P

STATION COTTS

5

East Close

Tilery
Wood

A689

Square
Plantation

West Carr
Plantation

28

Castle Eden Walkway

Cockpit

4

Tinkler's Moor
Plantation

Brierley Beck

Black Squares Dr

Black
Squares

3

Cowley House
Farm

Brierley Wood

BRIERLEY DR

NURSERY DR

Seaham New
Plantation

27

Brierley
Cottage

THE RACECOURSE

Dial Hill

2

A177

Layton Lings

Woodend

Holmelands

STOCKTON RD

1

Thorpe
Larches

CASTLE EDEN WALKWAY

Spring Bank
Cottages

South Layton

A177

26

DURHAM RD

38 **A** **B** **39** **C** **D** **40** **E** **F**

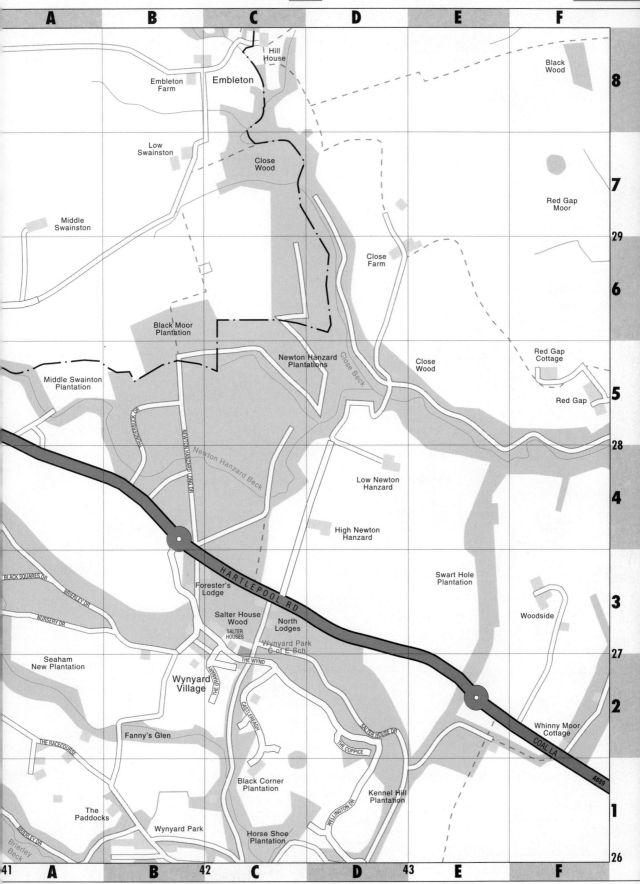

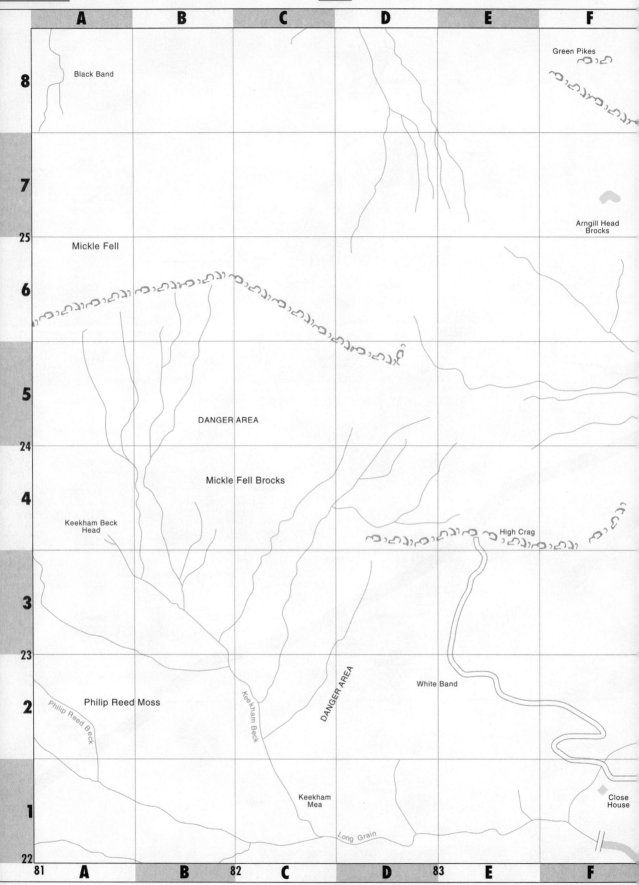

Black Band

Green Pikes

Arngill Head
Brocks

Mickle Fell

DANGER AREA

Mickle Fell Brocks

Keekham Beck
Head

High Crag

White Band

Philip Reed Moss

Philip Reed Beck

Keekham Beck

DANGER AREA

Keekham
Mea

Long Grain

Close
House

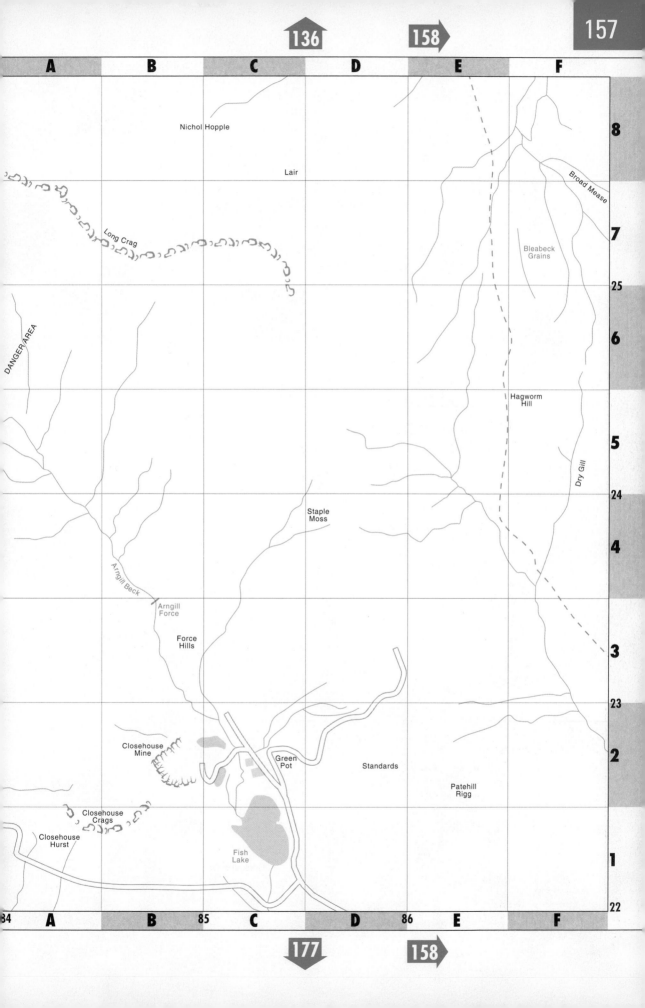

A B C D E F

8

Nichol Hopple

Lair

Broad Mease

Long Crag

7

Bleabeck
Grains

25

DANGER AREA

6

Hagworm
Hill

5

Dry Gill

24

Staple
Moss

4

Arngill Beck

Arngill
Force

Force
Hills

3

23

Closehouse
Mine

2

Green
Pot

Standards

Patehill
Rigg

Closehouse
Crags

Closehouse
Hurst

Fish
Lake

1

22

84 A B 85 C D 86 E F

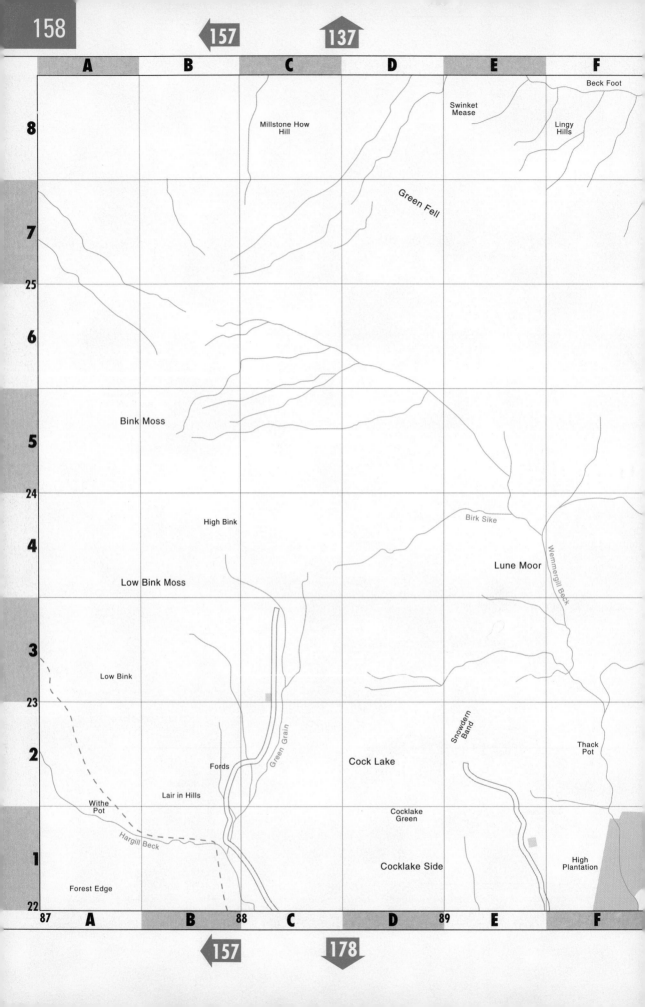

A B C D E F

8

Beck Foot

Swinket
Mease

Millstone How
Hill

Lingy
Hills

Green Fell

7

25

6

Bink Moss

5

24

High Bink

Birk Sike

4

Lune Moor

Wemmergill Beck

Low Bink Moss

3

Low Bink

23

Snowdern
Band

Thack
Pot

2

Green Grain

Fords

Cock Lake

Lair in Hills

Withe
Pot

Cocklake
Green

1

Hargill Beck

Cocklake Side

High
Plantation

22

Forest Edge

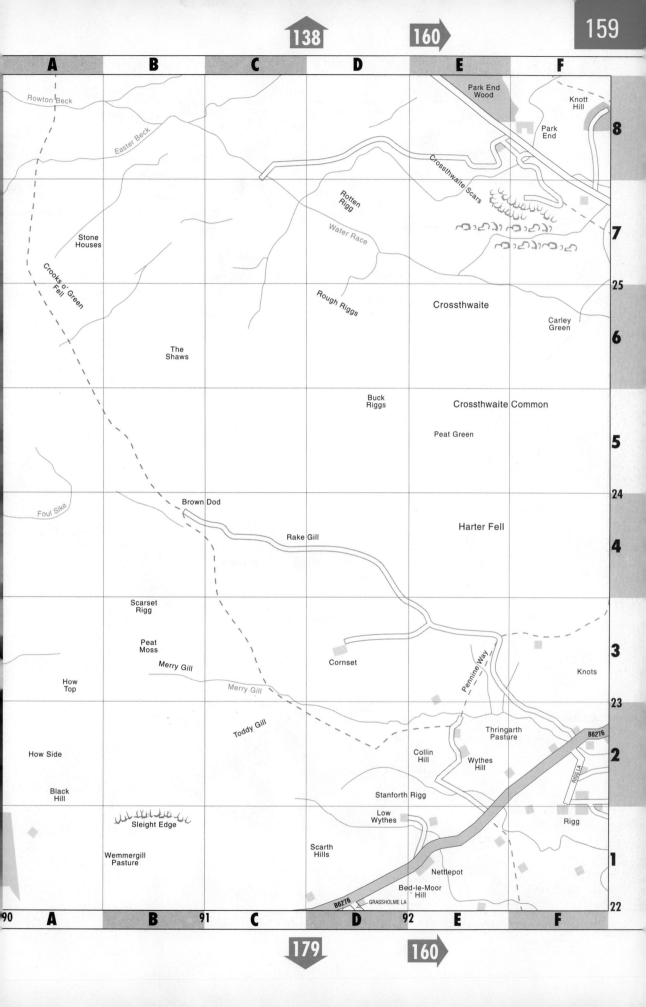

A B C D E F

Rowton Beck

Easter Beck

Park End Wood

Knott Hill

Park End

Crossthwaite Scars

8

Stone Houses

Crooks o' Green Fell

Rotten Rigg

Water Race

7

25

Rough Riggs

Crossthwaite

Carley Green

6

The Shaws

Buck Riggs

Crossthwaite Common

Peat Green

5

Foul Sike

Brown Dod

24

Harter Fell

Rake Gill

4

Scarset Rigg

Peat Moss

Merry Gill

Cornset

Pennine Way

Knots

3

How Top

Merry Gill

23

Toddy Gill

Thringarth Pasture

B6216

How Side

Collin Hill

Wythes Hill

RIGG LA

2

Black Hill

Stanforth Rigg

Sleight Edge

Low Wythes

Rigg

Wemmergill Pasture

Scarth Hills

Nettlepot

1

Bed-le-Moor Hill

B6216

GRASSHOLME LA

22

159
139

A **B** **C** **D** **E** **F**

8

Crook
Hill

B6277

Hudegate

The
Park

KING'S WK

Hudeshope B'CROOK

Stanhope
Gate

Spring
Hill

STACKS LA

Breckholm

HUDE

ROSE TERR

TOWN HEAD

ALSTON RD

Hotel
SHAW CRES

Middleton-in
-Teesdale

MARKET PL

Middle
Crosswhaite

Pennine Way

GOODBURN PL

B6282

WESLEY TERR

CHAPEL
ROW

CALIFORNIA ROW

B6282

Lane Side

HORSEMARKET

HILL TERR

TOWN END

JUBILEE PL

7

River Tees

BRIDGE ST

B6277

VICTORIA
TERR

GAS LA

LEEKWORTH

MEADOW CL

GDNS

Burnt
Scar

East
Crosswhaite

GARDEN TERR 1
DALE VIEW 2

NEWTOWN

WESTERMAN
PL

Middleton-in
-Teesdale
Jun & Inf Sch

LEEKWORTH LA

Leekworth

25

RIVER
TERR

Sewage
Works

Teesdale Way

Step
Ends

6

Intake
Hill

Daleview
Caravan Pk

Lonton

Lonton East
Farm

Moor Rigg

B6276

5

Pennine Way

Rams Gill

High Bowbank
Cottage

Laithkirk

B6277

24

Bowbank Fell

Spring
Top

4

Kirkcarrion

Bowbank

River Lune

COTE HOUSE RD

Eller Beck

Greengates

East
Park

Caravan
Site

3

Saddle
Bow

Limestone
Hill

Seed
Rigg

Cote
House

23

B6276

NOOK LA

Thringarth

West
Park

Thringarth
Park

Carl Beck

Low Nook

2

Low
Rigg

Stake
Hill

WEST PASTURE RD

Grassholme Resr

1

East
Close

Brock
Scar

West Pasture
Farm

Easter Beck

West Pasture

22

93 **A** 94 **B** **C** 95 **D** **E** **F**

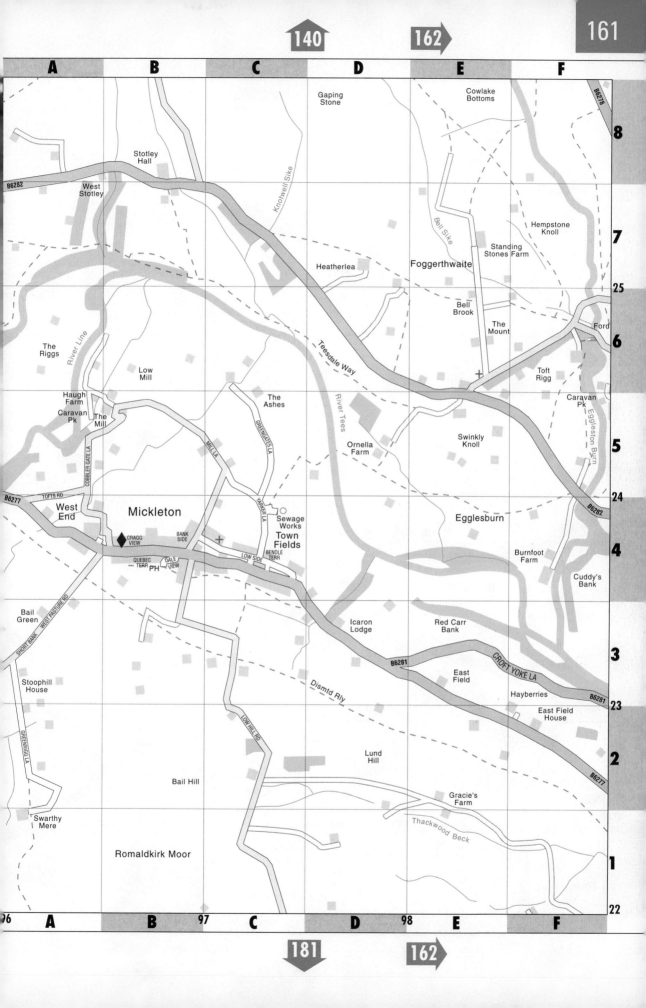

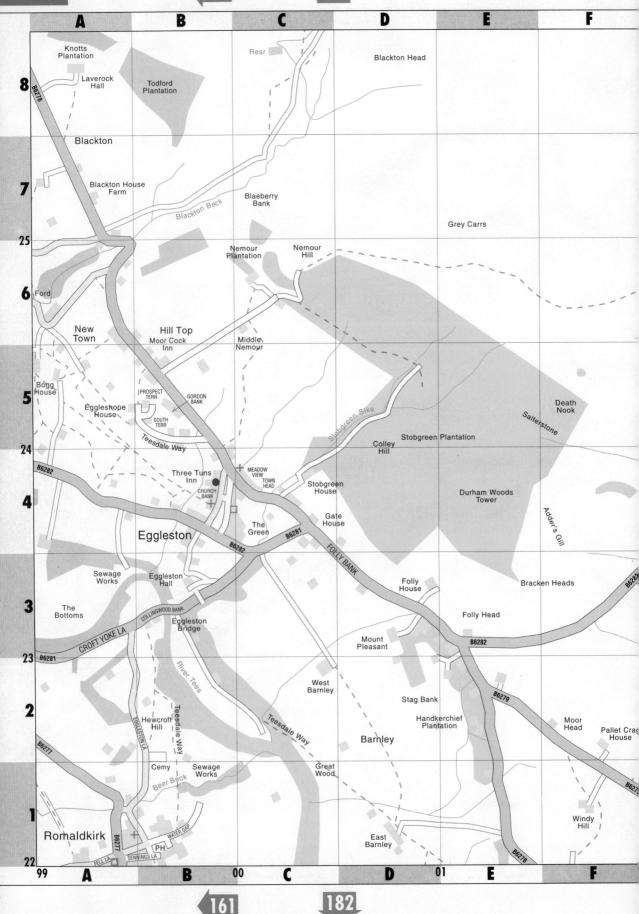

A B C D E F

8 Knotts Plantation

Laverock Hall

Todford Plantation

Blackton Head

B6278

Blackton

7 Blackton House Farm

Blaeberry Bank

Blackton Beck

Grey Carrs

25

Nemour Plantation

Nemour Hill

6 Ford

New Town

Hill Top

Moor Cock Inn

Middle Nemour

5 Bogg House

Eggleshope House

PROSPECT TERR

GORDON BANK

SOUTH TERR

Teesdale Way

Stobgreen Sike

Death Nook

Salterstone

Colley Hill

Stobgreen Plantation

24

Three Tuns Inn

MEADOW VIEW

TOWN HEAD

Stobgreen House

Durham Woods Tower

B6282

4 CHURCH BANK

The Green

B6281

Gate House

Adder's Gill

Eggleston

B6282

FOLLY BANK

Sewage Works

Eggleston Hall

Folly House

Bracken Heads

B6283

3 The Bottoms

Eggleston Bank COLLINGWOOD BANK

Eggleston Bridge

Folly Head

B6282

CROFT YOKE LA

Mount Pleasant

B6279

23 B6281

River Tees

West Barnley

Stag Bank

2 Hewcroft Hill

EGGLESTON LA

Teesdale Way

Teesdale Way

Handkerchief Plantation

Moor Head

Pallet Crag House

B6277

Barnley

Beer Beck

Cemy

Sewage Works

Great Wood

B627

1 Romaldkirk

WATER GAP

Windy Hill

B6278

B6277

FELL LA

B6277

PH

SENNINGS LA

22

99 A B 00 C 01 D E 01 F

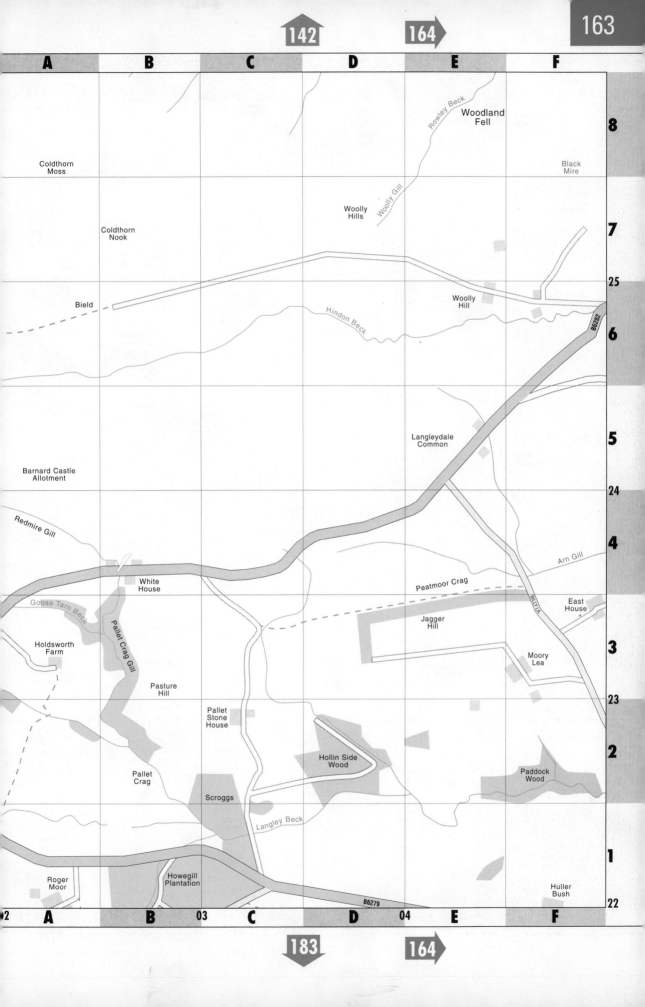

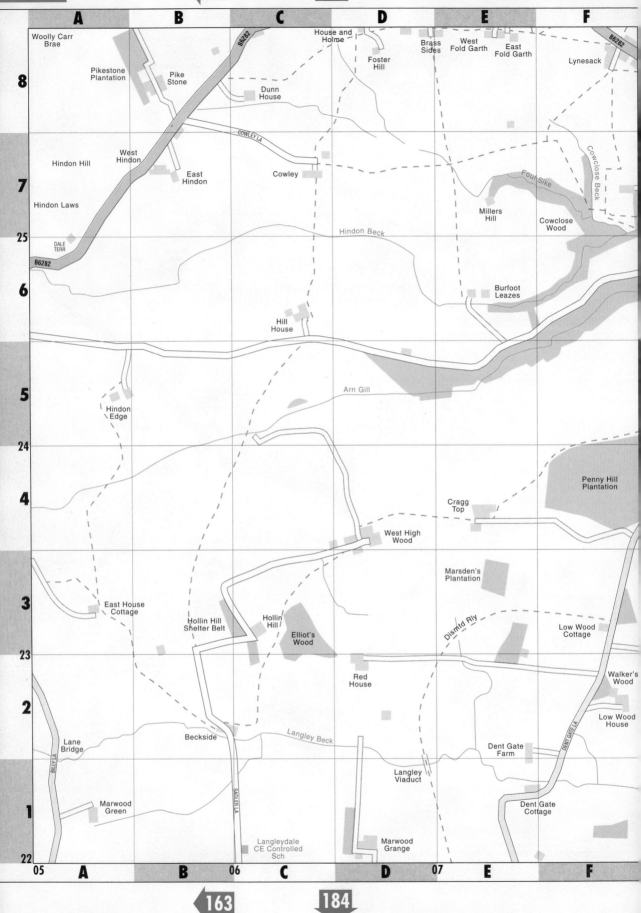

163
143

A **B** **C** **D** **E** **F**

Woolly Carr
Brae

Pikestone
Plantation

8

Pike
Stone

Dunn
House

House and
Holme

Foster
Hill

Brass
Sides

West
Fold Garth

East
Fold Garth

Lynesack

COWLEY LA

West
Hindon

Hindon Hill

East
Hindon

Cowley

Foul Sike

Cowclose Beck

7

Hindon Laws

Millers
Hill

Cowclose
Wood

25

DALE
TERR

Hindon Beck

B6282

Burfoot
Leazes

6

Hill
House

Arn Gill

5

Hindon
Edge

24

Penny Hill
Plantation

4

Cragg
Top

West High
Wood

Marsden's
Plantation

East House
Cottage

3

Hollin Hill
Shelter Belt

Hollin
Hill

Elliot's
Wood

Dismtd Rly

Low Wood
Cottage

23

Red
House

Walker's
Wood

2

BILLY LA

SADLER LA

Beckside

Langley Beck

Dent Gate
Farm

DENT GATE LA

Low Wood
House

Lane
Bridge

Langley
Viaduct

1

Marwood
Green

Dent Gate
Cottage

Langleydale
CE Controlled
Sch

Marwood
Grange

22

05 **A** **B** 06 **C** **D** 07 **E** **F**

163
184

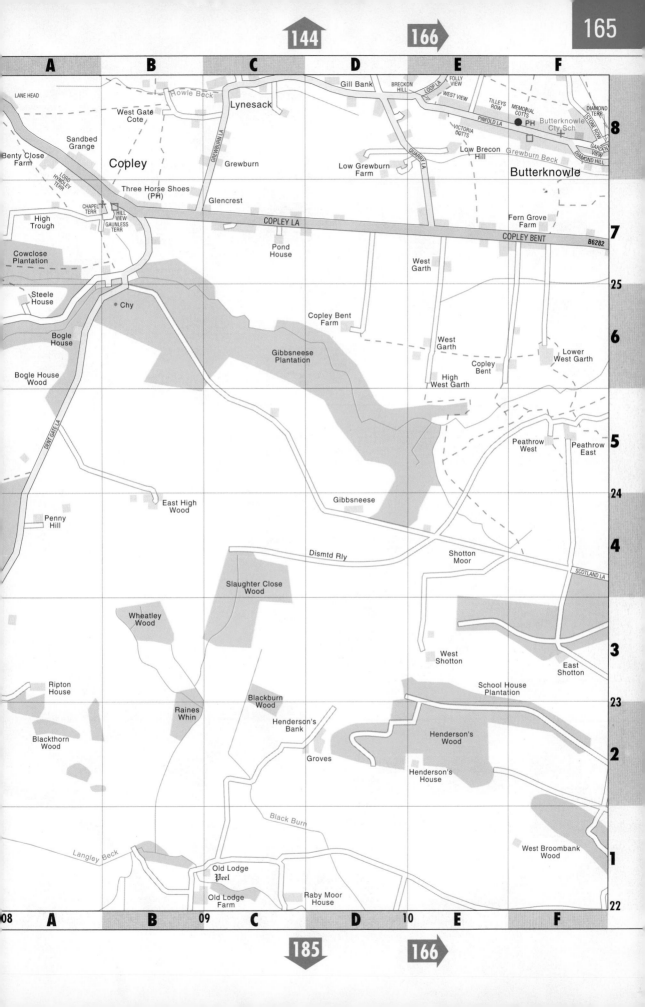

A **B** **C** **D** **E** **F**

8

Heather Dene Farm

Low Wham

GARDEN VIEW

Bowes Hill

LANDS RD

B6282

Low Butterknowle

High Lands

HIGH LANDS

Bluestone Farm

Dismtd Rly

DIAMOND HILL

THE SLACK

7

The Slack Inn

B6282

COPLEY BENT

Dismtd Rly

River Gaunless

Low Lands

Storey Lodge Colliery

Dismtd Rly

25

STATION COTTS

Lands Farm

Dismtd Rly

6

Cockfield Fell

1 YORK TERR
2 ST VINCENT TERR
3 PROSPECT TERR
4 BLEAK TERR
5 WEST END TERR
6 DIXON TERR
7 VANE TERR

Cemy

Blackburn Bridge

Sewage Works

ALPINE TERR

Cockfield Cty Sch

VICTORIA TERR

Cockfield

5

Wigglesworth

Hollymoor Farm

MOUNT PLEASANT

MOOR VIEW

KENSINGTON TERR

RABY TERR

GARDEN HOUSE LA

MINERS

BLING

ROYAL YARD

REST HAVEN

FRONT ST

THE GREEN

Liby

PH

STAINDROP RD

THE FALLOWS

CHURCH SQ

ESPERLEY LA

ESPERLEY

HAZELGROVE CRES

CORONATION TERR

MAYFIELD TERR

COMER TERR

MOSTYN TERR

24

1 PROSPECT SQ
2 MODEL TERR
3 OXFORD TERR
4 STANWIX COTTS

4

Raby Moor Farm

Hazelgrove Grounds

The Bungalow

LONG LA

Burnt Houses

SCOTLAND LA

BURNT HOUSES

PH

North Wood

3

The Folly

BURNT HOUSES LA

Ivy Cottage

23

Keverstone Grange

2

Low Shotton

Shotton Dean Wood

Raby Hill House

A688

KEVERSTONE BANK

Raby Park

The Laundry

Kennel Wood

Kennel House

Nursery

1

Kennel Wood Cottages

A688

North Lodge

22

Sandy Bank Wood

11 **A** **B** **12** **C** **D** **13** **E** **F**

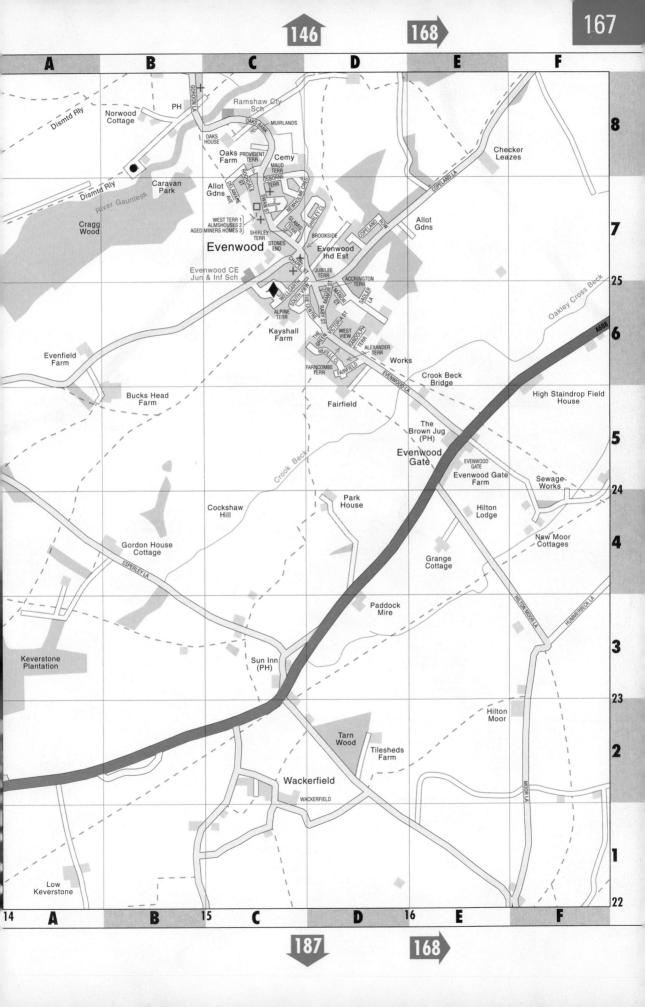

167
147

A B C D E F

8

7

25

6

5

24

4

3

23

2

1

22

Rosedene

DICKENSON RD
SIMPSON RD
COPELAND RD
ROBSON RD
STAINDROP RD
A68

West Auckland Cty Sch

Oakley Cross West Bridge

Wks

A68 DARLINGTON RD
Cemy

WEST VIEW

Bankfoot Farm

Fieldhouses

Hummerbeck Bridge

Hummerbeck Farm

Glenton Hall Farm

Backsandsides Farm

Oakley Cross Beck

Low Staindrop Field House

HUMMERBECK LA

Bridge House

Hummer Beck

LUTTERINGTON LA

Wheatside Lodge

Dial House

A688

Lutterington Hall

Wheatside Farm

Bildershaw Grange Farm

New Moors

Fair View

Lutterington

Brackenbury House

HUMMERBECK LA

Bolton Garths Plantation

Lutterington Beck

Lutterington Whin

Brackenbury Leases

The Lough

Bolton Garths

Sharpley Plantation

Lough House

Trunnelmire Plantation

Bolam Quarry (dis)

North Field

Bolam

CRAG LA

BROWNSIDE LA

Hindberries

STOBHILL LA

PH

West Leaside

DUNWELL LA

East Leaside

West Field

167
188

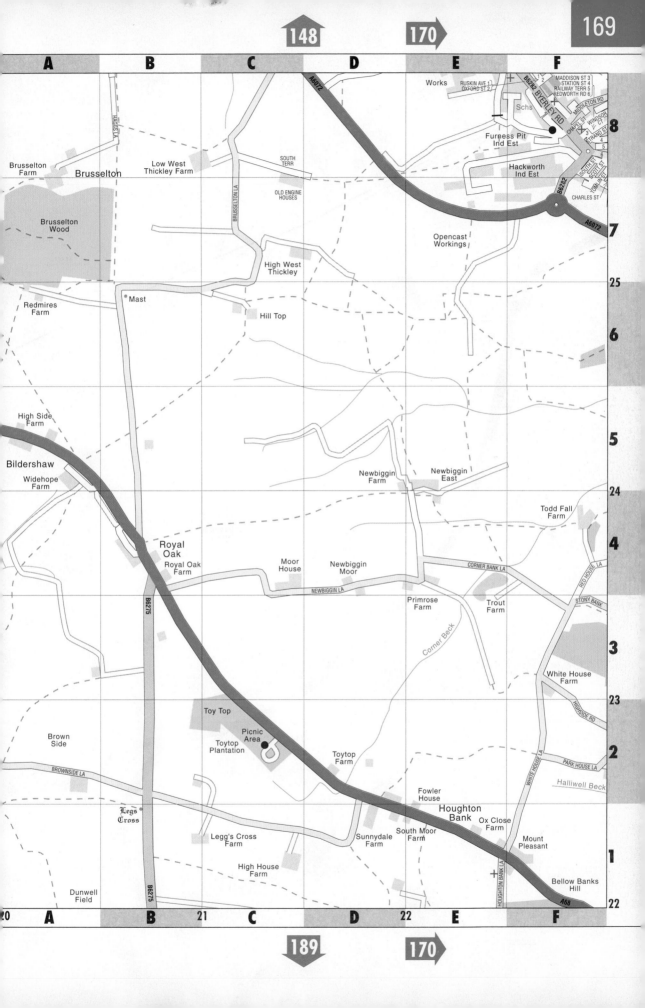

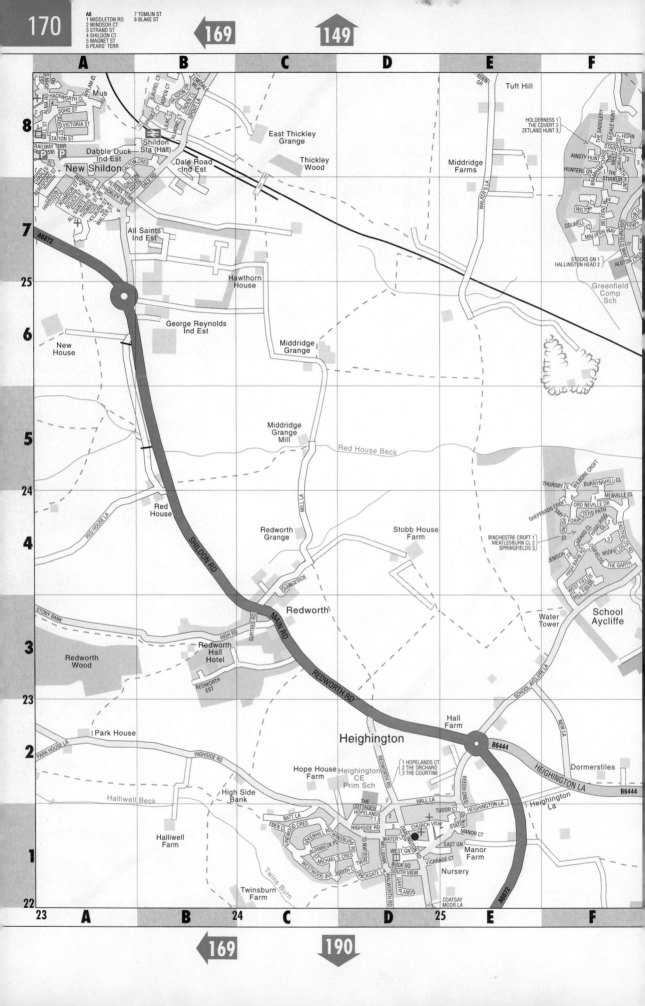

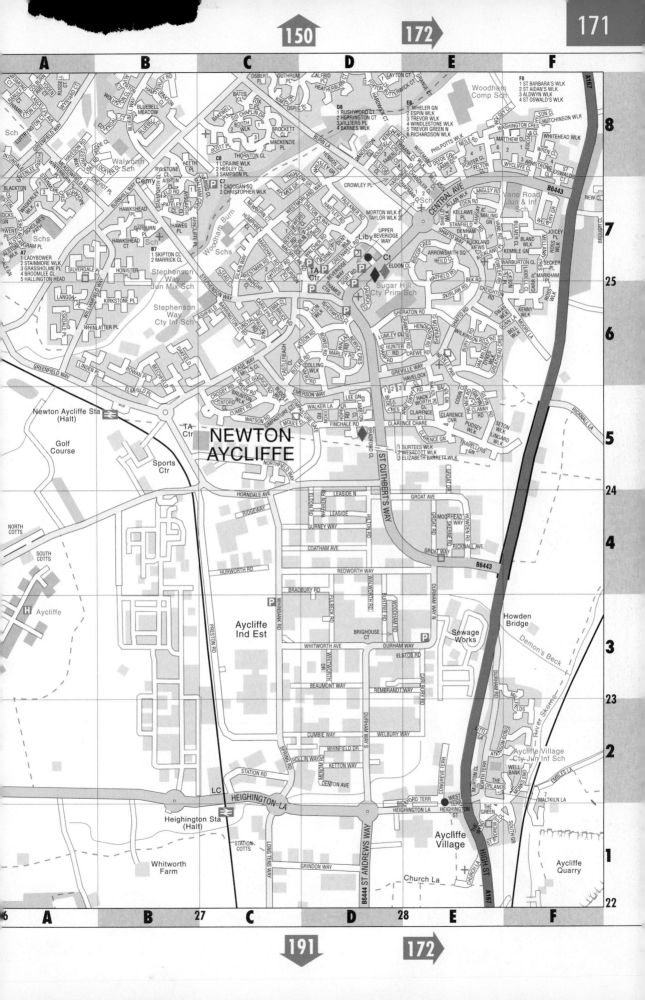

171
151

A B C D E F

8

Bradbury
Carrs

Woodham Burn

The Isle
Carrs

7

Ricknall
Carrs

Aycliffe Ctr
for Children

River Skerne

Preston
Carrs

25

6

High
Copelaw

Ricknall
Grange

CARR LA

Dismtd Rly

Ricknall
Lane End

5

Preston
West Farm

Preston
East Farm

WILDGOOSE LA

24

Dismtd Rly

Ricknall Mill
Farm

Blacksmiths
Arms
(PH)

Preston LA

Preston
Manor Farm

Preston-le-Skerne

LEEHALL LA

4

Hepworth
House

HEWORTH LA

RICKNALL LA

3

Rye Close
Farm

Lea
Hall

23

Preston
Tilery

2

EMBLES LA

Graham's
Wood

GREEN LA

Whinfield
House

The
Sycamores

Aycliffe
Quarry

LODGE LA

Preston
Lodge

1

High
Clump

LIME LA

SALTERS LA

Oat Hill
Farm

A1(M)

High
Grange

High
House

22

29 A 30 B C 30 D 31 E F

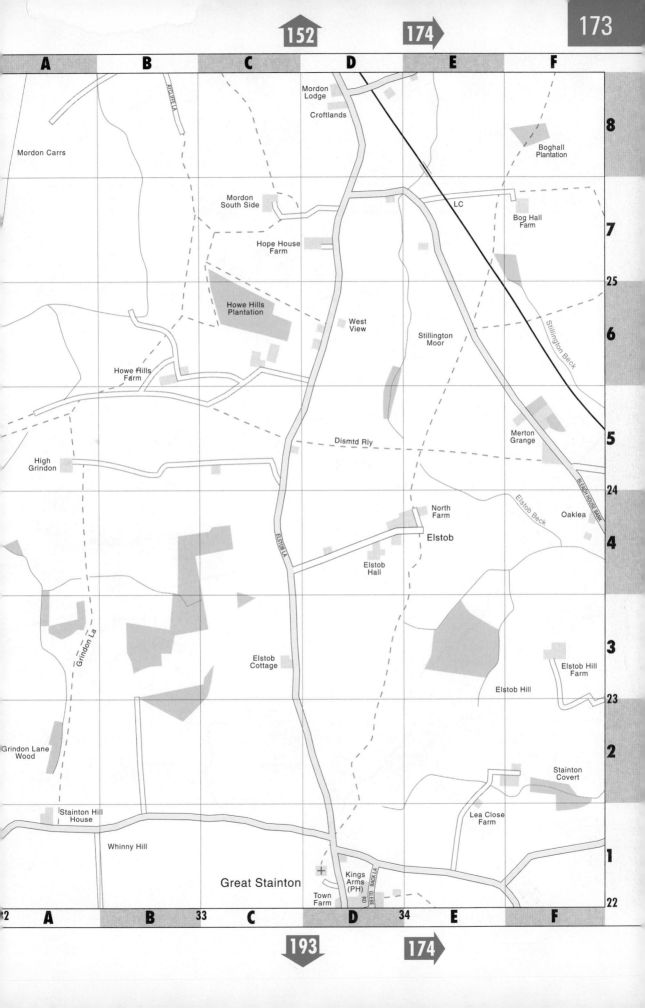

A   B   C   D   E   F

8

Mordon Carrs

Mordon Lodge

Croftlands

Boghall Plantation

Mordon South Side

LC

Bog Hall Farm

7

Hope House Farm

25

Howe Hills Plantation

West View

Stillington Moor

6

Stillington Beck

Howe Hills Farm

Dismtd Rly

Merton Grange

5

High Grindon

Elstob Beck

24

North Farm

Oaklea

Elstob

4

Elstob Hall

Grindon La

Elstob Cottage

Elstob Hill Farm

3

Elstob Hill

23

Grindon Lane Wood

Stainton Covert

2

Stainton Hill House

Lea Close Farm

Whinny Hill

1

Great Stainton

Kings Arms (PH)

Town Farm

22

173
153

A   B   C   D   E   F

8

Foxton
Wood

7

Crowdy
Hall

FOXTON LA

25

North
Farm

Foxton
Farm

South
Farm

Foxton

6

Shotton Beck

Shotton

Gilly
Hill

Shotton
Moor

Rafter Dene

Foxton Beck

5

Whitton
Three Gates

24

Lamb's
Hill

Stillington

Works

William Cassidi
(C of E)
Prim Sch

4

Moordale
Bottom

Stillington Beck

STILLINGTON
IND EST

IRONMASTERS WAY

LOWSON ST

MORRISON ST

BLEACH HOUSE BANK

Bleach House
Bridge

PH

MESSINES LA

BELL
SQ

PARK CRES

WETARE GR

THE
CROFTS

WEST

WEST

SOUTH ST

KIRK

MANOR DR

MANOR
WLK

3

SOUTH AVE

MOUNT
PLEASANT

MOUNT PLEASANT RD

MOUNT
PLEASANT
GR

23

Round
Hill

MOUNT
PLEASANT
CL

MOUNT
PLEASANT
WLK

Town
Farm

Old
Stillington

West House
Farm

Mill
Bridge

2

Stillington
Bridge

West
Farm

Bishopton
Mill

MILL LA

Stillington
Foot Bridge

Bishopton Beck

1

COBBY CASTLE LA

22

35   A   B   36   C   D   37   E   F

173
194

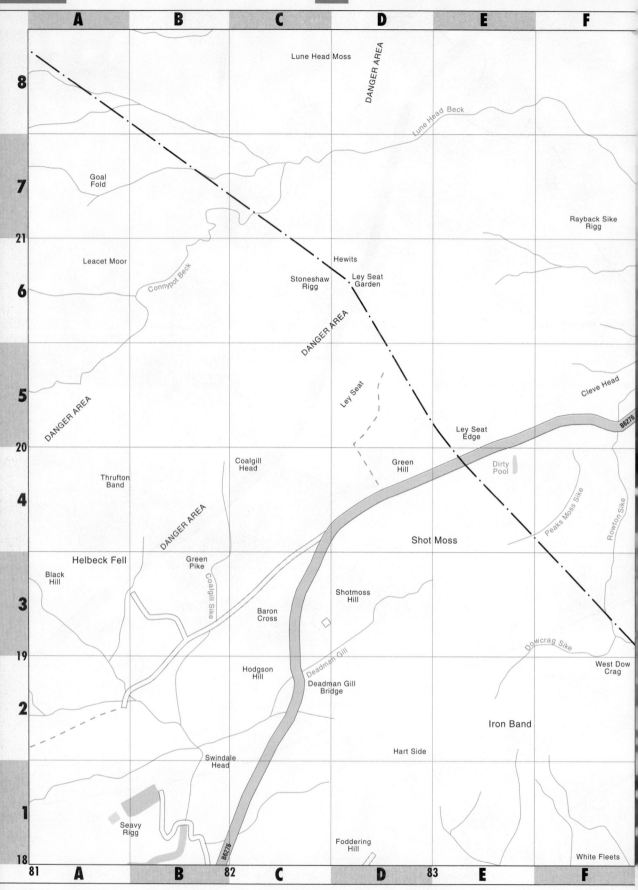

A B C D E F

8

7

21

6

5

20

4

3

19

2

1

18

Lune Head Moss

DANGER AREA

Lune Head Beck

Goal Fold

Rayback Sike Rigg

Leacet Moor

Connypot Beck

Hewits

Stoneshaw Rigg

Ley Seat Garden

DANGER AREA

Ley Seat

Cleve Head

Ley Seat Edge

DANGER AREA

Coalgill Head

Green Hill

Dirty Pool

B6276

Thrufton Band

Shot Moss

Peaks Moss Sike

Rowton Sike

DANGER AREA

Helbeck Fell

Green Pike

Coalgill Sike

Black Hill

Shotmoss Hill

Baron Cross

Deadman Gill

Dowcrag Sike

Hodgson Hill

Deadman Gill Bridge

West Dow Crag

Iron Band

Swindale Head

Hart Side

Seavy Rigg

B6276

Foddering Hill

White Fleets

81 A B 82 C D 83 E F

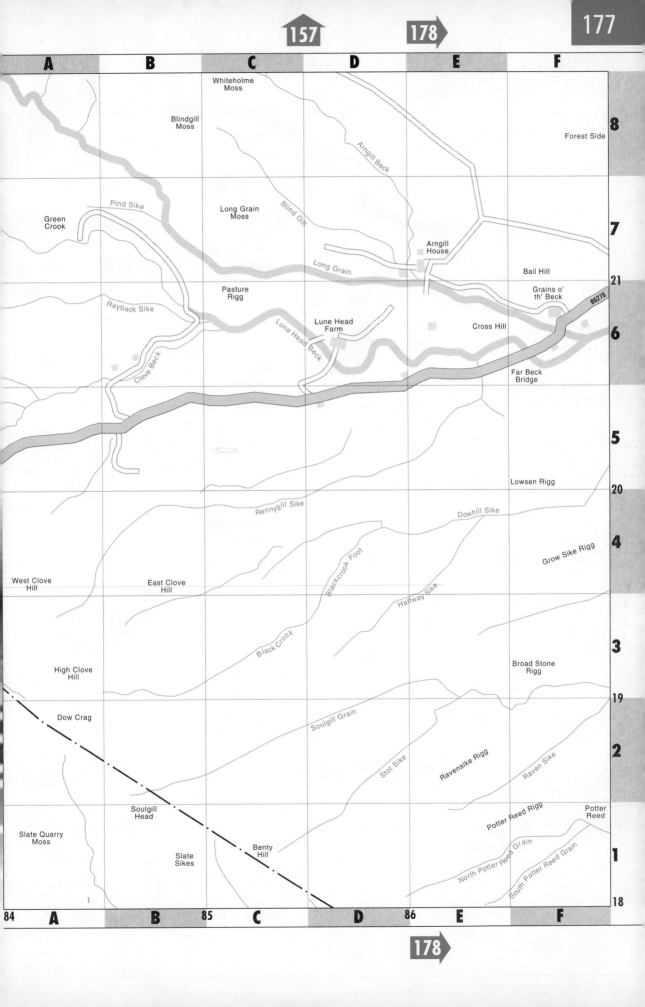

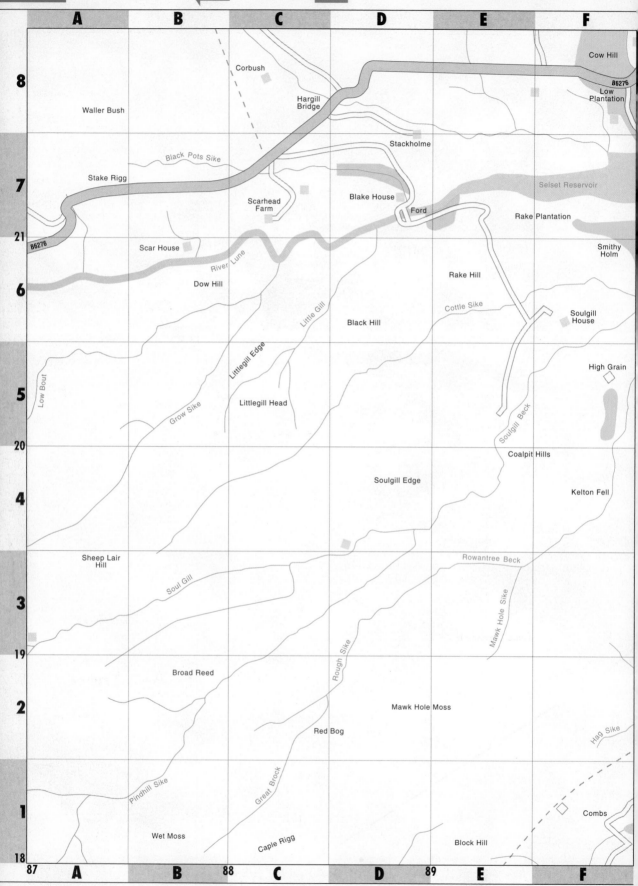

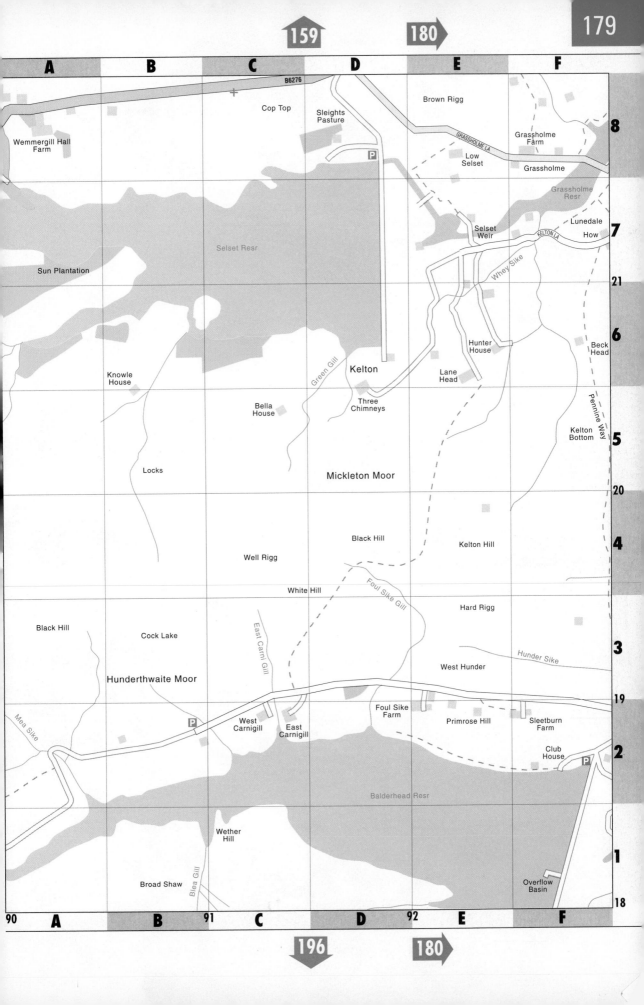

A B C D E F

8

Wemmergill Hall Farm

Cop Top

B6276

Sleights Pasture

Brown Rigg

GRASSHOLME LA

Low Selset

Grassholme Farm

Grassholme

P

Grassholme Resr

Selset Resr

Sun Plantation

Selset Weir

KELTON LA

Lunedale How

7

21

Whey Sike

Knowle House

Green Gill

Kelton

Hunter House

Lane Head

Beck Head

6

Bella House

Three Chimneys

Pennine Way

Kelton Bottom

5

Locks

Mickleton Moor

20

Black Hill

Kelton Hill

4

Well Rigg

White Hill

Foul Sike Gill

Hard Rigg

Black Hill

Cock Lake

East Carni Gill

Hunder Sike

3

Hunderthwaite Moor

West Hunder

19

Mea Sike

P

West Carnigill

East Carnigill

Foul Sike Farm

Primrose Hill

Sleetburn Farm

Club House

P

2

Balderhead Resr

Wether Hill

1

Broad Shaw

Blea Gill

Overflow Basin

18

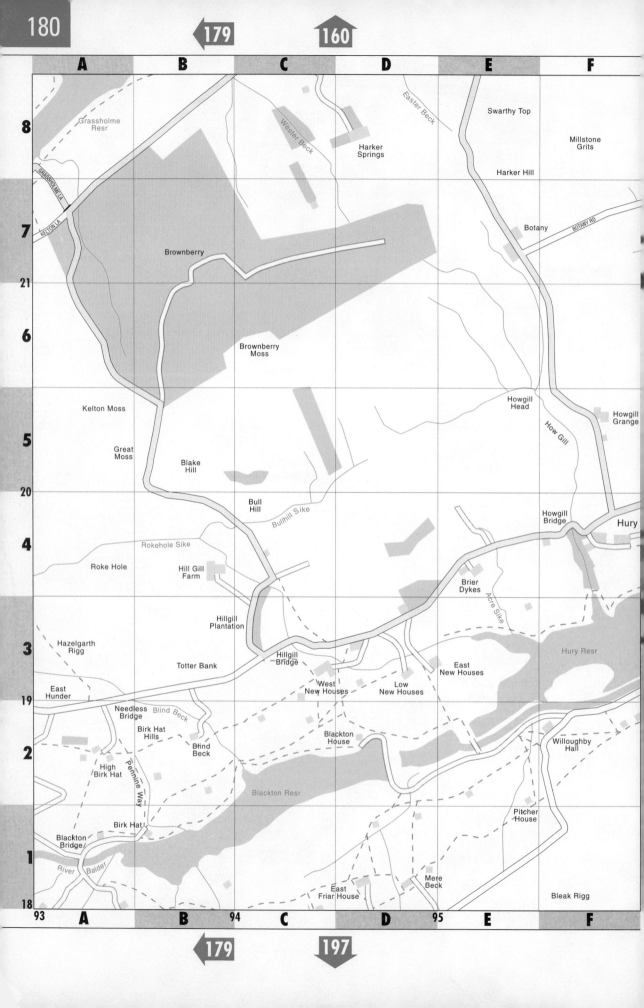

179
160

A   B   C   D   E   F

8

Grassholme Resr

Swarthy Top

Millstone Grits

Wester Beck

Easter Beck

Harker Springs

Harker Hill

KELTON LA

GRASSHOLME LA

7

Botany

BOTANY RD

Brownberry

21

6

Brownberry Moss

Kelton Moss

Howgill Head

How Gill

Howgill Grange

5

Great Moss

Blake Hill

Howgill Bridge

Hury

20

Bull Hill

Bullhill Sike

Acre Sike

4

Rokehole Sike

Roke Hole

Hill Gill Farm

Brier Dykes

Hury Resr

Hillgill Plantation

3

Hazelgarth Rigg

Totter Bank

Hillgill Bridge

East New Houses

East Hunder

West New Houses

Low New Houses

19

Needless Bridge

Blind Beck

Willoughby Hall

Birk Hat Hills

Blind Beck

Blackton House

2

High Birk Hat

Pennine Way

Blackton Resr

Pitcher House

Birk Hat

Blackton Bridge

1

River Balder

East Friar House

Mere Beck

Bleak Rigg

18

93   A   B   94   C   D   95   E   F

179
197

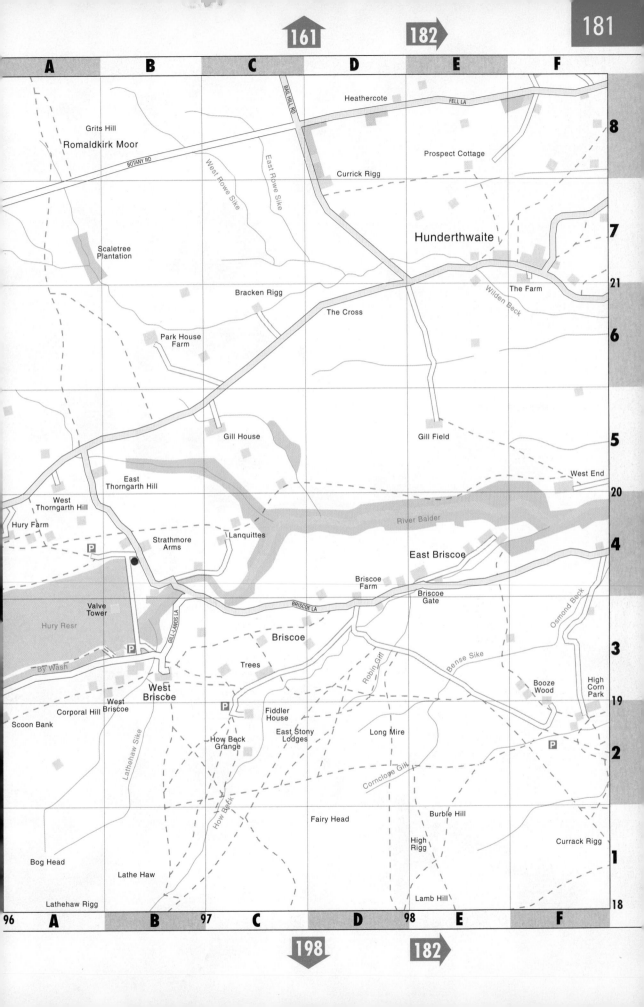

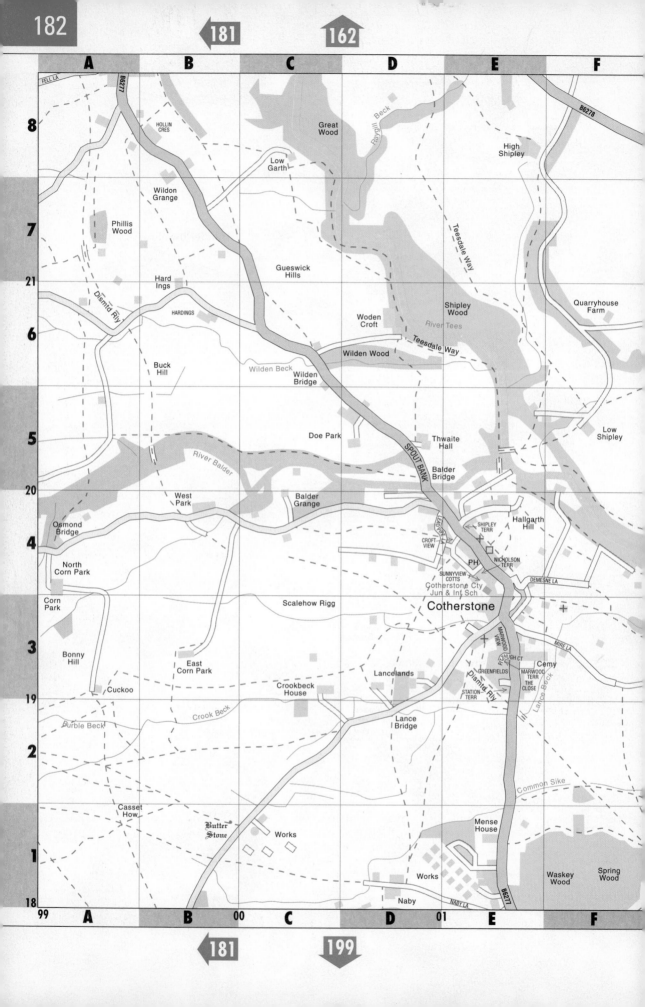

A   B   C   D   E   F

FELL LA
B6277
HOLLIN CRES
Low Garth
Great Wood
Raygill Beck
High Shipley
B6278

8

Wildon Grange
Phillis Wood

7

Teesdale Way

Dismid Rly
Hard Ings
HARDINGS
Gueswick Hills
Shipley Wood
Quarryhouse Farm

21

Woden Croft
River Tees

6

Buck Hill
Wilden Beck
Wilden Bridge
Wilden Wood
Teesdale Way

Doe Park
Thwaite Hall
Low Shipley

5

River Balder
Balder Bridge

SPOUT BANK

West Park
Balder Grange
Balder Bridge

20

Osmond Bridge
SHIPLEY TERR
Hallgarth Hill

4

North Corn Park
CROFT VIEW
PH
NICHOLSON TERR
DEMESNE LA

Corn Park
SUNNYVIEW COTTS
Cotherstone Cty Jun & Inf Sch

Scalehow Rigg
Cotherstone

Bonny Hill
East Corn Park
MARWOOD VIEW
HUGH CT
Cemy
MIRE LA

3

Cuckoo
Lancelands
GREENFIELDS
MARWOOD TERR
THE CLOSE

Crookbeck House
STATION TERR
Dismid Rly
Lance Beck

19

Durble Beck
Crook Beck
Lance Bridge

2

Common Sike

Casset How
Mense House

Butter Stone
Works
Works

1

Waskey Wood
Spring Wood

B6277
Naby
NABY LA

18

99   A   B   00   C   D   01   E   F

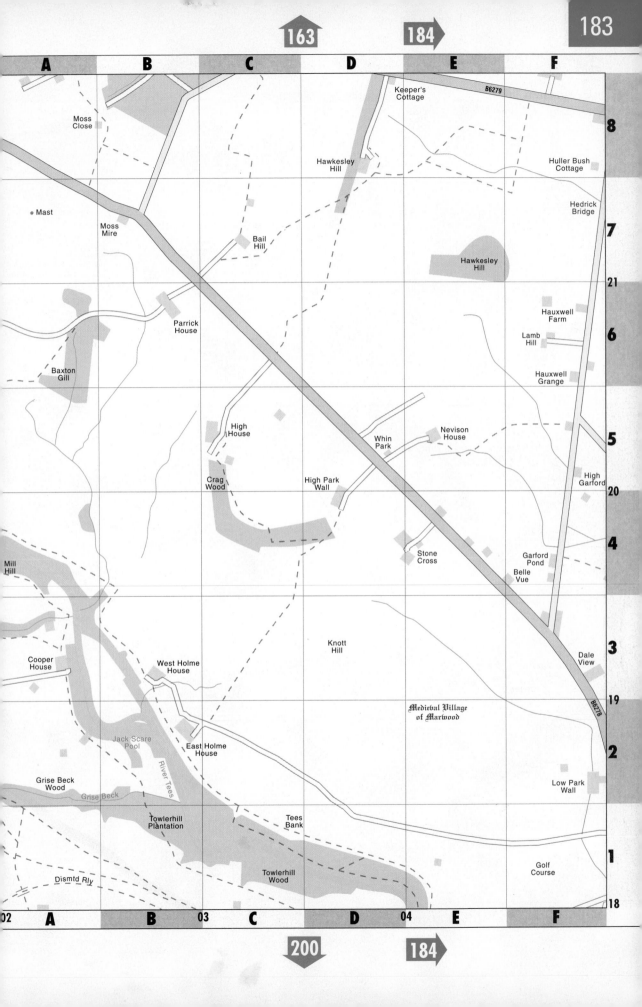

A   B   C   D   E   F

A   B   03   C   D   04   E   F

Keeper's
Cottage

B6279

Moss
Close

8

Huller Bush
Cottage

Hawkesley
Hill

Hedrick
Bridge

Mast

7

Moss
Mire

Bail
Hill

Hawkesley
Hill

21

Parrick
House

Hauxwell
Farm

6

Lamb
Hill

Baxton
Gill

Hauxwell
Grange

High
House

Whin
Park

Nevison
House

5

Crag
Wood

High Park
Wall

High
Garford

20

Mill
Hill

Stone
Cross

Garford
Pond

4

Belle
Vue

Knott
Hill

Dale
View

3

Cooper
House

West Holme
House

Medieval Village
of Marwood

B6278

19

Jack Scare
Pool

East Holme
House

2

River Tees

Low Park
Wall

Grise Beck
Wood

Grise Beck

Towlerhill
Plantation

Tees
Bank

1

Golf
Course

Dismtd Rly

Towlerhill
Wood

18

02   A   B   03   C   D   04   E   F

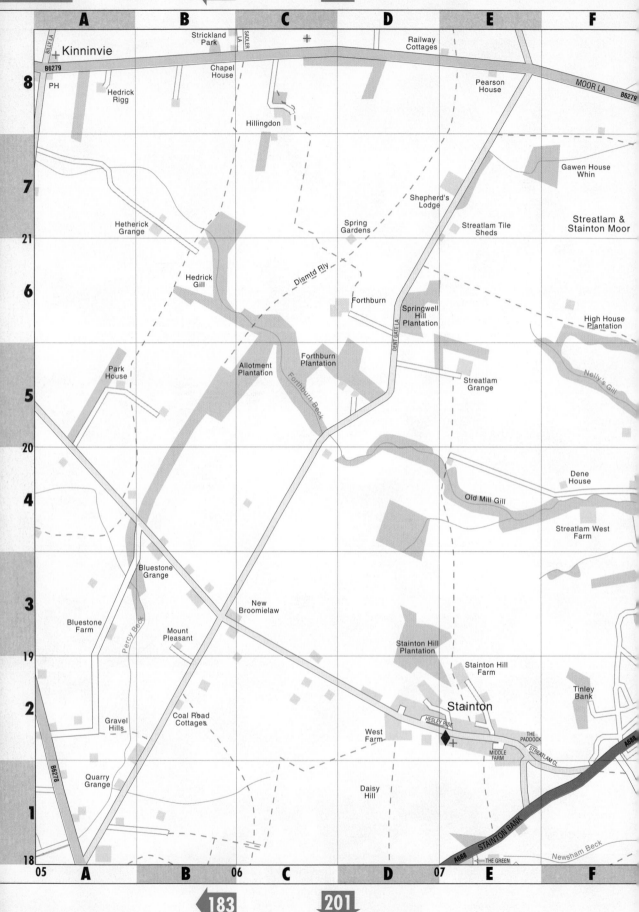

A **B** **C** **D** **E** **F**

Kinninvie

Strickland Park

BILLY LA

SADLER LA

Chapel House

Railway Cottages

MOOR LA

B6279

B6279

8

PH

Hedrick Rigg

Hillingdon

Pearson House

7

Hetherick Grange

Shepherd's Lodge

Gawen House Whin

Streatlam & Stainton Moor

21

Spring Gardens

Streatlam Tile Sheds

6

Hedrick Gill

Dismtd Rly

Forthburn

Springwell Hill Plantation

High House Plantation

DENT GATE LA

Park House

Allotment Plantation

Forthburn Plantation

Forthburn Beck

Streatlam Grange

Nelly's Gill

5

20

Dene House

4

Old Mill Gill

Streatlam West Farm

Bluestone Grange

3

New Broomielaw

Percy Beck

Bluestone Farm

Mount Pleasant

Stainton Hill Plantation

Stainton Hill Farm

Tinley Bank

19

2

Gravel Hills

Coal Road Cottages

Stainton

HESLEY RISE

West Farm

THE PADDOCK

STREATLAM CL

A688

B6278

Quarry Grange

MIDDLE FARM

Daisy Hill

STAINTON BANK

Newsham Beck

1

18

A688

← THE GREEN

05 **A** **B** **06** **C** **D** **07** **E** **F**

A **B** **C** **D** **E** **F**

Raby Home
Farm

Raby Moor
House

West
Farm

West Bulrush
Wood

Langley Beck

8

Gawen
House

Bolton
Hill

Ladyclose
Wood

7

Bolton Hill
Plantation

Long Ride

21

MOOR LA

Friars' Cote
House

Staindrop
Moor

West
Lodge

6

B6279

Moor Beck

Blakeley

Friars' Cote
Gill

Scaife
House

High
House

Ford

5

East Fog
Close

SNOTTERTON LA

Stud
Farm

North Drive
Clump

Streatlam
Grove

20

Snotterton
Hall

4

Sudburn Beck

Ford

Woodend
Farm

Streatlam
Park

Forthburn Beck

Sewage
Works

Great
Wood

Dun House
Wood

Dunn House
Farm

3

A688

Streatlam Home
Farm

Ralston
House

19

East
Lodge

CLEATLAM BACK LA

Oak
Lea

Lodge
Plantation

2

Picnic
Area

Depot

South
View

Barford
Camp

High
Barford

1

Broomielaw

Newsham Beck

18

A **B** 09 **C** **D** 10 **E** **F**

08

8

East Bulrush Wood

Raby Home Farm

Quarry Clump

Bath Cottage

High Pond

Raby Castle

Low Pond

Malt Kiln Cottages

New Raby Wood

A688

Raby Park

Deer Park

Burton House Plantation

Bath Wood

7

The Cabin

Silver Wedding Clump

21

B6279

Ladyclose Wood

Long Ride

Park Clump

Scarth Plantation

Church Bridge

6

Moor Beck

Langley Beck

Ladyclose Croft

Ladyclose

NORTH GN

QUEENS HEAD WYND

DUKE ST

DOVECOTE ST

BARNARD ST

FRONT ST

B6279

Cemy

Cemy

B6279

B6274

Moor Close Farm

WEST TERR

MOOR RD

B6279

Moor Bridge

CORONATION GDNS

SOUTH TERR

THE ORCHARDS

SOUTH GN

OFFICE SQ

SOUTH GN

Staindrop

ALMSHOUSES

CHURCH ST

SWAN WYND

PH

BROUMLEY CT

HARTLEY CL

WINSTON CT

BEECHSIDE

WINSTON RD

Doctor's Wood

Woodcroft Farm

ST GREGORY CL

SUDBURN AVE

Staindrop C of E Jun Mix & Inf Sch

LANGLEY GDNS

Saw Mills

MOOR LA

5

SNOTTERTON LA

Morton House

Staindrop Comp Sch

Council Depot

Bow Bridge

20

Sudburn Beck

Alwent

4

Sudburn Bridge

Cleatlam Bridge

Bell House

Dunhouse Quarry

3

A688

Quarry Plantation

19

Cleatlam East Farm

Cleatlam Hall

Bell House Fox Covert

2

CLEATLAM BACK LA

Cleatlam

Cleatlam High Farm

Toll Gate Cottage

South Cleatlam

Early Bank Plantation

1

Newsham Grange

SOUTH CLEATLAM

B6274

18

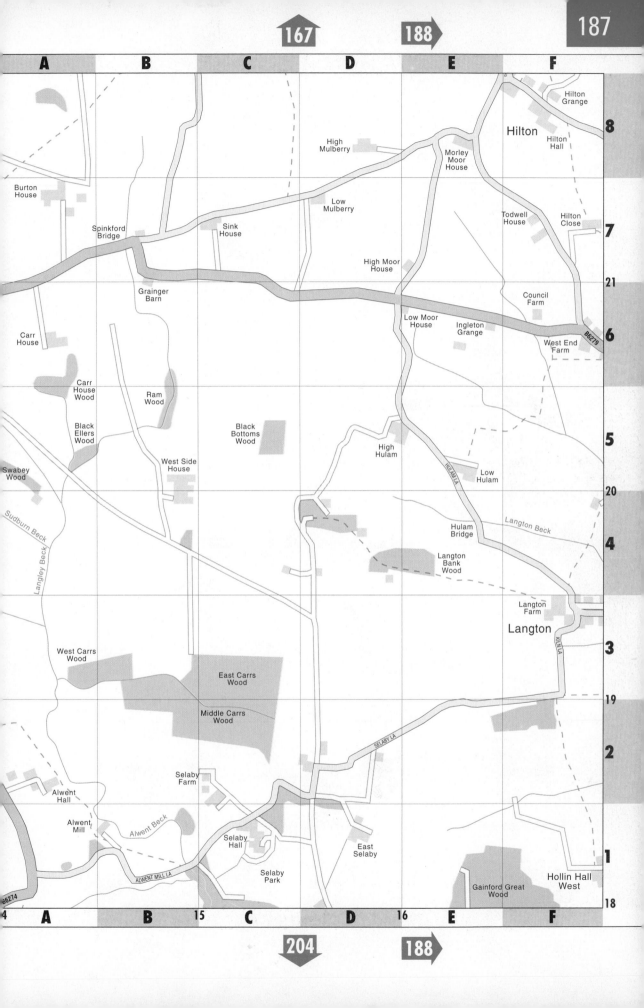

A   B   C   D   E   F

Hilton Grange

Hilton

Hilton Hall

High Mulberry

Morley Moor House

Todwell House

Hilton Close

Burton House

Low Mulberry

Spinkford Bridge

Sink House

Council Farm

High Moor House

Grainger Barn

Low Moor House

Ingleton Grange

West End Farm

B6279

Carr House

Carr House Wood

Ram Wood

Black Bottoms Wood

High Hulam

HULAM LA

Low Hulam

Black Ellers Wood

West Side House

Swabey Wood

Langton Beck

Hulam Bridge

Sudburn Beck

Langton Bank Wood

Langton Farm

Langley Beck

Langton

KILN LA

West Carrs Wood

East Carrs Wood

Middle Carrs Wood

SELABY LA

Alwent Hall

Selaby Farm

Alwent Mill

Alwent Beck

Selaby Hall

East Selaby

Hollin Hall West

ALWENT MILL LA

Selaby Park

Gainford Great Wood

B6274

8 7 21 6 5 20 4 3 19 2 1 18

14 15 16

187 168

A B C D E F

8

Hilton
Plantation

Quarry
House

Morton
Heads

7

Morton
Tinmouth

Hilton
Whin

West
Farm

East
Farm

21

6

Black Horse
(PH)

MANOR
COTTS

SCHOOL
HOUSES

B6279

HILLSIDE

CHURCH VIEW

MANOR RD

SPRINGWELL

CHURCH
ROW

THE GARTH

RAPSON CT

FRONT ST

GAINFORD RD

Killerby Beck

KIRK LA

Ingleton C of E
Controlled Sch

Ingleton

5

The
Mill

New House
Farm

Killerby Hall
Farm

NORTH LA

Woodside

20

Middleton
House

Morley
Hill

Killerby
Garths

Killerby

4

LANGTON BECK

Langton

CAKESMIRE LA

Killerby
Bridge

B6279

3

BACK LA

THE GREEN

19

Headlam

2

Ford Dike

Headlam
Hall

Headlam Beck

Dyance
Plantation

Ford Dike
Bridge

FORD DIKE LA

RIGG HEAD

1

Hollin Hall
East

COCK LA

Hillhouse
Hill

Dyance
Bridge

Dyance Beck

Dyance Bottom

18

17 A B 18 C D 19 E F

187 205

189
170

A B C D E F

8

Elm Grange

A68

Westholme

Page Farm

HUMBLE CARR LA

Deneville

COATSAY MOOR LA

A6072

Dene Bridge Farm

Broom Dykes North

Dene Bridge

7

Cock Inn Farm

Burrell Moor

CROSS LANES

The Dog (PH)

21

Walworth Moor Farm

Coatsay Moor

COATSAY MOOR LA

New House Farm

Dene Beck

6

Grimshaw Cottage

WEST AUCKLAND RD

Greystones

Cowfold Farm

A6072

5

COWFOLD LA

Walworth Gate

Ivy Cottage

WALWORTH RD

20

Throstle Nest

Cowfold Plantation

4

New Moor Farm

Throstle Nest Plantation

Swan House Farm

WEST AUCKLAND RD

Silver Hill

BACK LA

Silverhill Plantation

3

Humbleton Farm

North Farm

19

A68

The Rookery

Coldsides

2

Walworth

Walworth Grange

Peel Acres

Weezey Hill

1

Walworth Park

Cuckoo House

NEWTON LA

18

23 A B 24 C D 25 E F

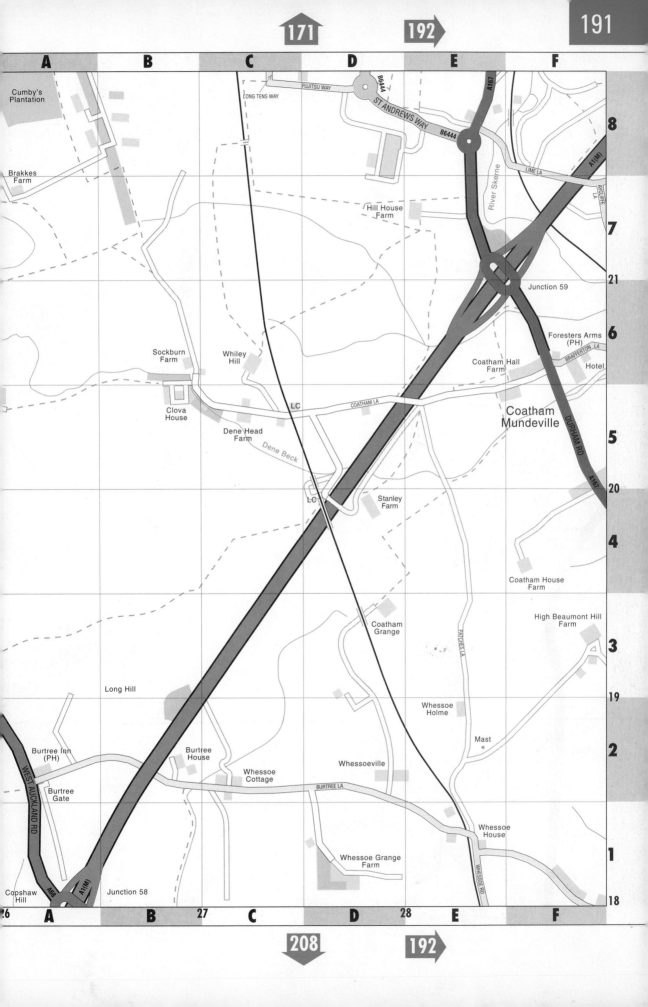

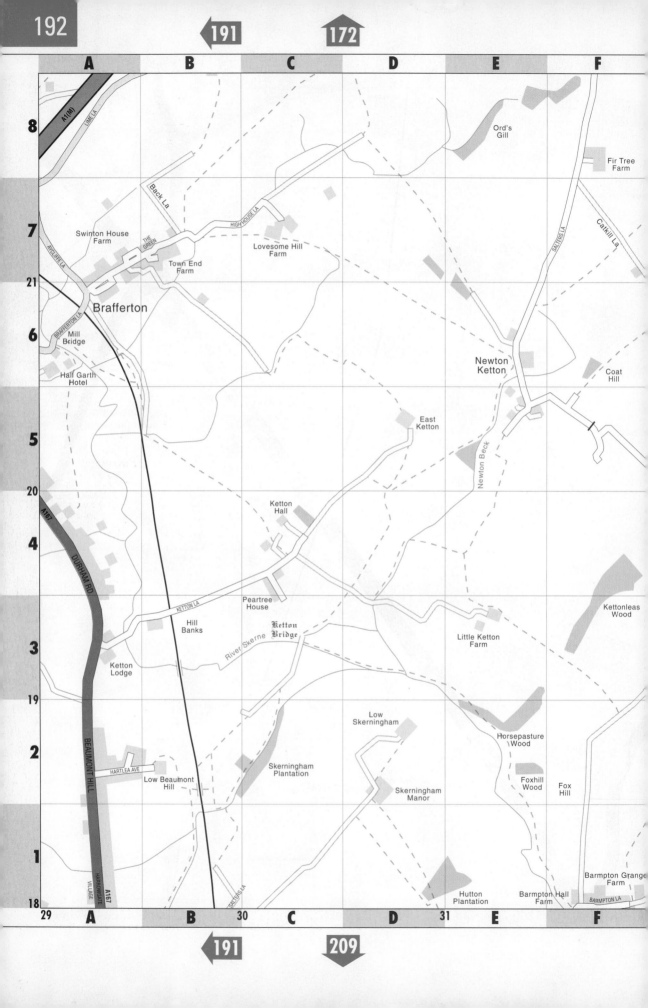

A B C D E F

8

Ord's Gill

Fir Tree Farm

7

Back La

High House La

21

Swinton House Farm

THE GREEN

Town End Farm

Lovesome Hill Farm

Catkill La

Salters La

AYCLIFFE LA

Brafferton

6

Mill Bridge

BRAFFERTON LA

Newton Ketton

Hall Garth Hotel

Coat Hill

5

East Ketton

Newton Beck

20

A167

DURHAM RD

Ketton Hall

4

Ketton La

Peartree House

Kettonleas Wood

Hill Banks

Ketton Bridge

River Skerne

Little Ketton Farm

3

Ketton Lodge

19

Low Skerningham

Horsepasture Wood

2

BEAUMONT HILL

HARTLEA AVE

Low Beaumont Hill

Skerningham Plantation

Skerningham Manor

Foxhill Wood

Fox Hill

1

Barmpton Grange Farm

18

A167

HARROWGATE VILLAGE

SALTERS LA

Hutton Plantation

Barmpton Hall Farm

BARMPTON LA

29 A 30 B C 30 D 31 E F

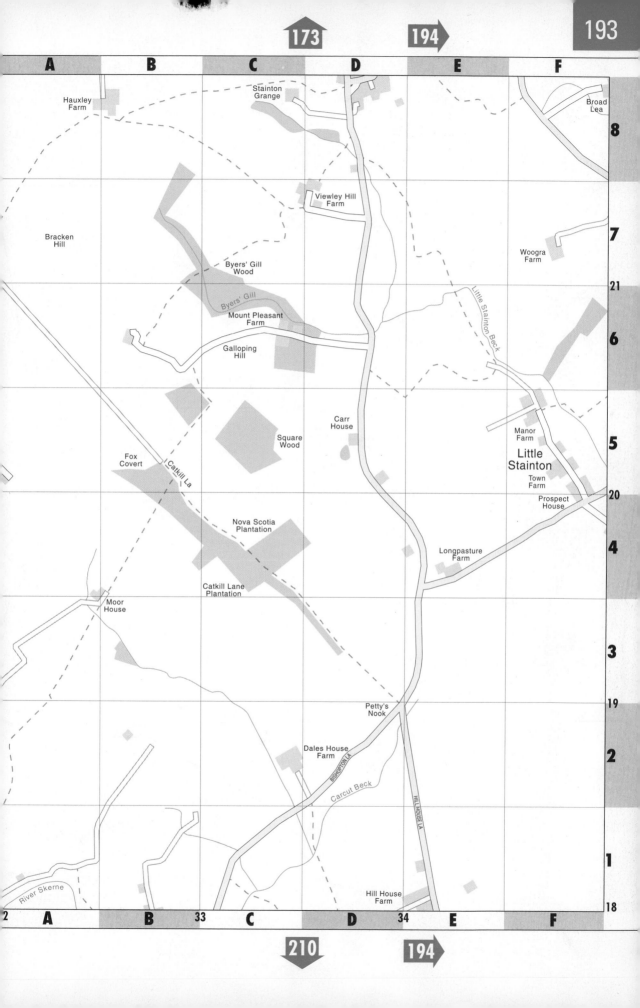

A   B   C   D   E   F

Hauxley
Farm

Stainton
Grange

Broad
Lea

8

Viewley Hill
Farm

Bracken
Hill

7

Woogra
Farm

Byers' Gill
Wood

21

Byers' Gill

6

Mount Pleasant
Farm

Galloping
Hill

Little Stainton Beck

Fox
Covert

Catkill La

Square
Wood

Carr
House

Manor
Farm

Little
Stainton

5

Town
Farm

Prospect
House

20

Nova Scotia
Plantation

Longpasture
Farm

4

Catkill Lane
Plantation

Moor
House

3

Petty's
Nook

19

Dales House
Farm

BISHOPTON LA

2

Carcut Beck

HILL HOUSE LA

River Skerne

1

Hill House
Farm

18

193
174

A B C D E F

8

Broad
Lea

Bulmerside
Hill

Downland
Farm

COBBY CASTLE LA

MILL LA

7

Sundial
Farm

Coal
Bank

Galloping
Hills

FARM
CT

THE GREEN

ANESTY
CT

PH.

HIGH ST

CHURCH VIEW

Bishopton & Redmarshall
C of E Sch

Bishopton

Redmarshall
Bridge

Karamea

21

FOLLY BANK

Castle
Hill

Bishopton Beck

Out
House

REDMARSHALL RD

6

Hambleton
View

Gately Moor
Resr

5

Windsurfing
Centre

Stoney Flatt
Farm

Newstead
Farm

20

4

Gillyflatts

Sauf Hall

3

Pitfield
House

19

East
Newbiggin

Woodbine

2

Newbiggin Beck

Wayside

Oak Lea

DARLINGTON BACK LA

BACK LA

Stone
Gables

1

West
Newbiggin

Fox Hill

Helsay

The
Grange

18

35

A B 36 C D 37 E F

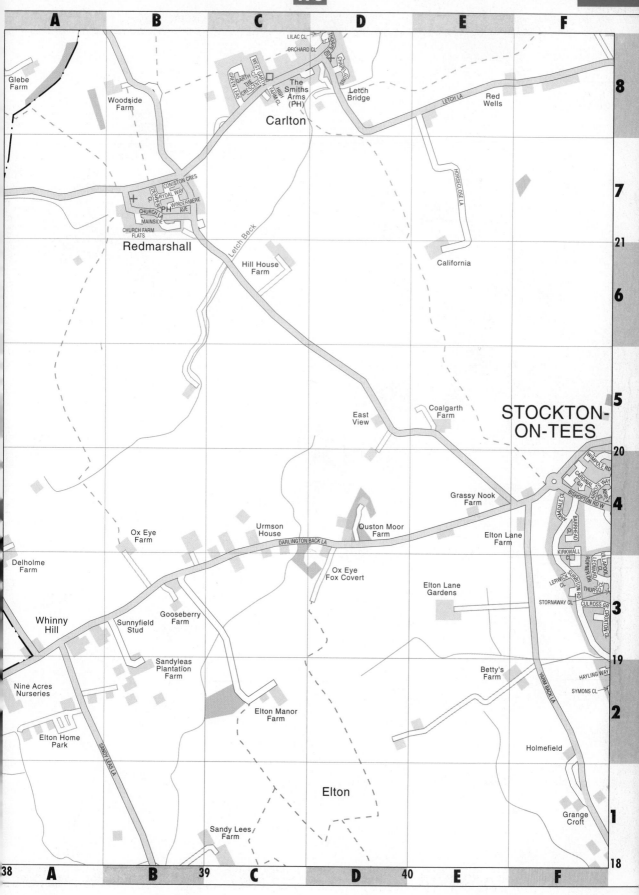

A B C D E F

8

Glebe
Farm

LILAC CL
ORCHARD CL

THORPE RD

CHAPEL GDNS

WEST GARTH
THE
GREEN LEAS
GARTH CL
HIGH FARM CL
THE CRESCENT

Woodside
Farm

The Smiths
Arms
(PH)

Letch
Bridge

LETCH LA

Red
Wells

Carlton

7

CONISTON CRES
RYDAL WAY
DERWENT CL
WINDERMERE AVE
PH
CHURCH LA
MAINSIDE
CHURCH FARM
FLATS

HORSECLOSE LA

21

Redmarshall

Letch Beck

Hill House
Farm

California

6

5

East
View

Coalgarth
Farm

STOCKTON-
ON-TEES

20

WIMPOLE RD
CARDINAL GR
ST MARYS WAY
DERBY CL
ABBE

Grassy Nook
Farm

4

Ox Eye
Farm

Urmson
House

Ouston Moor
Farm

Elton Lane
Farm

ARMDALE CL
BARRHEAD CL
KIRKWALL CL
LERWICK CL
ULLAPOOL CL
LEONARD
ROPNER DR
SURBITON RD
THURSO
CROXTON CL

Delholme
Farm

DARLINGTON BACK LA

Ox Eye
Fox Covert

Elton Lane
Gardens

STORNAWAY CL
CULROSS GR

3

19

Whinny
Hill

Sunnyfield
Stud

Gooseberry
Farm

Betty's
Farm

YARM BACK LA

HAYLING WAY
SYMONS CL

Nine Acres
Nurseries

Sandyleas
Plantation
Farm

2

Elton Home
Park

SANDY LEAS LA

Elton Manor
Farm

Holmefield

Elton

1

Grange
Croft

Sandy Lees
Farm

18

38 A B 39 C D 40 E F

179

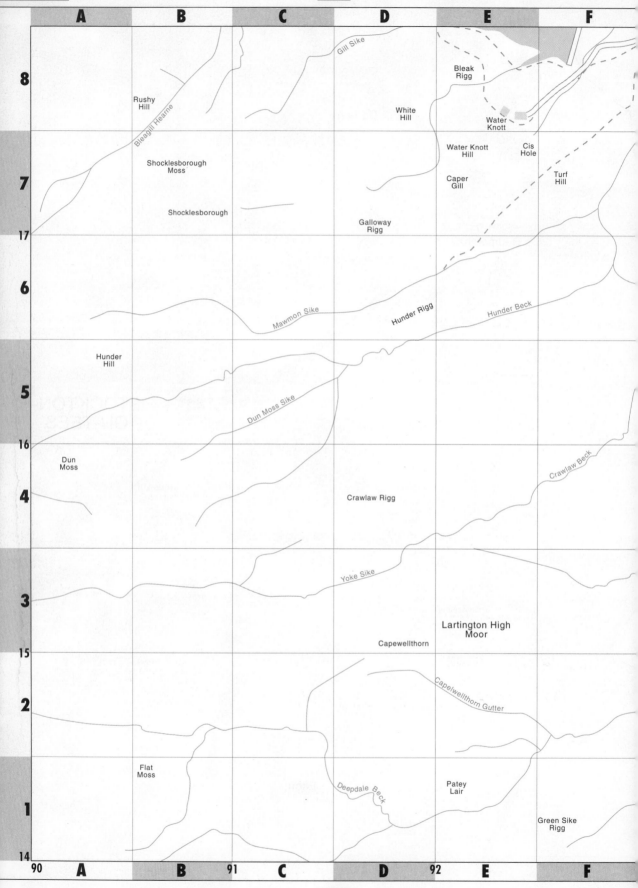

A B C D E F

8

Gill Sike

Bleak
Rigg

Rushy
Hill

White
Hill

Water
Knott

Bleagill Hearne

Water Knott
Hill

Cis
Hole

Shocklesborough
Moss

Caper
Gill

Turf
Hill

7

Shocklesborough

Galloway
Rigg

17

6

Mawmon Sike

Hunder Rigg

Hunder Beck

Hunder
Hill

Dun Moss Sike

5

16

Crawlaw Beck

Dun
Moss

4

Crawlaw Rigg

Yoke Sike

3

Lartington High
Moor

Capewellthorn

15

Capelwellthorn Gutter

2

Flat
Moss

Deepdale Beck

Patey
Lair

Green Sike
Rigg

1

14

90   A   B   91   C   D   92   E   F

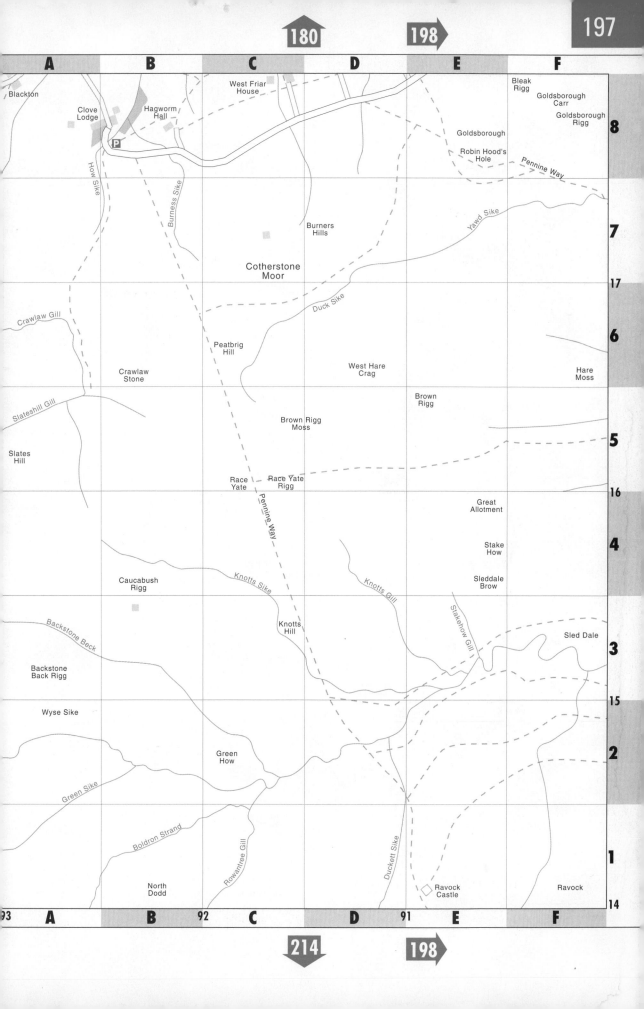

197
181

A **B** **C** **D** **E** **F**

8

Bowbank
Hill

How Beck

How Beck
Head

Loups's
Hill

Long Rigg

Sunny Brow

East
Loups's

Scur Beck

Ravock
Plantation

7

West
Loups's

Ravock Rigg

DANGER AREA

Gill
Feet

Whitstone
Rigg

Gill Beck

17

Hare Sike

Stonefold Rigg

6

Kearton Rigg

Blackpool Sike

Loups's Plantation

Battle
Hill

Stable Sike

Kirkstreveland Rigg

5

Ladyfold Rigg

Hazelgill Beck

Scotty Rigg

16

Hazelgill Rigg

Nova
Scotia

4

Pennine Way

Deep Dale

Deepdale Beck

Hazelgill

3

Levy
Pool

Strand
Foot

15

West Stoney
Keld

Stoney
Keld

East Stoney Keld

Water Knott

Stony
Keld

2

Tute
Hill

Bessy
Sike

Layer
Tree

Storage Site
(disused)

1

Philip
Hill

Clint
Farm

14

The Old Moss

CLINT LANE

A **B** **C** **D** **E** **F**
96 97 98

197
215

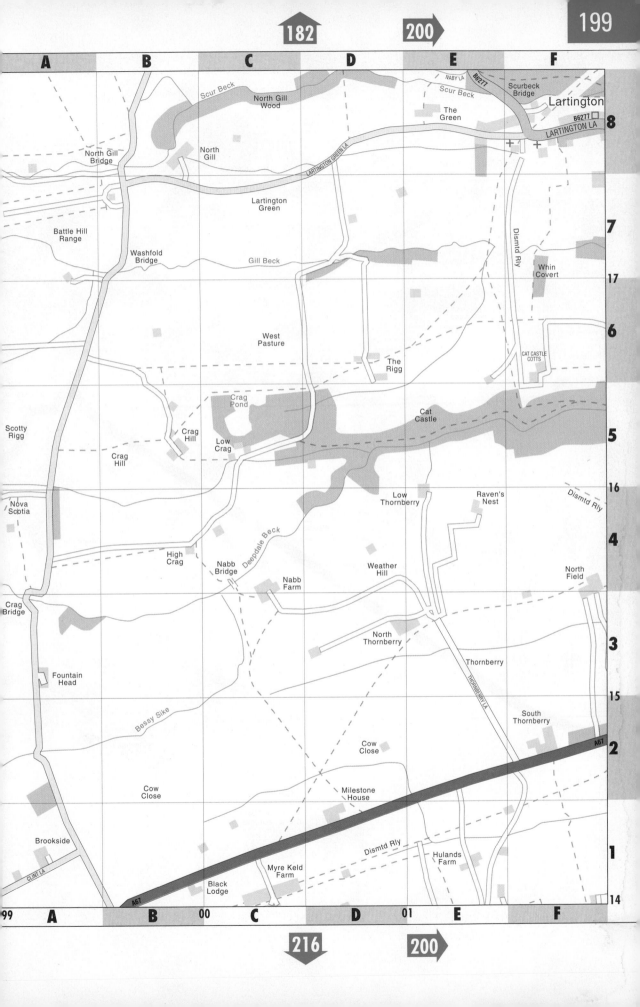

201
185

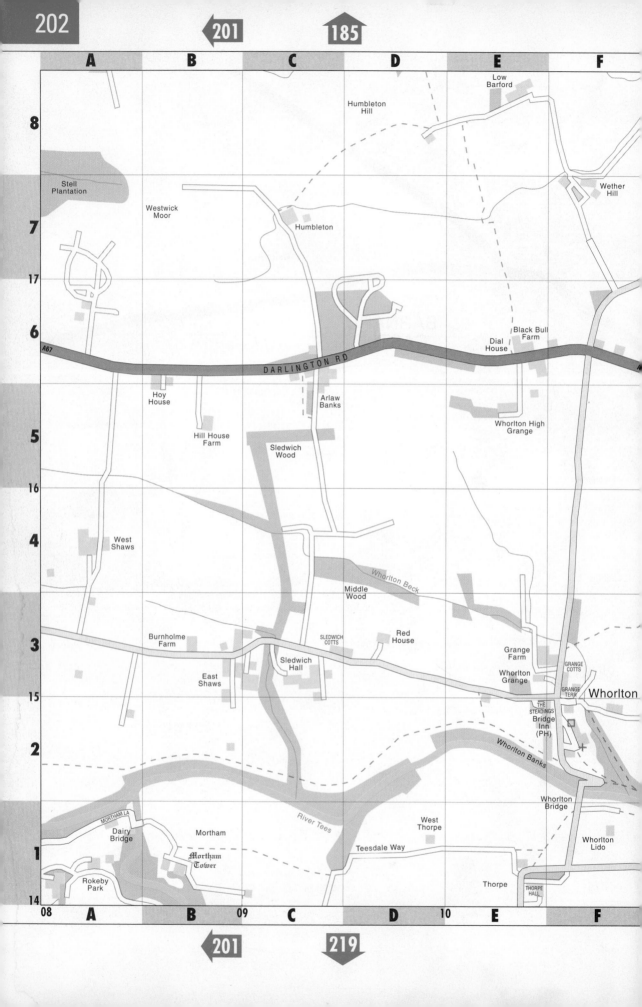

201
219

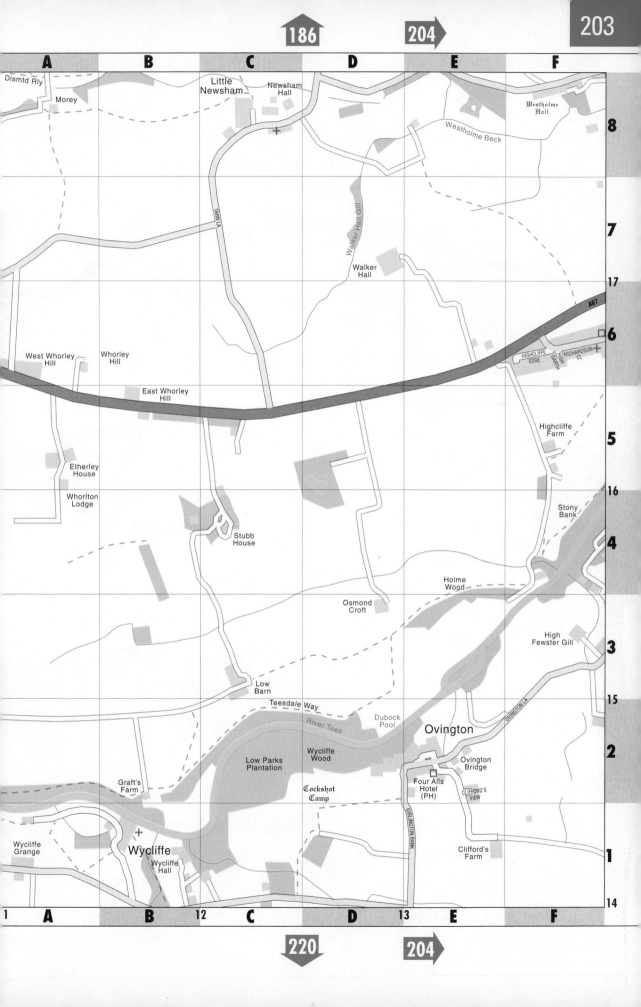

203
187

A   B   C   D   E   F

8

Westholme Beck
Westholme Bridge

Gainford Great Wood

B6274

Selaby Basses

Winfield

Alwent Beck

Dismtd Rly

7

Primrose Hill Farm

Station Farm

Vicarage Farm

River Tees

West Tees Bridge

BALMER HILL

B6274

17

A67

A67   SPA RD

PH   B6274

PIGGY LA   HIGH RD
LOW RD

CHURCH MEWS

Church Farm

Hedgeholme Wood

Gainford Controlled Prim Sch

6

Sewage Works

Winston

Hedgeholme

Barforth Hall

Cemy

5

Winston Bridge

Winston Gate

Hedgeholme Bank

Hill Top

St Lawrence's Chapel

16

Winston Bridge Caravan Pk

OVINGTON LA

BERRY BANK

Barforth Whins

4

Moor Row

Chapel Gill

Greener Hill

3

Barforth Grange

Ovington Grange

Pudding Hill

PUDDING HILL RD

15

2

Greystone West

Main Moor Hill

Cote Hill

1

Greystone

B6274

Sough Hill

14

14   A   B   15   C   D   16   E   F

203
221

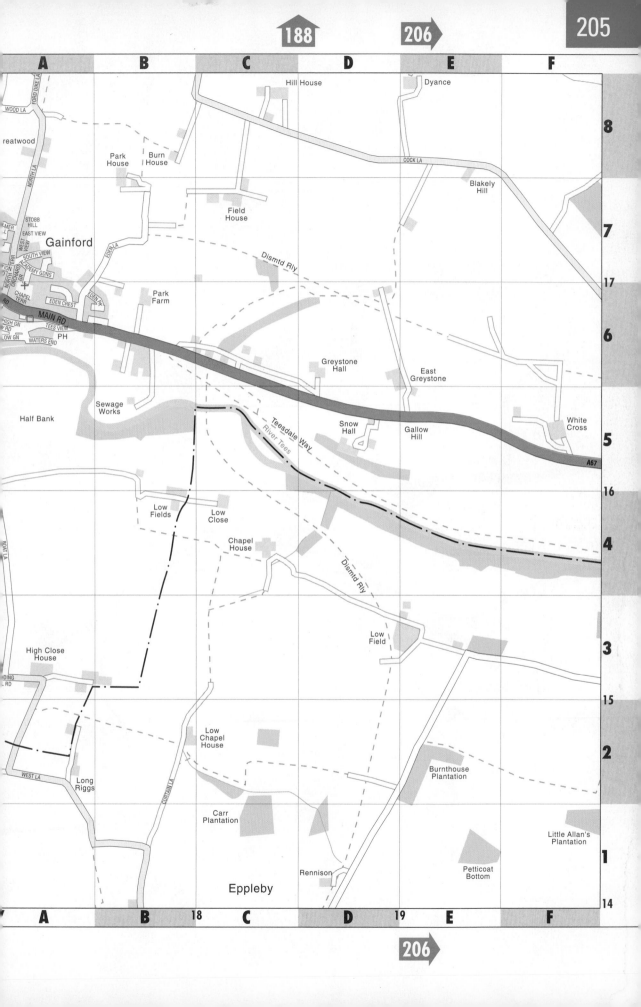

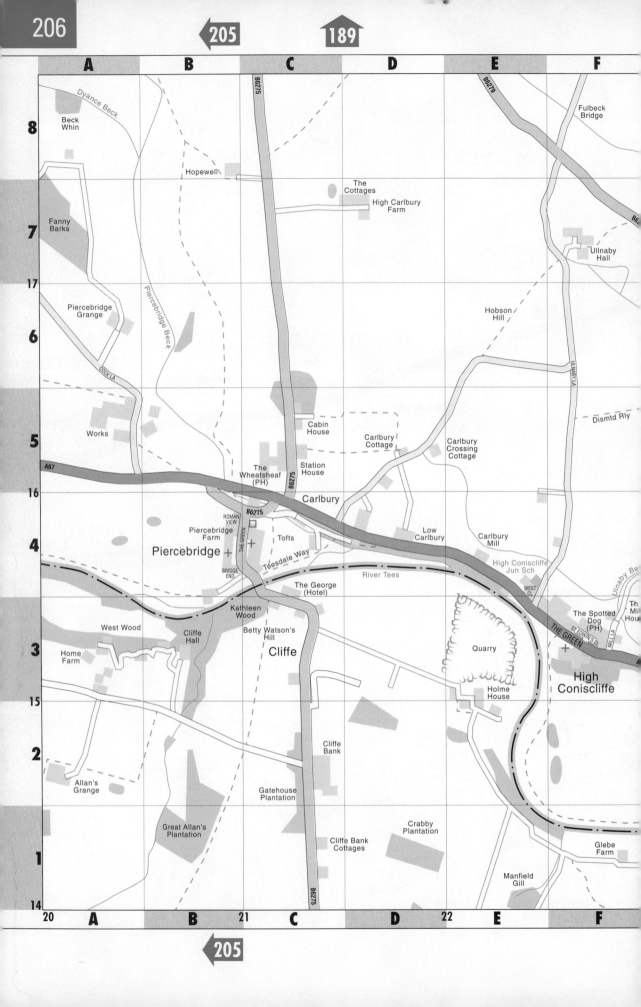

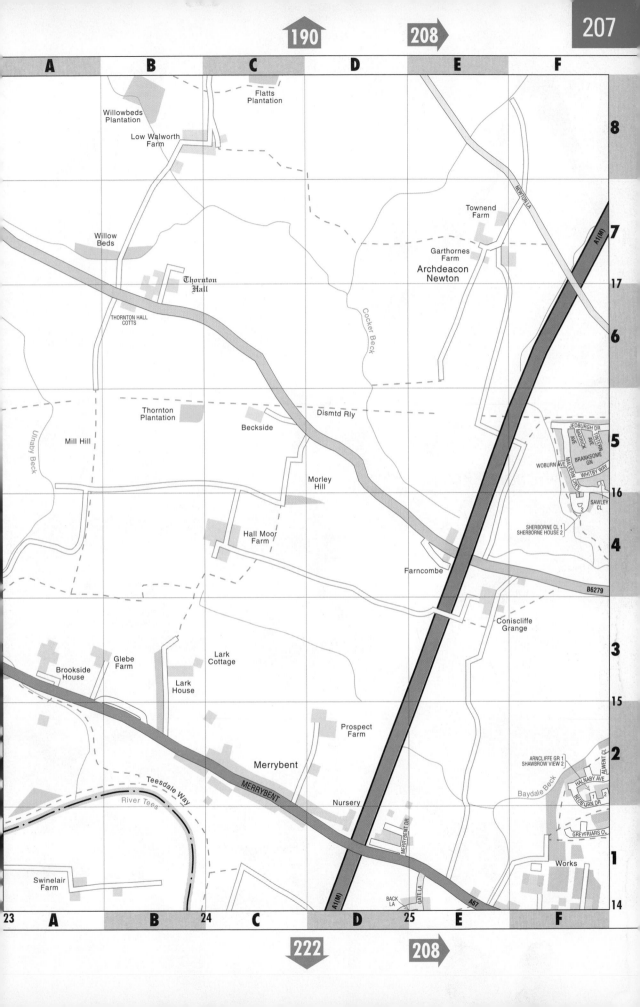

Flatts
Plantation

Willowbeds
Plantation

Low Walworth
Farm

Willow
Beds

Townend
Farm

NEWTON LA

A1(M)

8

7

Thornton
Hall

Garthornes
Farm

Archdeacon
Newton

17

THORNTON HALL
COTTS

Cocker Beck

6

Ulnaby Beck

Thornton
Plantation

Beckside

Dismtd Rly

Mill Hill

Morley
Hill

JEDBURGH DR
TINTERN AVE
MARRICK AVE
MALVERN CRES
WOBURN AVE
BRANKSOME
GN
WHITBY WAY

5

16

SAWLEY
CL

Hall Moor
Farm

SHERBORNE CL 1
SHERBORNE HOUSE 2

4

Farncombe

B6279

Coniscliffe
Grange

Lark
Cottage

Brookside
House

Glebe
Farm

Lark
House

3

15

Prospect
Farm

ARNCLIFFE GR 1
SHAWBROW VIEW 2

ALWENT CL

2

HALNABY AVE

BEDBURN DR

Merrybent

Teesdale Way

MERRYBENT

River Tees

Nursery

GREYFRIARS CL

Baydale Beck

Works

Swinelair
Farm

MERRYBENT DR

BACK
LA

GATE LA

A1(M)

A67

1

14

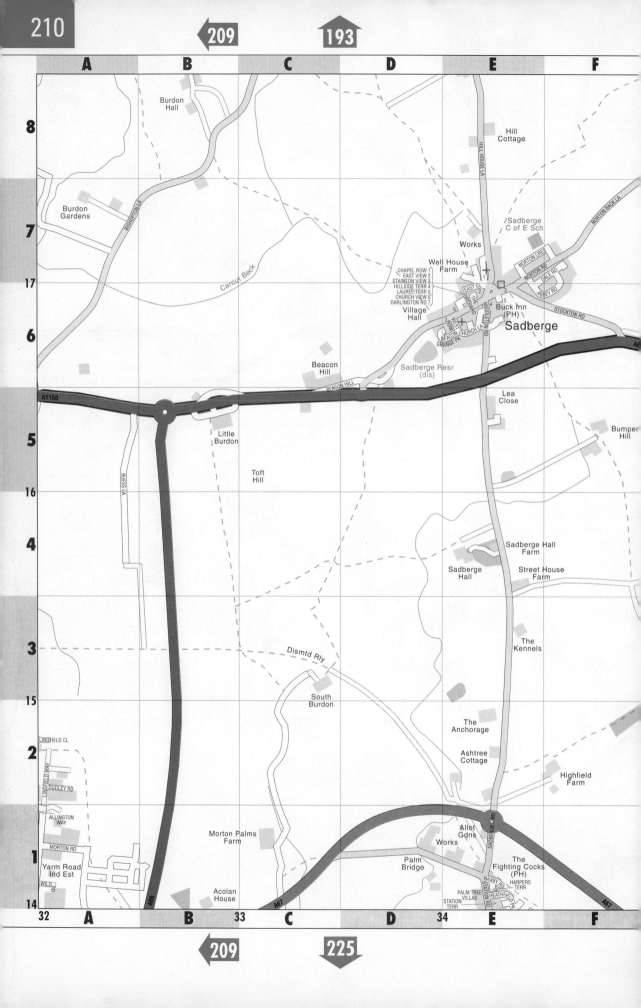

A B C D E F

8

Burdon
Hall

Hill
Cottage

HILL HOUSE LA

NORTON BACK LA

Burdon
Gardens

7

BISHORTON LA

Sadberge
C of E Sch

Works

Carcut Beck

Well House
Farm

NORTON CRES
NORTON RD
DALE RD
ABBEY RD

17

CHAPEL ROW 1
EAST VIEW 2
STAINTON VIEW 3
HILLSIDE TERR 4
LAUREL TERR 5
CHURCH VIEW 6
DARLINGTON RD 7

EAST CL

MIDDLETON RD

Buck Inn
(PH)

STOCKTON RD

Village
Hall

6

WEST VIEW

BEACON
GRANGE PK

CHURCH LA

Sadberge

A1150

Beacon
Hill

Sadberge Resr
(dis)

Lea
Close

A67

5

BEACON HILL

Little
Burdon

Bumper
Hill

16

BUESS LA

Toft
Hill

4

Sadberge Hall
Farm

Sadberge
Hall

Street House
Farm

3

Dismtd Rly

The
Kennels

15

South
Burdon

The
Anchorage

2

LINGFIELD CL

LINGFIELD WAY

DUDLEY RD

Ashtree
Cottage

Highfield
Farm

ALLINGTON WAY

MORTON RD

Morton Palms
Farm

SADBERGE RD

Allot
Gdns

Works

The
Fighting Cocks
(PH)

1

Yarm Road
Ind Est

WILD RD

A66

Palm
Bridge

HAXBY RD
STATION RD

HARPERS
TERR
HEATHFIELD

14

Acolan
House

A67

PALM TREE
VILLAS

STATION
TERR

A67

32 A B 33 C D 34 E F

A B C D E F

8
7
17
6
5
16
4
3
15
2
1
14

DARLINGTON
BACK LA

Salter Carr
Farm

NORTON BACK LA

Bewley
Hill

Longnewton
Resr

LARBERRY
Larberry
Pastures

BACK LA

Newton Grange
Farm

Rectory
Farm

Eddlethorpe
Farm

Ivanhoe

Newton South
Grange

Hang Thorn
Farm

Farfields
Farm

Longnewton

A66

THE WILLOW CHASE
THE YEW WLK
WOODLAND WAY
PARKSIDE
DARLINGTON RD
FAIRFIELDS CL

Vane
Arms
(PH)

West End
Farm

Middle Town
Farm

Londonderry
Cottage

Spring House
Farm

Hardstones
Farm

White House
Farm

Mill Hill
Farm

Lyndale

MILL LA

West
Moor

West Gate
Fox Covert

Burnwood Beck

High
Goosepool
Farm

Long
Plantation

Westgate
Farm

West Hartburn
Farm

Sewage
Works

35 A B 36 C D 37 E F A67

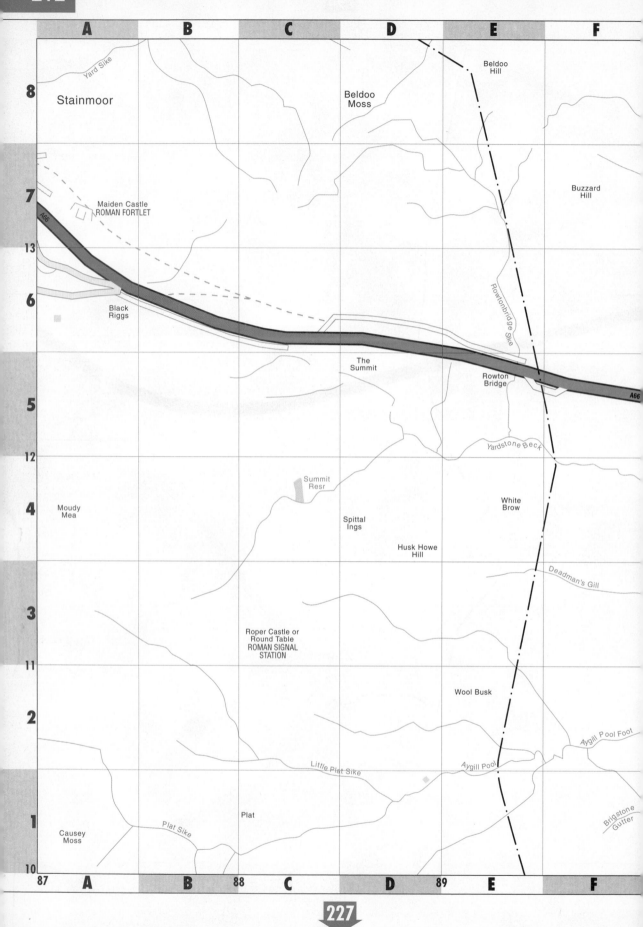

8

Stainmoor

Yard Sike

Beldoo
Moss

Beldoo
Hill

7

Maiden Castle
ROMAN FORTLET

A66

Buzzard
Hill

13

6

Black
Riggs

Rowtonbridge Sike

The
Summit

Rowton
Bridge

A66

5

Yardstone Beck

12

Summit
Resr

White
Brow

4

Moudy
Mea

Spittal
Ings

Husk Howe
Hill

Deadman's Gill

3

Roper Castle or
Round Table
ROMAN SIGNAL
STATION

11

Wool Busk

2

Aygill Pool Foot

Little Plat Sike

Aygill Pool

Brigstone
Gutter

1

Plat

Plat Sike

Causey
Moss

10

A B C D E F

8

Black Beck

Glasgow How

Glasgow Gill

North Ings

7

North Moor

North Ings Sike

13

Sandy Hill

Black Hill

Gate Gutter

6

Spital Sike

A66

Rey Cross

Spital Hill

Gate Gutter

Spital Bridge

5

Bowes Moor Hotel

Old Spital

12

Aygill Cottages

Valley Farm

Spital

White Brow

Aygill Bottom

4

Spital High Cottages

Dismtd Rly

Quart Gill

River Greta

Ay Gill

3

Bowes Moor

Foddering Gill

11

Red Gill

Deep Gill

Adam Gill

2

Collinson's Hill

1

Black Sike

Middle Moor

10

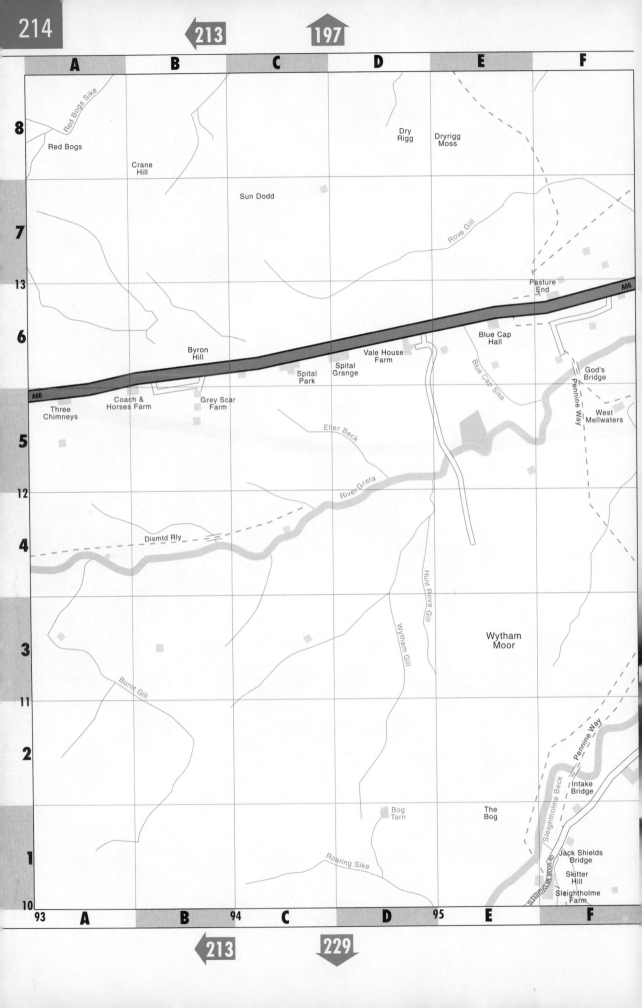

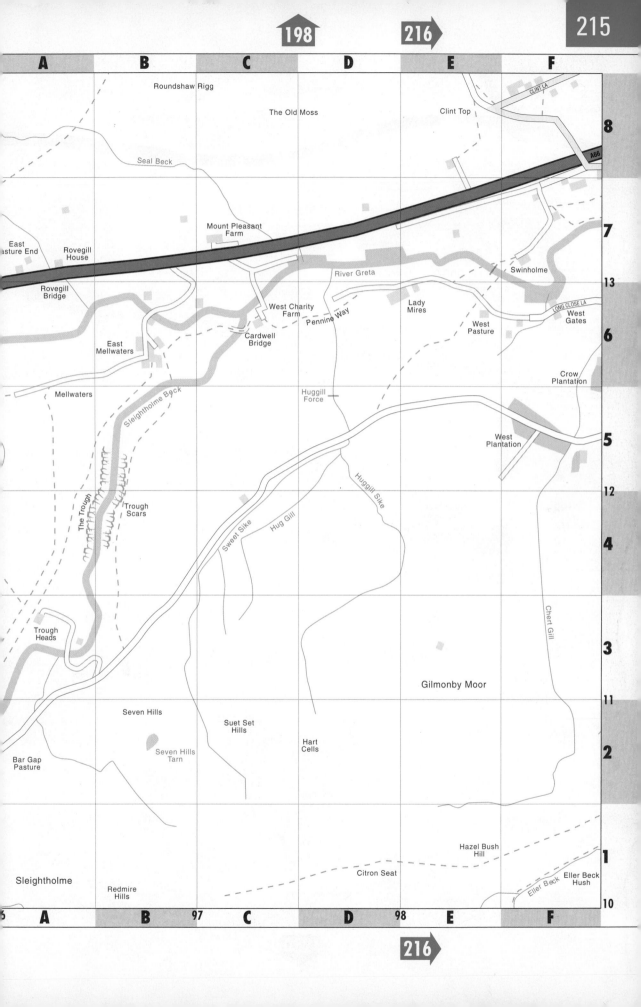

A **B** **C** **D** **E** **F**

Roundshaw Rigg

The Old Moss

Clint Top

8

Seal Beck

A66

Mount Pleasant
Farm

7

East
Pasture End   Rovegill
House

Swinholme

13

Rovegill
Bridge

River Greta

West Charity
Farm

Lady
Mires

LONG CLOSE LA

West
Gates

East
Mellwaters

Cardwell
Bridge

Pennine Way

West
Pasture

6

Crow
Plantation

Mellwaters

Sleightholme Beck

Huggill
Force

West
Plantation

5

The Trough

Trough
Scars

Sweet Sike

Hug Gill

Huggill Sike

12

Chert Gill

4

Trough
Heads

3

Gilmonby Moor

11

Seven Hills

Suet Set
Hills

Hart
Cells

2

Bar Gap
Pasture

Seven Hills
Tarn

Hazel Bush
Hill

1

Sleightholme

Redmire
Hills

Citron Seat

Eller Beck

Eller Beck
Hush

10

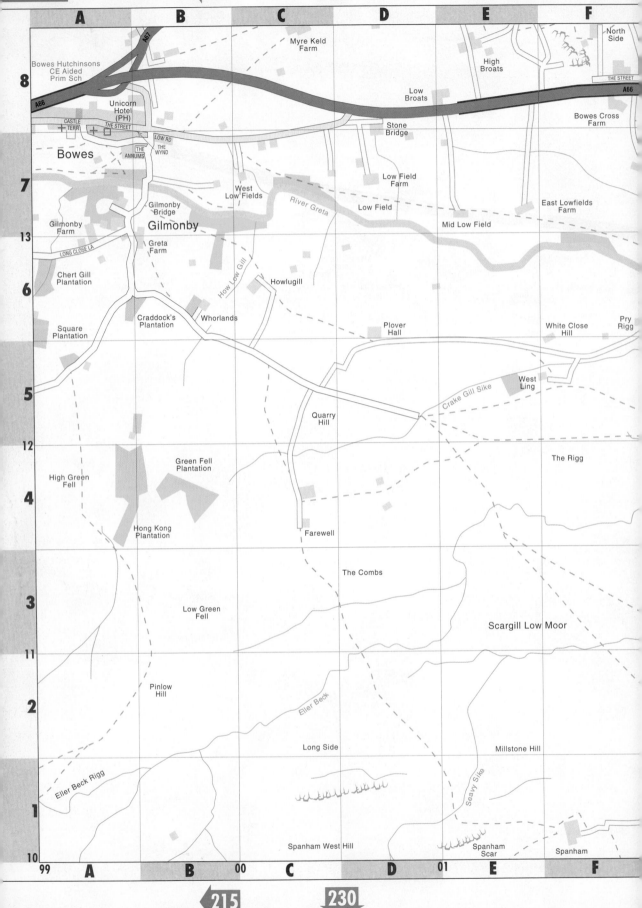

A B C D E F

8

North Side

Bowes Hutchinsons CE Aided Prim Sch

Myre Keld Farm

High Broats

Low Broats

A66

THE STREET

A66

Unicorn Hotel (PH)

CASTLE TERR

THE STREET

Stone Bridge

Bowes Cross Farm

Bowes

LOW RD

THE WYND

THE ANNUMS

7

Low Field Farm

West Low Fields

River Greta

Low Field

East Lowfields Farm

13

Gilmonby Bridge

Gilmonby

Mid Low Field

Gilmonby Farm

LONG CLOSE LA

Greta Farm

Chert Gill Plantation

6

How Low Gill

Howlugill

Plover Hall

White Close Hill

Pry Rigg

Square Plantation

Craddock's Plantation

Whorlands

5

Crake Gill Sike

West Ling

Quarry Hill

12

Green Fell Plantation

The Rigg

High Green Fell

4

Hong Kong Plantation

Farewell

The Combs

3

Low Green Fell

Scargill Low Moor

11

Pinlow Hill

2

Eller Beck

Long Side

Millstone Hill

Eller Beck Rigg

Seavy Sike

1

10

Spanham West Hill

Spanham Scar

Spanham

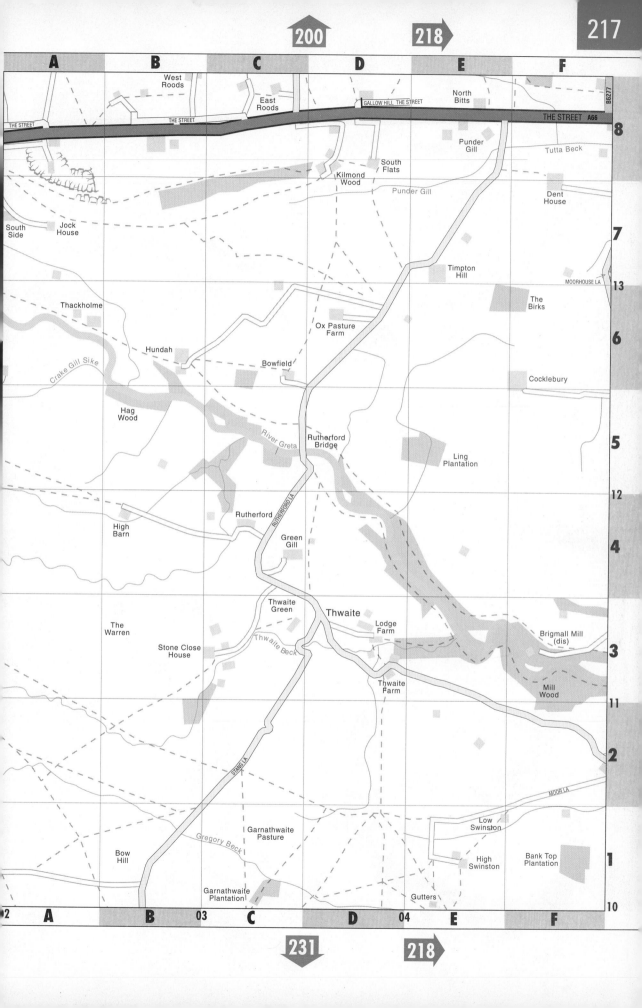

West
Roods

East
Roods

GALLOW HILL THE STREET

North
Bitts

THE STREET

THE STREET

B6277

THE STREET A66

8

Punder
Gill

Tutta Beck

South
Flats

Kilmond
Wood

Punder Gill

Dent
House

South
Side

Jock
House

7

Timpton
Hill

MOORHOUSE LA

13

Thackholme

The
Birks

Ox Pasture
Farm

6

Hundah

Bowfield

Cocklebury

Crake Gill Sike

Hag
Wood

River Greta

Rutherford
Bridge

Ling
Plantation

5

12

High
Barn

Rutherford

RUTHERFORD LA

Green
Gill

4

Thwaite
Green

Thwaite

Lodge
Farm

Brigmall Mill
(dis)

The
Warren

Stone Close
House

Thwaite Beck

Mill
Wood

3

Thwaite
Farm

11

STANG LA

MOOR LA

2

Low
Swinston

Garnathwaite
Pasture

High
Swinston

Bank Top
Plantation

1

Bow
Hill

Gregory Beck

Garnathwaite
Plantation

Gutters

10

A   B   03   C   D   04   E   F

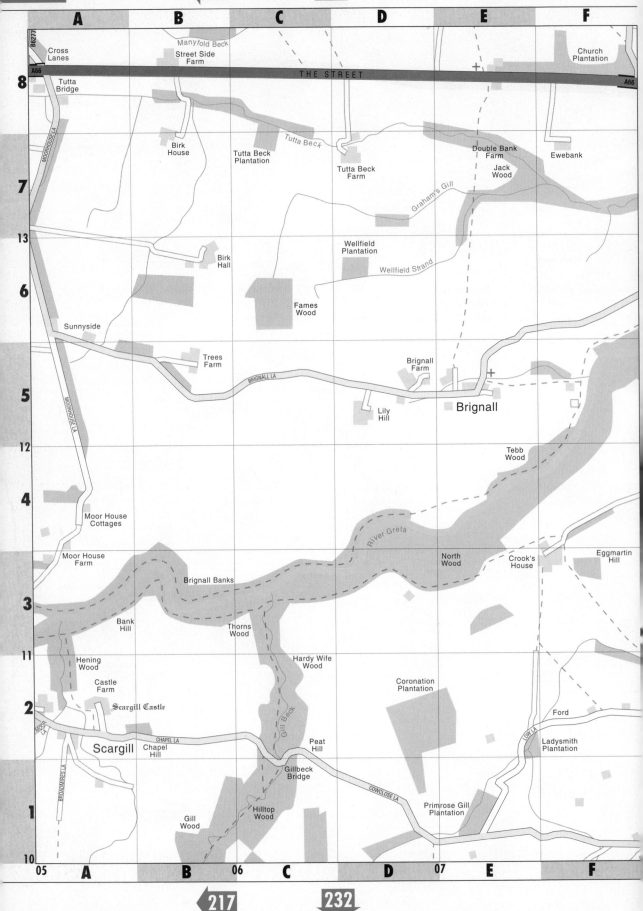

A B C D E F

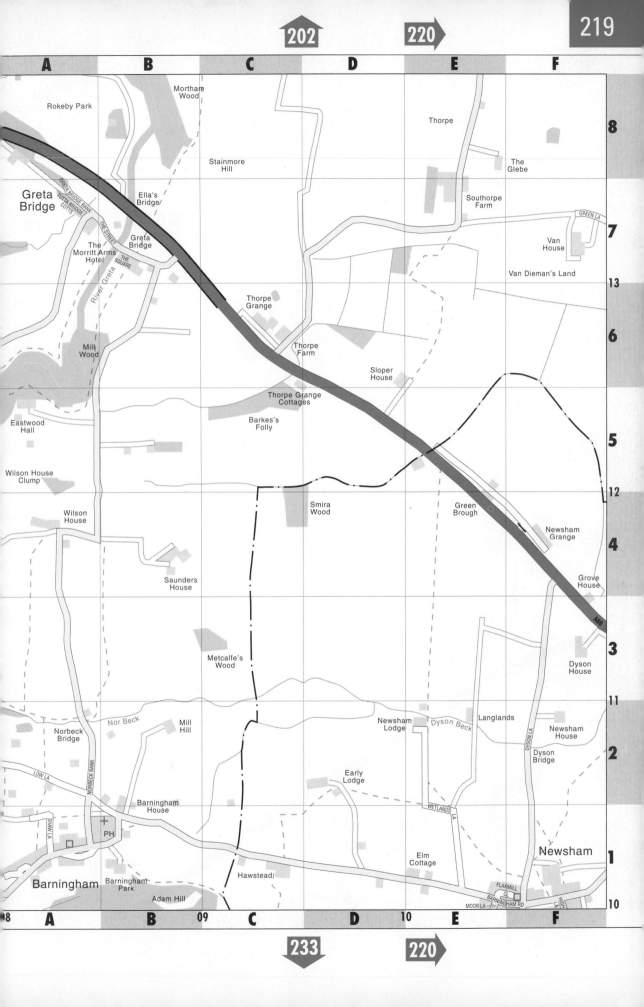

219
203

A **B** **C** **D** **E** **F**

8

Little Biltons
Plantation

Girlington
Hall

Low Moor
Plantation

New
Plantation

GIRLINGTON BANK

Bartle
Gate

7

LITTLE HUTTON LA

13

GREEN LA

Hutton Beck

Little
Hutton

6

West
Middleton

Hutton
Bridge

Smallways Beck

Hutton Hall
Bridge

Hutton
Hall

Hutton Magna

Oak Tree
Inn
(PH)

5

Holm
Hills

Hutton
Farm

12

Lane
Head

4

Hutton
Fields

NEWSHAM HILL

LANEHEAD LA

LANEHEAD LA

NEW RD

A66

Smallways New
Bridge

3

Rokeby
Close

Tefit
Hall

Smallways
Bridge

Smallways
Inn

11

STEPHEN BANK

2

LOW LA

Hareclose
Plantation

Black
Plantation

Cottonmill Beck

1

Browson
Bank

A66

10

219

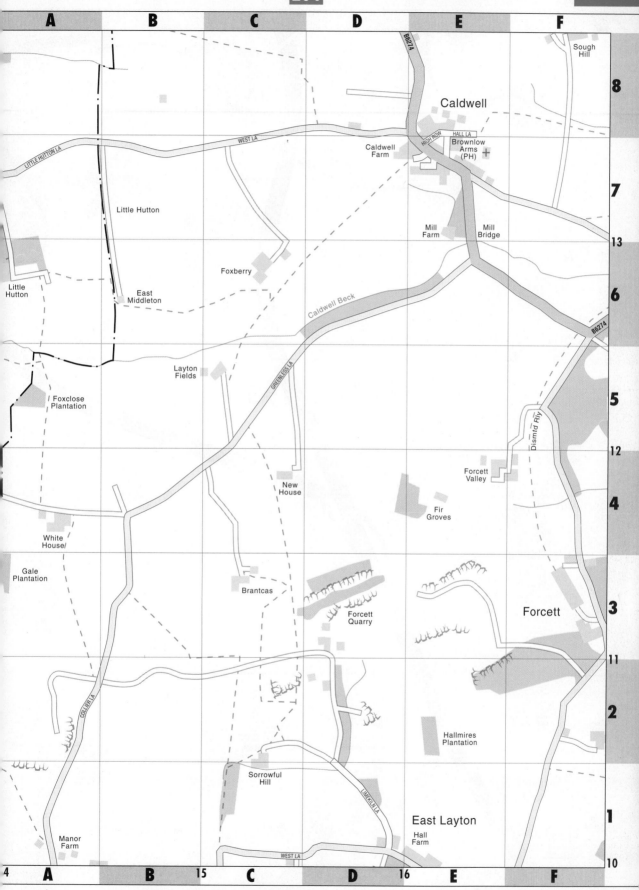

A   B   C   D   E   F

8

Sough
Hill

B6274

Caldwell

7

High Row   Hall La

West La   Caldwell   Brownlow
                                 Farm   Arms
                                             (PH)

Little Hutton La

Little Hutton

Mill   Mill
Farm   Bridge

13

Little
Hutton   East
              Middleton

Foxberry

6

Caldwell Beck

B6274

Layton
Fields

Greenless La

Dismtd Rly

5

Foxclose
Plantation

12

Forcett
Valley

New
House

4

Fir
Groves

White
House

Gale
Plantation

Brantcas

Forcett
Quarry

Forcett

3

Collier La

Hallmires
Plantation

11

2

Sorrowful
Hill

Limekiln La

East Layton

1

Manor
Farm

Hall
Farm

West La

10

4   A   B   15   C   D   16   E   F

Low Conniscliffe

The Holmes

Manfield Scar

JUBILEE COTTS

A67 CONISCLIFFE RD A67

P

Howden Hill Wood

Teesdale Way

River Tees

The Green

Cleasby

Teesdale Way

8

7

13

Manfield

Howden Hill Farm

Four Winds

The Green

CHAPEL LA

BOATHOUSE LA

6

Pinkney Carr Farm

West View

Downholme

A1(M)

BACK LA

GATE LA

WOODLAND

BANK

5

Cold Knuckles

High House

MOOR LA

A66(M)

12

A66(M)

4

Junction 57

New Wood

Old Wood

Wild Duck Farm

Grange View

Cowclose House

3

CLEASBY LA

Cleasby Grange

11

Clowbeck Farm

Beckmoor Plantation

Beck House

Jolby Grange

2

1

Bow Bridge

A1(M)

Clow Beck

Willow Bridge

Jolby Manor

JOLBY LA

10

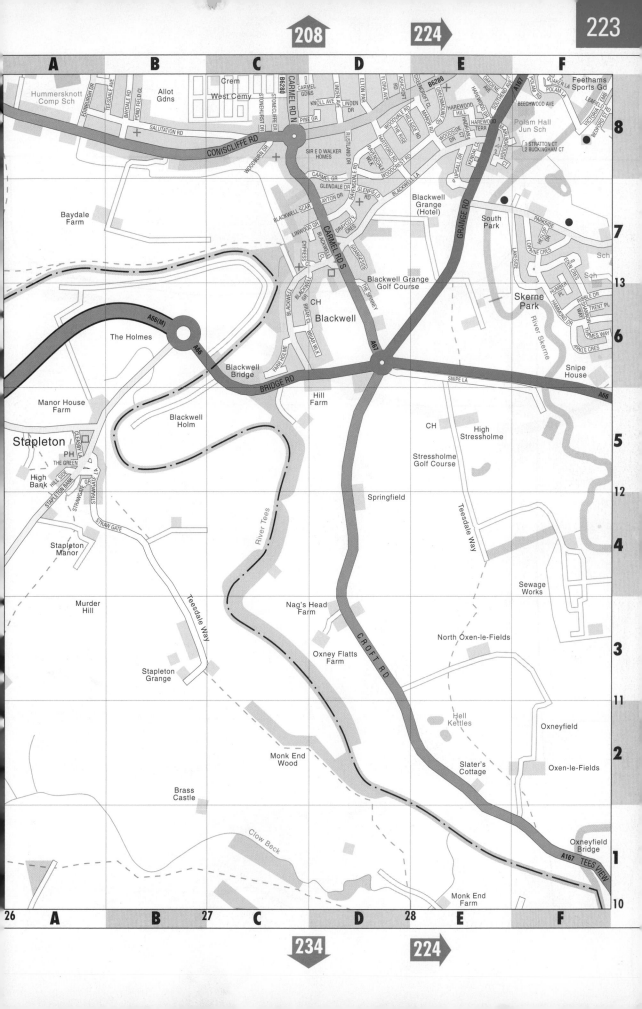

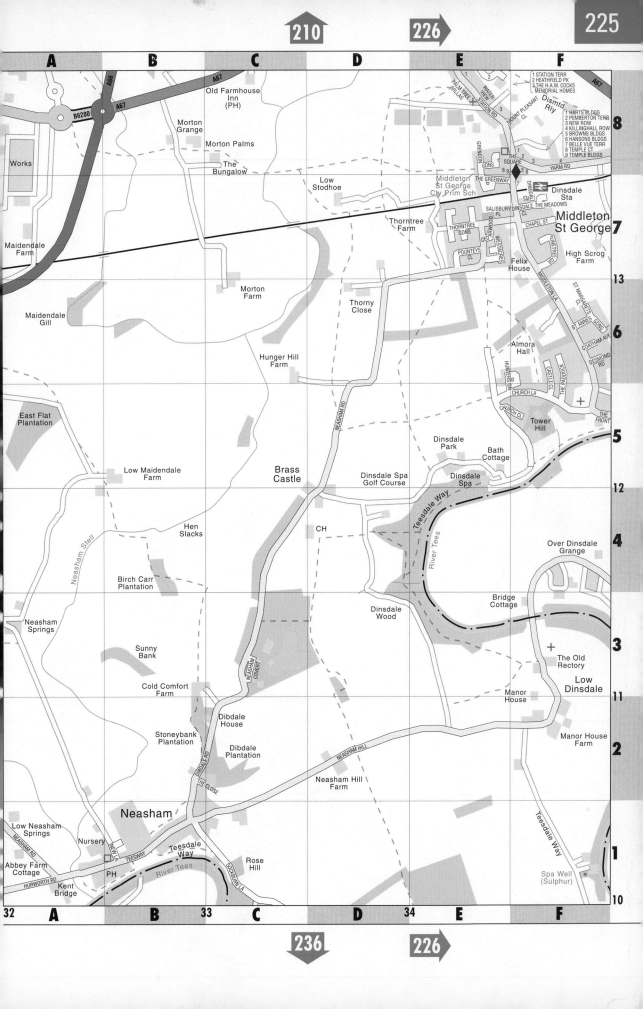

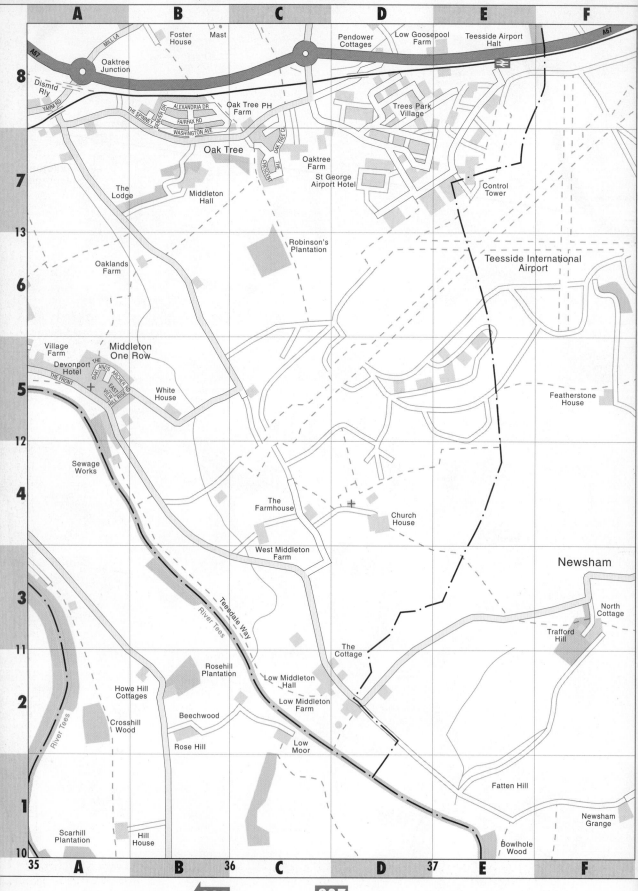

A67

A B C D E F

8

Dismtd Rly

Oaktree Junction

MILL LA

Foster House

Mast

Pendower Cottages

Low Goosepool Farm

Teesside Airport Halt

A67

YARM RD

THE SPINNEY
DENVER DR
ALEXANDRIA DR
FAIRFAX RD
WASHINGTON AVE

Oak Tree PH

Oak Tree Farm

Trees Park Village

7

13

The Lodge

Oak Tree

Middleton Hall

THE CRESCENT

OAK TREE CL

Oaktree Farm

St George Airport Hotel

Control Tower

Robinson's Plantation

Teesside International Airport

6

Oaklands Farm

5

Village Farm

Devonport Hotel

THE FRONT

THE OAKLANDS
ARCHER RD
EAST VIEW
HILL RISE

Middleton One Row

White House

Featherstone House

12

Sewage Works

The Farmhouse

Church House

Newsham

4

West Middleton Farm

3

11

Teesdale Way

River Tees

The Cottage

Trafford Hill

North Cottage

2

Howe Hill Cottages

Rosehill Plantation

Low Middleton Hall

Crosshill Wood

Beechwood

Low Middleton Farm

Rose Hill

Low Moor

Fatten Hill

1

River Tees

Newsham Grange

10

Scarhill Plantation

Hill House

Bowlhole Wood

35 A B 36 C D 37 E F

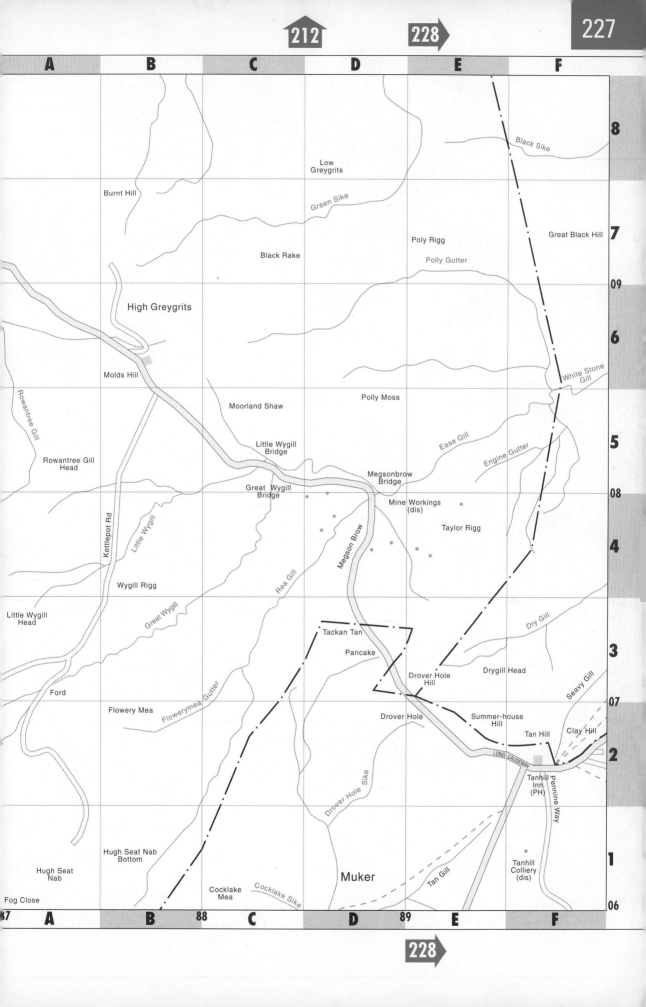

8

Black Sike

Burnt Hill

Low
Greygrits

Green Sike

Great Black Hill

7

Poly Rigg

Black Rake

Polly Gutter

09

High Greygrits

6

Rowantree Gill

Molds Hill

White Stone
Gill

Moorland Shaw

Polly Moss

Rowantree Gill
Head

Little Wygill
Bridge

Ease Gill

Engine Gutter

5

Kettlepot Rd

Little Wygill

Great Wygill
Bridge

Megsonbrow
Bridge

08

Mine Workings
(dis)

Rea Gill

Megson Brow

Taylor Rigg

4

Wygill Rigg

Great Wygill

Dry Gill

Little Wygill
Head

Tackan Tan

Drygill Head

3

Pancake

Seavy Gill

Drover Hole
Hill

Ford

07

Flowery Mea

Flowerymea Gutter

Drover Hole

Summer-house
Hill

Tan Hill

Clay Hill

2

LONG CAUSEWAY

Drover Hole Sike

Pennine Way

Tanhill
Inn
(PH)

Hugh Seat Nab
Bottom

1

Hugh Seat
Nab

Muker

Tan Gill

Tanhill
Colliery
(dis)

Fog Close

Cocklake
Mea

Cocklake Sike

06

227
213

A B C D E F

8

Black Sike

Little Black Hill

Bog Moss

7

09

White Stone Gill

Drygill Pasture

6

Dry Gill

Washfold Rigg

5

Frumming Beck

Pennine Way

08

Sleightholme Moor

4

Brook's Hill Swang

Great Cocker

SLEIGHTHOLME MOOR RD.

Brook's Hill

Cocker Top

LONG CAUSEWAY

Seavy Sike

3

07

Black Gutters

Coal Gill Sike

Coal Gill

Mirk Fell Gill

Mirk Fell Side

2

Mirk Fell
End

Mirk Fell

William Gill

Scollit Side

1

King's Pit
Colliery
(dis)

Mirk Fell Edge

Lad Gill

Little Scollit Hill

06

90 A B 91 C D 92 E F

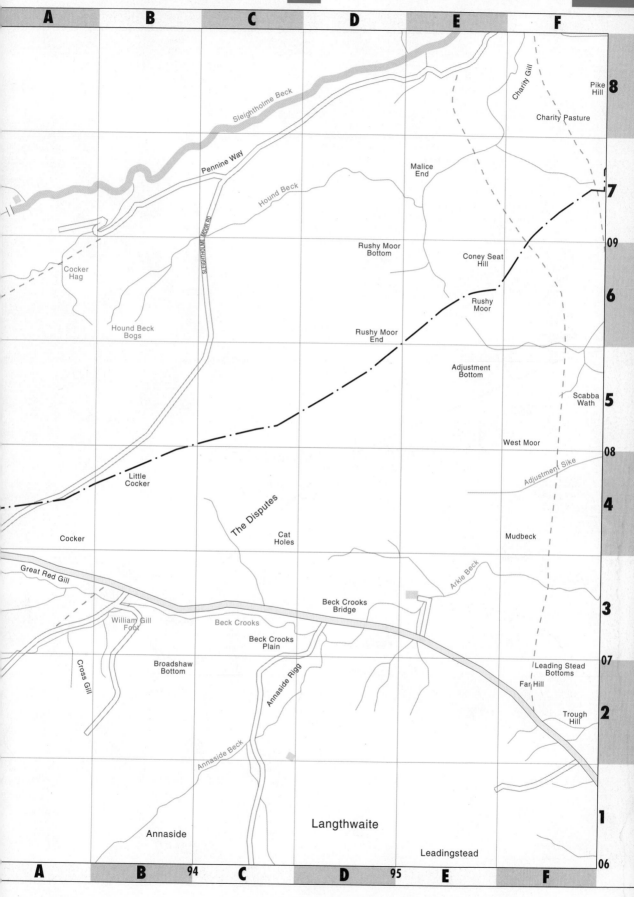

A B C D E F

8 Pike Hill

Charity Gill

Charity Pasture

Sleightholme Beck

Pennine Way

Malice End

7 09

Hound Beck

SLEIGHTHOLME MOOR RD

Rushy Moor Bottom

Coney Seat Hill

6

Cocker Hag

Rushy Moor

Hound Beck Bogs

Rushy Moor End

Adjustment Bottom

Scabba Wath

5 08

West Moor

Little Cocker

Adjustment Sike

4

The Disputes

Cocker

Cat Holes

Mudbeck

Great Red Gill

Arkle Beck

Beck Crooks Bridge

3

William Gill Foot

Beck Crooks

Leading Stead Bottoms

07

Beck Crooks Plain

Broadshaw Bottom

Far Hill

Cross Gill

Annaside Rigg

Trough Hill

2

Annaside Beck

Langthwaite

1 06

Annaside

Leadingstead

A B C D E F

94 95

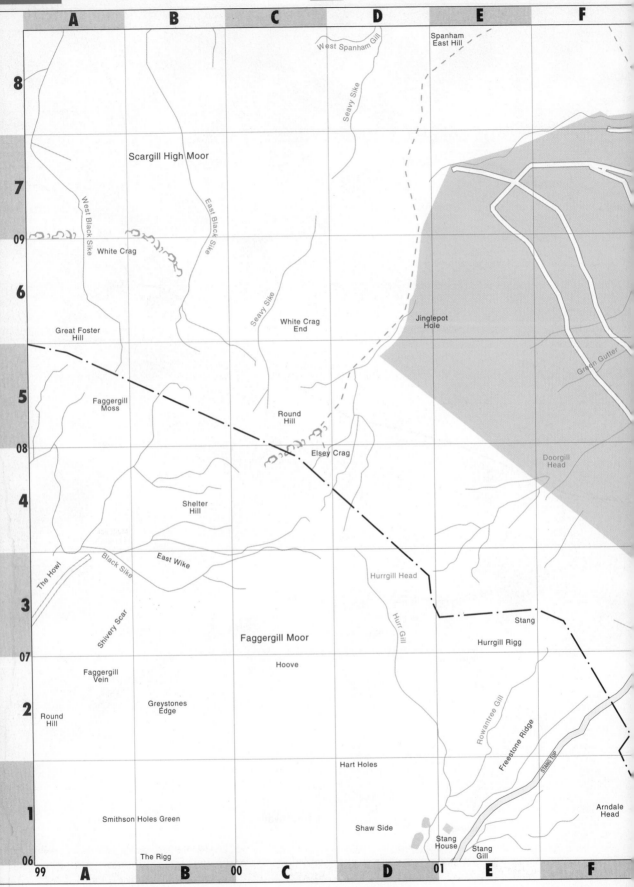

A   B   C   D   E   F

8

Scargill High Moor

West Spanham Gill

Spanham
East Hill

Seavy Sike

7

West Black Sike

East Black Sike

09   White Crag

6

Seavy Sike

White Crag
End

Jinglepot
Hole

Green Gutter

Great Foster
Hill

5   Faggergill
Moss

Round
Hill

08   Elsey Crag

Doorgill
Head

4   Shelter
Hill

East Wike

Black Sike

The Howl

Hurrgill Head

Hurr Gill

3   Shivery Scar

Stang

Faggergill Moor

Hurrgill Rigg

07   Hoove

Faggergill
Vein

Rowantree Gill

Freestone Ridge

STANG TOP

2   Greystones
Edge

Round
Hill

Hart Holes

1   Arndale
Head

Smithson Holes Green

Shaw Side

Stang
House

Stang
Gill

06   The Rigg

99   A   B   00   C   D   01   E   F

A B C D E F

Gregory Beck

Tad Hill

Summer Hill

Garnathwaite

Gutters Bridge

Gutters Plantation

Hurst Hill

8

Scargill Beck

Stang Foot

Peak Hole

West Hope

Hope Plantation

STANG LA

Hill Beck

7

Middle Rigg

East Hope

In Pasture Hill

09

Far East Hope

Murker Hill

Stoneuckley Hill

East Hope

6

Marl Hill

Doorgill Bridge

Woodclose Gill

Door Gill

The Stang

Black Hill Gate

5

Stang Gill

Long Gill

08

Cross Gill

P

Hope Scar

Hope Edge

High Band

4

Cold Seal Gill

STANG TOP

P

Hush Head

3

Peat Moor

Rowantree Hole

07

Cocker Hill

Hope Moor

Black Sike

Cocker Stake Nook

2

Arndale Hill

Black Hag

Arndale Beck

Arndale Bog

1

06

231
218

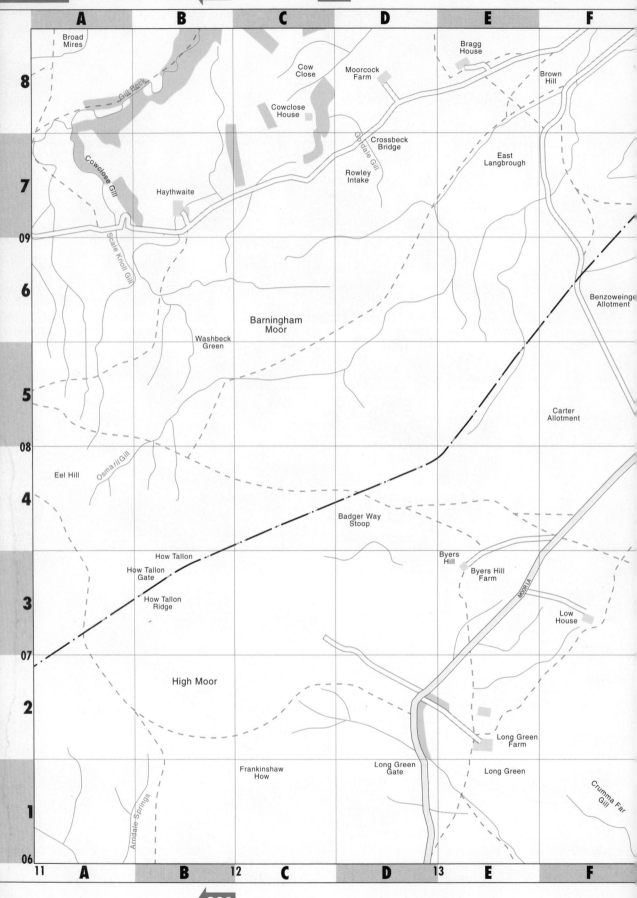

231

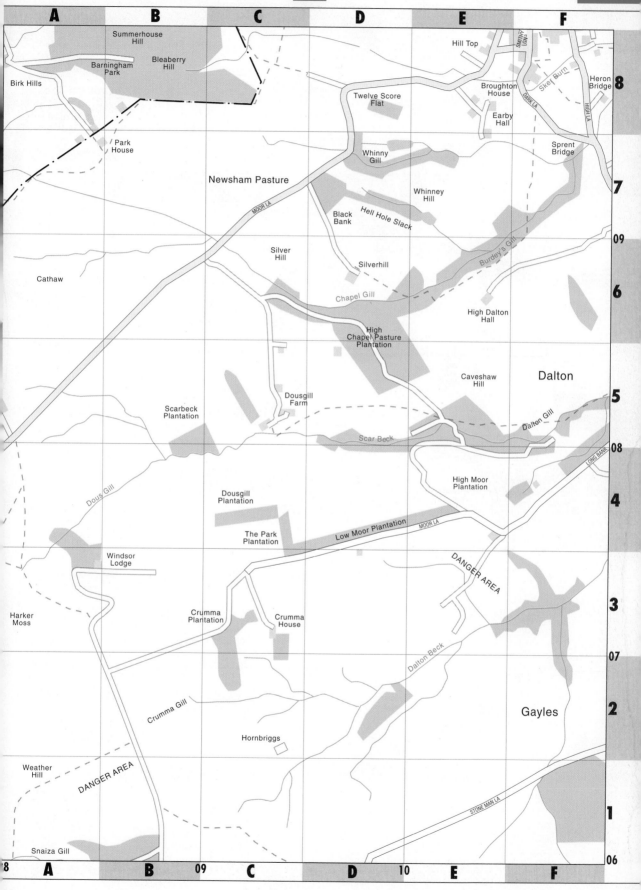

A B C D E F

8

Summerhouse
Hill

Bleaberry
Hill

Barningham
Park

Birk Hills

Hill Top

SMITHY LOW

Broughton
House

Sker Burn

Heron
Bridge

Earby
Hall

PARK LA

HIGH LA

Twelve Score
Flat

Park
House

Sprent
Bridge

Whinny
Gill

Newsham Pasture

7

Whinney
Hill

MOOR LA

Black
Bank

Hell Hole Slack

09

Burdey's Gill

Silver
Hill

Silverhill

Cathaw

Chapel Gill

6

High Dalton
Hall

High
Chapel Pasture
Plantation

Caveshaw
Hill

Dalton

5

Scarbeck
Plantation

Dousgill
Farm

Dalton Gill

Scar Beck

08

Dous Gill

Dousgill
Plantation

High Moor
Plantation

LONG BANK

4

The Park
Plantation

Low Moor Plantation

MOOR LA

Windsor
Lodge

DANGER AREA

Harker
Moss

Crumma
Plantation

Crumma
House

3

Dalton Beck

07

Crumma Gill

Gayles

2

Hornbriggs

Weather
Hill

DANGER AREA

STONE MAN LA

1

Snaiza Gill

06

8 A B 09 C D 10 E F

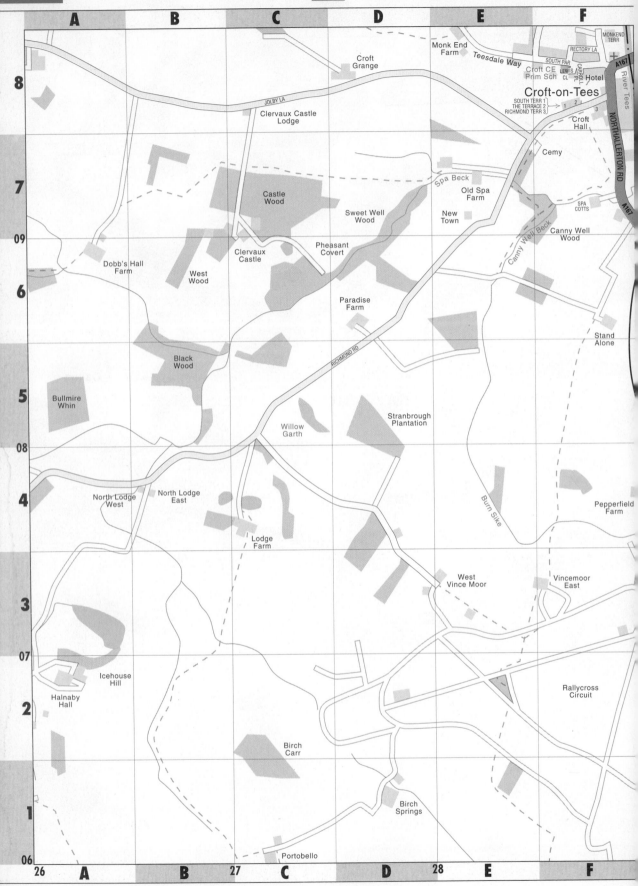

A B C D E F

8

7

09

6

5

08

4

3

07

2

1

06

26 A B 27 C D 28 E F

Monk End Farm
Teesdale Way
MONKEND TERR
RECTORY LA
SOUTH PAR
A161
Croft CE Prim Sch
LEWIS CL
CARROLL PL
Hotel
Croft-on-Tees
SOUTH TERR 1
THE TERRACE 2
RICHMOND TERR 3
1 2 3
Croft Hall
River Tees
NORTHALLERTON RD
Cemy
A167
SPA COTTS

Croft Grange

JOLBY LA

Clervaux Castle Lodge

Castle Wood

Spa Beck
Old Spa Farm

Sweet Well Wood

New Town

Canny Well Wood

Clervaux Castle

Pheasant Covert

Canny Well Beck

Dobb's Hall Farm

West Wood

Stand Alone

Paradise Farm

Black Wood

Bullmire Whin

Richmond Rd

Willow Garth

Stranbrough Plantation

North Lodge West

North Lodge East

Lodge Farm

Burn Sike

Pepperfield Farm

West Vince Moor

Vincemoor East

Icehouse Hill

Halnaby Hall

Rallycross Circuit

Birch Carr

Birch Springs

Portobello

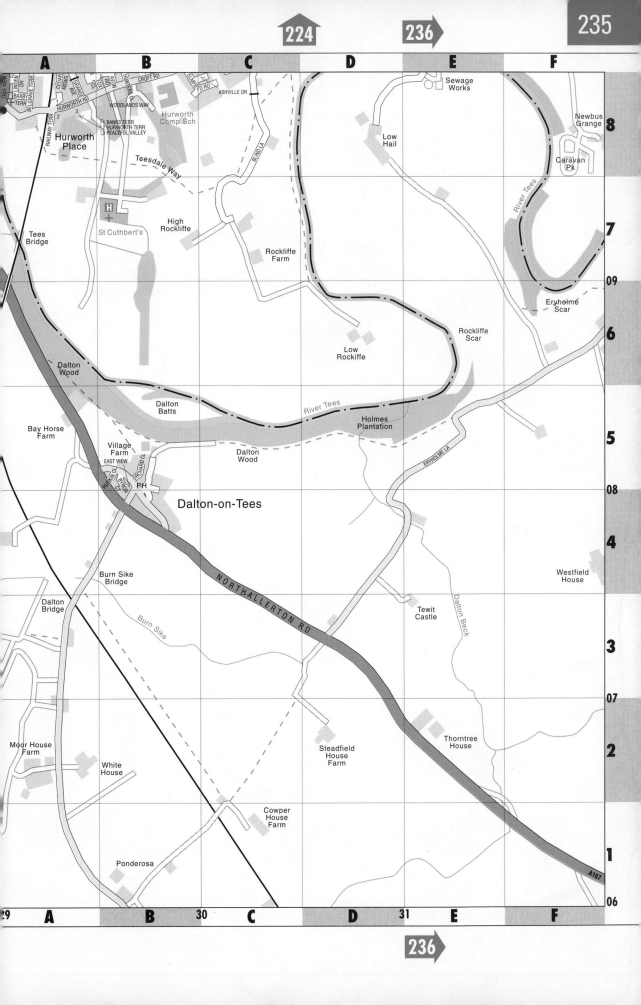

Map labels:

LINDEN VIEW
BAXBY TERR
BELGRAVE TERR
CEDAR MEWS
GRANGE AVE
HUNTERS CL
FOX CL
AVON RD
CROFT RD
ELMS YD RD
ASHVILLE DR
HURWORTH RD
WOODLANDS WAY
Hurworth Comp Sch
RAILWAY TERR
1 BANKS TERR
2 HURWORTH TERR
3 PEACEFUL VALLEY
Hurworth Place
Teesdale Way
BLIND LA

Sewage Works

Low Hail

Newbus Grange

Caravan Pk

River Tees

8

Tees Bridge

St Cuthbert's

High Rockliffe

Rockliffe Farm

7

09

Eryholme Scar

Low Rockliffe

Rockliffe Scar

6

Dalton Wood

Dalton Batts

River Tees

Holmes Plantation

Bay Horse Farm

Village Farm
EAST VIEW
RUSKIN CL
BYRON CT
ORCHARD CL
P H

Dalton Wood

Eryholme La

5

08

Dalton-on-Tees

4

Burn Sike Bridge

NORTHALLERTON RD

Tewit Castle

Dalton Beck

Westfield House

Dalton Bridge

Burn Sike

3

07

Moor House Farm

White House

Steadfield House Farm

Thorntree House

2

Cowper House Farm

Ponderosa

A167

1

06

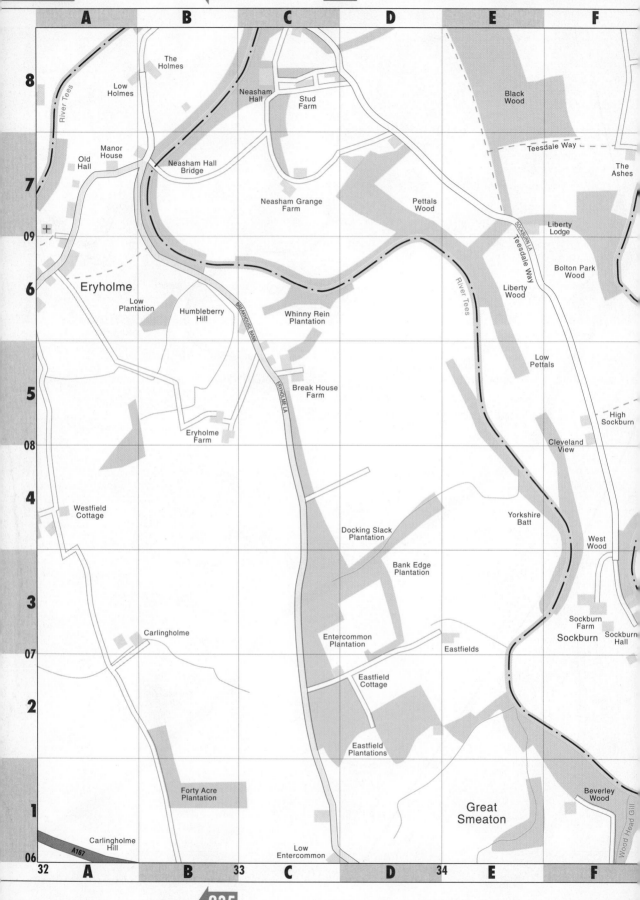

A · B · C · D · E · F

8

7

09

6

5

08

4

3

07

2

1

06

32 · A · B · 33 · C · D · 34 · E · F

River Tees

The Holmes

Low
Holmes

Neasham
Hall

Stud
Farm

Black
Wood

Teesdale Way

The
Ashes

Manor
House

Old
Hall

Neasham Hall
Bridge

Neasham Grange
Farm

Pettals
Wood

Liberty
Lodge

Eryholme

Low
Plantation

Humbleberry
Hill

Whinny Rein
Plantation

BREAKHOUSE BANK

SOCKBURN LA

Teesdale Way

River Tees

Liberty
Wood

Bolton Park
Wood

Low
Pettals

Break House
Farm

ERYHOLME LA

High
Sockburn

Eryholme
Farm

Cleveland
View

Westfield
Cottage

Docking Slack
Plantation

Bank Edge
Plantation

Yorkshire
Batt

West
Wood

Carlingholme

Entercommon
Plantation

Eastfields

Sockburn
Farm

Sockburn

Sockburn
Hall

Eastfield
Cottage

Eastfield
Plantations

Forty Acre
Plantation

Great
Smeaton

Beverley
Wood

Wood Head Gill

Carlingholme
Hill

A167

Low
Entercommon

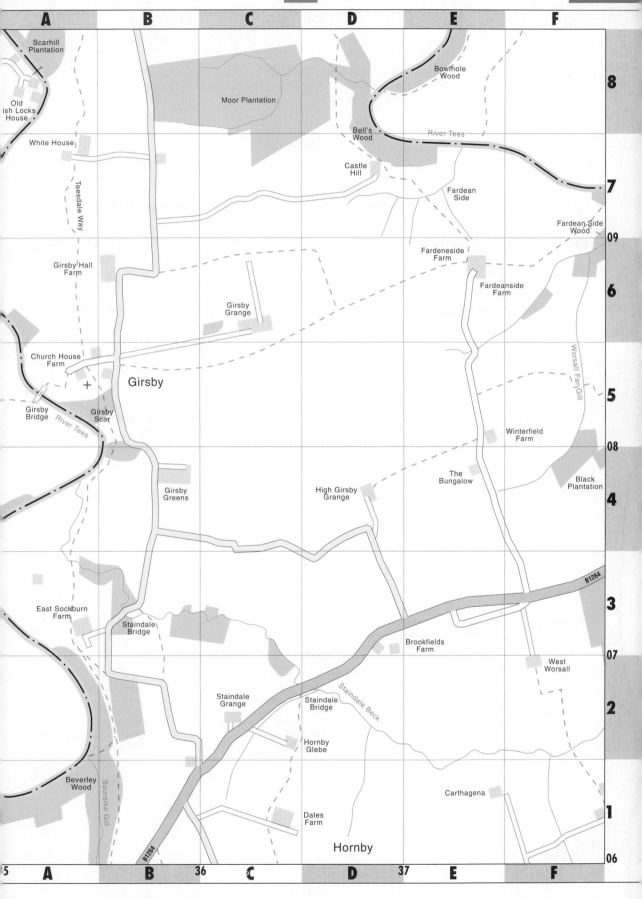

A | B | C | D | E | F

8

Scarhill
Plantation

Moor Plantation

Bowlhole
Wood

Old
ish Locks
House

Bell's
Wood

River Tees

White House

Castle
Hill

7

Teesdale Way

Fardean
Side

Fardean Side
Wood

09

Fardeneside
Farm

Girsby Hall
Farm

Fardeanside
Farm

6

Girsby
Grange

Church House
Farm

Winterfield
Farm

Girsby

08

Girsby
Bridge

River Tees

Girsby
Scar

Black
Plantation

The
Bungalow

Girsby
Greens

High Girsby
Grange

4

Worsall Far Gill

5

B1264

East Sockburn
Farm

3

Staindale
Bridge

Brookfields
Farm

West
Worsall

07

Staindale
Grange

Staindale
Bridge

Staindale Beck

2

Hornby
Glebe

Beverley
Wood

Soursike Gill

Carthagena

Dales
Farm

1

B1264

Hornby

06

5 | A | B | 36 | C | D | 37 | E | F

EXPLANATION OF THE STREET INDEX REFERENCE SYSTEM

Street names are listed alphabetically and show the locality, the Post Office Postcode District, the page number and a reference to the square in which the name falls on the map page.

Example: **Winston St.** **6** Darl DL3 .... **208** F2

Winston St. This is the full street name, which may have been abbreviated on the map.

6 In congested areas numbers may have been used to indicate the location of a street. In certain circumstances, the number used to represent a street will follow the reference in the gazetteer entry.

Darl This is the abbreviation for the town, village or locality in which the street falls.

DL3 This is the Post Office Postcode District for the street name.

208 This is the page number of the map on which the street name appears.

F2 The letter and figure indicate the square on the map in which the centre of the street falls. The square can be found at the junction of the vertical column carrying the appropriate letter and the horizontal row carrying the appropriate figure.

ABBREVIATIONS USED IN THE INDEX

Road Names

Approach............................App	Corner .... Cnr	Heights .... Hts	Road .... Rd
Arcade......................................Arc	Cottages .... Cotts	Industrial Estate .... Ind Est	Roundabout .... Rdbt
Avenue .... Ave	Court .... Ct	Interchange .... Intc	South .... S
Boulevard .... Bvd	Courtyard .... Ctyd	Junction .... Junc	Square .... Sq
Buildings .... Bldgs	Crescent .... Cres	Lane .... La	Stairs .... Strs
Business Park .... Bsns Pk	Drive .... Dr	North .... N	Steps .... Stps
Business Centre .... Bsns Ctr	Drove .... Dro	Orchard .... Orch	Street,Saint .... St
Bungalows .... Bglws	East .... E	Parade .... Par	Terrace .... Terr
Causeway .... Cswy	Embankment .... Emb	Park...................................... Pk	Trading Estate .... Trad Est
Centre .... Ctr	Esplanade .... Espl	Passage .... Pas	Walk .... Wlk
Circle .... Circ	Estate .... .Est	Place .... Pl	West .... W
Circus .... Cir	Gardens .... Gdns	Precinct .... Prec	Yard .... Yd
Close Cl	Green .... Gn	Promenade .... Prom	
Common .... Comm	Grove .... Gr	Retail Park .... Ret Pk	

Key to abbreviations of Town, Village and Rural locality names used in the index of street names.

A. J. Cook Terr. Shot Co DH6 ..... 84 C5
A. J. Cook's Cotts. R Gill NE39 ..... 1 B2
Abbey Cl. St on T TS21 ..... 195 F4
Abbey Cty Jun Sch. Darl DL3 ... 208 C1
Abbey Inf Sch. Darl DL3 ..... 208 D1
Abbey La. Gr Br DL12 ..... 201 A3
Abbey La. Start DL12 ..... 201 B3
Abbey Rd. Bish Au DL14 ..... 148 B5
Abbey Rd. Darl DL2 ..... 210 F6
Abbey Rd. Darl DL3 ..... 208 D1
Abbey Rd. Durham DH1 ..... 58 B8
Abbey Road Ind Est. Durham DH1 ..... 58 C8
Abbey Terr. Start DL12 ..... 201 A4
Abbeywoods. Durham DH1 ..... 58 B8
Abbots' Row. Belm DH1 ..... 58 F3
Abbots Way. St on T TS21 ..... 195 F4
Abbots Wlk. Beam DH9 ..... 18 F8
Abbotsfield Way. Darl DL3 ..... 208 B7
Abbotside Cl. Urpeth DH2 ..... 8 D2
Abercorn Ct. Darl DL3 ..... 208 B7
Aberdeen. Ouston DH2 ..... 8 F1
Aberdeen Rd. Darl DL1 ..... 209 E7
Aberfoyle Ct. Stanl DH9 ..... 18 B6
Aberfoyle. Ouston DH2 ..... 8 F1
Abernethy. Ouston DH2 ..... 8 F2
Abingdon. Ouston DH2 ..... 8 F1
Acacia Ave. Peter SR8 ..... 86 B6
Acacia Gdns. Crook DL15 ..... 100 D4
Acacia Rd. Bish Au DL14 ..... 148 B7
Acacia St. Darl DL3 ..... 208 E4
Academy Gdns. Gain DL2 ..... 205 A7
Accrington Terr. Even DL14 ..... 167 D6
Acer Dr. Hasw DH6 ..... 61 F3
Acle Burn. New Ay DL17 ..... 150 C3
Acle Meadows. New Ay DL17 ... 150 C3
Aclet Cl. Bish Au DL14 ..... 148 B4
Acorn Cl. Sacr DH7 ..... 35 B4
Acorn Dr. Will DL15 ..... 102 A6
Acorn Pl. Brand DH7 ..... 79 B4
Acorn St. Beam DH9 ..... 19 B7
Acornclose La. Sacr DH7 ..... 34 F4
Acornclose La. Wit Gil DH7 ..... 34 F4
Acre Rigg Rd. Peter SR8 ..... 85 B8
Acton Dene. Stanl DH9 ..... 18 C7
Acton Rd. Esh W DH7 ..... 77 E8
Ada St E. Murton SR7 ..... 40 D2
Ada St W. Murton SR7 ..... 40 D2
Adam St. 3 Peter SR8 ..... 86 B6
Adams Terr. Medom DH8 ..... 4 A2
Adamson St. Shild DL4 ..... 170 A7
Addison Rd. Cound DL14 ..... 127 C1
Addison Rd. Hunw DL14 ..... 125 D3
Addison St. Bish Au DL14 ..... 148 F5
Addison St. Crook DL15 ..... 100 E4
Adelaide Bank. Shild DL14 & DL4 ..... 148 E3
Adelaide Row. 4 Seaham SR7 .. 41 D7
Adelaide St. 5 Bish Au DL14 ... 148 C8
Adelaide St. C le S DH3 ..... 20 C2
Adelaide St. 11 Darl DL1 ..... 209 B1
Adelaide Terr. Shild DL4 ..... 148 E3
Adelphi Ct. 18 Darl DL1 ..... 209 B1
Adfrid Pl. Peter SR8 ..... 85 D7
Adolphus St W. Seaham SR7 ..... 41 D7
Adrian Pl. Peter SR8 ..... 85 E5
Adventure La. W Rain DH4 ..... 37 F2
Aged Miner's Home. Shild DL14 ..... 149 A3
Aged Miner's Homes. Bear DH7 ..... 57 A3
Aged Miner's Homes. Burnop NE16 ..... 6 A6
Aged Miner's Homes. C le St DH2 ..... 36 B7
Aged Miner's Homes. E Rain DH5 ..... 38 C4
Aged Miner's Homes. H le H DH5 ..... 38 F6
Aged Miner's Homes. H le H DH5 ..... 39 A2
Aged Miner's Homes. 5 H le Sp DH4 ..... 38 C8
Aged Miner's Homes. 3 H le Sp DH5 ..... 38 F8
Aged Miner's Homes. Quebec DH7 ..... 55 B4
Aged Miner's Homes. Ryhope SR2 ..... 22 E7
Aged Miner's Homes. Sacr DH7 35 D3
Aged Miner's Homes. 2 Seaham SR7 ..... 22 F1
Aged Miner's Homes. Seaham SR7 ..... 41 D6
Aged Miners' Homes. Bourn DH4 ..... 21 E2
Aged Miners' Homes. Brand DH7 ..... 79 B5
Aged Miners' Homes. Brand DH7 ..... 79 C3
Aged Miners' Homes. Even DL14 ..... 167 C7
Aged Miners' Homes. Fishb TS21 ..... 131 D5
Aged Miners' Homes. Gr Lum DH3 ..... 21 B1
Aged Miners' Homes. H Spen NE39 ..... 1 A4
Aged Miners' Homes. Kibble NE11 ..... 8 C6
Aged Miners' Homes. Kimble DH2 ..... 35 F4
Aged Miners' Homes. 8 Lang Pk DH7 ..... 56 C6
Aged Miners' Homes. Leadg DH8 ..... 15 C5
Aged Miners' Homes. Murton SR7 ..... 40 B3
Aged Miners' Homes. Pelton DH2 ..... 19 C6
Aged Miners' Homes. Peter SR8 85 F7
Aged Miners' Homes. Qua Hi DH6 ..... 106 D7
Aged Miners' Homes. R Gill NE39 1 F1
Aged Miners' Homes. S Hill DH6 ..... 60 C1
Aged Miners' Homes. Spenny DL16 ..... 127 C6
Aged Miners' Homes. The Mid DH9 ..... 18 B4
Aged Workers' Homes. Crook DL15 ..... 100 D4
Agnes St. Stanl DH9 ..... 17 F7
Agnew Way. New Ay DL5 ..... 150 D1
Agricola Ct. Darl DL3 ..... 208 C7
Aidan Cl. Stanl DH9 ..... 18 B7
Aidans Wlk. Ferry DL17 ..... 129 A7
Aiden Way. H le H DH5 ..... 39 A5
Ainsley Gr. Darl DL3 ..... 208 C7
Ainsley St. Durham DH1 ..... 58 B2
Ainsty Hunt. New Ay DL5 ..... 170 F8
Ainthorpe Cl. N Silk SR3 ..... 22 B7
Aintree Ct. Darl DL1 ..... 209 F3
Aintree Dr. Cons DH8 ..... 14 D7
Airedale Gdns. H le H DH5 ..... 38 F2
Aireys Cl. H le Sp DH4 ..... 38 C8
Airton Pl. New Ay DL5 ..... 171 B7
Airville Mount. Silk SR3 ..... 22 A4
Ajax St. Darl DL1 ..... 209 C6
Alamein Ave. H le Sp DH5 ..... 38 F8
Albatross Way. Darl DL1 ..... 209 D1
Albert Cl. Bar Cas DL12 ..... 201 A6
Albert Hill. Bish Au DL14 ..... 148 C7
Albert Hill Ind Est. Darl DL1 ..... 209 B4
Albert Rd. Cons DH8 ..... 14 F2
Albert Rd. Darl DL1 ..... 209 A4
Albert St. C le S DH3 ..... 20 C3
Albert St. Chilt DL17 ..... 151 A7
Albert St. Crook DL15 ..... 100 E4
Albert St. 12 Darl DL1 ..... 209 B1
Albert St. Durham DH1 ..... 58 B2
Albert St. Eas SR8 ..... 63 F5
Albert St. Esh W DH7 ..... 77 E8
Albert St. R Gill NE39 ..... 1 A1
Albert St. Seaham SR7 ..... 41 E6
Albert St. Shild DL4 ..... 149 A2
Albert St. Thorn DH6 ..... 83 D4
Albert St. W Pel DH2 ..... 19 A5
Albert Terr. Billy R DL15 ..... 100 E7
Albert Terr. Stanh DL13 ..... 71 B2
Albery Pl. 16 Darl DL1 ..... 209 B1
Albion Ave. Shild DL4 ..... 148 F2
Albion Gdns. Burnop NE16 ..... 5 F5
Albion Pl. Will DL15 ..... 101 F3
Albion St. Spenny DL16 ..... 127 C6
Albion Terr. Bish Au DL14 ..... 148 C7
Albion Terr. Wit Pk DL14 ..... 125 A1
Alcote Gr. Shot Co DH6 ..... 84 D6
Aldam St. Darl DL1 ..... 209 A4
Aldbrough Cl. 11 Ryhope SR2 ..... 22 F6
Aldbrough Wlk. 4 Darl DL2 ..... 224 C8
Alder Cl. H le H DH5 ..... 38 F3
Alder Cres. Tant DH9 ..... 5 F2
Alder Gr. Leadg DH8 ..... 15 D3
Alder Lea Cl. Belm DH1 ..... 59 A3
Alder Pk. Brand DH7 ..... 79 A3
Alder Rd. Peter SR8 ..... 86 B6
Alderdene Cl. Ush M DH7 ..... 57 B1
Alderdene. Lanch DH8 ..... 32 E3
Alderman Leach Cty Jun Sch. Darl DL3 ..... 208 C5
Alderman Wood Rd. Tanf L DH9 17 E8
Alderside Cres. Lanch DH7 ..... 32 E4
Alderson St. 4 Bish Au DL14 ..... 148 B6
Alderwood. Wash NE38 ..... 21 B8
Alderwood Cl. Darl DL1 ..... 209 E6
Alderwood Cl. Hartle TS27 ..... 111 C4
Aldhome Ct. Durham DH1 ..... 58 A6
Aldhun Cl. Bish Au DL14 ..... 148 B4
Aldin Grange Terr. Bear DH7 ..... 57 C3
Aldridge Ct. Ush M DH7 ..... 57 A2
Aldwin Cl. Chilt DL17 ..... 151 A8
Aldwyn Wlk. 3 New Ay DL5 ..... 171 F8
Alexander Dr. H le H DH5 ..... 38 F3
Alexander St. Darl DL1 ..... 209 C3
Alexander Terr. Even DL14 ..... 167 D6
Alexandra Cl. Durham DH1 ..... 58 A6
Alexandra Gdns. 5 Shild DL4 .. 149 A2
Alexandra St. Cons DH8 ..... 14 F2
Alexandra St. Pelton DH2 ..... 19 C6
Alexandra St. R Gill NE39 ..... 1 A1
Alexandra St. Shild DL4 ..... 149 A2
Alexandra Terr. Crook DL15 ..... 100 F4
Alexandra Terr. Hasw DH6 ..... 61 F3
Alexandra Terr. Wh Hi DH6 ..... 83 F3
Alexandria Cres. Durham DH1 ... 58 B1
Alexandria Dr. M St G DL2 ..... 226 B8
Alexandrina St. 1 Seaham SR7 . 41 D6
Alford. Ouston DH2 ..... 8 F2
Alfred St. Darl DL1 ..... 209 A4
Alfred St. Eas SR8 ..... 63 E4
Alfred St. Seaham SR7 ..... 41 E6
Alfred St E. Seaham SR7 ..... 41 E6
Alfreton Cl. Brand DH7 ..... 79 A2
Alfrid Pl. New Ay DL5 ..... 171 D8
Alhambra Terr. Fishb TS21 ..... 131 C5
Alice St. Pelton DH2 ..... 19 F8
Aline St. N Silk SR3 ..... 22 B7
Aline St. Seaham SR7 ..... 41 E7
Alington Cl. Chilt DL17 ..... 151 A8
Alington Pl. Durham DH1 ..... 59 A2
Alington Rd. New Ay DL5 ..... 171 C7
All Saints Dr. H le H DH5 ..... 39 A5
All Saints Ind Est. Shild DL4 ..... 170 B7
All Saints' Rd. Shild DL4 ..... 170 A7
Allan St. Darl DL1 ..... 209 B3
Allen St. C le S DH3 ..... 20 C2
Allen St. Eas SR8 ..... 63 F5
Allendale Rd. Brand DH7 ..... 79 C4
Allendale St. H le H DH5 ..... 39 A2
Allendale Terr. Ann Pl DH9 ..... 16 F4
Allendale Terr. Hasw DH6 ..... 61 F3
Allensford Bank. Cons DH8 ..... 29 F8
Allergate. Durham DH1 ..... 58 B1
Allerton Pl. Whick NE16 ..... 2 F5
Alliance Ind Est. Darl DL1 ..... 209 B4
Alliance St. Darl DL3 ..... 208 F4
Allington Way. Darl DL1 ..... 209 F2
Allison Gdns. Cons DH8 ..... 14 F4
Allison St. Cons DH8 ..... 14 F4
Alloy Terr. R Gill NE39 ..... 1 C1
Alma Pl. Belm DH1 ..... 59 B3
Alma Rd. Shild DL4 ..... 170 A8
Alma St. Eas SR8 ..... 63 F5
Alma Terr. Durham DH1 ..... 80 A8
Alma Terr. Stan Cr DL15 ..... 100 E8
Almond Cl. Hasw DH6 ..... 61 F3
Almond Cl. Shild DL4 ..... 170 B8
Almond Terr. 5 Peter SR8 ..... 86 B6
Almoner's Barn. Durham DH1 ..... 80 A7
Almshouses. Even DL14 ..... 167 C7
Almshouses. Staind DL2 ..... 186 D6
Alnwick Ave. Trim TS29 ..... 107 E4
Alnwick Cl. Bish Au DL14 ..... 148 A6
Alnwick Cl. C le S DH2 ..... 20 A1
Alnwick Cl. Ferry DL17 ..... 129 B5
Alnwick Cl. Hartle TS27 ..... 111 D3
Alnwick Gr. New Ay DL17 ..... 150 E1
Alnwick Pl. Darl DL1 ..... 209 C5
Alnwick Rd. Durham DH1 ..... 58 C7
Alnwick St. Eas SR8 ..... 63 E4
Alnwick St. Peter SR8 ..... 85 F8
Alpine Terr. Cockf DL13 ..... 166 C5
Alpine Terr. Even DL14 ..... 167 C6
Alpine Way. Tow Law DL13 ..... 75 C2
Alston Cres. New Ay DL5 ..... 171 A7
Alston Moor Cl. Darl DL1 ..... 224 D8
Alston Rd. Cons DH8 ..... 14 C4
Alston Rd. Mid in T DL12 ..... 160 C8
Alston Terr. Cons DH8 ..... 14 C4
Alston Way. Brand DH7 ..... 79 C4
Alston Wlk. New Ay DL5 ..... 171 A7
Alston Wlk. Peter SR8 ..... 85 E7
Alston Wlk. Sherb DH6 ..... 60 A1
Alum Waters. N Bran DH7 ..... 79 A8
Alverton Ct. New Ay DL5 ..... 150 B1
Alverton Dr. Darl DL3 ..... 208 C7
Alwent Cl. Darl DL3 ..... 207 F2
Alwent Mill La. Winst DL2 ..... 187 B1
Alwin Cl. Bourn DH4 ..... 21 E3
Alwin. Wash NE38 ..... 9 F1
Alwinton Dr. C le S DH2 ..... 20 A1
Alwyn Gdns. Cons DH8 ..... 14 F1
Alwyn Rd. Darl DL3 ..... 209 A7
Amberwood Cl. 2 Hartle TS27 ..... 111 C4
Ambleside Ave. Seaham SR7 ..... 40 F8
Ambleside Cl. Peter SR8 ..... 85 E7
Ambleside Mews. Leadg DH8 ..... 15 D4
Amersham Cres. Peter SR8 ..... 85 D7
Amiens Cl. Darl DL3 ..... 208 C5
Ampleforth Way. Darl DL3 ..... 208 A5
Ancaster Rd. Whick NE16 ..... 2 F6
Anchorage Terr. Durham DH1 ..... 80 D8
Anchorage Terr. The. C le S DH3 ..... 20 D3
Ancroft Garth. H Shin DH1 ..... 81 B4
Ancrum Way. Whick NE16 ..... 2 F5
Andrew St. Eas SR8 ..... 63 E4
Andrew Terr. Wh Hi DH6 ..... 83 E1
Andrew's La. Eas SR8 ..... 63 B2
Anesty Ct. Bish TS21 ..... 194 C7
Anfield Ct. Darl DL1 ..... 209 F3
Angate Sq. Wols DL13 ..... 97 F7
Angate St. Wols DL13 ..... 97 F7
Anglesey Gr. Hartle TS26 ..... 111 E1
Angus. Ouston DH2 ..... 8 F2
Angus Sq. Brand DH7 ..... 79 D5
Angus St. Eas SR8 ..... 63 F4
Angus Terr. Peter SR8 ..... 63 F3
Ann Ave. Kelloe DH6 ..... 106 D6
Ann St. 2 Cons DH8 ..... 14 F2
Ann's Terr. Darl DL3 ..... 208 F4
Annand Rd. Durham DH1 ..... 58 F3
Annandale. Darl DL1 ..... 209 E7
Annandale Cres. Hartle TS24 ..... 111 F2
Annaside Mews. Leadg DH8 ..... 15 D4
Anne Swyft Rd. New Ay DL5 ..... 171 E5
Annfield Pl. Ann Pl DH9 ..... 16 E4
Annfield Plain Cty Inf Sch. Ann Pl DH9 ..... 16 F3
Annfield Plain Cty Jun Sch. Ann Pl DH9 ..... 17 A3
Annfield Terr. Ann Pl DH9 ..... 16 E5
Annums The. Bowes DL12 ..... 216 B7
Anson Wlk. Cound DL4 ..... 149 B8
Anthony St. Eas SR8 ..... 63 F5
Anthony St. Stanl DH9 ..... 17 E7
Antliff Terr. Ann Pl DH9 ..... 16 F4
Antrim Gdns. Seaham SR7 ..... 41 C8
Apperley Ave. H Shin DH1 ..... 81 C4
Appleby St. Bish Au DL14 ..... 148 D5
Appleby Way. Peter SR8 ..... 85 A3
Appledore Gdns. C le S DH3 ..... 20 D4
Appledore Gdns. Edmon DH7 ..... 35 B7
Applegarth. Coxhoe DH6 ..... 106 A3
Appleton Cl. Darl DL3 ..... 208 F5
Appleton Cres. Will DL15 ..... 101 F3
Appletree Cl. Hur on T DL2 ..... 224 D1
Applewood Cl. Hartle TS27 ..... 111 B4
Aquinas Ct. Darl DL3 ..... 209 A6
Arbourcourt Ave. Esh W DH7 ..... 77 D8
Arbroath. Ouston DH2 ..... 8 F1
Arcadia Ave. C le S DH3 ..... 20 C5
Arcadia. Ouston DH2 ..... 8 F1
Archdeacon Cres. Darl DL3 ..... 208 B4
Archer Ave. Bish Au DL14 ..... 148 A4
Archer Rd. M St G DL2 ..... 226 A5
Archer St. Darl DL3 ..... 208 F2
Archery Rise. Durham DH1 ..... 80 A8
Arden St. Shot Co DH6 ..... 84 C7
Ardmore Dr. Darl DL1 ..... 209 D7
Ardrossan. Ouston DH2 ..... 8 F1
Arena Bsns Pk. H le Sp DH4 ..... 38 C7
Argent St. Eas SR8 ..... 63 F5
Argyle Ct. Tanf DH9 ..... 7 A1
Argyle Pl. S Hett DH6 ..... 61 F7
Argyll Cl. Darl DL1 ..... 209 D7
Argyll. Ouston DH2 ..... 8 F1
Arisaig. Ouston DH2 ..... 8 F1
Arkendale St. Darl DL1 ..... 209 A5
Arkle Cres. Darl DL1 ..... 223 F6
Arlington Cl. Bourn DH4 ..... 21 E3
Armadale Cl. St on T TS21 ..... 195 F4
Armondside Rd. B Mill NE17 ..... 4 C6
Armoury St. 5 Spenny DL16 ..... 103 F1
Armstrong Ave. Wing TS28 ..... 108 E8
Armstrong Cl. New Ay DL5 ..... 171 F8
Armstrong Ct. Darl DL3 ..... 208 D4
Armstrong Ind Est. Wash NE37 ... 9 F7
Armstrong Rd. Peter SR8 ..... 85 D8
Arncliffe Gr. Darl DL2 ..... 207 F2
Arncliffe Pl. New Ay DL5 ..... 171 B7
Arndale House. 11 Birt DH3 ..... 9 C4
Arnison Ctr The. Durham DH1 ..... 58 C8
Arnold Cl. Stanl DH9 ..... 18 A6
Arnold Rd. Darl DL1 ..... 209 C3
Arnold St. Bish Au DL14 ..... 147 C2
Arran Ct. Silk SR3 ..... 22 A6
Arran Wlk. Darl DL1 ..... 209 D7
Arrowsmith Sq. New Ay DL5 ..... 171 E7
Arthur Ave. Ryhope SR2 ..... 23 A6
Arthur St. Beam DH9 ..... 19 A7
Arthur St. Bish Au DL14 ..... 148 F4
Arthur St. Chilt DL17 ..... 151 A7
Arthur St. Crook DL15 ..... 100 F4
Arthur St. Darl DL3 ..... 208 F4
Arthur St. Eas SR8 ..... 63 F5
Arthur St. 11 Ryhope SR2 ..... 23 A6
Arthur St. Ush M DH7 ..... 56 F2
Arthur Terr. Bish Au DL14 ..... 148 B5
Arthur Terr. Ferry DL17 ..... 129 C4
Arthur Terr. Stan Cr DL15 ..... 76 E1
Arun Cl. Peter SR8 ..... 85 C5
Arundel Cl. Bish Au DL14 ..... 148 A6
Arundel Dr. Darl DL3 ..... 208 B5
Arundel Way. Brand DH7 ..... 79 C4
Arundel Wlk. Pelton DH2 ..... 19 F7
Ascot Pl. Pelton DH2 ..... 19 F7
Ascot Rd. Cons DH8 ..... 14 E7
Ascot St. Eas SR8 ..... 63 F4
Ascot View. Darl DL1 ..... 209 E4
Ash Ave. Durham DH1 ..... 59 A1
Ash Ave. Ush M DH7 ..... 57 A2
Ash Cres. Seaham SR7 ..... 41 C5
Ash Dr. Will DL15 ..... 102 C3
Ash Gr. Chilt DL17 ..... 150 E8
Ash Gr. Shild DL4 ..... 149 A1
Ash Gr. Spenny DL16 ..... 127 E7
Ash Gr. Wing TS29 ..... 108 A5
Ash Meadows. C le S DH3 ..... 20 E7
Ash St. Cons DH8 ..... 14 F2
Ash St. 12 Lang Pk DH7 ..... 56 C6
Ash Terr. Ann Pl DH9 ..... 16 E5
Ash Terr. Bowb DH6 ..... 105 D8
Ash Terr. Cornf DL17 ..... 129 E8
Ash Terr. Leadg DH8 ..... 15 D4
Ash Terr. Murton SR7 ..... 40 D3
Ash Terr. Tant DH9 ..... 6 B2
Ash Terr. The Mid DH9 ..... 18 B3
Ash Tree Cl. Darl DL3 ..... 208 B2
Ash Tree Terr. Holm DH7 ..... 34 D7
Ashbrook Cl. Brand DH7 ..... 78 F3
Ashbrooke Est. Hut Hen TS27 ..... 109 C4
Ashbrooke Est. Shot Co DH6 ..... 84 C6
Ashby Cres. Cons DH8 ..... 14 D5
Ashby La. Cons DH8 ..... 14 D4
Ashcroft Gdns. Bish Au DL14 ..... 148 C6
Ashcroft Rd. Darl DL3 ..... 223 D8
Ashcroft. Stanh DL13 ..... 71 A4
Ashdale. Pens DH4 ..... 21 E8
Ashdale Rd. Cons DH8 ..... 15 A3
Ashdown Ave. Belm DH1 ..... 59 B3
Ashfield. Cons DH8 ..... 14 D6
Ashfield Ct. H Spen NE39 ..... 1 A4
Ashfield. New Ay DL5 ..... 171 C6
Ashfield Terr. C le S DH3 ..... 20 D2
Ashford Dr. Sacr DH7 ..... 35 B4
Ashford Gr. Thorn DH6 ..... 83 E4
Ashgrove Terr. Birt DH3 ..... 9 B5
Ashkirk Cl. C le S DH2 ..... 20 A1
Ashleigh Ave. Durham DH1 ..... 58 B5
Ashleigh. C le S DH2 ..... 20 A5
Ashleigh Gr. Lanch DH7 ..... 32 E4
Ashley Ct. Tanf L DH9 ..... 17 C8
Ashley Terr. C le S DH3 ..... 20 C4
Ashmore Terr. Wh Hi DH6 ..... 83 F3
Ashton Rise. Peter SR8 ..... 85 E7
Ashton St. Eas SR8 ..... 63 F4
Ashtree Cl. R Gill NE39 ..... 1 F3
Ashtree La. H Spen NE21 & NE39 ... 1 B5
Ashvale Ave. Kibble NE11 ..... 8 C6
Ashville Dr. Hur on T DL2 ..... 235 C8
Ashwood Cl. Hartle TS27 ..... 111 C4
Askerton Dr. Peter SR8 ..... 85 A3
Askrigg Cl. New Ay DL5 ..... 171 C8
Askrigg Cl. Urpeth DH2 ..... 8 E2
Askrigg St. Darl DL1 ..... 209 A5
Aspen Ave. 7 Peter SR8 ..... 86 B6
Aspen Cl. Belm DH1 ..... 59 A3
Aspen Ct. Cons DH8 ..... 14 E4
Aspen Ct. Gr Lum DH3 ..... 37 A7
Aspen Ct. Shild DL4 ..... 170 B8
Aspley Cl. Silk SR3 ..... 22 A6
Asquith St. Thorn DH6 ..... 83 E4
Asquith Terr. Ann Pl DH9 ..... 16 E5
Association St. Shild DL4 ..... 148 F2
Aston Terr. Darl DL3 ..... 208 C3
Aston Way. Whick NE16 ..... 2 F5
Athelstan Rigg. Ryhope SR2 ..... 23 A7
Atherstone Way. Darl DL3 ..... 208 A5
Atherton Cl. Spenny DL16 ..... 127 F7
Atherton Dr. Fence DH4 ..... 38 A7
Atherton St. Durham DH1 ..... 58 B2
Atherton Terr. Bish Au DL14 ..... 148 E5
Athlone Pl. Birt DH3 ..... 9 D1
Athol Gdns. Ryhope SR2 ..... 23 A6
Athol Gr. N Silk SR3 ..... 22 A7
Atholl Cl. Darl DL1 ..... 209 D6
Atholl. Ouston DH2 ..... 8 F2
Atkinson Gdns. New Ay DL5 ..... 171 E2
Atkinson Gr. Shot Co DH6 ..... 84 B7
Atkinson Rd. C le S DH3 ..... 20 D5
Atlee Sq. Sherb DH6 ..... 59 F2
Attlee Ave. B Rocks TS27 ..... 86 F1
Attlee Cres. Hasw DH6 ..... 61 E1
Attlee Ct. Tow Law DL13 ..... 75 C1
Attlee Est. Tow Law DL13 ..... 75 C1
Attlee Gr. Sland SR2 ..... 22 E8
Attwood Pl. Tow Law DL13 ..... 75 B2
Attwood Rd. Tow Law DL13 ..... 75 B3
Attwood Terr. Spenny DL16 ..... 104 B4
Attwood Terr. Wols DL13 ..... 98 A7
Auckland Ave. Darl DL3 ..... 208 D4
Auckland. C le S DH2 ..... 20 A3
Auckland Mews. New Ay DL5 ..... 171 E7
Auckland Oval. Darl DL3 ..... 208 D5
Auckland Pl. New Ay DL5 ..... 171 E7
Auckland Rd. Bish Au DL14 ..... 148 D5
Auckland Rd. Durham DH1 ..... 58 D7
Auckland Rd. Ferry DL17 ..... 129 B6
Auckland Terr. Shild DL4 ..... 148 E2
Auckland View. Hi Eth DL14 ..... 146 F5
Auckland Wynd. Shild DL4 ..... 148 E2
Audrey Gr. Darl DL1 ..... 209 D1
Augusta Cl. Darl DL1 ..... 209 E6
Austen Pl. Stanl DH9 ..... 18 B4
Austen Way. Crook DL15 ..... 100 C3
Austin St. Eas SR8 ..... 63 F5
Auton Cl. Bear DH7 ..... 57 B3
Auton Field. Bear DH7 ..... 57 C3
Auton Stile. Bear DH7 ..... 57 B3
Avenue 1. Chilt DL17 ..... 128 E1
Avenue 2. Chilt DL17 ..... 128 E1
Avenue 3. Chilt DL17 ..... 128 E1
Avenue 4. Chilt DL17 ..... 128 D1
Avenue St. H Shin DH1 ..... 81 B4
Avenue The. Ann Pl DH9 ..... 16 E3
Avenue The. Birt DH3 ..... 9 C4
Avenue The. Bourn DH3 & DH4 ... 21 E6
Avenue The. Burnh DH7 ..... 33 E5
Avenue The. C le S DH2 ..... 20 B3
Avenue The. Cons DH8 ..... 15 A2
Avenue The. Coxhoe DH6 ..... 106 A4
Avenue The. Durham DH1 ..... 58 A7
Avenue The. Durham DH1 ..... 58 B1
Avenue The. H le H DH5 ..... 39 B4
Avenue The. Murton SR7 ..... 40 D3
Avenue The. Pelton DH2 ..... 19 F7
Avenue The. R Gill NE39 ..... 1 F1
Avenue The. Seaham SR7 ..... 41 A7
Avenue The. Staint DL12 ..... 201 D8
Avenue The. Wh Hi DH6 ..... 83 E3
Avenue Vivian. Gr Lum DH4 ..... 21 F1
Aviemore Ct. Darl DL1 ..... 209 F3
Avon Cl. R Gill NE39 ..... 1 F3
Avon Cres. Fence DH4 ..... 38 A8
Avon Rd. Hur on T DL2 ..... 235 B8
Avon Rd. Peter SR8 ..... 85 C5
Avon Rd. Stanl DH9 ..... 17 F5
Avon St. Eas SR8 ..... 63 E4
Avon Way. Darl DL1 ..... 224 A6
Avoncroft Cl. Seaton SR7 ..... 40 D8
Avondale Rd. 2 Cons DH8 ..... 14 F3
Avondale Terr. C le S DH2 & DH3 20 C3
Axford Terr. Hams NE17 ..... 4 B6
Aycliffe Ctr for Children. New Ay DL5 ..... 172 A7
Aycliffe Hospl. New Ay DL5 ..... 171 A3
Aycliffe Ind Est. New Ay DL5 ..... 171 C3
Aycliffe La. Braf DL1 ..... 192 A7
Aycliffe La. Mordon TS21 ..... 152 B1
Aycliffe Village Cty Jun Inf Sch. New Ay DL5 ..... 171 E2
Aykley Ct. Durham DH1 ..... 58 A4
Aykley Gn. Durham DH1 ..... 58 A4
Aykley Heads Sports Gd. Durham DH1 ..... 58 C4
Aykley Rd. Durham DH1 ..... 58 B6
Aykley Vale. Durham DH1 ..... 58 B5
Aylesbury Dr. Silk SR3 ..... 22 A5
Aylmer Gr. New Ay DL5 ..... 171 C7
Aylsham Ct. Silk SR3 ..... 22 A4
Aylward Pl. Stanl DH9 ..... 18 B5
Aynsley Terr. Cons DH8 ..... 14 F3
Ayresome Way. Darl DL1 ..... 209 D3
Aysgarth Cl. New Ay DL5 ..... 171 B7
Aysgarth Rd. Darl DL1 ..... 224 B8
Ayton Dr. Darl DL3 ..... 223 D7
Ayton Prim Sch. Wash NE38 ..... 9 F3
Ayton Rd. Wash NE38 ..... 9 F4
Azalea Ave. 6 Peter SR8 ..... 86 B6
Babbacombe Dr. Ferry DL17 ..... 129 C5
Back Church St. Cound DL14 ..... 149 B8
Back Coronation Terr. Coxhoe DH6 ..... 105 F5
Back Coronation Terr. H le H DH5 ..... 39 A2
Back East Par. Cons DH8 ..... 15 A2
Back Eldon Terr. Ferry DL17 ..... 129 C4
Back La. G Stain TS21 ..... 173 D1
Back La. Gr Lum DH3 ..... 37 A8
Back La. Head DL2 ..... 188 B3
Back La. L Con DL2 ..... 222 D8
Back La. Lang DL2 ..... 188 B3
Back La. Leadg DH8 ..... 15 F2
Back La. Longn TS21 ..... 211 F7
Back La. Satley DH7 & DL13 ..... 53 C3
Back La. Walw DL2 ..... 190 C3
Back Mount Joy. Durham DH1 ... 80 D8
Back North Railway St. Seaham SR7 ..... 41 D8
Back North Terr. Seaham SR7 ... 41 D8

Bondisle Terr. Stanh DL13 71 B2
Bondisle Way. Stanh DL13 71 A2
Bone Mill Bank. Bish Au DL14 148 E6
Bonemill La. Bourn NE38 & DH3 20 F8
Bonemill La. C le S NE38 & DH3 20 F8
Bonemill La. Wash NE38 & DH3 21 C8
Bonemill La. Wash NE38 & DH3 20 F8
Booth Wlk. New Ay DL5 171 C8
Borough Rd. Darl DL1 209 A2
Borough Road Ind Est. Darl DL1 209 A2
Borrowdale. Leadg DH8 15 D4
Borrowdale Cl. Belm DH1 59 E4
Borrowdale Cres. Blay NE21 2 B8
Borrowdale Dr. Belm DH1 59 C4
Borrowdale Gr. Crook DL15 100 F2
Borrowdale St. H le H DH5 39 A2
Boston Cl. Darl DL1 209 C6
Boston St. Eas SR8 63 F4
Botany Rd. Romald DL12 181 B8
Botham Gr. 3 Darl DL3 209 A7
Bottle Works Rd. Seaham SR7 41 E6
Bouch St. Shild DL4 170 A7
Boulby Cl. N Silk SR3 22 C7
Boulmer Ct. C le S DH2 20 C2
Boundary La. Newl DH8 3 A3
Bourne Ct. Stanl DH9 18 B7
Bourne St. Eas SR8 63 F4
Bourne Terr. Ann Pl DH9 16 F4
Bourne Way. Will DL15 102 A3
Bournemouth Dr. Hartle TS24 111 D4
Bournemouth Dr. Seaham SR7 40 F6
Bournmoor Cty Jun & Inf Sch. Bourn DH4 21 E3
Bousfield Cres. New Ay DL5 171 D8
Bow La. Durham DH1 58 C1
Bow Sch. Durham DH1 80 C8
Bow St. Bowb DH6 81 D1
Bow St. Thorn DH6 83 D4
Bowburn Cty Inf Sch. Bowb DH6 105 D8
Bowburn Cty Jun Sch. Bowb DH6 81 D1
Bowburn South Ind Est. Bowb DH6 105 C8
Bowen Rd. Darl DL3 208 C5
Bowes Ave. H le H DH5 39 B1
Bowes Ave. Seaham SR7 40 F6
Bowes Cl. Ferry DL17 129 B6
Bowes Cres. Byer NE16 6 D8
Bowes Ct. Durham DH1 58 D7
Bowes Gr. Bish Au DL14 148 A6
Bowes Gr. Hartle TS24 111 D4
Bowes Gr. Spenny DL16 103 F2
Bowes Hill. Even DL14 146 B3
Bowes Hutchinson CE Aided Prim Sch. Bowes DL12 216 A8
Bowes Lea. S Row DH4 21 F4
Bowes Moor Cl. Darl DL1 224 E7
Bowes' Mus. Bar Cas DL12 201 B5
Bowes Rd. New Ay DL5 171 D6
Bowes Rd. Start DL12 200 E5
Bowes Rly. Spring NE9 9 E8
Bowesville. Burnop NE16 6 B5
Bowles Terr. Dipton DH9 16 D8
Bowman St. Darl DL3 209 A7
Bowmont Dr. Tanf L DH9 17 C8
Bowmont Wlk. C le S DH2 20 A1
Bowness Cl. Peter SR8 85 E7
Bowness Gr. Ferry DL17 128 F6
Boyd St. Cons DH8 15 A1
Boyd St. Durham DH1 80 D8
Boyd St. Eas SR8 63 F4
Boyd Terr. Stanl DH9 17 D5
Boyden Cl. Bish Au DL14 147 C2
Boyes Hill Gr. Darl DL3 208 D2
Boyne Ct. Brand DH7 79 D5
Boyne Ct. Sedge TS21 153 A7
Boyne St. Will DL15 102 A4
Boyne View. Trim TS29 107 E1
Boyne View. Trim TS29 131 E8
Boynston Gr. Sedge TS21 153 B7
Boyntons. Kimble DH2 35 F4
Brack's Rd. Bish Au DL14 148 E7
Bracken Cl. Stanl DH9 17 E6
Bracken Ct. Ush M DH7 57 A2
Bracken Field Rd. Durham DH1 58 B5
Bracken Hill Rd. Hunw DL15 125 C7
Bracken Hill. Shot Co SR8 84 F5
Bracken Rd. Darl DL3 208 D3
Brackenbeds Cl. Pelton DH2 19 F6
Brackendale Ct. Hut Hen TS28 108 F5
Brackendale Rd. Belm DH1 59 D4
Brackenhill Ave. Shot Co DH6 84 E6
Brackenridge. Burnop NE16 5 E6
Bracknell Cl. N Silk SR3 22 C8
Bradbury Cl. Tanf L DH9 17 C8
Bradbury Rd. New Ay DL5 171 D4
Bradford Cl. New Ay DL5 171 D5
Bradford Cres. Durham DH1 58 F3
Bradley Ave. H le Sp DH5 38 E6
Bradley Bglws. Leadg DH8 15 C6
Bradley Cl. Urpeth DH2 8 E2
Bradley Cotts. Leadg DH8 15 C6
Bradley Ct. 5 Bish Au DL14 148 B8
Bradley Lodge Dr. Dipton DH9 16 E8
Bradley St. Eas SR8 63 F4
Bradley St. Leadg DH8 15 C4
Bradley Terr. Dipton DH9 16 E7
Bradley Terr. E Lane DH5 39 C1
Bradley Workshops Ind Est. Leadg DH8 15 C4
Bradman Dr. C le S DH3 20 E1
Bradshaw Ct. Hartle TS24 111 F2
Braemar Ct. Darl DL1 209 E7
Braemar Terr. 1 Peter SR8 86 B6
Braes The. Cons DH8 14 C1
Braeside. Burnh DH7 33 D4
Braeside. Edmon DH7 35 B7
Brafferton Cl. New Ay DL5 150 E1
Brafferton La. Coat Mu DL1 192 A6
Braithwaite Rd. Peter SR8 85 F6
Braithwaite St. 10 Bish Au DL14 148 B8
Braithwaite St. Shild DL4 148 E1
Brakespeare Pl. Peter SR8 85 E5
Bramall La. Darl DL1 209 F3
Bramham Chase. New Ay DL5 170 F8
Brampton Ct. Eas SR8 63 B3
Bramwell Terr. Cons DH8 15 A4
Brancepath Wlk. Hartle TS24 111 F3
Brancepeth Castle Golf Course. Brance DH7 102 F7
Brancepeth Chare. Peter SR8 85 B3
Brancepeth Cl. Durham DH1 58 E6
Brancepeth Cl. New Ay DL17 150 E1
Brancepeth Gr. Bish Au DL14 148 A6
Brancepeth Rd. Ferry DL17 129 A6
Brancepeth Terr. Will DL15 102 A4
Brancepeth View. Brand DH7 78 F3
Brancpeth Cl. Ush M DH7 57 C1
Brandlings Way. Peter SR8 85 D6
Brandon Cl. Blay NE21 2 A8
Brandon Cl. C le St DH2 19 F1
Brandon Cl. H le Sp DH4 38 D7
Brandon Cty Jun & Inf Sch. Brand DH7 79 C4
Brandon La. Brand DH7 79 C5
Brandon La. N Bran DH7 & DL15 78 B5
Brandon Rd. Esh W DH7 77 E8
Brandon View. Ush M DH7 79 C8
Brankin Dr. Darl DL1 224 C7
Brankin Rd. Darl DL1 224 C7
Branksome Gn. Darl DL3 207 F5
Branksome Hall Dr. Darl DL3 208 A5
Branksome Lodge. Darl DL3 208 B5
Branksome Sch. Darl DL3 208 A4
Branksome Terr. Darl DL3 208 F3
Bransdale. Pens DH4 21 E8
Bransdale. Spenny DL16 103 E1
Brantwood. C le St DH2 19 F2
Brantwood Cres. Bish Au DL14 148 A3
Brass Thrill. Durham DH1 58 B1
Braunespath Est. N Bran DH7 78 F8
Brawton Gr. Darl DL3 208 E4
Breakhouse Bank. Ery DL2 236 C6
Breamish Dr. Wash NE38 20 F8
Breck Rd. Darl DL3 208 D2
Brecken Way. Brand DH7 79 C4
Breckon Hill. Butter DL13 165 E8
Breckon Terr. Fishb TS21 131 C5
Brecon Cl. Peter SR8 85 B5
Brecon Pl. Pelton DH2 19 F8
Brecon Rd. Durham DH1 58 E7
Brecon Side. Darl DL1 209 E5
Brendon Pl. Peter SR8 85 B7
Brentwood Ct. Stanl DH9 18 C6
Brewer St. Bish Au DL14 148 B6
Brewer Terr. Ryhope SR2 23 A6
Brewery Sq. Stanl DH9 17 F7
Brian Rd. Darl DL1 209 A6
Briar Ave. Brand DH7 79 A3
Briar Ave. 2 H le Sp DH4 38 D8
Briar Cl. Darl DL3 223 C6
Briar Cl. Gr Lum DH4 21 E1
Briar Cl. Kimble DH2 35 F3
Briar Cl. S Row DH4 21 F4
Briar Cl. Spenny DL16 127 D6
Briar Dale. Cons DH8 31 C8
Briar Gdns. Crook DL15 100 D3
Briar Gr. Trim TS29 131 D8
Briar Hill. St J Ch DL13 66 F2
Briar Lea. Wit Gil DH7 35 B1
Briar Mews. Cons DH8 14 D5
Briar Rd. Belm DH1 59 D4
Briar Rd. R Gill NE39 1 D2
Briar Terr. Burnop NE16 6 C6
Briar Wlk. Darl DL3 223 D6
Briardene. Burnop NE16 5 E6
Briardene. Durham DH1 58 B1
Briardene. Esh W DH7 55 C1
Briardene. Lanch DH7 32 E3
Briarhill. C le S DH2 20 A5
Briarside. Cons DH8 14 D5
Briarsyde Cl. Whick NE16 2 E5
Briarwood Ave. C le St DH2 19 E3
Briarwood St. Gr Lum DH4 21 E1
Briary Gdns. Cons DH8 14 C6
Briary The. Cons DH8 14 D6
Brick Garth. E Lane DH5 39 C1
Brick Row. Ryhope SR2 22 E7
Bridge Ct. Shadf DH6 82 E7
Bridge End. Coxhoe DH6 105 F5
Bridge End. Pier DL2 206 B4
Bridge House Est. Ferry DL17 128 F5
Bridge Inn Yd. Bar Cas DL12 201 A5
Bridge Rd. Bish Au DL14 148 A8
Bridge Rd. Cornf DL17 105 E2
Bridge Rd. Shot Co DH6 84 D6
Bridge Rd. Stapl DL2 223 C6
Bridge Rd Bglws. Shot Co DH6 84 D5
Bridge St. Bish Au DL14 126 B1
Bridge St. Cons DH8 14 D3
Bridge St. Durham DH1 58 B2
Bridge St. Ferry DH6 & DL17 105 B2
Bridge St. How le W DL15 124 E7
Bridge St. Lang Pk DH7 56 C7
Bridge St. Mid in T DL12 160 D7
Bridge St. Stanl DH9 17 E4
Bridge St. Tow Law DL13 75 C2
Bridge St. Will DL15 101 E1
Bridge Terr. Darl DL1 209 B1
Bridge Terr. Hut Hen TS28 108 F5
Bridge View. Fishb TS21 131 D4
Bridge Way. Lang Pk DH7 56 D6
Bridgegate. Bar Cas DL12 200 F5
Bridgemere Dr. Durham DH1 58 A6
Bridle The. New Ay DL17 150 D2
Brier Ave. Peter SR8 85 F8
Brierley Dr. Sedge TS21 & TS22 154 D3
Brierville. 4 Durham DH1 58 B1
Brighouse Ct. New Ay DL5 171 D3
Bright St. Cons DH8 14 F4
Bright St. Darl DL1 209 C1
Brighton Rd. Darl DL1 224 B8
Brighton Terr. S Hill DH6 60 D1
Brignall Cl. Gr Lum DH3 37 B7
Brignall La. Brig DL12 218 C5
Brignall Moor Cres. Darl DL1 224 D8
Brindley Rd. Shot Co SR8 84 F6
Brinkburn. C le S DH2 20 A3
Brinkburn Ave. Darl DL3 208 D4
Brinkburn Cl. Bish Au DL14 147 E5
Brinkburn Cl. Blay NE21 2 A8
Brinkburn Dr. Darl DL3 208 D5
Brinkburn Rd. Darl DL3 208 E4
Briscoe La. Coth DL12 181 C3
Britannia Rd. N Silk SR3 22 A7
Britannia Terr. Fence DH4 38 A8
Britten Cl. Stanl DH9 18 A5
Brixham Cl. Seaham SR7 41 A6
Broadgate Rd. Lang Pk DH7 56 C3
Broadmeadows. Bowb DH6 81 E1
Broadmeadows. Darl DL3 208 B2
Broadmires La. Scar DL12 218 A1
Broadmires Terr. Kimble DH2 35 E4
Broadoak Dr. Lanch DH7 32 E3
Broadoaks. Bish Mi DL17 130 B3
Broadview Villas. Sherb DH6 60 A1
Broadviews. Gr Lum DH3 37 A7
Broadway. C le S DH3 20 D5
Broadway. Cons DH8 31 B7
Broadway Ave. Trim TS29 107 C1
Broadway S The. Darl DL1 209 E2
Broadway The. Darl DL1 209 D2
Broadway The. H le Sp DH4 38 E8
Broadwood La. Satley DH7 & DL13 53 D8
Broadwood View. C le S DH3 20 D2
Broadwood View. Cons DH8 14 C5
Brockett Cl. New Ay DL5 171 C8
Brockwell Cl. New Ay DL5 150 C1
Brockwell Ct. Bish Au DL14 149 A5
Brockwell Rd. Wash NE38 9 F5
Broken Banks. Bish Au DL14 148 B8
Broken Way. St J Ch DL13 67 C1
Bromley Cl. H Shin DH1 81 B4
Brompton Cl. Urpeth DH2 8 E2
Brompton Wlk. Darl DL3 208 C1
Bronte Ct. Crook DL15 100 C2
Bronte Pl. Stanl DH9 18 B4
Brook Cl. New Ay DL17 150 E1
Brook St. Bish Au DL14 148 F5
Brook St. 2 Spenny DL16 103 F1
Brook Terr. Bish Au DL14 148 F4
Brook Terr. Darl DL3 208 F4
Brook View. Lanch DH7 32 E3
Brookdale. Belm DH1 59 E4
Brookes Rise. Brand DH7 79 D5
Brooklands. Bish Au DL14 148 B4
Brooklyn Rd. Chilt DL17 150 F7
Brooklyn St. Murton SR7 40 D2
Brooklyn Terr. Murton SR7 40 D2
Brooks Cl. Stanl DH9 18 A6
Brookside. Even DL14 167 D7
Brookside. H le Sp DH5 38 D6
Brookside. Sacr DH7 35 C4
Brookside. Wit Gil DH7 57 B8
Brookside Ave. Crook DL15 100 E2
Broom Cl. Blay NE21 2 B8
Broom Cl. Stanl DH9 18 B7
Broom Cottages Cty Jun & Inf Sch. Ferry DL17 129 A6
Broom Cotts. 5 Ferry DL17 129 A5
Broom Cres. Ush M DH7 57 B1
Broom Ct. Spring NE9 9 F8
Broom Farm West. Ush M DH7 79 C8
Broom Hall Dr. Ush M DH7 57 C1
Broom La. Ush M DH1 & DH7 79 D8
Broom Rd. Ferry DL17 129 A6
Broom St. Spenny DL16 104 C1
Broom Terr. Burnop NE16 6 C6
Broom Terr. Crook DL15 100 E4
Broome Ct. Ush M DH7 79 C8
Broome Rd. Belm DH1 59 D4
Broomfield Cres. Chopw NE17 4 B8
Broomhill. Tanf L DH9 17 E7
Broomhill Est. H le H DH5 38 F6
Broomhill Terr. H le H DH5 38 F5
Broomhill Terr. Medom DH8 15 A8
Broomlee Cl. 6 New Ay DL5 171 A7
Brooms La. Leadg DH8 15 F4
Brooms RC Jun & Inf Sch. Leadg DH8 15 D4
Brooms RC Jun Mix Sch. Leadg DH8 15 F5
Brooms The. Ouston DH2 8 F2
Broomside. Ferry DL17 129 A5
Broomside Ct. Belm DH1 59 D4
Broomside La. Belm DH1 59 D4
Brough Cl. New Ay DL5 172 A7
Brough Ct. Hartle TS27 111 D3
Brough Gr. Bish Au DL14 148 A6
Brougham Ct. Peter SR8 85 B3
Brougham St. Darl DL3 209 A5
Broumley Ct. Staind DL2 186 E5
Browbank. Sacr DH7 35 D2
Brown Ave. Will DL15 101 F2
Brown St. R Gill NE39 1 C2
Brown St. Shild DL4 148 F2
Brown's Bldgs. Birt DH3 9 C1
Brown's Terr. 3 Lang Pk DH7 56 C6
Browney Bank. Satley DH7 53 F7
Browney Cty Jun & Inf Sch. Brand DH7 79 D3
Browney La. Brand DH7,DH1 & DH6 79 E2
Browning Cl. Stanl DH9 18 A6
Browning Hill. Coxhoe DH6 106 A4
Browning Pl. Crook DL15 100 C3
Browning St. Eas SR8 63 F4
Browney Ct. Lang Pk DH7 56 C7
Browns Bldgs. M St G DL2 225 F8
Browns Cl. Coxhoe DH6 106 A5
Brownside La. Bolam DL2 169 A2
Bruce Cres. Wing TS28 108 D8
Bruce Glasier Terr. Shot Co DH6 84 C5
Bruce Kirkup Rd. Peter SR8 85 F8
Bruce Pl. Peter SR8 85 C8
Bruce Rd. New Ay DL5 171 C6
Bruce St. Edmon DH7 35 B6
Brunel Rd. Darl DL1 209 B2
Brunel St. Ferry DL17 128 E6
Brunel Way. Darl DL1 209 B2
Brunswick St. Darl DL1 209 A2
Brunswick St N. Darl DL1 209 A2
Bruntoft Ave. Hartle TS24 111 F3
Brunton St. Darl DL1 209 B1
Brunton Wlk. New Ay DL5 171 C5
Brusselton La. Shild DL4 169 C7
Bryan Cl. Hur on T DL2 224 D1
Bryan St. Spenny DL16 104 A1
Bryan's Leap. Burnop NE16 6 A7
Brydon Cres. S Hett DH6 62 B6
Buck Sq. Heigh DL5 170 D1
Buckham St. Cons DH8 14 E4
Buckingham Ave. Hart TS27 110 F2
Buckingham Ct. Darl DL1 223 E8
Buckingham Rd. Peter SR8 85 B8
Buckingham Terr. Cound DL14 149 D8
Buckinghamshire Rd. Belm DH1 59 C3
Buckton's Yd. 3 Darl DL3 208 F1
Buddle Cl. Peter SR8 85 D8
Buddle St. Cons DH8 15 A2
Buddle Wlk. New Ay DL5 171 C5
Bude Sq. Murton SR7 40 D4
Buess La. Darl DL1 210 A5
Bull Wynd. Darl DL1 208 F1
Bullion La. C le S DH2 20 B3
Bulmer Cl. New Ay DL5 171 F7
Bulmer Pl. Hartle TS24 111 F2
Bulmers Sq. Darl DL3 208 F5
Bungalows The. Birt DH3 9 B6
Bungalows The. Cons DH8 30 B7
Bungalows The. Crook DL15 100 E4
Bungalows The. Ebch DH8 3 F4
Bungalows The. H le H DH5 38 F6
Bungalows The. Kibble NE11 8 E8
Bungalows The. Medom NE17 4 B4
Bungalows The. N Bran DH7 78 F8
Bungalows The. Peter SR8 85 F8
Bungalows The. S Hett DH6 62 B6
Bungalows The. Tanf L DH9 17 C8
Burdon Ave. H le Sp DH5 39 A8
Burdon Cl. New Ay DL5 171 C7
Burdon Cres. Ryhope SR2 22 E6
Burdon Cres. Seaham SR7 22 F1
Burdon Cres. Wing TS28 84 E1
Burdon Dr. Eas SR8 84 E7
Burdon Gr. N Silk SR3 22 B7
Burdon La. Burdon SR2 & SR3 22 C5
Burdon La. Ryhope SR2 & SR3 22 C5
Burdon Pl. Peter SR8 85 E6
Burdon Plain. Sunn NE16 7 B7
Burdon Rd. Burdon SR3 22 B5
Burdon Rd. N Silk SR3 22 B6
Burghley Mews. New Ay DL17 150 E1
Burke St. Shild DL4 148 F1
Burlawn Cl. 3 Sland SR2 22 F8
Burleigh Pl. Darl DL3 208 E1
Burma Rd. Hur on T DL2 224 E4
Burn Crook. H le Sp DH5 38 D6
Burn Foot. St J Ch DL13 67 D1
Burn Gdns. Eas SR8 63 C4
Burn La. H le H DH5 39 A3
Burn La. New Ay DL5 171 D8
Burn Oval. Trim TS29 107 C1
Burn Park Rd. H le Sp DH4 38 D8
Burn Pl. Will DL15 101 F3
Burn Prom. 5 H le Sp DH4 38 E8
Burn St. Bowb DH6 81 D1
Burn Terr. 1 Spenny DL16 103 F1
Burn Valley Gdns. Hut Hen TS28 108 F5
Burn's Cl. Hart TS27 110 F3
Burn's Terr. Shot Co DH6 84 D6
Burnbeck Pl. Heigh DL5 170 C1
Burnell Rd. Esh W DH7 77 E8
Burnett Cres. Kelloe DH6 106 E5
Burnhall Dr. Seaham SR7 23 A1
Burnhill Way. New Ay DL5 & DL17 171 B7
Burnhills La. Green NE40 1 B8
Burnhope. New Ay DL5 171 A7
Burnhope Cl. Crook DL15 100 D2
Burnhope Cty Jun & Inf Sch. Burnh DH7 33 D4
Burnhope Way. Peter SR8 85 C6
Burnhopeside Ave. Lanch DH7 33 A3
Burnie Gdns. Shild DL4 149 A1
Burnigill. Brand DH7 79 C3
Burnington Dr. Will DL15 101 E3
Burnip Rd. Murton SR7 40 C4
Burnlea. 4 H le Sp DH4 38 C8
Burnmere. Spenny DL16 103 E2
Burnmill Bank. Shot DH8 13 D6
Burnop Terr. H Spen NE39 1 A2
Burnopfield Cty Jun Mix & Inf Sch. Burnop NE16 6 A6
Burnopfield RC Mix & Inf Sch. Byer NE16 6 D7
Burnopfield Rd. R Gill NE39 1 F1
Burns Ave N. H le Sp DH5 38 E7
Burns Ave S. H le Sp DH5 38 E7
Burns Cl. Stanl DH9 18 A6
Burns Cl. W Rain DH4 38 A2
Burns Rd. Chilt DL17 150 E8
Burns St. Wh Hi DH6 83 E2
Burnshouse La. Shild DL14 168 E8
Burnside. Esh W DH7 55 D1
Burnside. Lanch DH7 32 E4
Burnside. Peter SR8 85 D6
Burnside. Wit Gil DH7 57 B8
Burnside Ave. Peter SR8 86 A6
Burnside Cotts. Rook DL13 47 A2
Burnside Rd. Darl DL1 224 D7
Burnside Rd. R Gill NE39 1 D2
Burnt Ho. Cockf DL13 166 C3
Burnt Houses La. Cockf DL13 & DL2 166 E3
Burnthouse Bank. C le St DH2 19 F4
Burnthouse Cl. Blay NE21 2 A8
Burnway. Seaham SR7 23 A1
Burnynghill Cl. New Ay DL5 170 F5
Burt Cl. Hasw DH6 61 E3
Burt Cl. Peter SR8 85 D8
Burtree Ford. Cows DL13 66 C6
Burtree La. Coat Mu DL2 191 D2
Burtree La. Darl DL3 191 D2
Burtree Rd. New Ay DL5 171 D3
Bury Rd. New Ay DL5 171 E6
Bushblades La. Ann Pl DH9 16 F7
Bushel Hill Ct. Darl DL3 208 B3
Bushel Hill Dr. Darl DL3 208 B2
Busty Bank. Burnop NE16 6 B7
Busty Bank. Burnop NE16 & NE39 6 A8
Busty Terr. Shild DL4 148 E3
Butchers Race. Spenny DL16 104 C2
Bute Ct. 3 Silk SR3 22 A6
Bute St. Tant DH9 6 A2
Butler Rd. New Ay DL5 171 D6
Butler St. Eas SR8 63 F4
Butsfield La. Cons DH8 31 C6
Butsfield La. Satley DL13 52 F7
Butterknowle Cty Sch. Butter DL13 165 F8
Buttermere. Peter SR8 85 A3
Buttermere. Spenny DL16 103 E2
Buttermere Ave. E Lane DH5 61 C8
Buttermere Cl. C le S DH2 20 C2
Buttermere Cres. Blay NE21 2 B8
Buttermere Cres. S Hett DH6 61 E8
Buttermere Gr. Bish Au DL14 147 B1
Buttermere Gr. Crook DL15 100 F2
Butterwick Ct. New Ay DL5 171 D8
Butterwick Rd. Fishb TS21 131 D5
Butterwick Rd. Hartle TS24 111 E3
Butterwick Rd. Sedge TS21 131 F2
Butterwick Rd. Sedge TS21 153 D8
Button's Bank. Esh W DH7 & DL15 77 B5
Butts Cr. Stanh DL13 71 B3
Butts La. Hart TS27 110 F3
Butts The. Stanh DL13 71 B3
Buxton Moor Cres. Darl DL1 224 D7
Bye The. Cons DH8 30 C8
Byer Sq. H le H DH5 39 A6
Byer St. H le H DH5 39 A6
Byerley Park Cty Jun Sch. New Ay DL5 171 A8
Byerley Rd. Shild DL4 169 F8
Byerleyhouse La. Satley DL13 52 E5
Byers Ct. N Silk SR3 22 B8
Byers Green Cty Jun & Inf Sch. By Gr DL14 102 D1
Byland Cl. Bish Au DL14 147 D2
Byland Ct. Bear DH7 57 B3
Byland Towers. Spenny DL16 128 A8
Bylands Way. Darl DL3 208 A4
Byony Toft. Ryhope SR2 23 A7
Byrne Terr. 4 N Silk SR3 22 B7
Byrne Terr W. 2 N Silk SR3 22 B7
Byron Ave. Bish Au DL14 148 B6
Byron Ave. C le St DH2 19 E3
Byron Cl. Stanl DH9 18 A6
Byron Ct. Crook DL15 100 C2
Byron Ct. Da on T DL2 235 B5
Byron Lodge Est. 6 Seaham SR7 22 E1
Byron Rd. Chilt DL17 150 E8
Byron Rd. Darl DL1 209 C3
Byron St. Eas SR8 63 F4
Byron St. Ouston DH2 8 F2
Byron St. Wh Hi DH6 83 F2
Byron Terr. H le Sp DH5 38 E7
Byron Terr. Seaham SR7 22 F1
Byron Terr. Shot Co DH6 84 D6
Byway The. Darl DL1 209 D1
Bywell Dr. Peter SR8 85 C3

Cadger Bank. Lanch DH7 32 E3
Cadogan Sq. 1 New Ay DL5 171 C7
Cadwell La. Eas SR8 63 B4
Caedmon Cres. Darl DL3 208 B1
Cain Terr. Wh Hi DH6 83 E2
Cairngorm Dr. Darl DL1 209 C6
Cairns Rd. Murton SR7 40 A3
Caithness Way. Darl DL1 209 E7
Cakesmire La. Head DL2 188 C3
Calder Cl. Bish Au DL14 147 E6
Caldermere. Spenny DL16 103 E2
Caldew Ct. H le H DH5 39 B2
Caldwell Gn. 2 Darl DL2 224 C8
Caledonia. Gr Lum DH3 37 A8
Caledonian Way. Darl DL1 209 E7
California. Escomb DL14 147 C8
California Row. Mid in T DL12 160 F6
Callaley Ave. Whick NE16 2 F6
Callander. Ouston DH2 9 A2
Callerton Pl. Crag DH9 18 D2
Callerton Rise. New Ay DL5 150 C1
Calley Cl. Peter SR8 85 C3
Callington Cl. Bourn DH4 21 E2
Callington Dr. Sland SR2 22 F8
Calow Way. Whick NE16 2 F5
Calvert St. Crook DL15 100 E4
Calvert Terr. Murton SR7 40 C3
Cam Mead. Silk SR3 22 A4
Camberley Cl. N Silk SR3 22 C8
Camberley Dr. Brand DH7 78 F3
Cambridge Ave. Cons DH8 30 A6
Cambridge Ave. Will DL15 101 F3

Cambridge Dr. Gr Lum DH3 37 A6
Cambridge Pl. Birt DH3 9 C1
Cambridge Rd. N Silk SR3 22 A7
Cambridge Rd. Peter SR8 85 C8
Cambridge St. Cound DL14 127 D1
Cambridge St. Spenny DL16 127 F8
Cambridge Terr. Bar Cas DL12 201 A6
Cambridge Terr. Bowb DH6 105 D8
Cambridgeshire Dr. Belm DH1 59 C2
Camden Sq. Seaham SR7 41 C6
Camelot Cl. Seaham SR7 41 C8
Camp St. Eas SR8 63 F4
Campbell St. Eas SR8 63 F4
Campbell St. Tow Law DL13 75 C2
Campbell Terr. H le H DH5 39 B1
Camperdown Ave. C le S DH3 20 D5
Campion Ct. New Ay DL17 150 E2
Campion Dr. Tanf L DH9 17 D8
Campion Rd. Darl DL1 209 B5
Candlish Terr. Seaham SR7 41 E6
Cann Rd. Peter SR8 85 D7
Cann St. Eas SR8 63 C4
Canney Hill. Bish Au DL14 148 F8
Cannobie Cl. Darl DL3 208 C1
Canterbury Cl. Gr Lum DH3 37 A6
Canterbury Cl. Spenny DL16 103 E3
Canterbury Cres. Will DL15 101 F2
Canterbury Gr. Darl DL1 209 E5
Canterbury Rd. Durham DH1 58 E7
Caradoc Rd. Wing TS28 108 E8
Caragh Rd. C le S DH2 20 C1
Cardigan Gr. Hartle TS26 111 E1
Cardinal Gdns. Darl DL3 208 C2
Cardinal Gr. St on T TS21 195 F4
Carey Cl. Bowb DH6 105 D8
Caribbees. Cons DH8 31 C7
Carileph Cl. New Ay DL5 171 C6
Carisbrooke Cres. Bish Au DL14 147 E6
Carisbrooke Wlk. Darl DL3 208 A2
Carlbury Cres. Darl DL3 208 B2
Carlbury Rd. New Ay DL5 171 E3
Carleton Dr. Darl DL3 208 B2
Carleton Gr. Darl DL3 208 B2
Carlingford Rd. C le S DH2 20 B1
Carlisle Gr. Bish Au DL14 148 A6
Carlisle Rd. Durham DH1 58 F7
Carlton Cl. Urpeth DH2 8 E2
Carlton Ct. 5 Darl DL1 209 B1
Carlton Moor Cres. Darl DL1 224 D7
Carlton St. Ferry DL17 129 C3
Carlton Terr. Eas SR8 63 B3
Carlyle Cres. Shot Co DH6 84 D6
Carmel Ct. Darl DL3 208 C2
Carmel Gdns. Darl DL3 223 C8
Carmel Gr. Darl DL3 223 D7
Carmel RC Comp Sch. Darl DL3 208 B1
Carmel Rd. Stanl DH9 17 D6
Carmel Rd N. Darl DL3 208 C2
Carmel Rd S. Darl DL3 223 D7
Carnaby Rd. Darl DL1 209 D1
Carnation Ave. Bourn DH4 21 E3
Carnforth Gdns. R Gill NE39 1 E3
Carnoustie. Ouston DH2 9 A1
Carnoustie Gr. Darl DL1 209 C7
Carnoustie Gr. Hartle TS27 111 C4
Carole Dunes. Qua Hi DH6 106 D7
Caroline St. Bish Au DL14 148 B6
Caroline St. H le H DH5 39 A4
Caroline St. Seaham SR7 41 D7
Carr Ave. Brand DH7 79 B4
Carr House Dr. Durham DH1 58 D7
Carr La. Mordon DL1 & DL5 172 E6
Carr La. Spenny DL16 103 E2
Carr Pl. New Ay DL5 171 F6
Carr Row. W Rain DH4 37 E3
Carr Side. Darl DL3 208 F6
Carr St. Spenny DL16 103 E1
Carr's Terr. Wit le W DL14 124 B3
Carrhouse La. H le H DH5 & SR7 39 F4
Carrick St. Hartle TS24 111 F2
Carrmere Rd. 1 Sland SR2 22 E8
Carrmyers. Ann Pl DH9 16 E6
Carrock Cl. Peter SR8 85 D4
Carroll Pl. Cr on T DL2 234 F8
Carroll Rd. Darl DL3 208 B1
Carrowmore Rd. C le S DH2 20 C1
Carrs The. Durham DH1 58 C7
Carrsdale. Belm DH1 59 D5
Carrside Rd. Trim TS29 131 D7
Carrsides La. New Ay DL17 150 F4
Carrsway. Belm DH1 59 D5
Carrsyde Cl. Whick NE16 2 F5
Cartington Cl. Peter SR8 85 D3
Cartington Rd. Durham DH1 58 D5
Cartmel Ct. C le S DH2 20 A2
Cartmel Ct. Spenny DL16 103 E3
Cartmel Terr. Beam DH9 19 B7
Cartmell Terr. Darl DL3 208 E4
Carville Est. Will DL15 101 E4
Carville Terr. Will DL15 101 E4
Carvis Cl. Brand DH7 79 A3
Carwardine Cl. New Ay DL17 150 C2
Carway Bank. St J Ch DL13 66 F3
Cassel Bank. Mid in T DL12 139 A1
Cassop Cty Jun & Inf Sch. Qua Hi DH6 106 D8
Castle Ave. Bowb DH6 81 C1
Castle Bank. Tow Law DL13 75 C3
Castle Chare. 3 Bish Au DL14 148 C8
Castle Chare. 2 Durham DH1 58 C2
Castle Cl. C le S DH3 20 D2
Castle Cl. H le H DH5 39 B2
Castle Cl. M St G DL2 225 F6
Castle Close Flats. Stanh DL13 71 B3
Castle Dene Gr. H le Sp DH4 38 D8
Castle Eden Dene (Nature Reserve) Ca Eden TS27 85 E3
Castle Eden Walkway. Grind TS21 175 E8
Castle Howard Cl. Hartle TS27 111 D3
Castle Riggs. C le S DH2 20 B3
Castle St. Eas SR8 63 F4
Castle Terr. Bowes DL12 216 A8
Castle View. C le S DH3 20 C5
Castle View. Esh W DH7 55 D1
Castle View. How le W DL15 125 A6
Castle View. Ush M DH7 57 C1
Castle View. Wit le W DL14 124 B3
Castlebay Ct. Darl DL1 209 E7
Castledene Rd. Cons DH8 15 B1
Castlegarth. Spenny DL16 127 C5
Castlereagh. Grind TS22 155 C2
Castlereagh Cl. New Ay DL5 171 C6
Castlereagh Homes The. Seaham SR7 23 D1
Castlereagh Rd. Seaham SR7 41 D7
Castlereagh St. N Silk SR3 22 A7
Castlereigh Cl. Bourn DH4 21 D3
Castleside Cty Jun & Inf Sch. Cons DH8 29 F6
Castleside Ind Est. Cons DH8 30 B7
Cat Castle Cotts. Lart DL12 199 F6
Catchgate Cty Jun & Inf Schs. Ann Pl DH9 16 E4
Catchwell Rd. Dipton DH9 16 D8
Caterhouse Rd. Durham DH1 58 C6
Cathedral View. Sacr DH7 35 D2
Catherine Cl. Spenny DL16 128 A8
Catherine Terr. Ann Pl DH9 17 B4
Catherine Terr. Stanl DH9 17 F8
Causeway Rd. St J Ch DL13 66 D2
Causeway The. Darl DL1 209 D2
Causeway The. Wols DL13 97 E7
Causey Arch. Tanf DH9 7 A4
Causey Dr. Stanl DH9 18 A8
Causey Rd. Tanf DH9 & NE16 7 A3
Causey View. Stanl DH9 18 B7
Cavell Pl. Stanl DH9 18 A5
Cavell Sq. Eas SR8 63 D5
Cavendish Cl. Brand DH7 79 A3
Cavendish Ct. 4 Darl DL1 209 B6
Cavendish Ct. Ferry DL17 128 E5
Cavendish Dr. 3 Darl DL1 209 B6
Cavendish Pl. Burnop NE16 6 A4
Cavendish Pl. 2 N Silk SR3 22 A7
Cawthorne Terr. Burnop NE16 6 A4
Caxton Way. C le S DH3 20 D8
Cecil Cres. Lanch DH7 32 F3
Cecil Rd. Bar Cas DL12 200 F6
Cedar Ave. Kimble DH2 35 F3
Cedar Cl. Belm DH1 59 A3
Cedar Cres. Burnop NE16 5 F6
Cedar Cres. E Lane DH5 39 D1
Cedar Cres. Seaham SR7 41 C6
Cedar Cres. Will DL15 102 C3
Cedar Ct. Lang Pk DH7 56 A6
Cedar Dr. Durham DH1 80 B5
Cedar Gdns. Cons DH8 14 C1
Cedar Gdns. Crook DL15 100 D4
Cedar Gr. Shild DL4 149 A1
Cedar Mews. Hur on T DL2 235 A8
Cedar Rd. Bish Au DL14 148 C7
Cedar Rd. Darl DL3 208 D4
Cedar St. Peter SR8 86 B6
Cedar St. Wald DH2 19 E1
Cedar Terr. Cornf DL17 129 E8
Cedar Terr. 7 Fence DH4 38 A8
Cedars. C le S DH2 20 B5
Cedars Cres. Murton SR7 40 D3
Cedars The. Coxhoe DH6 106 A3
Cedars The. Darl DL3 208 D3
Cedarwood. Gr Lum DH4 21 E1
Cedarwood. M St G DL2 225 E7
Cemetery La. Darl DL3 208 C1
Cemetery Rd. Stanl DH9 17 F7
Cemetery Rd. Wh Hi DH6 83 F2
Cemetery Rd. Wit le W DL14 124 B3
Central Ave. Bish Au DL14 147 D3
Central Ave. Brand DH7 79 C3
Central Ave. New Ay DL5 171 E7
Central Dr. Spenny DL16 127 D6
Central Par. Shild DL4 149 A1
Centre The. Even DL14 167 D6
Century Terr. Ann Pl DH9 16 E5
Cestria Way. New Ay DL5 171 A8
Chains The. 3 Durham DH1 58 D2
Chair La. Spenny DH6 & DL16 104 A5
Chalfont Way. Brand DH7 79 C4
Challener Way. Bish Au DL14 147 D2
Chancery La. 11 Darl DL1 208 F1
Chandler Cl. New Ay DL5 171 E8
Chandlers Ford. Pens DH4 21 F8
Chandos. Silk SR3 22 A4
Chandos St. Darl DL3 208 F4
Chantilly Ave. Darl DL1 209 E6
Chantry Cl. W Rain DH4 38 A2
Chapel Ave. Burnop NE16 6 B6
Chapel Cl. Hamst DL13 123 B3
Chapel Cl. Kibble NE11 8 D6
Chapel Ct. Sherb DH6 60 A1
Chapel Gdns. Carl TS21 195 D8
Chapel Hill Rd. Peter SR8 85 F6
Chapel La. Cleas DL2 222 E7
Chapel La. Hasw DH6 61 F3
Chapel La. Scar DL12 218 B2
Chapel Row. Birt DH3 9 E3
Chapel Row. Mid in T DL12 160 D7
Chapel Row. Sadb DL2 210 E7
Chapel Row. Thor DL13 99 B7
Chapel St. Bish Au DL14 147 C1
Chapel St. Even DL14 167 C7
Chapel St. H le H DH5 39 B4
Chapel St. Hunw DL15 125 D7
Chapel St. Kir Me DL16 128 A3
Chapel St. M St G DL2 225 F7
Chapel St. Shild DL4 169 F8
Chapel St. Stan Cr DL15 100 F8
Chapel St. Stanh DL13 71 B3
Chapel St. Tant DH9 6 B2
Chapel St. Toro DL14 125 F2
Chapel St. Will DL15 101 F3
Chapel St. Wing TS28 108 E6
Chapel Terr. Copley DL13 165 A7
Chapel Terr. Gain DL2 205 A6
Chapel Terr. Rook DL13 47 C2
Chapel View. R Gill NE39 1 E3
Chapel View. W Rain DH4 37 F1
Chapel Wlk. Will DL15 101 F3
Chaplin St. Seaham SR7 41 D5
Chapman Cl. New Ay DL5 171 E7
Chare La. Shadf DH6 82 E7
Chare The. Peter SR8 85 D6
Charlaw Cl. Sacr DH7 35 B4
Charlaw La. Wit Gil DH7 34 E4
Charlaw Terr. Sacr DH7 35 B3
Charles Perkins Memorial Cottage Homes. Birt DH3 9 C3
Charles Row. Midd DL4 149 E1
Charles St. Darl DL1 209 A4
Charles St. Eas SR8 63 F4
Charles St. 12 Ryhope SR2 23 A6
Charles St. Seaham SR7 41 D7
Charles St. Shild DL4 170 A8
Charles St. Spenny DL16 127 F8
Charles St. Stanl DH9 17 E5
Charles Terr. Pelton DH2 19 E6
Charlotte St. Stanl DH9 17 E4
Charlotte Terr. Chilt DL17 150 F8
Charnwood. Stanl DH9 17 E8
Charters Cres. S Hett DH6 61 F7
Charters Cres. S Hett DH6 62 A7
Chartwell Pl. Cons DH8 14 F4
Chase Cl. Darl DL3 208 A4
Chase End. Hur on T DL2 224 C1
Chase The. Hur on T DL2 224 C1
Chase The. Wash NE38 9 F1
Chatsworth Ave. 7 Bish Au DL14 148 B6
Chatsworth Terr. Darl DL1 224 A8
Chatton Cl. C le S DH2 20 A1
Chaucer Cl. Stanl DH9 18 A6
Chaucer Rd. Darl DL1 224 A7
Chaucer St. 9 H le Sp DH4 38 D8
Chaytor Ct. Darl DL3 208 F7
Chaytor Rd. Cons DH8 14 C4
Chaytor Terr. Fishb TS21 131 C4
Chaytor Terr N. The Mid DH9 18 C3
Chaytor Terr S. The Mid DH9 18 C3
Cheapside. Shild DL4 149 A2
Cheapside. Spenny DL16 127 F8
Cheddar Ct. Ann Pl DH9 16 F3
Chelmsford St. 4 Darl DL3 208 F3
Chelmsford St. 5 N Silk SR3 22 A8
Chepstow Cl. Cons DH8 14 D7
Chepstow Ct. Darl DL1 209 F4
Chepstow Wlk. Hartle TS26 111 E1
Cherribank. Ryhope SR2 22 E6
Cherry Banks. C le S DH3 20 D5
Cherry Cotts. Tant DH9 6 B2
Cherry Knowle Hospl. Ryhope SR2 22 E4
Cherry Pk. Brand DH7 79 A3
Cherry Tree Dr. Sedge TS21 153 B7
Cherry Tree Dr. Will DL15 101 E2
Cherry Tree Sq. Sland SR2 22 E8
Cherrytree Rd. C le S DH2 20 A5
Cherwell Rd. Peter SR8 85 B5
Cheshire Ave. Birt DH3 9 C1
Cheshire Dr. Belm DH1 59 C2
Cheshire Pl. Bish Au DL14 148 B5
Chesnut St. Darl DL1 209 A3
Chester Cres. Cornf DL17 129 F8
Chester Dr. Will DL15 101 F2
Chester Gdns. Wit Gil DH7 35 A1
Chester Gr. Darl DL3 208 B3
Chester Pl. Peter SR8 85 B7
Chester Rd. Bourn DH3 & DH4 21 D3
Chester Rd. C le S DH3 20 F5
Chester Rd. Cons DH8 30 A7
Chester Rd. S Row DH3 & DH4 21 D3
Chester Rd. Stanl DH9 18 A7
Chester Road Est. Stanl DH9 18 A7
Chester St. Bish Au DL14 148 C7
Chester St. Wald DH2 19 E1
Chester Terr. Eas SR8 63 D4
Chester-le-Street RC (Aided) Jun & Inf Sch. C le S DH3 20 D2
Chester-le-Street Sta. C le S DH3 20 C3
Chester-le-Street Bullion La Sch. C le S DH2 20 B3
Chester-le-Street C of E Jun Sch. C le S DH2 20 B5
Chester-le-Street Cestria Cty Jun & Inf Sch. C le S DH3 20 D3
Chester-le-Street General Hospl. C le S DH3 20 C2
Chester-le-Street Hermitage Comp Sch. C le S DH2 20 A2
Chester-le-Street Newker Cty Jun Sch. C le S DH2 20 B2
Chester-le-Street Park View Comp Sch. C le S DH3 20 D3
Chester-le-Street Pelaw Cty Inf Sch. C le S DH2 20 B5
Chester-le-Street Red Rose Cty Jun & Inf Sch. C le S DH3 20 D1
Chester-le-Street West La Sch. C le S DH2 20 B2
Chesters Dene. Ebch DH8 3 E3
Chesters The. Ebch DH8 3 E3
Chestnut Ave. Ferry DL17 129 A6
Chestnut Ave. Spenny DL16 127 E7
Chestnut Cl. Shild DL4 149 A1
Chestnut Dr. Hasw DH6 62 A3
Chestnut Gr. Billy R DL15 100 D7
Chestnut Gr. Ush M DH7 57 A1
Chestnut Rd. Sedge TS21 153 B7
Cheveley Park Jun & Inf Schs. Belm DH1 59 E4
Cheveley Park Sh Ctr. Belm DH1 59 D4
Cheveley Wlk. Belm DH1 59 D3
Cheviot Ct. Ann Pl DH9 16 F3
Cheviot Ct. 3 Darl DL1 209 C6
Cheviot Ct. Seaham SR7 41 A8
Cheviot Gdns. Seaham SR7 41 B8
Cheviot La. Ryhope SR2 22 E7
Cheviot Pl. New Ay DL5 171 B7
Cheviot Pl. Peter SR8 85 B6
Cheviot Rd. C le S DH2 20 B1
Cheviot Terr. Stanl DH9 18 A5
Cheviot View. C le St DH2 36 A8
Cheviot Wlk. Cound DL14 149 C8
Cheyne The. Silk SR3 22 A5
Chichester Rd. Durham DH1 58 D8
Chichester Wlk. Darl DL1 209 F5
Chillingham Dr. C le S DH2 20 A1
Chillingham Gr. New Ay DL17 150 E1
Chillingham Rd. Durham DH1 58 D6
Chiltern Ave. C le S DH2 20 B2
Chiltern Gdns. Stanl DH9 18 B5
Chiltern Rd. Cound DL14 149 C8
Chilton Cl. Darl DL3 208 B1
Chilton Cl. New Ay DL5 150 E1
Chilton Cty Inf Sch. Chilt DL17 150 F8
Chilton Cty Jun Sch. Chilt DL17 150 F7
Chilton Garth. Peter SR8 85 F5
Chilton Gdns. 10 Fence DH4 38 A8
Chilton Ind Est. Chilt DL 17 128 E2
Chilton La. Ferry DL17 129 C4
Chilton Way. Chilt DL17 128 E1
China St. Darl DL3 209 A6
Chipchase. Wash NE38 9 F4
Chirnside Terr. Ann Pl DH9 16 E3
Chisholm Rd. Trim TS29 131 D8
Chopwell Rd. B Mill NE17 4 C6
Christchurch Cl. 5 Darl DL1 209 B6
Christchurch Pl. Peter SR8 85 C5
Christopher Wlk. 2 New Ay DL5 171 C7
Church Bank. Cons DH8 14 C6
Church Bank. Egg DL12 162 B4
Church Bank. Stanl DH9 17 F7
Church Bank. Start DL12 200 F4
Church Chare. C le S DH3 20 D3
Church Cl. Ebch DH8 3 E3
Church Cl. Kir Me DL16 128 A3
Church Cl. M St G DL2 225 F5
Church Cl. New Ay DL5 171 D6
Church Cl. Peter SR8 85 E5
Church Cl. Seaham SR7 41 C8
Church Ct. Seaham SR7 41 A8
Church Dr. Bish Au DL14 148 D6
Church Farm Flats. Redmar TS21 195 B7
Church Gn. Seaham SR7 41 C8
Church Gr. Cound DL14 149 B8
Church Hill. Crook DL15 100 F4
Church La. Durham DH1 58 E2
Church La. Durham DH1 80 D8
Church La. Ferry DL17 128 F6
Church La. Hunw DL15 125 E6
Church La. M St G DL2 225 F5
Church La. Murton SR7 40 C2
Church La. Nent CA9 42 A4
Church La. New Ay DL5 171 E1
Church La. Redmar TS21 195 B7
Church La. Sadb DL2 210 E6
Church La. Shadf DH6 82 F7
Church La. Stanh DL13 71 B3
Church La. Tow Law DL13 75 C2
Church La. Wols DL13 97 E7
Church La N. Murton SR7 40 B3
Church Mews. Winst DL2 204 A6
Church Par. Sacr DH7 35 B4
Church Rd. Cons DH8 14 D4
Church Rd. Ferry DL17 128 F6
Church Rd. H le H DH5 39 A5
Church Rd. Pelton DH2 19 D6
Church Rd. Trim TS29 107 D1
Church Row. 5 Darl DL1 208 F1
Church Row. Hur on T DL2 224 E1
Church Row. Ingle DL2 188 A6
Church Row. Stanh DL13 71 A5
Church Sch. Hur on T DL2 224 C1
Church Sq. Cockf DL13 166 D5
Church Sq. Hi Eth DL14 146 F5
Church St. Ann Pl DH9 16 F4
Church St. Birt DH3 9 C4
Church St. Bish Mi DL17 130 B3
Church St. By Gr DL16 126 F8
Church St. Cons DH8 14 F2
Church St. Cons DH8 29 F5
Church St. Cound DL14 149 B8
Church St. Crook DL15 100 F4
Church St. Durham DH1 80 D8
Church St. Ferry DL17 129 C3
Church St. 7 H le Sp DH4 & DH5 38 E8
Church St. Hasw DH6 61 E3
Church St. Hesl TS27 86 A1
Church St. Hi Eth DL14 146 F5
Church St. How le W DL15 124 E7
Church St. Hut Hen TS28 108 F6
Church St. 1 Lang Pk DH7 56 C6
Church St. Leadg DH8 15 C4
Church St. Murton SR7 40 D2
Church St. 1 Qua Hi DH6 106 D8
Church St. Sacr DH7 35 B3
Church St. Seaham SR7 41 D7
Church St. Shild DL4 148 F2
Church St. Spenny DL16 127 F8
Church St. Staind DL2 186 E6
Church St. Stanl DH9 17 F7
Church St. W Rain DH4 38 A2
Church St. Wh Hi DH6 84 A3
Church St. Will DL15 101 C3
Church St E. Coxhoe DH6 106 A4
Church Street Head. Durham DH1 80 D8
Church Street Villas. Durham DH1 80 D8
Church Vale. H Pitt DH6 60 C4
Church View. Belm DH1 59 D4
Church View. Bish TS21 194 D7
Church View. Cons DH8 14 E2
Church View. Hasw DH6 61 F3
Church View. Heigh DL5 170 D1
Church View. 2 Hi Eth DL14 146 F5
Church View. Hur on T DL2 224 D1
Church View. Ingle DL2 188 A6
Church View. Kimble DH2 36 A3
Church View. Lanch DH7 32 F3
Church View. N Silk SR3 22 A7
Church View. Quebec DH7 55 B4
Church View. Sadb DL2 210 E6
Church View. Sedge TS21 153 A6
Church View. Shot Co DH6 84 C7
Church View. Thor DL13 99 B7
Church View. Thorn DH6 83 D4
Church View. Will DL15 102 B3
Church Wlk. Eas SR8 63 A3
Church Wynd. Sherb DH6 59 F1
Churchgarth La. Rook DL13 47 C1
Churchill Ave. Durham DH1 58 F2
Churchill Cl. Cons DH8 14 C6
Churchill Rd. Bar Cas DL12 201 B6
Churchill Sq. Durham DH1 58 F3
Churchill Sq. Fence DH4 38 B8
Churchill Terr. S Hill DH6 82 E8
Cinnamon Dr. Wing TS29 108 A5
Clanny Rd. New Ay DL5 171 E5
Clap Shaw. Blanch DH8 10 A1
Clappersgate. Eas SR8 63 A3
Clara St. Seaham SR7 41 B8
Clare Ave. Darl DL3 208 B2
Clare Rd. Peter SR8 85 B5
Claremont Gr. Sedge TS21 153 A5
Claremont Rd. Darl DL1 224 C7
Clarence Chare. New Ay DL5 171 E5
Clarence Cl. New Ay DL5 171 E5
Clarence Cnr. New Ay DL5 171 E5
Clarence Gdns. Bish Au DL14 148 B8
Clarence Gdns. Cons DH8 14 F4
Clarence Gdns. Crook DL15 101 A3
Clarence Gn. New Ay DL5 171 E5
Clarence House. Spenny DL16 127 F8
Clarence St. Bish Au DL14 148 B8
Clarence St. Bowb DH6 105 D8
Clarence St. Bowb DH6 105 F6
Clarence St. 3 Seaham SR7 41 D7
Clarence St. Spenny DL16 127 F8
Clarence St. Tant DH9 6 B2
Clarence Terr. C le S DH3 20 C3
Clarence The. 11 Bish Au DL14 148 B8
Clarence Villas. Bowb DH6 105 F6
Clarendon Rd. Darl DL1 209 E6
Clarendon St. 13 Cons DH8 14 F3
Clareville Rd. Darl DL3 208 C2
Clark Terr. Leadg DH8 15 B6
Clark Terr. Stanl DH9 17 F8
Clark's Terr. 2 Seaham SR7 22 E1
Clarke Terr. Murton SR7 40 C3
Claude St. H le H DH5 39 A3
Claude Terr. Murton SR7 40 D3
Clavering Pl. Ann Pl DH9 16 F3
Clavering Prim Sch. Hartle TS24 111 C3
Clavering Rd. Hartle TS27 111 D3
Claxton Ave. Darl DL3 208 B3
Claxton Ct. New Ay DL5 150 A1
Claxton St. 5 Peter SR8 86 A7
Clay La. Durham DH1 80 A8
Clay La. Durham DH1 80 B8
Claypath. Durham DH1 58 D2
Claypath Rd. H le H DH5 39 B2
Claypool Farm Cl. Hut Hen TS27 109 D5
Clayton Ct. Bish Au DL14 126 B1
Clayton St. 1 Bish Au DL14 148 B8
Cleadon St. 8 Cons DH8 14 F3
Cleasby La. Stapl DL2 222 E3
Cleasby La. Stapl DL2 223 A5
Cleasby View. Darl DL3 208 B4
Cleatlam Back La. Cleat DL2 185 F2
Clemmy Bank. Wit le W DL14 124 B3
Clervaux Terr. Fishb TS21 131 D5
Cleve Cotts. 1 Ferry DL17 129 B5
Clevecoat Wlk. Hart TS27 110 F2
Cleveland Ave. Bish Au DL14 148 B6
Cleveland Ave. C le S DH2 20 B2
Cleveland Ave. Darl DL3 208 E1
Cleveland Ave. Shild DL4 149 B1
Cleveland Ave. Trim TS29 107 D1
Cleveland Ct. Ferry DL17 129 C5
Cleveland Pl. Peter SR8 85 B6
Cleveland Rd. Bar Cas DL12 201 B7
Cleveland St. Darl DL1 209 A4
Cleveland Terr. Darl DL3 208 D1
Cleveland Terr. Stanl DH9 18 A5
Cleveland Trad Est. Darl DL1 209 A4
Cleveland View. Cound DL14 149 C8
Cleveland View. Ferry DL17 129 B5
Cleveland View. Fishb TS21 131 C4
Cleves Ave. Ferry DL17 129 C5
Cleves Cl. Ferry DL17 129 B6
Cleves Cross Cty Jun & Inf Sch. Ferry DL17 129 B6
Cleves Cross Grange. Ferry DL17 129 B6
Cleves Ct. Ferry DL17 129 B7
Cliff Rd. Ryhope SR2 23 A6
Cliff Terr. Eas SR8 63 B4
Cliff Terr. Ryhope SR2 23 A6
Cliff View. Ryhope SR2 23 A7
Cliffe Way. Darl DL1 224 C8
Clifford Ave. Bish Au DL14 148 B5

Gladstone Terr. Binch DL14 127 A4
Gladstone Terr. Birt DH3 9 B4
Gladstone Terr. Coxhoe DH6 105 F3
Gladstone Terr. 9 Ferry DL17 129 B5
Gladstone Terr. Pens DH4 21 F8
Gladstone Villas. Ferry DL17 129 B4
Glaisdale. Spenny DL16 103 E1
Glaisdale Gdns. Shild DL4 149 B1
Glamis Cres. R Gill NE39 2 B4
Glamis Rd. Darl DL1 209 D6
Glamis Terr. Even DL14 167 C7
Glamis Villas. Birt DH3 9 C6
Glanton Cl. C le S DH2 20 A2
Glanton Terr. 2 Peter SR8 86 B6
Glastonbury Cl. Spenny DL16 103 E3
Gleaston Ct. Peter SR8 85 B3
Glebe Ave. Eas SR8 63 D4
Glebe Dr. Seaham SR7 22 F2
Glebe Est. Seaham SR7 22 F2
Glebe Houses. Ferry DL17 128 F6
Glebe Rd. Darl DL1 209 B8
Glebe Rd. G Stain TS21 173 D1
Glebe Sch. Darl DL1 209 B8
Glebe Terr. Eas SR8 63 D4
Glebe View. Frost DL13 96 B6
Glebe View. Murton SR7 40 E4
Glebe Villas. Cornf DL17 105 E1
Glebeside. Satley DL13 53 B3
Glebeside. Wit Gil DH7 57 B8
Glen Barr. C le S DH2 20 B4
Glen Cl. R Gill NE39 1 E3
Glen Hill Sch. Eas SR8 63 A4
Glen Hill Sch. Eas SR8 63 D5
Glen Terr. C le S DH2 20 A4
Glen's Flats. H Pitt DH6 60 B5
Glenavon Ave. C le S DH2 20 B4
Glenburn Cl. Wash NE38 9 F3
Glencoe Ave. C le S DH2 20 B4
Glencoe Terr. R Gill NE39 1 C1
Glencot Gr. Haw SR7 63 A7
Glendale Cl. Blay NE21 1 F8
Glendale Dr. Darl DL3 223 D7
Gleneagles Rd. Darl DL1 209 E7
Gleneagles Rd. 8 Hartle TS27 111 C4
Glenfield Rd. Darl DL3 223 D7
Glenholme Cl. Wash NE38 9 F3
Glenholme Dr. Crook DL15 100 F3
Glenhurst Cotts. Eas SR8 63 D4
Glenhurst Dr. Whick NE16 2 F4
Glenhurst Rd. Eas SR8 63 D4
Glenhurst Terr. Murton SR7 40 D3
Glenlude Ct. Cons DH8 14 C3
Glenmeads. Kimble DH2 35 F4
Glenmere. Spenny DL16 103 E2
Glenmore. Cons DH8 31 C8
Glenmore Ave. C le S DH2 20 C4
Glenroy Gdns. C le S DH2 20 B4
Glenside. Cons DH8 14 D6
Glenside Terr. C le St DH2 19 F4
Glenuce. Birt DH3 9 E3
Globe Cl. 19 Darl DL1 209 B1
Gloucester Cl. Gr Lum DH3 37 A6
Gloucester Pl. Darl DL1 209 C4
Gloucester Pl. Peter SR8 85 B7
Gloucester Rd. Cons DH8 15 B1
Gloucester Terr. Hasw DH6 61 E1
Gloucestershire Dr. Belm DH1 59 C3
Goatbeck Terr. Brand DH7 79 D5
Goathland Cl. N Silk SR3 22 C7
Goathland Dr. N Silk SR3 22 B6
Goldcrest Rd. Wash NE38 9 F3
Golden Acre. Cons DH8 14 D5
Golden Gr. Chilt DL17 150 F8
Goldhill La. Mugg DH8 29 A4
Goldsmith Ave. Hartle TS24 111 E4
Golf Course Rd. S Row DH4 21 F5
Gomer Terr. Bish Au DL14 126 B1
Gonville Ct. Darl DL1 209 B6
Good Ave. Trim TS29 107 E4
Good St. Tanf L DH9 17 E8
Goodburn Pl. Mid in T DL12 160 D7
Goodison Way. Darl DL1 209 E3
Goodwell Lea. Brance DH7 78 E1
Goodwood Cl. Cons DH8 14 E6
Goodyear Cres. Durham DH1 59 B1
Gordon Ave. Peter SR8 85 F7
Gordon Bank. Egg DL12 162 B5
Gordon Cl. Darl DL1 209 E7
Gordon La. Even DL14 167 B8
Gordon Terr. 3 Bish Au DL14 148 B8
Gordon Terr. Ferry DL17 129 A5
Gordon Terr. 3 Ryhope SR2 23 A6
Gordon Terr. Stanl DH9 17 F8
Gordon Terr. Wols DL13 97 F7
Gore Hill Est. Thorn DH6 83 C4
Gorecock La. M Law DH7 & DH9 32 B8
Gorleston Way. Silk SR3 22 A4
Gorsedale Gr. Belm DH1 59 D3
Gort Pl. Durham DH1 58 F3
Gort Rd. New Ay DL5 171 D7
Gouldsmith Gdns. Darl DL1 209 E5
Goundry Ave. Ryhope SR2 23 A6
Gower Wlk. Hartle TS26 111 E1
Gowland Sq. Murton SR7 40 B3
Graham Ct. 1 Darl DL1 209 B1
Graham Ct. Sacr DH7 35 C3
Graham Sports Ctr The. Durham DH1 80 E7
Graham St. Stanh DL13 71 B3
Graham Terr. H Pitt DH6 60 B5
Graham Way The. Seaham SR7 41 B6
Graham's Cotts. Sunni DL13 76 A1
Grainger St. Bish Au DL14 126 B1
Grainger St. Darl DL1 224 A8
Grainger St. Spenny DL16 104 B1
Grampian Ave. C le S DH2 20 B2
Grampian Ct. Ann Pl DH9 16 E3
Grampian Dr. Peter SR8 85 B5
Grampian Way. Chilt DL17 151 A8
Granaries The. Fence DH4 38 B8
Granary The. Grind TS22 155 C2
Granby Terr. Wing TS28 84 E1
Grand View. Sherb DH6 81 F8
Grange Ave. Bish Au DL14 148 E6
Grange Ave. Eas SR8 63 B3
Grange Ave. Hur on T DL2 235 A8
Grange Bank. Hunw DL15 125 A4
Grange Cl. Peter SR8 85 D8
Grange Cotts. Whorl DL12 202 F3
Grange Cres. Coxhoe DH6 106 A4
Grange Ct. New Ay DL5 171 E8
Grange Ct. W Pel DH2 19 B5
Grange Est. Kibble NE11 8 C6
Grange Park Cres. Bowb DH6 105 E8
Grange Rd. Belm DH1 59 C4
Grange Rd. Darl DL1 & DL2 223 E7
Grange Rd. Stanl DH9 17 D6
Grange St. Cons DH8 31 B7
Grange St. Pelton DH2 19 E7
Grange Terr. C le St DH2 19 D4
Grange Terr. Kibble NE11 8 C6
Grange Terr. Medom DH8 4 B1
Grange Terr. Shot Co DH6 84 C7
Grange Terr. Trim TS29 107 D3
Grange Terr. Whorl DL12 202 F3
Grange The. New Ay DL17 150 D2
Grange The. Tanf L DH9 17 C8
Grange View. Bish Au DL14 148 F8
Grange View. E Rain DH5 38 D5
Grangeside. Darl DL3 223 D7
Grangeside. Heigh DL5 170 C4
Grant St. 3 Peter SR8 86 A7
Grantham Ave. Seaham SR7 41 A7
Granton Cl. Darl DL3 208 B1
Grants Cres. Seaham SR7 41 D7
Granville Ave. Ann Pl DH9 16 F4
Granville Ave. 3 Shild DL4 148 F1
Granville Cl. Chilt DL17 151 A8
Granville Cl. Shild DL4 148 F1
Granville Rd. Bish Au DL14 148 A6
Granville Rd. Peter SR8 85 F5
Granville Terr. Binch DL14 126 F5
Granville Terr. Wh Hi DH6 83 F3
Grape La. Durham DH1 58 C1
Grasmere. Birt DH3 9 E2
Grasmere. Spenny DL16 103 E2
Grasmere Ave. Bish Au DL14 147 B1
Grasmere Ave. E Lane DH5 61 C8
Grasmere Cres. Blay NE21 2 B8
Grasmere Gr. Crook DL15 100 F3
Grasmere Mews. Leadg DH8 15 D4
Grasmere Rd. C le S DH2 20 B1
Grasmere Rd. Darl DL1 224 B8
Grasmere Rd. Ferry DL17 128 F5
Grasmere Rd. Peter SR8 85 E7
Grasmere Terr. Murton SR7 40 D2
Grasmere Terr. S Hett DH6 62 B7
Grasmere Terr. Stanl DH9 17 D4
Grass St. Darl DL1 209 A4
Grassdale. Belm DH1 59 D3
Grasshill Cswy. St J Ch DL13 90 A8
Grassholme. 12 Darl DL2 224 C8
Grassholme La. Holw DL12 179 E8
Grassholme Pl. 3 New Ay DL5 171 A7
Grasslees. Wash NE38 20 F8
Gravel Wlks. 1 H le Sp DH5 38 F8
Gray Ave. C le S DH2 20 B2
Gray Ave. Durham DH1 58 B5
Gray Ave. Murton SR7 40 C3
Gray Ave. Sherb DH6 59 F2
Gray Ct. Eas SR8 63 D4
Gray La. Bar Cas DL12 201 A5
Gray Sq. Wing TS28 108 E8
Gray St. Bish Au DL14 148 F4
Gray St. Cons DH8 14 E3
Gray Terr. Ann Pl DH9 17 C5
Gray's Terr. Durham DH1 58 A1
Graylands. Wash NE38 20 E8
Grayson Rd. Spenny DL16 127 D6
Graythwaite. C le St DH2 19 F3
Great Gates. Bish Au DL14 148 C8
Great North Rd. Darl DL1 209 A8
Greathead Cres. New Ay DL5 171 E6
Green Cres. Coxhoe DH6 106 A4
Green Ct. Esh DH7 55 F4
Green La. Bar Cas DL12 201 C6
Green La. Bish Au DL14 148 B3
Green La. Bish Au DL14 148 B8
Green La. Darl DL1 209 B8
Green La. Darl DL1 209 C7
Green La. Durham DH1 58 E1
Green La. Durham DH1 58 F2
Green La. Hasw DH6 61 B3
Green La. Holm DH7 & DH9 33 E7
Green La. Hunw DL15 125 B5
Green La. New Ay DL5 172 A2
Green La. Satley DL13 52 E5
Green La. Satley DL13 52 E8
Green La. Seaton DH5 & SR7 39 F6
Green La. Shild DL14 148 F4
Green La. Shild DL4 149 A2
Green La. Spenny DL16 104 C1
Green La. Wing TS29 107 E8
Green La. Wycl DL12 220 B7
Green Lane Ind Est. Spenny DL16 104 C2
Green Law. Wit Gil DH7 35 B1
Green Leas. Carl TS21 195 C8
Green Rise. By Gr DL16 102 E1
Green Rising. Hunw DL15 125 D5
Green St. Cons DH8 14 C7
Green St. Cons DH8 14 F3
Green St. Darl DL1 209 B1
Green St. Leadg DH8 15 C4
Green St. Seaham SR7 41 D7
Green The. Bish TS21 194 C7
Green The. Bish Mi DL17 130 C4
Green The. Braf DL1 192 B7
Green The. C le S DH2 20 B3
Green The. Chopw NE17 4 B8
Green The. Cleas DL2 222 E7
Green The. Cockf DL13 166 D5
Green The. Cornf DL17 105 E2
Green The. Elwick TS27 134 D5
Green The. Even DL14 167 D6
Green The. H Con DL2 206 F3
Green The. 2 H le Sp DH5 38 F8
Green The. H Shin DH1 81 B4
Green The. Haw SR7 63 B7
Green The. Head DL2 188 B2
Green The. Hett DH6 104 E6
Green The. Hur on T DL2 224 D1
Green The. Kimble DH2 35 F4
Green The. New Ay DL5 171 E1
Green The. Peter SR8 85 A4
Green The. R Gill NE39 1 C2
Green The. Spenny DH1 104 A3
Green The. Staint DL12 201 E8
Green The. Stapl DL2 223 A5
Green The. Wit Pk DL14 125 A1
Green's Bank. Beam DH9 19 A7
Greenacres. Pelton DH2 19 D7
Greenacres Rd. Cons DH8 14 D5
Greenbank Cl. Trim TS29 131 D8
Greenbank Hospl. Darl DL3 208 E3
Greenbank Rd. Darl DL3 208 E3
Greenbank St. C le S DH3 20 D4
Greencroft. S Hett DH6 62 B7
Greencroft Cl. Darl DL3 208 D1
Greencroft Comp Lower Sch. Ann Pl DH9 17 B4
Greencroft Comp Sch. Ann Pl DH9 16 E4
Greencroft Ind Est. Ann Pl DH9 16 E2
Greencroft Ind Pk. Ann Pl DH9 16 E2
Greencroft Rd. Cons DH8 31 C8
Greencroft Terr. Ann Pl DH9 16 E3
Greendale Gdns. H le H DH5 38 F2
Greenfield Cl. Hur on T DL2 224 C2
Greenfield Comp Sch. New Ay DL5 170 F7
Greenfield Cotts. Crook DL15 100 F4
Greenfield St. By Gr DL16 102 E1
Greenfield Terr. Ann Pl DH9 16 F4
Greenfield Way. New Ay DL5 170 F7
Greenfields. Bish Au DL14 147 A4
Greenfields. Coth DL12 182 E3
Greenfields. 7 Ferry DL17 129 A6
Greenfields. Ouston DH2 9 A2
Greenfields Ind Est. Bish Au DL14 147 F4
Greenfields Rd. Bish Au DL14 147 D5
Greenfinch Cl. Wash NE38 9 F3
Greenford. Kibble NE11 8 D6
Greenford La. Kibble DH2 & NE11 8 F6
Greengates La. Mick DL12 161 C5
Greenhead. Crook DL15 100 E1
Greenhead. Wash NE38 9 F4
Greenhill Rd. Heigh DL5 170 C1
Greenhills Est. Wing TS28 84 E1
Greenhills Terr. Wh Hi DH6 83 F3
Greenland Rd. Esh DH7 55 D4
Greenlands. Stanl DH9 17 D4
Greenlea. Elwick TS27 134 C5
Greenlea Cl. H Spen NE39 1 A3
Greenlee Garth. New Ay DL5 171 A8
Greenless La. E Lay DL11 221 C5
Greenless La. Force DL11 221 C5
Greenmount Rd. Darl DL3 223 E8
Greenrigg La. Mick DL12 161 A2
Greenside Ave. Peter SR8 85 F7
Greenside Ct. Hur on T DL2 224 C1
Greenside Pl. Crook DL15 101 A2
Greentree La. Ann Pl DH9 16 E5
Greenway Ct. Cons DH8 31 C8
Greenway The. M St G DL2 225 E7
Greenways. Cons DH8 31 C8
Greenways. Will DL15 101 E2
Greenways. Wols DL13 97 F8
Greenwell Rd. New Ay DL5 171 D7
Greenwell St. Darl DL1 224 A8
Greenwells Garth. Cound DL14 149 C8
Greenwood Ave. Burnh DH7 33 D4
Greenwood Cl. Wh Hi DH6 84 A3
Gregory Terr. 4 Fence DH4 38 A8
Gregory Terr. 10 Ferry DL17 129 A6
Gregson St. Sacr DH7 35 C3
Gregson Terr. S Hett DH6 62 B6
Gregson Terr. Seaham SR7 22 F1
Grendon Gdns. M St G DL2 225 E8
Grenwood Ave. H le Sp DH4 38 C8
Gresham Cl. Darl DL1 209 B5
Gresley Rd. Shot Co SR8 85 A6
Greta Bridge Bank. Gr Br DL12 219 A7
Greta Pl. Lanch DH7 32 F3
Greta Rd. Bar Cas DL12 201 B6
Greta St N. Pelton DH2 19 C6
Greta St S. Pelton DH2 19 C6
Greville Way. New Ay DL5 171 E6
Grewburn La. Copley DL13 165 C8
Grey Coll. Durham DH1 80 C7
Grey Gables. Brand DH7 79 C5
Grey Gdns. Cound DL14 149 B8
Grey Ridges. Brand DH7 79 C4
Grey St. Bish Au DL14 148 B8
Grey St. Crook DL15 100 F4
Grey St. Darl DL1 209 B3
Grey St. Newf DL14 126 B7
Grey Terr. 3 Ferry DL17 129 B5
Grey Terr. 10 Ryhope SR2 22 F6
Grey Terr. 2 Ryhope SR2 23 A6
Greyfriars Cl. Darl DL3 208 A1
Greylingstadt Terr. The Mid DH9 18 A3
Greystones. Ludw DH6 83 C7
Greywood Cl. Hartle TS27 111 C5
Grindon Ct. New Ay DL5 150 E1
Grindon Way. New Ay DL5 171 D1
Grinstead Way. Belm DH1 59 D5
Grinton Park Way. 4 Darl DL1 224 C7
Grisedale Rd. Peter SR8 85 E6
Groat Ave. New Ay DL5 171 E4
Groat Dr. New Ay DL5 171 E5
Groat Rd. New Ay DL5 171 E4
Groat Way. New Ay DL5 171 E4
Grosmont. Gr Lum DH3 37 A7
Grosvener Terr. Cons DH8 15 A3
Grosvenor Cl. Stanh DL13 71 A3
Grosvenor St. Darl DL1 224 A8
Grosvenor Terr. Trim TS29 107 F5
Grove Cotts. 8 Birt DH3 9 C4
Grove Ct. Hett DH6 104 E5
Grove Ct. Shot Co DH6 84 C5
Grove Pk. Bar Cas DL12 201 A6
Grove Rd. Bish Au DL14 148 A7
Grove Rd. Brand DH7 79 B3
Grove Rd Flats. Brand DH7 79 A3
Grove Rd. Tow Law DL13 75 B3
Grove St. Durham DH1 58 B1
Grove Terr. Brand DH1 & DH7 79 E6
Grove Terr. Burnop NE16 6 B6
Grove The. Burnh DH7 33 D4
Grove The. Chilt DL17 150 F7
Grove The. Cornf DL17 105 E1
Grove The. Coxhoe DH6 106 A3
Grove The. Durham DH1 58 A3
Grove The. Eas SR8 63 A4
Grove The. H le Sp DH5 38 D6
Grove The. R Gill NE39 1 F1
Grove The. Ryhope SR2 22 F6
Gudmunsen Ave. Bish Au DL14 148 A4
Guildford Cl. Darl DL1 209 E5
Gullane Cl. Stanl DH9 18 B6
Gully Rd. Wing TS28 108 E8
Gunn La. New Ay DL5 171 F6
Gurlish Terr. Cound DL14 127 B1
Gurney Pease Cty Prim Sch. Darl DL1 209 B4
Gurney St. Darl DL1 209 A4
Gurney Terr. Bish Au DL14 149 A5
Gurney Valley. Bish Au DL14 149 A5
Gurney Way. New Ay DL5 171 D4
Guthrum Pl. New Ay DL5 150 C1

H. W. Cocks Memorial Homes The. M St G DL2 225 E8
Hackworth Cl. Ferry DL17 128 E5
Hackworth Cl. New Ay DL5 171 E5
Hackworth Cl. Shild DL4 170 A8
Hackworth Ind Est. Shild DL4 169 F8
Hackworth Rd. B Coll TS27 86 D4
Hackworth Rd. Eas SR8 62 F1
Hackworth St. Ferry DL17 128 E5
Hackworth St. Shild DL4 149 A1
Hadleigh Cl. Sedge TS21 153 A5
Hadrian Ave. C le S DH3 20 D5
Hadrian Ct. Darl DL3 223 E8
Hadrians Way. Ebch DH8 3 E3
Hagg La. By Gr DL16 103 A1
Hagg Rd. By Gr DL16 126 F8
Haggs La. Shild DL14 & DL4 169 B8
Haig Cres. Durham DH1 59 A1
Haig St. Darl DL3 208 F5
Haig St. Ferry DL17 129 C4
Haig Terr. Ferry DL17 128 E6
Haldon Pl. Peter SR8 85 B5
Hale Rise. Peter SR8 85 E6
Hales Cl. B Coll TS27 86 D3
Half Moon La. Spenny DL16 104 C1
Hall Ave. Ush M DH7 57 A2
Hall Cl. Seaton SR7 22 D1
Hall Cl. W Rain DH4 38 A2
Hall Cres. Peter SR8 63 F1
Hall Farm Ct. Trim TS29 107 D1
Hall Farm. H Shin DH1 80 F6
Hall Farm Rd. Silk SR3 22 A5
Hall Gdns. Sherb DH6 60 A1
Hall La. Cald DL11 221 E8
Hall La. H le Sp DH5 38 F7
Hall La. H Shin DH1 80 F5
Hall La. Hasw DH6 61 F3
Hall La. Heigh DL5 170 D2
Hall La. W Rain DH4 38 A2
Hall Lane Est. Will DL15 101 F2
Hall Lea. Sedge TS21 153 A7
Hall Rd. Cons DH8 14 C2
Hall Rd. Esh DH7 55 F4
Hall St. Bar Cas DL12 201 A5
Hall Terr. Will DL15 102 A2
Hall View Gdns. How le W DL15 124 D8
Hall View Gr. Darl DL3 208 A3
Hall View. Hunw DL15 125 D7
Hall Wlks. Eas SR8 63 A3
Hallam Rd. Peter SR8 85 D7
Hallfield Cl. Silk SR3 22 A5
Hallfield Dr. Eas SR8 63 A3
Hallgarth. Kir Me DL16 128 A3
Hallgarth La. H Pitt DH6 60 B5
Hallgarth Rd. Trim TS29 131 D8
Hallgarth St. Durham DH1 80 D8
Hallgarth St. Sherb DH6 59 F1
Hallgarth Terr. Ferry DL17 129 A6
Hallgarth Terr. Lanch DH7 32 F3
Hallgarth The. Durham DH1 80 D8
Hallgarth View. Durham DH1 80 D8
Hallgarth View. H Pitt DH6 60 C5
Hallgarth Villas. Sherb DH6 60 A1
Halliday Gr. Brand DH7 79 D5
Hallimond Rd. Escomb DL14 147 D7
Hallington Head. New Ay DL5 170 F7
Halnaby Ave. Darl DL3 207 F2
Halton Rd. Durham DH1 58 D5
Hambledon Ave. C le S DH2 20 B2
Hambledon Pl. Peter SR8 85 A5
Hambleton Ct. New Ay DL5 171 A8
Hambleton Dr. Seaham SR7 41 B8
Hambleton Gr. 4 Darl DL1 209 C6
Hambleton Rd. Cound DL14 149 C8
Hambleton Way. Chilt DL17 151 A8
Hamilton Ct. Shot Co DH6 84 C6
Hamilton Ct. Thor Th TS21 175 E3
Hamilton Dr. Darl DL1 209 C7
Hamilton St. Peter SR8 85 F7
Hamilton Terr. Edmon DH7 35 B6
Hammer Square Bank. Beam DH9 7 F1
Hammermill La. Shot DH8 13 D7
Hammond Dr. Darl DL1 223 F6
Hampshire Pl. Bish Au DL14 148 C5
Hampshire Pl. Peter SR8 85 B7
Hampshire Rd. Belm DH1 59 C3
Hampton Ct. C le S DH3 20 D7
Hamsteels Bank. Lanch DH7 55 A6
Hamsteels Cty Jun & Inf Sch. Esh W DH7 55 C1
Hamsteels La. Lanch DH7 55 B6
Hamsterley Cl. Gr Lum DH3 37 B7
Hamsterley Cres. Durham DH1 58 D6
Hamsterley Ct. 6 Silk SR3 22 A6
Hamsterley Cty Jun Mix & Inf Sch. Hamst DL13 123 A3
Hamsterley Dr. Crook DL15 100 D3
Hamsterley Gdns. Ann Pl DH9 16 F4
Hamsterley Rd. New Ay DL5 171 B8
Hamsterley St. Darl DL3 208 E4
Handel Terr. Wh Hi DH6 83 E2
Handley Cres. E Rain DH5 38 C4
Handley St. Peter SR8 85 F7
Hangingstone La. Ann Pl DH8 & DH9 16 C3
Hanover Cl. Darl DL3 208 A1
Hanover Ct. Bish Au DL14 148 C6
Hanover Ct. 1 Durham DH1 58 B1
Hanover Gdns. Bish Au DL14 148 C6
Hansard Cl. New Ay DL5 170 F4
Hansons Bldgs. M St G DL2 225 F8
Harap Rd. Fishb DL17 & TS21 131 B7
Harap Rd. Kelloe DL17 130 E8
Harbour Wlk. Seaham SR7 41 C7
Harcourt St. Darl DL3 208 F4
Harding Terr. Darl DL3 208 E4
Hardinge Rd. New Ay DL5 171 D8
Hardings. Hunw DL12 182 B6
Hardisty Cres. Bish Au DL14 148 A5
Hardwick Cl. Darl DL1 209 D6
Hardwick Ct. New Ay DL5 171 D8
Hardwick Hall Ctry Pk. Sedge TS21 152 F7
Hardwick Rd. Sedge TS21 153 A7
Hardwick St. B Coll TS27 86 C3
Hardwick St. Peter SR8 86 A6
Hardy St. Seaham SR7 41 D7
Hardy Terr. Crook DL15 100 E4
Hardy Terr. Stanl DH9 17 C4
Hare Law Sch. Ann Pl DH9 16 E6
Harebell Meadows. New Ay DL17 150 D2
Harelaw. Pelton DH2 19 D6
Harelaw Gdns. Ann Pl DH9 16 E6
Harelaw Ind Est. Dipton DH9 16 E7
Harewood Gr. Darl DL3 223 E8
Harewood Hill. Darl DL3 223 E8
Harewood Terr. Darl DL1 & DL3 223 E8
Hargill Dr. Wash NE38 21 A8
Hargill Gr. How le W DL15 124 D7
Hargill Haven. How le W DL15 124 D7
Hargill Rd. How le W DL15 124 D7
Hargreave Terr. Darl DL1 209 A1
Harker St. 5 Shild DL4 148 F1
Harlech Wlk. Hartle TS26 111 E1
Harley Gr. Darl DL1 209 E6
Harley St. Brand DH7 79 D3
Harley Terr. Sherb DH6 59 F2
Harmire Cl. Bar Cas DL12 201 A7
Harmire Enterprise Pk. Bar Cas DL12 201 A8
Harmire Rd. Bar Cas DL12 201 A7
Harold Wilson Dr. Hesl TS27 85 F1
Harper Bglws. Wh Hi DH6 83 E1
Harperley Gdns. Ann Pl DH9 16 E5
Harperley La. Tant DH9 17 B7
Harperley Rd. Ann Pl DH9 16 F5
Harperley Terr. Fir T DL15 100 A1
Harpers Terr. M St G DL2 210 E1
Harpington View. Mordon TS21 152 C1
Harras Bank. Birt DH3 9 C3
Harraton Terr. 12 Birt DH3 9 C4
Harraton Terr. Bourn DH3 21 C7
Harringay Cres. Darl DL1 209 E3
Harris St. Darl DL1 224 D8
Harrison Cl. Peter SR8 85 E5
Harrison Cl. Shild DL4 170 A7
Harrison Cres. Bish Au DL14 147 F4
Harrison Ct. Birt DH3 9 C3
Harrison Garth. Sherb DH6 59 F2
Harrison Pl. Hartle TS24 111 F2
Harrison St. Tow Law DL13 75 B2
Harrison Terr. Darl DL3 208 E4
Harrison Terr. Eas SR8 63 D4
Harrogate Terr. Murton SR7 40 C3
Harrowgate Hill Cty Inf Sch. Darl DL3 209 A6
Harrowgate Hill Cty Jun Sch. Darl DL3 208 F6
Harrowgate Hill Cty Jun Sch. Darl DL3 209 A6
Harrowgate Village. Darl DL1 209 A8
Harry St. Darl DL3 208 F5
Hart Cres. B Rocks TS27 86 F1
Hart Pastures. Hart TS27 111 A2
Hart Rd. Hartle TS24 & TS27 111 D3
Hart View. Trim TS29 131 E8
Hart Village Prim Sch. Hart TS27 110 F3
Hartbrigg La. Hi Eth DL14 146 E3
Hartford Rd. Darl DL3 223 D8
Harthope Cl. Wash NE38 20 F8
Harthope Gr. Bish Au DL14 147 F5
Harthope Rd. St J Ch DL13 91 C8
Hartington St. Cons DH8 15 A3
Hartland Dr. Birt DH3 9 D3
Hartlea Ave. Darl DL1 192 A2

Langdale Terr. Hams NE17 4 A5
Langdale Way. Lang Pk DH7 56 D6
Langdale Wlk. Bish Au DL14 147 F4
Langdon Gdns. Ann Pl DH9 16 E5
Langholm Cres. Darl DL3 208 E1
Langhurst. Sland SR2 22 E8
Langley Ave. Burnh DH7 33 D4
Langley Cres. Brand DH7 79 D5
Langley Dr. Spenny DL16 128 A8
Langley Garth. Staind DL2 186 F5
Langley Gr. Bish Au DL14 148 A6
Langley La. Lang Pk DH7 34 B2
Langley Moor Ind Est. Brand DH7 79 E5
Langley Moor Jun & Inf Sch. Brand DH7 79 E6
Langley Park Cty Inf Sch. Lang Pk DH7 56 C7
Langley Park Sch. Lang Pk DH7 56 C6
Langley Rd. Durham DH1 58 C6
Langley Rd. New Ay DL5 171 E7
Langley St. Lang Pk DH7 56 C7
Langley Terr. Ann Pl DH9 17 A4
Langley Terr. Burnh DH7 33 D5
Langley View. Stanl DH9 17 C3
Langleydale CE Controlled Sch. Kinn DL12 164 C1
Langmere. Spenny DL16 103 E2
Langthorne Ave. 10 Peter SR8 86 B6
Langton. Lang DL2 188 A3
Langton Lea. H Shin DH1 81 C5
Langton Terr. Bourn DH4 21 E2
Langton Wlk. 11 Darl DL2 224 C8
Lanivet Cl. 4 Sland SR2 22 F8
Lansbury Cl. Birt DH3 9 B6
Lansbury Dr. Birt DH3 9 B5
Lansbury Dr. Murton SR7 40 C3
Lansdown Way. Will DL15 101 E1
Lansdowne. Sland SR2 22 E7
Lansdowne St. Darl DL3 209 A5
Lapwing Cl. Wash NE38 9 F3
Lapwing Ct. Burnop NE16 6 C5
Larch Ave. 2 H le Sp DH4 38 C8
Larch Ave. Shild DL4 149 B1
Larch St. Cons DH8 14 F3
Larch Terr. Tant DH9 6 A1
Larch Terr. The Mid DH9 18 B3
Larches Rd. Durham DH1 58 A3
Larches The. Burnop NE16 6 B7
Larches The. Esh W DH7 77 D8
Larchfield Gdns. Crook DL15 100 D4
Larchfield House. 13 Darl DL3 208 F1
Larchfield St. Darl DL3 208 F1
Larkspur Cl. Tanf L DH9 17 D8
Larkspur Dr. Darl DL1 209 C2
Lartington Cl. Gr Lum DH3 37 B6
Lartington Green La. Lart DL12 199 D8
Lartington La. Lart DL12 200 C7
Larwood Ct. Ann Pl DH9 16 E3
Lascelles Ave. New Ay DL5 171 A8
Latimer Rd. Darl DL1 209 D5
Laude Bank. Esh DH7 55 D4
Launceston. Gr Lum DH3 37 A7
Laura St. Seaham SR7 41 D6
Laurel Ave. Durham DH1 59 A1
Laurel Ave. Seaham SR7 41 B7
Laurel Avenue Cty Inf Sch. Durham DH1 59 A1
Laurel Avenue Cty Jun Sch. Durham DH1 58 F1
Laurel Cres. Beam DH9 19 B7
Laurel Cres. Thorn DH6 83 C3
Laurel Cres. Trim TS29 107 F5
Laurel Ct. C le S DH2 20 B5
Laurel Ct. Shild DL4 170 B8
Laurel Dr. Leadg DH8 15 D3
Laurel Gdns. Crook DL15 100 D4
Laurel Rd. Chilt DL17 129 C2
Laurel St. Darl DL3 208 E3
Laurel Terr. Burnop NE16 5 F6
Laurel Terr. Sadb DL2 210 E6
Lauren Ct. Eas SR8 63 C4
Lauriston Cl. Darl DL3 208 A1
Lavender Gdns. Sacr DH7 35 D3
Laverick Terr. Ann Pl DH9 17 A3
Lavers Rd. Birt DH3 9 C5
Lawnhead Sq. Silk SR3 22 B6
Lawns The. E Lane DH5 39 C1
Lawns The. Seaham SR7 41 A6
Lawnswood. H le Sp DH5 38 F7
Lawrence St. Darl DL1 209 B1
Lawson Ct. 4 C le S DH2 20 C2
Lawson Rd. Bowb DH6 81 D1
Lawson Terr. Durham DH1 58 B1
Lawson Terr. H le H DH5 39 B1
Lawson's St. Trim TS29 108 A4
Lax Terr. Crook DL15 100 D3
Laxford. Birt DH3 9 D2
Laxford Ct. Silk SR3 22 A5
Layburn Pl. Peter SR8 85 C7
Layton Ct. New Ay DL5 150 D1
Lazenby Cl. Darl DL3 208 B3
Lazenby Cres. Darl DL3 208 B3
Lazenby Gr. Darl DL3 208 B3
Lazenby Rd. Hartle TS24 111 E4
Lea Gn. Birt DH3 9 E1
Lea Gn. Wols DL13 97 E7
Lea La. Eas SR8 63 B6
Lea Riggs. W Rain DH4 38 A2
Lea Side. Cons DH8 31 B8
Leach Gr. Darl DL3 208 C5
Lead La. Newl DH8 & NE43 3 C6
Leadenhall St. Darl DL1 209 A3
Leadgate Cty Inf Sch. Leadg DH8 15 C3
Leadgate Cty Jun Sch. Leadg DH8 15 D3
Leadgate Ind Est. Leadg DH8 15 E2
Leadgate Rd. Cons DH8 15 B4
Leadgate Rd. Leadg DH8 15 B4
Leadgate Terr. Wols DL13 98 A7
Leadpipe La. Coth DL12 182 D4
Leafield Rd. Darl DL1 224 A8
Leamside Cty Jun Sch. W Rain DH4 37 F1
Leander Ave. C le S DH3 20 D7
Leas The. Darl DL1 209 A6
Leas The. Sedge TS21 153 B5
Leases The. Bowb DH6 105 D8
Leaside. New Ay DL5 171 D4
Leaside N. New Ay DL5 171 D4
Leasyde Wlk. Whick NE16 2 F5
Leatham. Sland SR2 22 E8
Leazes Ct. Durham DH1 58 D2
Leazes Hospl. Wols DL13 97 D8
Leazes La. Bish Au DL14 147 C3
Leazes La. Durham DH1 58 E2
Leazes La. Wols DL13 97 D7
Leazes Pl. Durham DH1 58 D2
Leazes Rd. Durham DH1 58 D2
Leazes Rise. Peter SR8 85 F5
Leazes The. Burnop NE16 5 F6
Leazes View. R Gill NE39 1 D2
Leazes View. Wols DL13 97 E7
Leazes Villas. Burnop NE16 6 A6
Lee Gn. New Ay DL5 171 D5
Lee Hill Ct. Lanch DH7 32 E3
Lee Terr. Eas SR8 63 C4
Lee Terr. H le H DH5 39 B2
Lee Terr. Shot Co DH6 84 C6
Leechmere Cres. Seaham SR7 22 F1
Leechmere Ind Est. Sland SR2 22 F8
Leechmere View. 5 Sland SR2 22 F8
Leechmere Way. Sland SR2 22 F8
Leechmire Terr. Hut Hen TS27 109 C5
Leehall La. Mordon DL1 & DL5 172 E4
Leeholme. H le Sp DH5 38 F7
Leeholme Ct. Ann Pl DH9 17 A3
Leeholme Rd. Cound DL14 149 D8
Leekworth Gdns. Mid in T DL12 160 E7
Leekworth La. Mid in T DL12 160 F7
Leeman's La. Hett DH6 104 F5
Lees St. Stanl DH9 17 F7
Lees Wlk. Cound DL14 149 C8
Leesfield Dr. Brand DH7 79 C3
Leesfield Gdns. Brand DH7 79 C3
Leesfield Rd. Brand DH7 79 C3
Leicester Gr. Darl DL1 209 E5
Leicester Wlk. Peter SR8 85 C8
Leicestershire Dr. Belm DH1 59 D3
Leighton Terr. Birt DH3 9 B5
Leith Gdns. Tanf L DH9 6 D1
Leith Rd. Darl DL3 208 B1
Lendings The. Start DL12 201 A4
Lenin Terr. Chopw NE17 4 C8
Lenin Terr. Stanl DH9 17 F5
Leonard Ropner Dr. St on T TS21 195 F3
Leonard St. Darl DL1 224 B8
Leopold Pl. Bish Au DL14 148 C7
Lerwick Cl. St on T TS21 195 F3
Lesbury Cl. C le St DH2 19 F1
Lesbury Terr. Chopw NE17 4 B8
Leslie St. Bish Au DL14 147 D2
Letch Ave. Haw SR7 63 B8
Letch La. Carl TS19 & TS21 195 E8
Leuchars Ct. Birt DH3 9 C3
Leven Ave. C le S DH2 20 B1
Leven Rd. Bish Au DL14 147 B1
Leven Wlk. Peter SR8 85 C4
Levisham Cl. N Silk SR3 22 C7
Lewes Rd. Darl DL1 224 B8
Lewis Cl. Cr on T DL2 234 F8
Lexington Ct. Brand DH7 79 A2
Leybourne Hold. Birt DH3 9 C6
Leyburn Cl. Urpeth DH2 8 D1
Leyburn Pl. Birt DH3 9 B6
Leyburn Rd. Darl DL1 209 A6
Leyfield Cl. Burdon SR3 22 B5
Leyland Cl. Bowb DH6 81 E2
Liberty Terr. Tant DH9 6 B2
Library Terr. Ann Pl DH9 16 F4
Library Wlk. Ann Pl DH9 16 F4
Lichfield Cl. Gr Lum DH3 37 A6
Lichfield Rd. Cornf DL17 129 F8
Lidcombe Cl. N Silk SR3 22 C7
Liddell Cl. New Ay DL5 171 F6
Liddell Terr. Kibble NE11 8 C6
Liddle Ave. Sherb DH6 59 F1
Liddle Cl. Peter SR8 85 B8
Lidell Terr. Wh Hi DH6 83 E1
Lightfoot Cres. Hartle TS24 & TS26 111 F2
Lightfoot Rd. New Ay DL5 171 C7
Lightfoot Terr. Ferry DL17 128 E5
Lilac Ave. B Rocks TS27 86 F2
Lilac Ave. Durham DH1 58 B5
Lilac Ave. 10 H le Sp DH5 38 E8
Lilac Ave. N Silk SR3 22 B8
Lilac Ave. Sacr DH7 35 C3
Lilac Ave. Sedge TS21 153 B7
Lilac Cl. Carl TS21 175 D1
Lilac Cres. Burnop NE16 6 A6
Lilac Cres. Wing TS29 108 B5
Lilac Ct. Shild DL4 170 B8
Lilac Gdns. Beam DH9 19 B7
Lilac Gdns. Crook DL15 100 D3
Lilac Gr. C le S DH2 20 A5
Lilac Gr. Trim TS29 107 D1
Lilac Pk. Ush M DH7 57 A1
Lilac Pl. Leadg DH8 15 D3
Lilac Rd. Chilt DL17 129 C2
Lilac Sq. Bourn DH4 21 E3
Lilac Terr. Ann Pl DH9 16 E5
Lilac Terr. Shot Co DH6 84 C6
Lilac Way. Hi Eth DL14 146 E5
Lilburn Cl. C le St DH2 36 A8
Lilburn Cl. Shild DL4 148 F1
Lilburne Cres. New Ay DL5 171 D7
Lile Gdns. Sedge TS21 153 B6
Lilian Ave. Sland SR2 22 E8
Lilian Terr. 4 Lang Pk DH7 56 C6
Lilley Terr. R Gill NE39 1 F3
Lilleycroft. R Gill NE39 1 F2
Lillie Terr. Trim TS29 107 D3
Lily Bglws. Dipton DH9 16 E8
Lilywhite Terr. H le H DH5 39 B1
Lime Ave. B Rocks TS27 86 E3
Lime Ave. Darl DL1 209 A8
Lime Ave. H le Sp DH4 38 C8
Lime Gr. Bish Au DL14 148 B4
Lime Gr. Shild DL4 149 B1
Lime La. Mordon DL1 172 C1
Lime La. New Ay DL1 191 F8
Lime Pk. Brand DH7 79 B4
Lime Rd. Ferry DL 17 128 F6
Lime St. Stanl DH9 17 D4
Lime Terr. Bish Au DL14 148 F4
Limecragg Ave. Belm DH1 59 B3
Limehurst Rd. Darl DL3 208 E3
Limekiln La. E Lay DL11 221 D1
Limes The. E Lane DH5 39 D1
Linacre Ct. Peter SR8 85 B5
Linacre Way. Darl DL1 209 B6
Linburn. Wash NE38 21 B8
Linburn Dr. Bish Au DL14 147 F5
Lincoln Ave. N Silk SR3 22 A8
Lincoln Cl. New Ay DL5 171 C7
Lincoln Cres. H le H DH5 38 F4
Lincoln Ct. Darl DL1 209 E4
Lincoln Dr. Will DL15 101 F2
Lincoln Pl. Cons DH8 30 A7
Lincoln Rd. Cons DH8 30 A7
Lincoln Rd. Durham DH1 58 D7
Lincoln St. Cound DL14 149 D8
Lincoln Wlk. Gr Lum DH3 37 A7
Lincoln Wlk. Peter SR8 85 C8
Lincolnshire Cl. Belm DH1 59 C3
Linden Ave. Darl DL3 223 D8
Linden Cl. Shild DL4 170 B8
Linden Ct. Spenny DL16 128 A8
Linden Dr. Darl DL3 223 D8
Linden Dr. Hur on T DL2 235 A8
Linden Gr. Coxhoe DH6 105 F4
Linden Gr. H le Sp DH4 38 D8
Linden Pk. Brand DH7 79 B4
Linden Pl. New Ay DL5 171 A6
Linden Rd. Bear DH7 57 B3
Linden Rd. Bish Au DL14 148 C6
Linden Rd. Cornf DL17 129 E8
Linden Rd. Ferry DL17 129 B5
Linden Terr. Coxhoe DH6 105 F4
Linden Way. Cons DH8 14 E4
Lindesfarne. H Shin DH1 81 B5
Lindisfarne. Peter SR8 85 D4
Lindisfarne. Ryhope SR2 22 E6
Lindisfarne Ave. C le S DH3 20 D3
Lindisfarne Cl. Bish Au DL14 147 E6
Lindisfarne Cl. C le S DH3 20 A1
Lindisfarne Cl. Hartle TS27 111 D3
Lindisfarne Rd. Durham DH1 58 D5
Lindom Ave. C le S DH3 20 D3
Lindon Rd. Stanl DH9 17 E5
Lindrick Dr. Hartle TS27 111 C4
Lindsay St. Bish Au DL14 148 B7
Lindsay St. H le H DH5 39 B5
Lingard Wlk. New Ay DL5 171 E5
Lingdale. Belm DH1 59 D3
Lingey Cl. Sacr DH7 35 B4
Lingfield Cl. Darl DL1 209 F2
Lingfield Gn. Darl DL1 209 E1
Lingfield Rd. Cons DH8 14 E3
Lingfield Way. Darl DL1 209 F1
Lingholme. C le S DH2 20 A4
Lingmell Dene. Cound DL14 127 B1
Links The. Belm DH1 59 D3
Linkway. Sacr DH7 35 C3
Linley Hill. Whick NE16 2 E4
Linskell. Sland SR2 22 E8
Lintfort. C le S DH3 20 E7
Linton Terr. Crook DL15 100 F4
Lintz Green La. Burnop NE16 & NE39 5 C6
Lintz La. Burnop NE16 5 C6
Lintz Terr. Burnop NE16 5 F6
Lintz Terr. Stanl DH9 17 C5
Lintzford Gdns. R Gill NE39 5 D8
Lintzford La. R Gill NE39 1 B1
Lintzford Rd. H Mill NE39 5 C7
Lintzford Rd. R Gill NE39 5 C7
Linwood Gr. Darl DL3 223 D7
Lishman Ave. Crook DL15 100 E4
Lisle Rd. New Ay DL5 171 A8
Lismore Dr. Darl DL1 209 D7
Lister Cl. H le Sp DH5 38 D6
Lister Rd. Peter SR8 85 A8
Lister Terr. Crook DL15 100 E5
Lister Terr E. Wols DL13 97 F7
Lister Terr. Wols DL13 97 F7
Litchfield Rd. Durham DH1 58 D8
Little Eden. Peter SR8 85 D7
Little Hutton La. Hut Ma DL11 220 E7
Little La. New Ay DL5 171 E2
Littlebeck Dr. Darl DL1 209 C5
Littleburn Ind Est. Brand DH7 79 F4
Littleburn La. Brand DH7 79 E5
Littleburn Rd. Brand DH7 79 E4
Littletown La. H Pitt DH6 60 D3
Livingstone St. 17 Cons DH8 14 F3
Lloyd Ave. E Rain DH5 38 C4
Lloyds Terr. 5 Lang Pk DH7 56 C6
Lobley Hill Rd. Brand DH7 79 D4
Lobleyhill Rd. Byer NE16 6 D8
Lobleyhill Rd. Sunn NE16 6 D8
Local Ave. S Hill DH6 60 C1
Lochfield Gdns. Kibble NE11 8 C6
Lock St. Darl DL3 208 F5
Lockhaugh Rd. R Gill NE39 2 A4
Lockyer Cl. New Ay DL5 171 B8
Locomotive St. Darl DL1 209 C6
Lodge Cl. H Mill NE39 5 A5
Lodge La. Mordon DL1 & TS21 172 E1
Lodge St. By Gr DL16 102 E1
Lodge St. Darl DL1 209 A2
Loefield. Gr Lum DH3 37 A8
Logan St. H le H DH5 39 A3
Logan St. Lang Pk DH7 56 C7
Logan Terr. S Hett DH6 61 E8
Lombard Dr. C le S DH3 20 D7
Lomond Ct. 8 Silk SR3 22 A6
Lomond Pl. C le S DH2 20 B1
Lomond Wlk. Bish Au DL14 147 C1
Londonderry Ave. Durham DH1 59 A1
Londonderry Bglws. Eas SR8 63 D5
Londonderry St. N Silk SR3 22 A7
Londonderry St. Seaham SR7 41 E5
Londonderry Terr. Eas SR8 63 D5
Londonderry Terr. N Silk SR3 22 B7
Long Acres. Durham DH1 58 F3
Long Bank. Birt DH3 9 C7
Long Bank. Dalton DL11 233 F4
Long Burn Dr. C le St DH2 19 F2
Long Close La. Gilm DL12 216 A6
Long Close Rd. H Mill NE39 4 F5
Long Cswy. Langth DL11 228 B3
Long Edge. Burnh DH7 34 C4
Long Edge. Sacr DH7 34 C4
Long Gair. Blay NE21 2 A8
Long Garth. Durham DH1 57 F4
Long La. Cockf DL13 & DL2 166 E4
Long La. Newf DL14 126 D7
Long Row. How le W DL15 125 A6
Long Tens Way. New Ay DL3 & DL5 171 C1
Longacre. H le Sp DH4 38 C8
Longclose Bank. Medom DH8,DH9,NE17 & NE39 4 E3
Longdale Gr. St J Ch DL13 67 C1
Longdean Pk. C le S DH3 20 D6
Longedge La. Heal DH7 & DH8 31 C2
Longedge La. Lanch DH7 & DH8 31 C2
Longfellow Ct. Crook DL15 100 C2
Longfellow St. H le Sp DH5 38 E7
Longfield Comp Sch. Darl DL3 208 F7
Longfield Rd. Bish Au DL14 148 D5
Longfield Rd. Darl DL3 208 F6
Longfield Stad. Darl DL3 208 F7
Longhorn Ends. Cows DL13 66 D6
Longlands Dr. H le Sp DH5 38 E7
Longnewton St. Seaham SR7 41 D5
Longshank La. Kibble DH3 9 A6
Lonsdale Ave. Trim TS29 107 E4
Lonsdale. Birt DH3 9 E1
Loop La. Butter DL13 144 F2
Loraine Cres. Darl DL1 223 F7
Loraine Wlk. 1 New Ay DL5 171 C8
Lord Byrons Wlk. Seaham SR7 23 B1
Lord Hyndley Terr. Copley DL13 165 A8
Lord Neville Dr. New Ay DL5 170 F4
Lord St. N Silk SR3 22 B7
Lord St. Seaham SR7 41 D7
Lorimers Cl. Peter SR8 85 B4
Lorn Wlk. Darl DL1 209 D7
Lorne St. E Lane DH5 61 B8
Lorne Terr. Cound DL14 149 C8
Lothian Cl. Birt DH3 9 D1
Lothian Cl. Spenny DL16 127 E7
Loud Terr. Ann Pl DH9 16 D4
Loud View Terr. Ann Pl DH9 16 E3
Lough House Bank. Ferry DL17 129 D4
Louisa Ctr The. Stanl DH9 17 E6
Louisa St. Darl DL1 209 B1
Louisa Terr. Bish Au DL14 147 E3
Louisa Terr. Stanl DH9 17 E6
Louisa Terr. Wit Gil DH7 57 B8
Louise Terr. C le S DH3 20 C3
Louvain Terr. Crook DL15 100 D3
Louvain Terr. H le H DH5 39 A5
Louvain Terr W. H le H DH5 39 A5
Lovaine St. Pelton DH2 19 C6
Lovaine Terr. 8 Ferry DL17 129 B5
Low Albert Terr. Billy R DL15 100 D7
Low Bowes Cl. Even DL14 146 B1
Low Chare. C le S DH3 20 D3
Low Church St. Ann Pl DH9 16 F5
Low Dowfold. Crook DL15 101 A5
Low Downs Rd. H le H DH5 39 A6
Low Dyke St. Trim TS29 108 A4
Low Etherley. Hi Eth DL14 146 F6
Low Flatts Rd. C le S DH2 & DH3 20 C6
Low Gn. Gain DL2 205 A6
Low Gn. H Shin DH1 80 F6
Low Gn. New Ay DL17 150 E2
Low Graham St. Sacr DH7 35 C3
Low Grange Rd. Spenny DL16 104 A1
Low Greenfields. Bish Au DL14 147 B4
Low Hogg St. Trim TS29 108 A4
Low La. Barn DL11 218 E2
Low La. Newsh DL11 220 A1
Low La. Wit le W DL14 & DL15 124 D4
Low Melbourne St. Bish Au DL14 148 B5
Low Mill. Bar Cas DL12 201 A5
Low Moor Cotts. Durham DH1 36 D1
Low Moor Rd. Lanch DH7 55 E6
Low Moor Rd. Lang Pk DH7 56 B6
Low Queen St. Wit Pk DL14 125 A1
Low Rd. Bowes DL12 216 B7
Low Rd. Cound DL14 127 E3
Low Rd. Eas SR8 63 B3
Low Rd. Gain DL2 204 F6
Low Rd. H Shin DH1 81 D4
Low Redgate Bank. Wols DL13 74 A1
Low Side. Mick DL12 161 C4
Low Startforth Rd. Start DL12 200 F5
Low Station Rd. W Rain DH4 37 E2
Low West Ave. R Gill NE39 1 D1
Low Willington. Will DL15 102 B2
Lowdale La. Hartle TS24 111 C4
Lowe St. Darl DL3 208 F2
Lowe's Barn Bank. Durham DH1 80 A7
Lower Bridge St. Bish Au DL14 126 B1
Lowery La. Crag DH7 & DH9 18 D1
Lowery Rd. New Ay DL5 171 C5
Lowes Ct. Durham DH1 80 A8
Lowes Fall. Durham DH1 80 A8
Lowes Rise. Durham DH1 80 A8
Loweswater Ave. C le S DH2 20 B1
Loweswater Ave. E Lane DH5 61 C8
Lowfields. New Ay DL5 170 F4
Lowhills Rd. Peter SR8 85 B8
Lowick Cl. Birt DH3 9 D1
Lowland Cl. Silk SR3 22 A5
Lowland Rd. Brand DH7 79 B4
Lowmoor Rd. Darl DL1 224 D7
Lowson St. Darl DL3 209 A7
Lowson St. Still TS21 174 F4
Lowther Ave. C le S DH2 20 B2
Lowther Cl. Peter SR8 85 D7
Lowther Ct. Peter SR8 85 B2
Lowther Dr. New Ay DL17 150 E1
Lowther Rd. Bish Au DL14 148 A4
Lucknow St. Darl DL1 209 B4
Lucy St. C le S DH3 20 C4
Ludworth Cty Sch. Ludw DH6 83 B7
Luke Ave. Cassop DH6 82 E1
Luke Cres. Murton SR7 40 B3
Luke St. Wing TS29 107 F5
Luke Terr. Wh Hi DH6 83 E2
Lulworth Gr. Hartle TS24 111 D4
Lumley Cl. C le S DH2 20 B3
Lumley Cl. New Ay DL5 171 D6
Lumley Cl. Spenny DL16 104 A2
Lumley Cres. Ferry DL17 129 B5
Lumley Cty Jun Sch. Gr Lum DH3 37 B7
Lumley Dr. Cons DH8 31 C8
Lumley Dr. Peter SR8 85 D3
Lumley Gdns. Burnop NE16 5 E5
Lumley Gr. Bish Au DL14 148 A6
Lumley Medway Cty Inf Sch. Gr Lum DH3 37 A8
Lumley New Rd. Gr Lum DH3 & DH4 21 C1
Lumley Rd. Durham DH1 58 C7
Lumley Terr. C le S DH3 20 D2
Lumley Terr. Coxhoe DH6 105 F3
Lumley Terr. 1 Ryhope SR2 22 F6
Lumsden Sq. Murton SR7 40 B3
Lumsden Terr. Ann Pl DH9 16 E5
Lund Ave. Durham DH1 58 B6
Lund's La. Ives DH8 16 A1
Lunedale Dr. Gr Lum DH3 37 B6
Lunedale Rd. Darl DL3 208 B3
Lunesdale St. H le H DH5 39 A2
Lusby Cres. Bish Au DL14 147 F4
Lutterington La. Bolam DL14 168 D6
Luttryngton Ct. New Ay DL5 171 A8
Luxmoore Ave. Will DL15 101 F3
Lych Gate. Hur on T DL2 224 D1
Lydford Way. Birt DH3 9 D3
Lydgate Ave. Wols DL13 97 F8
Lydgate La. Wols DL13 97 F8
Lydgate Sq. Wols DL13 98 A7
Lydia St. Will DL15 101 F3
Lydia Terr. Newf DL14 126 B8
Lynden Rd. 6 Sland SR2 22 F8
Lyndhurst Ave. C le S DH3 20 C6
Lyndhurst Cl. Blay NE21 2 A8
Lyndhurst Dr. Durham DH1 58 A1
Lyndhurst Rd. Chilt DL17 150 F7
Lyndhurst Rd. Stanl DH9 17 D6
Lyne Cl. Pelton DH2 19 F8
Lyne Rd. Spenny DL16 127 D6
Lyne's Dr. Brand DH7 79 D5
Lyngrove. Sland SR2 22 F8
Lynn Cres. Cassop DH6 82 F1
Lynn Park Cres. Coxhoe DH6 105 F3
Lynn St. C le S DH3 20 C2
Lynn Terr. Wh Hi DH6 84 A4
Lynndale. Wols DL13 98 A7
Lynne Cl. Darl DL3 209 A7
Lynthorpe. Sland SR2 22 F8
Lynton Gdns. Darl DL1 209 D1
Lyon Wlk. New Ay DL5 171 D6
Lyonette Rd. Darl DL1 209 D6
Lyons Ave. H le H DH5 39 B2
Lyons La. H le H DH5 39 C1
Lyster Cl. Seaham SR7 22 E1
Lytham Rd. Darl DL1 209 B7
Maben Ave. Bish Au DL14 147 D3
Mackenzie Pl. New Ay DL5 171 C8
Macmillan Rd. New Ay DL5 171 C7
Maddison St. Shild DL4 169 F8
Mafeking Pl. Shild DL4 149 A1
Mafeking Terr. Sacr DH7 35 B2
Magdalene Ave. Belm DH1 59 D4
Magdalene Ct. 2 Durham DH1 58 E2
Magdalene Dr. Hart TS27 110 F3
Magdalene Hts. 1 Durham DH1 58 E2
Magdalene St. Durham DH1 58 E2
Magdalene Terr. 7 Ferry DL17 129 B5
Maglona St. Seaham SR7 41 D6
Magnet St. 5 Shild DL4 170 A8
Magnolia Way. Shild DL4 149 B1
Mahogany Row. Beam DH9 7 D1
Maiden Castle. Durham DH1 80 E8
Maiden Law. Fence DH4 38 A7
Maiden Law Hospl. M Law DH7 32 F6
Main Rd. Gain DL2 205 A6
Main Rd. Heigh DL5 170 C3
Main Rd. Shild DL4 149 A4
Main St. Bish Au DL14 148 D5
Main St. Cons DH8 15 B2
Main St. Ferry DL17 128 F6
Main St. Shild DL4 148 F1
Main St. Wit Pk DL14 147 B8

Mains Ct. Durham DH1 .... 58 A5
Mains Park Rd. C le S DH3 .... 20 D3
Mainsforth Front Row.
Ferry DL17 .... 129 C3
Mainsforth Rd. Ferry DL17 .... 129 D4
Mainside. Redmar TS21 .... 195 B7
Major St. Darl DL3 .... 208 E4
Malcolm Ave. Qua Hi DH6 .... 106 D7
Malcolm St. 5 Seaham SR7 .... 41 D6
Malham Cres. New Ay DL5 .... 171 C7
Malim Rd. Darl DL1 .... 209 E1
Maling Gn. New Ay DL5 .... 171 E7
Mallard Cl. Wash NE38 .... 9 F4
Mallard Rd. Darl DL1 .... 209 E1
Mallory Ct. Darl DL1 .... 209 E4
Malone Gdns. Birt DH3 .... 9 D6
Malt Cres. Peter SR8 .... 85 F7
Maltby Cl. Bish Au DL14 .... 148 E6
Maltings The. N Silk SR3 .... 22 C7
Maltkiln La. New Ay DL5 .... 171 E2
Malton Terr. Sedge TS21 .... 153 B6
Malvern. Chilt DL17 .... 151 A8
Malvern Ave. C le S DH2 .... 20 B2
Malvern Cl. Hur on T DL2 .... 224 D1
Malvern Cl. Peter SR8 .... 85 B5
Malvern Cres. Darl DL3 .... 207 F5
Malvern Cres. Seaham SR7 .... 41 A7
Malvern Cres. Wing TS29 .... 108 A5
Malvern Terr. Stanl DH9 .... 18 A5
Malvern Villas. Durham DH1 .... 58 F2
Malvern Way. New Ay DL5 .... 170 F7
Malvern Wlk. Cound DL14 .... 149 C8
Mandela Cl. Stanl DH9 .... 17 D5
Manfield House. 6 Darl DL2 .... 224 C8
Manisty Terr. Eas SR8 .... 63 D4
Mann Cres. Murton SR7 .... 40 D4
Manor Cl. Elwick TS27 .... 134 D5
Manor Cl. Trim TS29 .... 131 D8
Manor Cl The. H Shin DH1 .... 81 A6
Manor Cotts. Ingle DL2 .... 188 A6
Manor Cotts. Thor Th TS21 .... 175 E3
Manor Ct. Even DL14 .... 167 D6
Manor Ct. Ferry DL17 .... 129 A6
Manor Ct. Heigh DL5 .... 170 E1
Manor Ct. Lanch DH7 .... 33 A2
Manor Dr. Ann Pl DH9 .... 16 F5
Manor Dr. Still TS21 .... 174 F3
Manor Field. Dalt P TS27 .... 134 E3
Manor Gr. Cockf DL13 .... 166 D5
Manor Grange. Lanch DH7 .... 33 A3
Manor Hall Cl. Seaham SR7 .... 40 E8
Manor House Est.
Hut Hen TS27 .... 109 C5
Manor House Est.
Hut Hen TS27 .... 109 D6
Manor Rd. Bish Au DL14 .... 147 D2
Manor Rd. Darl DL3 .... 223 E8
Manor Rd. Hur on T DL2 .... 224 A1
Manor Rd. Ingle DL2 .... 188 A6
Manor Rd. Medom DH8 .... 4 C1
Manor Rd. Stanl DH9 .... 17 F7
Manor Rd. Will DL15 .... 102 B3
Manor St. Even DL14 .... 167 D6
Manor Terr. Win M NE21 .... 2 C7
Manor View. 3 Ferry DL17 .... 129 A6
Manor View. H Pitt DH6 .... 60 B4
Manor Way. Peter SR8 .... 85 E5
Manor Wlk. Still TS21 .... 174 F3
Manorfields. Hur on T DL2 .... 224 D1
Manse St. Cons DH8 .... 14 E4
Mansell Cres. Peter SR8 .... 85 E7
Maple Ave. Durham DH1 .... 59 A2
Maple Ave. N Silk SR3 .... 22 B8
Maple Ave. Shild DL4 .... 149 B1
Maple Cl. Will DL15 .... 101 E2
Maple Cres. Crook DL15 .... 100 D4
Maple Cres. Seaham SR7 .... 41 C4
Maple Ct. Brand DH7 .... 78 F3
Maple Ct. Hi Eth DL14 .... 146 E5
Maple Gdns. Cons DH8 .... 14 C4
Maple Gr. Cornf DL17 .... 105 E1
Maple Gr. Stanl DH9 .... 17 D4
Maple Grove. Sedge TS21 .... 153 B7
Maple Pk. Ush M DH7 .... 57 B1
Maple Rd. Darl DL1 .... 209 B8
Maple St. 18 Cons DH8 .... 14 F3
Maple St. Stanl DH9 .... 17 D4
Maple Terr. Ann Pl DH9 .... 16 E5
Maple Terr. Burnop NE16 .... 5 F6
Maplewood. C le S DH2 .... 20 B4
Maplewood St. Gr Lum DH4 .... 21 E1
Marcia Ave. Shot Co DH6 .... 84 C7
Mardale St. H le H DH5 .... 39 A2
Margaret Ct. Bowb DH6 .... 81 D1
Margaret St. Ludw DH6 .... 83 C7
Margaret St. 7 Seaham SR7 .... 41 D6
Margaret Terr. Bish Au DL14 .... 148 E4
Margaret Terr. R Gill NE39 .... 1 C1
Margaret Terr. Tanf L DH9 .... 6 C1
Margaret Terr. Wing TS29 .... 108 A5
Margate St. N Silk SR3 .... 22 A8
Margery La. Durham DH1 .... 58 B1
Maria St. N Silk SR3 .... 22 A7
Maria St. 8 Seaham SR7 .... 41 D7
Marigold Cres. Bourn DH4 .... 21 E3
Marigold Ct. Darl DL1 .... 209 C2
Marina Rd. Darl DL3 .... 209 A8
Marina Terr. 8 Ryhope SR2 .... 22 F6
Marine Cres. B Rocks TS27 .... 86 F2
Marine Dr. Sland SR2 .... 23 A8
Maritime Cres. Peter SR8 .... 63 F3
Mariville E. Ryhope SR2 .... 23 A5
Mariville W. Ryhope SR2 .... 23 A5
Mark Rise. H le H DH5 .... 39 A5
Mark St. R Gill NE39 .... 1 C2
Mark's La. W Rain DH4 .... 37 F4
Market Cres. Hut Hen TS28 .... 108 E6
Market Pl. Bar Cas DL12 .... 201 A5
Market Pl. Bish Au DL14 .... 126 C1
Market Pl. 8 Darl DL1 .... 208 F1
Market Pl. 4 Durham DH1 .... 58 C2
Market Pl. Esh W DH7 .... 77 E8
Market Pl. H le Sp DH5 .... 38 F8
Market Pl. Mid in T DL12 .... 160 D8
Market Pl. Shild DL4 .... 149 A2
Market St. Cons DH8 .... 14 D4
Market St. Ferry DL17 .... 128 F6
Market St. H le H DH5 .... 39 B4
Markham Pl. New Ay DL5 .... 171 F7
Markington Dr. Ryhope SR2 .... 22 F6
Markle Gr. E Rain DH5 .... 38 D5
Marlborough. 1 Seaham SR7 .... 41 D7
Marlborough Ct. Darl DL1 .... 223 E8
Marlborough Ct. H le Sp DH5 .... 38 E6
Marlbrough Cres. 8
Peter SR8 .... 86 B6
Marlene Ave. Bowb DH6 .... 81 D2
Marley Hill Cty Jun & Inf Sch.
Sunn NE16 .... 7 A8
Marley Rd. New Ay DL5 .... 171 D6
Marley Way. Hartle TS27 .... 111 D3
Marley Wlk. Hartle TS27 .... 111 D3
Marley's Cotts. Quebec DH7 .... 55 B4
Marlow Way. Whick NE16 .... 2 F5
Marlowe Pl. H le Sp DH5 .... 38 F7
Marmaduke St. Spenny DL16 .... 104 A1
Marrick Ave. Darl DL3 .... 207 F5
Marrick Cl. 2 New Ay DL5 .... 171 B7
Marsden Cl. H le Sp DH4 .... 38 C8
Marsden Wlk. Darl DL3 .... 208 F7
Marshall Cl. Hartle TS24 .... 111 E3
Marshall Rd. New Ay DL5 .... 171 C7
Marshall St. Bar Cas DL12 .... 201 A6
Marshall St. Darl DL3 .... 208 F3
Marshall Terr. Belm DH1 .... 59 A2
Marske Gr. Darl DL3 .... 208 F5
Marson Ave. Crook DL15 .... 100 E2
Marston Moor Rd. Darl DL1 .... 224 E8
Marston Wlk. Whick NE16 .... 2 F5
Martha St. Tant DH9 .... 6 B2
Martin Ct. Wash NE38 .... 9 F2
Martin St. Stanh DL13 .... 71 B3
Martindale Cl. Elwick TS27 .... 134 D6
Martindale Pk. H le Sp DH5 .... 38 E8
Martindale Rd. Darl DL1 .... 209 C5
Marwood Cres. Darl DL3 .... 208 D5
Marwood Dr. Bar Cas DL12 .... 201 A7
Marwood Gr. Peter SR8 .... 85 C3
Marwood Terr. Coth DL12 .... 182 E3
Marwood View. Coth DL12 .... 182 E3
Marx Cres. Stanl DH9 .... 17 F5
Marx Terr. Chopw NE17 .... 4 C8
Mary Ave. Birt DH3 .... 9 B6
Mary Cres. Kelloe DH6 .... 106 E6
Mary Ct. Darl DL3 .... 208 B4
Mary St. Ann Pl DH9 .... 17 A4
Mary St. N Silk SR3 .... 22 A8
Mary St. Seaham SR7 .... 41 E7
Mary St. Stanl DH9 .... 17 E6
Mary Terr. Bish Au DL14 .... 148 E4
Mary Terr. Bowb DH6 .... 81 C1
Masefield Cl. Stanl DH9 .... 18 B7
Masefield Cres. Will DL15 .... 101 F1
Masefields. C le St DH2 .... 19 E4
Masham Moor Way. Darl DL1 .... 224 D7
Mason Cres. Peter SR8 .... 85 F6
Mason St. Cons DH8 .... 14 F2
Masterman Pl. Mid in T DL12 .... 160 D7
Matfen Ct. C le S DH2 .... 20 A3
Matfen Ct. Sedge TS21 .... 153 A7
Matterdale Rd. Peter SR8 .... 85 F6
Matthew Cl. New Ay DL5 .... 171 F8
Matthews Cres. S Hett DH6 .... 62 B6
Matthews Rd. Cold He SR7 .... 40 E1
Maud Terr. Even DL14 .... 167 C8
Maud Terr. Tanf DH9 .... 6 D3
Maude St. Darl DL3 .... 208 F2
Maude Terr. Bish Au DL14 .... 147 E3
Maudlin St. H le H DH5 .... 39 B6
Maudville. Cons DH8 .... 30 A6
Maugham St. 7 Shild DL4 .... 148 F1
Maughan Cl. Cornf DL17 .... 105 D1
Maughan Terr. Fishb TS21 .... 131 C4
Maureen Terr. Belm DH1 .... 59 C6
Maureen Terr. Seaham SR7 .... 41 C7
Mavin St. Durham DH1 .... 80 D8
Maxwell Cl. Darl DL1 .... 224 D8
May Ave. Win M NE21 .... 2 C7
May Cres. Wing TS29 .... 108 B5
May Lea. Wit Gil DH7 .... 35 B1
May St. Birt DH3 .... 9 C4
May St. Bish Au DL14 .... 148 B8
May St. Durham DH1 .... 58 B1
May Terr. Lang Pk DH7 .... 56 C6
Mayfair Rd. Darl DL1 .... 209 A8
Mayfair Sch. Darl DL1 .... 209 B8
Mayfield. Bar Cas DL12 .... 201 A6
Mayfield. Darl DL3 .... 208 E1
Mayfield Terr. Cockf DL13 .... 166 C5
Maylands. Thor DL13 .... 99 A7
Maynard's Row. Durham DH1 .... 58 F2
Maynes Way. Stanl DH9 .... 18 B7
Mayorswell Cl. 7 Durham DH1 .... 58 D2
Mayorswell Field. 4
Durham DH1 .... 58 E2
Mayorswell St. 6 Durham DH1 .... 58 D2
Mazine Terr. Hasw DH6 .... 61 E2
McAteer Cl. Hasw DH6 .... 61 E1
McCullagh Gdns. Bish Au DL14 .... 148 C6
McCutcheon St. 7 Seaham SR7 .... 22 E1
McGuinness Ave. Peter SR8 .... 85 E8
McIntyre Terr. Bish Au DL14 .... 148 B6
McMullen Rd. Darl DL1 .... 209 E2
McNally Pl. Durham DH1 .... 58 F2
McNay St. Darl DL3 .... 208 F4
Mead The. Darl DL1 .... 209 C1
Meadhope St. Wols DL13 .... 97 F7
Meadow Cl. Coxhoe DH6 .... 105 F4
Meadow Cl. H le Sp DH5 .... 38 F7
Meadow Cl. Mid in T DL12 .... 160 E7
Meadow Dr. C le St DH2 .... 19 F2
Meadow Grange. Bourn DH4 .... 21 E2
Meadow Rd. Trim TS29 .... 131 D7
Meadow Rise. Darl DL3 .... 208 B2
Meadow St. E Rain DH5 .... 38 C3
Meadow View. Bish Au DL14 .... 147 C2
Meadow View. Cons DH8 .... 31 C7
Meadow View. Coxhoe DH6 .... 105 F3
Meadow View. Dipton DH9 .... 5 E1
Meadow View. Egg DL12 .... 162 C4
Meadow View. Sacr DH7 .... 35 C3
Meadow Way. Lanch DH7 .... 32 E3
Meadowbank. Lang Pk DH7 .... 56 B6
Meadowdale. Chilt DL17 .... 150 F7
Meadowfield. Cons DH8 .... 14 D3
Meadowfield Ave.
Spenny DL16 .... 104 D2
Meadowfield Ind Est.
Brand DH7 .... 79 D3
Meadowfield Rd. Darl DL3 .... 208 B5
Meadowfield Way.
New Ay DL5 .... 171 A8
Meadowfield Way. Tanf L DH9 .... 17 C8
Meadows La. W Rain DH4 & DH5 .... 38 B3
Meadows The. Bourn DH4 .... 21 D3
Meadows The. M St G DL2 .... 225 F7
Meadows The. Midd DL5 .... 149 E1
Meadows The. Sedge TS21 .... 153 B6
Meadows The. W Rain DH4 .... 38 A3
Meatlesburn Cl. New Ay DL5 .... 170 F4
Medomsley Cross Rds.
Medom DH8 .... 15 A8
Medomsley Rd. Cons DH8 .... 14 F4
Medway. Gr Lum DH3 .... 37 A7
Medway Cl. Peter SR8 .... 85 C4
Medway Gdns. Stanl DH9 .... 17 E4
Medwyn Cl. Bourn DH4 .... 21 E3
Meet The. New Ay DL5 .... 170 F8
Melbeck Dr. Urpeth DH2 .... 8 E2
Melbourne Pl. Wols DL13 .... 97 F7
Melbourne Terr. Sacr DH7 .... 35 B5
Melbury St. Seaham SR7 .... 41 E5
Meldon Ave. Sherb DH6 .... 60 A1
Meldon Cl. Darl DL1 .... 209 D5
Meldon Way. Ann Pl DH9 .... 17 B4
Meldon Way. Blay NE21 .... 1 F8
Meldon Way. H Shin DH1 .... 81 B5
Melgrove Way. Sedge TS21 .... 153 A5
Mellanby Cres. New Ay DL5 .... 171 F7
Melland St. Darl DL1 .... 209 A1
Mellbutts Bank. Frost DL13 .... 96 A1
Mellor Ct. Darl DL3 .... 209 A5
Melrose Ave. Darl DL3 .... 209 A7
Melrose Ave. Murton SR7 .... 40 A3
Melrose Cres. Seaham SR7 .... 40 F8
Melrose Ct. Cons DH8 .... 14 C4
Melrose Dr. Bish Au DL14 .... 147 D3
Melsonby Cres. Darl DL1 .... 224 C8
Melville St. C le S DH3 .... 20 C2
Melville St. 2 Darl DL1 .... 208 F3
Memorial Ave. Eas SR8 .... 63 E4
Memorial Cotts. Butter DL13 .... 165 F8
Memorial Homes. Tanf L DH9 .... 17 D8
Mendip Ave. C le S DH2 .... 20 C2
Mendip Cl. Peter SR8 .... 85 B6
Mendip Gn. Chilt DL17 .... 150 F8
Mendip Gr. Darl DL1 .... 209 C5
Mendip Terr. Stanl DH9 .... 18 A5
Mendip Wlk. Cound DL14 .... 149 C8
Menom Rd. New Ay DL5 .... 171 D2
Menville Cl. New Ay DL5 .... 170 F4
Mercantile Rd. H le Sp DH4 .... 38 C7
Mercia Ct. Darl DL3 .... 208 F2
Mercia Ret Pk. Durham DH1 .... 58 C8
Mere Dr. Durham DH1 .... 58 B7
Merlin Cl. Seaham SR7 .... 41 C8
Merlin Ct. Esh W DH7 .... 77 D8
Merlin Dr. C le S DH3 .... 20 D7
Merriman Gr. Hartle TS24 .... 111 D3
Merrington Cl. Kir Me DL16 .... 128 A3
Merrington Hts. Kir Me DL16 .... 127 F3
Merrington Lane Ind Est.
Spenny DL16 .... 128 B7
Merrington Rd.
Ferry DL16 & DL17 .... 128 C5
Merrington Rd. Kir Me DL17 .... 128 C5
Merrington View. Spenny DL16 .... 128 A8
Merrybent. L Con DL2 .... 207 C2
Merrybent Dr. L Con DL2 .... 207 D1
Mersey St. Leadg DH8 .... 15 D5
Merton Cl. Darl DL1 .... 209 B6
Merz Rd. New Ay DL5 .... 171 D6
Messenger Bank. Cons DH8 .... 14 C6
Messines La. Still TS21 .... 174 E3
Metcalfe Cres. Murton SR7 .... 40 B3
Metcalfe Rd. Cons DH8 .... 15 B1
Methold Houses. Beam DH9 .... 18 E8
Mewburn Ct. Darl DL3 .... 208 F7
Mewburn Rd. Darl DL3 .... 208 F7
Mews The. Fence DH4 .... 38 A7
Mews The. H Shin DH1 .... 80 F6
Meynell Rd. Darl DL3 .... 208 F5
Mickle Gr. Cound DL14 .... 149 C8
Mickle Hill Rd. B Rocks TS27 .... 86 D1
Mickle Hill Rd. Hesl TS27 .... 86 D1
Mickleton Cl. Gr Lum DH3 .... 37 B7
Middle Bank. Thor Th TS21 .... 175 E3
Middle Chare. C le S DH3 .... 20 D3
Middle Farm. Staint DL12 .... 184 E2
Middle St. B Coll TS27 .... 86 D4
Middle St. Cons DH8 .... 14 F2
Middlefield. Pelton DH2 .... 19 E7
Middlefield Terr. Ush M DH7 .... 56 F1
Middleham Cl. Urpeth DH2 .... 8 E1
Middleham Rd. Cornf DL17 .... 105 E1
Middleham Rd. Darl DL1 .... 209 B7
Middleham Rd. Durham DH1 .... 58 D7
Middleham Way. New Ay DL17 .... 150 E1
Middleham Wlk. Spenny DL16 .... 104 A2
Middlehope Gr. Bish Au DL14 .... 147 E5
Middles Rd. The Mid DH9 .... 18 B3
Middlestone Moor Cty Jun Mix
Sch. Spenny DL16 .... 127 C5
Middleton Ave. R Gill NE39 .... 1 F1
Middleton Cl. Seaham SR7 .... 22 E1
Middleton Ct. Darl DL1 .... 209 A2
Middleton La. M St G DL2 .... 225 F6
Middleton Rd. Sadb DL2 .... 210 E6
Middleton Rd. Shild DL4 .... 169 F8
Middleton Rd. Wood DL13 .... 143 C1
Middleton St. Darl DL1 .... 209 A2
Middleton St George Cty Prim
Sch. M St G DL2 .... 225 E7
Middleton-in-Teesdale Jun
& Inf Sch. Mid in T DL12 .... 160 E7
Middlewood Ave. Bish Au DL14 .... 147 D2
Middlewood Cl. 3 Hartle TS27 .... 111 C4
Middlewood Rd. Lanch DH7 .... 32 E3
Middridge La. Shild DL4 & DL5 .... 149 C1
Middridge Rd. Lang Pk DH7 .... 56 B6
Middridge Rd.
New Ay DL17 & DL5 .... 150 C4
Middridge Rd. New Ay DL5 .... 150 A1
Midfields. New Ay DL5 .... 170 F4
Midhill Cl. Brand DH7 .... 79 B5
Midhill Cl. 7 Lang Pk DH7 .... 56 C6
Miers Ave. Hartle TS24 .... 111 F2
Milbank Cres. Darl DL3 .... 208 D2
Milbank Ct. Darl DL3 .... 208 C2
Milbank Rd. Darl DL3 .... 208 D2
Milbank Terr. Hut Hen TS28 .... 108 F5
Milbank Terr. Shot Co DH6 .... 84 D6
Milbanke Cl. Ouston DH2 .... 8 F1
Milbanke St. Ouston DH2 .... 8 F1
Milbourne Ct. Sedge TS21 .... 153 A8
Milburn Cl. C le S DH3 .... 20 E2
Milburn St. Crook DL15 .... 100 E4
Mildred St. Darl DL3 .... 208 F3
Milford Meadow. Bish Au DL14 .... 148 D4
Milford Terr. 9 Ferry DL17 .... 129 A6
Milkwood Ct. Darl DL3 .... 208 E4
Mill Ct. Bourn DH4 .... 21 E2
Mill Farm Rd. H Mill NE39 .... 5 A5
Mill Hill. Eas SR8 .... 63 A1
Mill Hill. H le Sp DH5 .... 38 D6
Mill Hill. Peter SR8 .... 85 A8
Mill Hill Prim Sch. Silk SR3 .... 22 A5
Mill Hill Rd. Silk SR3 .... 22 A6
Mill House Ct. Belm DH1 .... 59 A2
Mill La. Bish TS21 .... 194 E8
Mill La. Bish Au DL14 .... 148 D5
Mill La. Darl DL1 .... 209 E4
Mill La. Durham DH1 .... 59 A2
Mill La. Ebch DH8 .... 3 E4
Mill La. Frost DL13 .... 96 B6
Mill La. H Con DL2 .... 206 F3
Mill La. H Shin DH1 .... 81 A7
Mill La. Heigh DL4 & DL5 .... 170 C4
Mill La. Kimble DH2 & DH3 .... 36 B4
Mill La. Longn DL2 & TS21 .... 211 D3
Mill La. M St G DL2 .... 211 D3
Mill La. Mick DL12 .... 161 C5
Mill La. N Bran DH7 .... 79 A8
Mill La. Sherb DH6 .... 60 A1
Mill La. Spenny DL16 .... 103 E4
Mill La. Urpeth DH2 & DH9 .... 8 D1
Mill La. Win M NE21 .... 2 B7
Mill Race Cl. B Mill NE17 .... 4 B6
Mill Rd. B Mill NE17 .... 4 B8
Mill Rd. Brand DH7 .... 79 E5
Mill Rd. Chopw NE17 .... 4 B8
Mill Rd. Seaham SR7 .... 40 F8
Mill St. Cons DH8 .... 31 B8
Mill St. Crook DL15 .... 100 F4
Mill St. Shild DL4 .... 170 A8
Mill St. Will DL15 .... 101 F3
Mill Terr. Eas SR8 .... 63 A4
Mill Terr. H le Sp DH5 .... 38 D6
Mill Terr. Thor Th TS21 .... 175 D3
Mill The. Hunst DH8 .... 25 E3
Mill Wynd. Staind DL2 .... 186 D6
Millbank. Heigh DL5 .... 170 D1
Millbank Cl. Bish Au DL14 .... 147 C1
Millbank Cl. Hart TS27 .... 111 A3
Millbank Ct. Durham DH1 .... 58 B3
Millbank Terr. Bish Au DL14 .... 148 F4
Millbank Terr. Still TS21 .... 175 A2
Millbeck Gr. H le Sp DH5 .... 38 D6
Millburngate. Durham DH1 .... 58 C2
Millburngate Sh Ctr.
Durham DH1 .... 58 C2
Milldale. Seaham SR7 .... 40 F8
Miller Cres. Hartle TS24 .... 111 D4
Miller Gdns. C le St DH2 .... 19 D4
Miller Terr. N Silk SR3 .... 22 A8
Millershill La. Heal DH8 .... 30 E2
Millfield. Lanch DH7 .... 32 E4
Millfield Cl. C le S DH2 .... 20 A1
Millfield Ct. Cons DH8 .... 14 C3
Millfield Gr. Crook DL15 .... 100 E4
Millfield Rd. Fishb TS21 .... 131 D4
Millfields. New Ay DL5 .... 171 F2
Millford Way. Bowb DH6 .... 81 E1
Millhill La. Durham DH1 .... 80 B7
Millom Ct. Peter SR8 .... 85 A3
Millrace Cl. Darl DL1 .... 209 F6
Millrace. Wols DL13 .... 97 E7
Mills Bldgs. Ferry DL17 .... 129 C4
Mills Cl. New Ay DL5 .... 171 C6
Milner Rd. Darl DL1 .... 224 A8
Milton Ave. Bish Au DL14 .... 148 B6
Milton Ave. H le Sp DH5 .... 38 F7
Milton Cl. Seaham SR7 .... 41 B7
Milton Cl. Stanl DH9 .... 18 B6
Milton Gr. Shot Co DH6 .... 84 D6
Milton La. Eas SR8 .... 63 C4
Milton St. Crook DL15 .... 100 E5
Milton St. Darl DL1 .... 224 C8
Minehead Gdns. 9 N Silk SR3 .... 22 A8
Miners' Bglws. Cockf DL13 .... 166 C5
Miners' Homes. Bish Au DL14 .... 147 E3
Miners' Homes. Will DL15 .... 102 A2
Mingarry. Birt DH3 .... 9 E2
Mingary Cl. E Rain DH5 .... 38 C4
Minors Cres. Darl DL3 .... 208 B5
Minstarley. Gr Lum DH3 .... 37 A7
Minster Ct. Belm DH1 .... 59 C3
Minster Wlk. Hur on T DL2 .... 224 D1
Mire La. Coth DL12 .... 182 F3
Miry La. Newb DL12 .... 138 D4
Mission Pl. Kir Me DL16 .... 128 A3
Mistletoe St. Durham DH1 .... 58 B1
Mistral Dr. Darl DL1 .... 209 B7
Mitchell Cl. Peter SR8 .... 85 B8
Mitchell St. Ann Pl DH9 .... 17 A4
Mitchell St. 3 Birt DH3 .... 9 C4
Mitchell St. 4 Durham DH1 .... 58 B2
Mitchell St. Stanl DH9 .... 17 D4
Mitchell Terr. Tant DH9 .... 6 B2
Mitford Cl. C le S DH3 .... 20 D8
Mitford Cl. H Shin DH1 .... 81 B5
Mitford Cl. Peter SR8 .... 85 D4
Mitford Ct. Sedge TS21 .... 153 A8
Mitford Dr. Sherb DH6 .... 60 A2
Model Pl. 4 Darl DL1 .... 209 A1
Model Terr. 2 Cockf DL13 .... 166 C5
Moffat Cl. Darl DL1 .... 209 D7
Mona St. Stanl DH9 .... 17 F7
Monarch Gn. Darl DL1 .... 209 B7
Moncreiff Terr. Eas SR8 .... 63 D4
Money Slack. Durham DH1 .... 80 B5
Monk Ct. Peter SR8 .... 85 B3
Monkend Terr. Cr on T DL2 .... 234 F8
Monks' Cres. Belm DH1 .... 58 F3
Monks End. New Ay DL5 .... 171 F2
Monkswood Sq. Silk SR3 .... 22 B6
Monmouth Gr. Hartle TS26 .... 111 E1
Montalbo Rd. Bar Cas DL12 .... 201 A7
Monteith Cl. Bish Au DL14 .... 147 C1
Montfalcon Cl. Peter SR8 .... 85 C6
Montgomery Rd. Bar Cas DL12 .... 200 F7
Montgomery Rd. Durham DH1 .... 58 F3
Montrose St. Darl DL1 .... 209 B3
Monument Terr. 10 Birt DH3 .... 9 C4
Moor Cotts. H Pitt DH6 .... 60 D4
Moor Cres. Belm DH1 .... 59 B3
Moor Cres. Ludw DH6 .... 83 C7
Moor Edge. Brand DH7 .... 79 B3
Moor Edge. Durham DH1 .... 57 F2
Moor Farm Est. Spenny DL16 .... 127 E6
Moor Houses. Stan Cr DL15 .... 76 E1
Moor La. Cleas DL2 .... 222 E5
Moor La. Dalton DL11 .... 233 E4
Moor La. Hilton DL14 & DL2 .... 167 F2
Moor La. Midd DL5 .... 150 A2
Moor La. Newsh DL11 .... 233 C7
Moor La. Scar DL12 .... 217 F2
Moor La. Shild DL4 & DL5 .... 149 E3
Moor La. Staind DL2 .... 185 C7
Moor La. Staint DL2 .... 185 C7
Moor La. Stapl DL2 .... 222 E5
Moor La. Wing TS28 .... 108 E7
Moor Rd. Staind DL2 .... 186 C5
Moor View. Cockf DL13 .... 166 C5
Moor View. Thorn DH6 .... 83 E4
Moor View. Wh Hi DH6 .... 83 E4
Moor View Terr. Ann Pl DH9 .... 16 E3
Moore Cres. Birt DH3 .... 9 C6
Moore Cres N. H le Sp DH5 .... 38 E7
Moore Cres S. H le Sp DH5 .... 38 E7
Moore La. New Ay DL5 .... 171 F6
Moore Sq. Wing TS28 .... 84 D1
Moore St. Bish Au DL14 .... 148 F4
Moore St. Stanl DH9 .... 17 E4
Moore St. Wh Hi DH6 .... 83 F2
Moore Terr. Shot Co DH6 .... 84 D5
Moorfield. Butter DL13 .... 144 E1
Moorfoot Ave. C le S DH2 .... 20 C2
Moorhead Way. New Ay DL5 .... 171 E4
Moorhouse Gdns. H le H DH5 .... 39 B2
Moorhouse La. Brig DL12 .... 218 A5
Moorland Cl. Will DL15 .... 101 E1
Moorland Cres. Cons DH8 .... 30 A6
Moorland View. Chopw NE17 .... 4 B8
Moorland View. Cons DH8 .... 29 F6
Moorlands. Cons DH8 .... 14 D5
Moorlands Cres. Cons DH8 .... 14 D4
Moorlands Rd. Darl DL3 .... 208 C4
Moorlands The. Dipton DH9 .... 5 E1
Moorlands The. Durham DH1 .... 59 A2
Moormill. Kibble NE11 .... 8 D6
Moormill La. Kibble NE11 .... 8 E6
Moors Cl. Fence DH4 .... 38 B8
Moorsfield. Fence DH4 .... 38 B8
Moorside. Spenny DL16 .... 127 D6
Moorside Cres. Fishb TS21 .... 131 D4
Moorsley Rd. H le H DH5 .... 38 F2
Moorview. Cons DH8 .... 14 E4
Moraine Cres. B Mill NE17 .... 4 B6
Moravian St. Crook DL15 .... 100 E4
Moray Cl. Birt DH3 .... 9 D1
Moray Cl. Darl DL1 .... 209 C7
Moray Cl. Peter SR8 .... 85 C5
Mordue Terr. Ann Pl DH9 .... 17 A3
Morland St. Bish Au DL14 .... 148 B5
Morley Cres. Kelloe DH6 .... 106 E6
Morley Gdns. 3 Cons DH8 .... 14 F4
Morley La. Brance DH7 .... 78 E3
Morley Terr. 3 Fence DH4 .... 38 A8
Morningside Ct. C le S DH3 .... 20 C4
Morningside. Sacr DH7 .... 35 C4
Morningside. Wash NE38 .... 20 E8
Mornington La. Darl DL3 .... 208 D4
Morpeth Ave. Darl DL1 .... 209 C6
Morpeth Cl. Ferry DL17 .... 129 B6
Morpeth Cl. Spenny DL16 .... 128 A8
Morpeth Cl. Wash DH3 .... 9 F4
Morpeth Gr. Bish Au DL14 .... 148 A6
Morpeth St. Peter SR8 .... 85 F8
Morris Cres. Thorn DH6 .... 83 C4
Morris Sq. Eas SR8 .... 63 C3
Morris St. Birt DH3 .... 9 C4

Poplars The. Chilt DL17 .... 150 E8
Poplars The. E Lane DH5 .... 39 C1
Poppyfields. C le St DH2 .... 19 F2
Popular Ct. C le S DH3 .... 20 C3
Porrett Cl. Hartle TS24 .... 111 E4
Porter Cl. New Ay DL5 .... 171 E8
Porter Terr. Murton SR7 .... 40 C3
Portland Ave. Seaham SR7 .... 41 A7
Portland Cl. C le S DH2 .... 20 A1
Portland Gr. Hartle TS24 .... 111 D4
Portland Pl. Darl DL3 .... 208 F2
Portmeads Rise. Birt DH3 .... 9 D4
Portobello Terr. Birt DH3 .... 9 E2
Portobello Way. Birt DH3 .... 9 D4
Portree Cl. Birt DH3 .... 9 D1
Portrush Cl. Darl DL1 .... 209 E6
Portsmouth Pl. Darl DL1 .... 209 E5
Post Horn. New Ay DL5 .... 170 F8
Post House Wynd. 2 Darl DL3 .... 208 F1
Post Office Row. Corn DH7 .... 54 B3
Post Office St. Wit le W DL14 .... 124 B3
Potter Pl. Stanl DH9 .... 18 B5
Potterhouse La. Wit Gil DH1 .... 57 F8
Potterhouse Terr. Durham DH1 .... 58 A8
Potters Bank. Durham DH1 .... 80 B7
Potters Cl. Durham DH1 .... 80 A7
Pottery Yd. 3 H le Sp DH4 .... 38 E8
Potto St. Shot Co DH6 .... 84 D6
Potts Rd. Cound DL14 .... 127 C1
Pounder Pl. Hartle TS24 .... 111 F2
Pounteys Cl. M St G DL2 .... 225 E7
Pow Hill Ctry Pk. Edmun DH8 .... 11 D4
Powburn Cl. C le S DH2 .... 20 A1
Powlett St. Darl DL3 .... 208 F1
Prebend Row. 8 Darl DL1 .... 208 F2
Prebend Row. Pelton DH2 .... 19 D7
Prebends Field. Belm DH1 .... 59 A4
Prendwick Cl. C le St DH2 .... 36 A8
Prescott St. Darl DL1 .... 209 B3
Preston La. Mordon DL5 .... 172 C4
Preston Rd. New Ay DL5 .... 171 C3
Price Ave. Bish Au DL14 .... 148 A4
Priestfield Gdns. Burnop NE16 .... 5 F6
Priestgate. Darl DL1 .... 209 A2
Priestman Ave. Cons DH8 .... 14 C1
Priestman Rd. New Ay DL5 .... 171 C7
Primitive St. Shild DL4 .... 148 F2
Primrose Ave. Peter SR8 .... 85 F7
Primrose Cres. Bourn DH4 .... 21 E3
Primrose Gdns. Ouston DH2 .... 8 F2
Primrose Hill. Newf DL14 .... 126 B8
Primrose St. Darl DL3 .... 208 F1
Primrose Terr. Birt DH3 .... 9 D4
Prince Charles Ave. Bowb DH6 .... 81 D1
Prince's St. Ann Pl DH9 .... 16 F5
Prince's St. Bish Au DL14 .... 148 B8
Prince's St. 13 Darl DL1 .... 209 B1
Princes' St. Durham DH1 .... 58 B2
Princes' St. Shild DL4 .... 148 E1
Princess Ave. Cons DH8 .... 14 D5
Princess Cl. B Rocks TS27 .... 86 E2
Princess Ct. Spenny DL16 .... 127 E8
Princess Gdns. H le H DH5 .... 39 A5
Princess Rd. Darl DL3 .... 209 A8
Princess Rd. Seaham SR7 .... 41 D6
Princess St. Spenny DL16 .... 127 E8
Pringle Cl. N Bran DH7 .... 78 E7
Pringle Gr. N Bran DH7 .... 78 F7
Pringle Pl. N Bran DH7 .... 78 F7
Prior Dene. Darl DL3 .... 208 C4
Prior St. Darl DL3 .... 208 C4
Priors Cl. Durham DH1 .... 58 A2
Priors Grange. H Pitt DH6 .... 60 B5
Priors Path. Ferry DL17 .... 129 A7
Priory Cl. Cons DH8 .... 14 C5
Priory Ct. Bar Cas DL12 .... 201 A5
Priory Gdns. Will DL15 .... 102 A3
Priory Rd. Durham DH1 .... 58 B6
Priory Road Flats. Durham DH1 .... 58 B5
Progress Way. Darl DL1 .... 209 A3
Promenade. Seaham SR7 .... 23 D1
Promenade The. Cons DH8 .... 14 F4
Prospect Cres. E Lane DH5 .... 61 C8
Prospect Pl. Bar Cas DL12 .... 201 B7
Prospect Pl. 9 Cons DH8 .... 14 F3
Prospect Pl. 7 Darl DL3 .... 208 F2
Prospect Pl. Darl DL3 .... 208 F5
Prospect Pl. N Bran DH7 .... 78 E8
Prospect Pl. Wing TS29 .... 107 F5
Prospect Rd. Crook DL15 .... 100 E2
Prospect Sq. 1 Cockf DL13 .... 166 C5
Prospect St. C le S DH3 .... 20 C4
Prospect St. 10 Cons DH8 .... 14 F3
Prospect Terr. Ann Pl DH9 .... 17 B4
Prospect Terr. Burnop NE16 .... 6 A4
Prospect Terr. C le S DH3 .... 20 C4
Prospect Terr. Chilt DL17 .... 151 A7
Prospect Terr. 3 Cockf DL13 .... 166 C5
Prospect Terr. Durham DH1 .... 80 A8
Prospect Terr. Egg DL12 .... 162 B5
Prospect Terr. H Shin DH1 .... 81 A6
Prospect Terr. Kibble NE11 .... 8 C6
Prospect Terr. Lanch DH7 .... 32 E3
Prospect Terr. N Bran DH7 .... 78 F8
Prospect Terr. Will DL15 .... 101 F3
Prospect View. W Rain DH4 .... 37 F2
Proudfoot Dr. Bish Au DL14 .... 148 A5
Providence Pl. Belm DH1 .... 59 B3
Providence Row. Durham DH1 .... 58 D2
Provident St. Pelton DH2 .... 19 C6
Provident Terr. Crag DH9 .... 18 D2
Provident Terr. Even DL14 .... 167 C8
Prudhoe Ave. Fishb TS21 .... 131 C4
Pudding Hill Rd. Oving DL11 .... 204 E3
Pudsey Ct. Durham DH1 .... 58 C6
Pudsey Wlk. New Ay DL5 .... 171 E5
Purvis Terr. Wing TS29 .... 108 B5

Quaker La. Darl DL1 .... 223 F8
Quantock Ave. C le S DH2 .... 20 A2
Quantock Cl. Darl DL1 .... 209 C5
Quantock Pl. Peter SR8 .... 85 A6
Quarrington Hill Ind Est.
Qua Hi DH6 .... 106 D7
Quarry Burn La. Hunw DL15 .... 125 B8
Quarry Cres. Bear DH7 .... 57 A3
Quarry Farm Cl. Hunw DL15 .... 125 D6
Quarry House Gdns.
E Rain DH5 .... 38 C4
Quarry House La. Durham DH1 .... 57 F1
Quarry House La. E Rain DH5 .... 38 D4
Quarry Houses. Cound DL14 .... 127 B3
Quarry La. Butter DL13 .... 165 E8
Quarry Rd. N Silk SR3 .... 22 B6
Quarry Rd. Stanl DH9 .... 17 F7
Quarry St. N Silk SR3 .... 22 A7
Quarry St. Shild DL4 .... 148 F1
Quarryheads La. Durham DH1 .... 80 C8
Quay The. H le H DH5 .... 39 A3
Quebec St. Darl DL1 .... 209 A2
Quebec St. 2 Lang Pk DH7 .... 56 C6
Quebec Terr. Mick DL12 .... 161 B4
Queen Alexandra Rd.
Seaham SR7 .... 41 D5
Queen Elizabeth Dr.
E Lane DH5 .... 61 D8
Queen St. Bar Cas DL12 .... 201 A5
Queen St. Birt DH3 .... 9 B4
Queen St. Cons DH8 .... 14 F2
Queen St. Crook DL15 .... 100 E3
Queen St. 4 Darl DL3 .... 208 F2
Queen St. H le H DH5 .... 39 A5
Queen St. Seaham SR7 .... 41 C7
Queen St. Shild DL4 .... 149 A2
Queen St. Sland SR2 .... 22 F8
Queen St. W Pel DH2 .... 19 A5
Queen's Ave. Seaham SR7 .... 40 F6
Queen's Pk. C le S DH3 .... 20 D2
Queen's Rd. Bish Au DL14 .... 148 C7
Queen's Rd. Cons DH8 .... 14 E5
Queen's Rd. Wing TS28 .... 108 D8
Queens Dr. Sedge TS21 .... 153 A5
Queens Garth. Sland B DH6 .... 104 B7
Queens Gr. Durham DH1 .... 80 A7
Queens Head Wynd.
Staind DL2 .... 186 D6
Queens Par. Ann Pl DH9 .... 16 F4
Queens Way. Cons DH8 .... 14 C5
Queensbury Rd. Seaham SR7 .... 41 A7
Queensmere. C le S DH3 .... 20 C7
Queensway. H le Sp DH5 .... 38 F8
Queensway. Shild DL4 .... 149 B1
Queensway. Will DL15 .... 102 B2
Quetlaw Rd. Wh Hi DH6 .... 83 E2
Quigley Terr. Birt DH3 .... 9 B6
Quilstyle Rd. Wh Hi DH6 .... 83 E2
Quin Cres. Wing TS28 .... 108 D8
Quin Sq. S Hett DH6 .... 62 A7
Quinn Cl. Peter SR8 .... 85 D5

Raby Ave. Bar Cas DL12 .... 200 F6
Raby Ave. Eas SR8 .... 63 E5
Raby Cotts. Denton DL2 .... 189 D2
Raby Dr. New Ay DL5 .... 150 E1
Raby Gdns. Bish Au DL14 .... 148 B6
Raby Gdns. Burnop NE16 .... 5 E6
Raby Gdns. 7 Shild DL4 .... 149 A2
Raby Rd. Durham DH1 .... 58 C7
Raby Rd. Ferry DL17 .... 129 A6
Raby St. Darl DL3 .... 208 E1
Raby St. Even DL14 .... 167 D6
Raby Terr. Bish Au DL14 .... 147 B1
Raby Terr. Chilt DL17 .... 150 E8
Raby Terr. Cockf DL13 .... 166 C5
Raby Terr. Darl DL3 .... 208 F2
Raby Terr. Will DL15 .... 101 E3
Raby Way. Spenny DL16 .... 128 A8
Racecourse The. Grind TS22 .... 154 F2
Rachel Cl. Ryhope SR2 & SR3 .... 22 C7
Radcliffe St. Birt DH3 .... 9 C3
Rafton Dr. Hartle TS27 .... 111 D3
Raglan Pl. Burnop NE16 .... 6 B6
Raglan St. Cons DH8 .... 14 F2
Ragpath La. Corn DH7 .... 54 C6
Railway Cotts. Darl DL2 .... 224 B6
Railway Cotts. Durham DH1 .... 57 F1
Railway Cotts. Gr Lum DH4 .... 37 F8
Railway Cotts. Wing TS28 .... 84 F1
Railway Cotts. Wit le W DL15 .... 124 F4
Railway Gdns. Ann Pl DH9 .... 16 F4
Railway Houses. Bish Au DL14 .... 148 F4
Railway Pl. Cons DH8 .... 14 D3
Railway St. Ann Pl DH9 .... 17 A3
Railway St. Bish Au DL14 .... 148 C7
Railway St. Cons DH8 .... 15 A2
Railway St. Crag DH9 .... 18 C2
Railway St. H le H DH5 .... 39 A4
Railway St. How le W DL15 .... 124 E7
Railway St. Lanch DH7 .... 32 F3
Railway St. Lang Pk DH7 .... 56 C7
Railway St. Leadg DH8 .... 15 D4
Railway St. Tow Law DL13 .... 75 C2
Railway Terr. Bar Cas DL12 .... 201 A7
Railway Terr. Cornf DL17 .... 105 E2
Railway Terr. Hunw DL15 .... 125 F6
Railway Terr. Hur on T DL2 .... 235 A8
Railway Terr. Shild DL4 .... 170 A8
Railway Terr. Stan Cr DL15 .... 100 F7
Railway Terr. Stanh DL13 .... 71 C1
Railway Terr. Will DL15 .... 102 A3
Railway Terr. Wit le W DL14 .... 124 C3
Raine St. Bish Au DL14 .... 148 B8
Rainton Bridge Ind Est.
H le Sp DH4 .... 38 C7
Rainton Gr. H le Sp DH5 .... 38 E6
Rainton St. Seaham SR7 .... 41 D6
Rainton View. W Rain DH4 .... 37 F2
Raisby Terr. Cornf DL17 .... 105 E1
Ralph Ave. Sland SR2 .... 22 E8
Ramilies. Ryhope SR2 .... 22 D6
Ramona Ave. Kelloe DH6 .... 106 C5
Ramsay Pl. New Ay DL5 .... 171 E7
Ramsay St. Bowb DH6 .... 105 C4
Ramsay St. H Spen NE39 .... 1 A5
Ramsay Terr. Cons DH8 .... 31 B8
Ramsey Cl. Durham DH1 .... 59 A2
Ramsey Cl. Peter SR8 .... 85 D8
Ramsey Cres. Bish Au DL14 .... 147 F4
Ramsey Dr. Ferry DL17 .... 128 E5
Ramsey St. C le S DH3 .... 20 C2
Ramsey Wlk. Darl DL1 .... 209 D5
Ramsgill. 1 Darl DL1 .... 224 C7
Ramsgill House. 2 Darl DL2 .... 224 C7
Ramshaw Cl. Lang Pk DH7 .... 56 A6
Ramshaw Cty Sch. Even DL14 .... 167 C8
Ramshaw La. Even DL14 .... 146 C2
Ramshaw Terr. Kir Me DL16 .... 128 A3
Ramside View. Belm DH1 .... 59 D5
Randolph St. Bish Au DL14 .... 148 F5
Randolph Terr. Even DL14 .... 167 D6
Ranksborough St. Seaham SR7 .... 41 B8
Rannoch Ave. C le S DH2 .... 20 B1
Ranulf Ct. New Ay DL5 .... 171 A8
Raven Ct. Esh W DH7 .... 77 C8
Ravenscar Cl. Whick NE16 .... 2 F5
Ravensdale Rd. Darl DL3 .... 223 D7
Ravensdale Wlk. Darl DL3 .... 223 D8
Ravenside Terr. Cons DH8 .... 14 D4
Ravensworth. Birt DH3 .... 9 D5
Ravensworth. Ryhope SR2 .... 22 D7
Ravensworth Ave. 8
Bish Au DL14 .... 148 B6
Ravensworth Cres. Byer NE16 .... 6 D8
Ravensworth Cres.
Hartle TS24 .... 111 D5
Ravensworth Ct. Crook DL15 .... 101 A3
Ravensworth Ct. S Hett DH6 .... 61 F7
Ravensworth Rd. Birt DH3 .... 9 B5
Ravensworth Rd. Fence DH4 .... 21 F1
Ravensworth Rd. Ferry DL17 .... 129 B6
Ravensworth Terr. 2
Durham DH1 .... 58 D2
Raventhorpe Prep Sch.
Darl DL3 .... 208 C1
Ravenwood Cl. Hartle TS27 .... 111 B4
Rayson Ct. Ingle DL2 .... 188 A6
Reading St. Cornf DL17 .... 105 D1
Reay Ct. 1 C le S DH2 .... 20 C2
Rectory Gdns. Will DL15 .... 102 B3
Rectory La. Blay NE21 .... 2 B8
Rectory La. Cr on T DL2 .... 234 F8
Rectory La. Wols DL13 .... 97 F7
Rectory Rd. H le H DH5 .... 39 A3
Rectory Row. Sedge TS21 .... 153 B6
Rectory View. Shadf DH6 .... 82 E7
Red Banks. C le St DH2 .... 19 F2
Red Barnes Way. Darl DL1 .... 209 D3
Red Cts. Brand DH7 .... 79 C4
Red Firs. Brand DH7 .... 79 B4
Red Hall Cty Prim Sch.
Darl DL1 .... 209 E4
Red Hall Dr. Darl DL1 .... 209 D3
Red Hills Terr. Durham DH1 .... 58 B1
Red House La. Heigh DL2 .... 170 A4
Red Houses. Hi Eth DL14 .... 146 E5
Red Ridges. Brand DH7 .... 79 C4
Red Rose Terr. C le S DH3 .... 20 D2
Redburn Cl. H le Sp DH4 .... 38 C8
Redesdale Ave. Blay NE21 .... 1 F8
Redesdale Ct. Trim TS29 .... 107 E4
Redesdale Rd. C le S DH2 .... 20 A1
Redford La. Hamst DL13 .... 122 D4
Redgate Bank. Wols DL13 .... 74 B1
Redhill Dr. Whick NE16 .... 2 E4
Redhills La. Durham DH1 .... 58 A2
Redhills Way. H le H DH5 .... 39 A2
Redhouse Cl. Sacr DH7 .... 35 D2
Redmarshall Rd. Bish TS21 .... 194 F6
Redmarshall St. Still TS21 .... 174 E3
Redmire Cl. Darl DL1 .... 209 A5
Redmires Cl. Urpeth DH2 .... 8 E1
Redshank Cl. Wash NE38 .... 9 F2
Redwing Cl. Wash NE38 .... 9 F3
Redwood. Brand DH7 .... 79 B4
Redwood. Esh W DH7 .... 77 D7
Redwood Cl. H le H DH5 .... 38 F4
Redwood Cl. Hartle TS27 .... 111 C5
Redwood Ct. Cons DH8 .... 14 E4
Redworth Est. Heigh DL5 .... 170 B3
Redworth Gr. Bish Au DL14 .... 148 E7
Redworth Rd. Darl DL3 .... 208 B4
Redworth Rd. Heigh DL5 .... 170 D2
Redworth Rd. Shild DL4 .... 170 A7
Redworth Way. New Ay DL5 .... 171 D4
Reed Ave. Will DL15 .... 102 A6
Reeth Moor Cl. Darl DL1 .... 224 E8
Reeth Pl. New Ay DL5 .... 171 B8
Regal Dr. Darl DL1 .... 209 B7
Regency Dr. N Silk SR3 .... 22 B8
Regency Dr. Whick NE16 .... 2 F6
Regent Dr. Whick NE16 .... 2 F4
Regent Rd. Ryhope SR2 .... 23 A5
Regent St. Ann Pl DH9 .... 16 F5
Regent St. Bish Au DL14 .... 148 C8
Regent St. Bish Au DL14 .... 148 F4
Regent St. H le H DH5 .... 39 A5
Regent St. Shild DL4 .... 148 F1
Regent Terr. Fishb TS21 .... 131 C4
Regents Ct. Darl DL1 .... 209 C1
Reid St. Darl DL3 .... 208 E3
Reid Street Cty Prim Sch.
Darl DL3 .... 208 E3
Relley Cl. Ush M DH7 .... 57 B1
Relley Garth. Brand DH7 .... 79 D5
Relly Path. Durham DH1 .... 80 A8
Relton Cl. Fence DH4 .... 38 A7
Relton Terr. C le S DH3 .... 20 C2
Rembrandt Way. New Ay DL5 .... 171 D3
Renfrew Pl. Birt DH3 .... 9 D2
Rennie Cl. Darl DL1 .... 209 B2
Rennie St. Ferry DL17 .... 128 E6
Renny St. 5 Durham DH1 .... 58 E2
Renny's La. Belm DH1 .... 59 B2
Rescue Station Cotts.
H le Sp DH5 .... 38 F6
Reservoir Terr. Stan Cr DL15 .... 100 F7
Reynolds Cl. Stanl DH9 .... 17 F6
Reynolds Ct. Peter SR8 .... 86 B6
Rhodes' Terr. Durham DH1 .... 79 F8
Ribble Dr. Darl DL1 .... 223 F6
Richard Ct. Darl DL1 .... 209 A4
Richard St. H le H DH5 .... 39 A3
Richard Terr. Bish Au DL14 .... 148 E4
Richardson Ave. Bish Au DL14 .... 147 F4
Richardson Cl. Winst DL2 .... 203 F6
Richardson Fields.
Bar Cas DL12 .... 201 A6
Richardson Hospl.
Bar Cas DL12 .... 201 A6
Richardson Pl. Kir Me DL16 .... 128 A3
Richardson Terr. 6
Ryhope SR2 .... 23 A6
Richardson Wlk. 6
New Ay DL5 .... 171 E8
Richmond. Ryhope SR2 .... 22 D7
Richmond Ave. Bish Au DL14 .... 148 A6
Richmond Cl. Darl DL3 .... 208 B5
Richmond Cl. Ferry DL17 .... 129 B5
Richmond Ct. Durham DH1 .... 58 D7
Richmond Fields. Spenny DL16 .... 128 B8
Richmond Rd.
Cr on T DL10 & DL2 .... 234 D5
Richmond Rd. Durham DH1 .... 58 D7
Richmond St. By Gr DL 16 .... 126 F8
Richmond Terr. Cr on T DL2 .... 234 F8
Richmond Terr. Hasw DH6 .... 61 F3
Rickleton Ave. C le S DH3 .... 20 D5
Rickleton Prim Sch.
Wash NE38 .... 20 F8
Rickleton Way. Wash NE38 .... 21 A8
Ricknall Ave. New Ay DL5 .... 171 E4
Ricknall La. Mordon DL1 & DL5 .... 172 C3
Ricknall La. New Ay DL1 & DL5 .... 172 C3
Riddell Ct. 5 C le S DH2 .... 20 C2
Ridding Ct. Esh W DH7 .... 77 D8
Ridding Rd. Esh W DH7 .... 77 D8
Ridgeside. Spenny DL16 .... 128 A5
Ridgeway. Birt DH3 .... 9 C6
Ridgeway. Darl DL3 .... 208 F7
Ridgeway. New Ay DL5 .... 171 C4
Ridgeway. Ryhope SR2 .... 22 C6
Riding Hill. Gr Lum DH3 .... 37 A7
Riding Hill Rd. Ann Pl DH9 .... 17 A5
Riding La. Kibble DH9 & NE11 .... 8 B4
Ridley Ave. C le S DH2 .... 20 B2
Ridley Ave. Sland SR2 .... 22 F7
Ridley St. Stanl DH9 .... 17 F7
Ridley Terr. Leadg DH8 .... 15 C3
Ridley Terr. Tow Law DL13 .... 75 B3
Ridlington Way. Hartle TS24 .... 111 E4
Ridsdale St. Darl DL1 .... 209 B1
Rievaulx Ct. Spenny DL16 .... 103 E3
Rigg Head. Lang DL2 .... 188 A2
Rigg La. Holw DL12 .... 159 F2
Riggs The. Brand DH7 .... 79 C5
Riggs The. H le Sp DH5 .... 38 F8
Riggs The. Hunw DL15 .... 125 D5
Ripon Dr. Darl DL1 .... 224 B7
Ripon Dr. Will DL15 .... 101 F2
Ripon Rd. Durham DH1 .... 58 D8
Ripon St. C le S DH3 .... 20 C1
Ripon Terr. Kimble DH2 .... 36 A3
Ripon Terr. Murton SR7 .... 40 C3
Rise Carr Cty Prim Sch.
Darl DL3 .... 208 F5
Rise The. Cons DH8 .... 30 A6
Rise The. Darl DL3 .... 223 D8
Ritson Ave. Bear DH7 .... 57 B3
Ritson Rd. New Ay DL5 .... 171 D6
Ritson St. Cons DH8 .... 14 D4
Ritson St. Stanl DH9 .... 17 F6
Ritson's Rd. Cons DH8 .... 14 D4
River Terr. Mid in T DL12 .... 160 D7
River View. B Mill NE17 .... 4 B6
River View. Will DL15 .... 102 B2
River View Ind Est. Darl DL1 .... 209 C4
River Wlk. Bish Au DL14 .... 147 C2
Riverbank Trad Est. Darl DL1 .... 209 A4
Riverdale. Wols DL13 .... 97 F6
Rivergarth. Darl DL1 .... 209 F6
Rivermead Ave. Darl DL1 .... 209 F6
Riversdale. B Mill NE17 .... 4 B6
Riverside. Bish Au DL14 .... 148 D6
Riverside. Cons DH8 .... 14 C6
Riverside Dr. Darl DL1 .... 209 F5
Riverside Ind Est. Lang Pk DH7 .... 56 C7
Riverside Way. Darl DL1 .... 209 C5
Roast Calf La. Bish Mi DL17 .... 130 C4
Robert Sq. Seaham SR7 .... 41 E6
Robert St. N Silk SR3 .... 22 B7
Robert St. Seaham SR7 .... 41 E6
Robert St. Spenny DL16 .... 127 E7
Robert Terr. Bowb DH6 .... 81 D2
Robert Terr. Stanl DH9 .... 17 F8
Roberts Sq. Cornf DL17 .... 105 D1
Roberts Wlk. 4 Darl DL1 .... 209 B1
Robin Ct. E Rain DH5 .... 38 C3
Robin La. E Rain DH4 & DH5 .... 38 C2
Robin La. W Rain DH4 & DH5 .... 38 C2
Robinson St. Cons DH8 .... 14 E4
Robinson Terr. Burnop NE16 .... 6 A4
Robinson Terr. By Gr DL16 .... 102 E1
Robinson Terr. N Silk SR3 .... 22 B7
Robson Ave. Peter SR8 .... 85 D7
Robson Cres. Bowb DH6 .... 81 D2
Robson Pl. 10 Ryhope SR2 .... 23 A6
Robson Rd. Bish Au DL14 .... 168 B8
Robson St. Cons DH8 .... 15 A3
Robson St. Shild DL4 .... 149 A2
Robson Terr. H Shin DH1 .... 80 F6
Robson Terr. H Spen NE39 .... 1 B3
Robson Terr. Tant DH9 .... 5 F1
Rochdale St. Even DL14 .... 167 C7
Rochdale St. H le H DH5 .... 39 A2
Roche Wlk. Darl DL3 .... 208 A5
Rochester Cl. Bish Au DL14 .... 147 E6
Rochester Rd. Durham DH1 .... 58 D7
Rochester Way. Darl DL1 .... 209 E5
Rock Rd. Spenny DL16 .... 127 E6
Rock Terr. Mid in T DL12 .... 139 E1
Rock Terr. N Bran DH7 .... 78 F8
Rockcliffe House. 3 Darl DL2 .... 224 C7
Rockcliffe Terr. Kir Me DL16 .... 128 A3
Rocket St. Darl DL1 .... 209 B1
Rockhope. Wash NE38 .... 20 F8
Rockingham Dr. Bish Au DL14 .... 147 E6
Rockingham Rd. Will DL15 .... 101 F1
Rockingham St. Darl DL1 .... 224 A8
Rockwell Ave. Darl DL1 .... 209 D6
Rockwell House. Darl DL1 .... 209 C5
Roddymoor Ct. Billy R DL15 .... 100 D7
Roddymoor Rd.
Billy R DL13 & DL15 .... 100 B5
Roddymoor Rd. Billy R DL15 .... 100 D7
Rodham Terr. Stanl DH9 .... 17 F8
Rodney Cl. Ryhope SR2 .... 22 C6
Rodney Wlk. Cound DL4 .... 149 B8
Rodwell St. Wing TS29 .... 107 F5
Roger St. Cons DH8 .... 14 E3
Rogeri Pl. Hartle TS24 .... 111 F3
Rogerley Terr. Ann Pl DH9 .... 16 E5
Rogers Cl. 1 Peter SR8 .... 86 A6
Rogerson Cl. Sland B DH6 .... 104 B7
Rogues La. H Spen NE39 .... 1 A5
Rokeby Pk. Gr Br DL12 .... 202 A1
Rokeby Sq. Durham DH1 .... 80 A7
Rokeby Terr. Hunw DL15 .... 125 E6
Roker Cl. Darl DL1 .... 209 E3
Roman Ave. C le S DH3 .... 20 D3
Roman Mews. W Rain DH4 .... 38 A2
Roman View. Pier DL2 .... 206 B4
Romanway Ind Est.
Bish Au DL14 .... 148 A3
Romney Dr. Belm DH1 .... 59 D5
Ronaldsay Cl. 4 Sland SR2 .... 22 E8
Rookery Gdns. Chilt DL17 .... 150 E6
Rookery La. Whick NE16 .... 2 E4
Rookhope Cty Jun Mix & Inf Sch.
Rook DL13 .... 47 B2
Rookhope Gr. Bish Au DL14 .... 147 E5
Rookswood Gdns. R Gill NE39 .... 1 E3
Rookwood Hunt. New Ay DL5 .... 171 A8
Roosevelt Rd. Durham DH1 .... 58 F3
Roper's Terr. Trim TS29 .... 107 D3
Ropery La. Bourn DH3 .... 20 F3
Ropery La. C le S DH3 .... 20 D2
Ropery Wlk. Seaham SR7 .... 41 E6
Rosa St. Spenny DL16 .... 127 E8
Rosa Street Jun & Inf Sch.
Spenny DL16 .... 127 E8
Rose Ave. Fence DH4 .... 21 F1
Rose Ave. Stanl DH9 .... 17 D5
Rose Cotts. Burnop NE16 .... 5 E5
Rose Cotts. S Hett DH6 .... 62 A7
Rose Cotts. Shot Co SR8 .... 84 E7
Rose Cres. Bourn DH4 .... 21 D3
Rose Cres. Sacr DH7 .... 35 D3
Rose Ct. Esh W DH7 .... 55 C2
Rose Ct. Peter SR8 .... 85 B3
Rose Gdns. Kibble NE11 .... 8 C6
Rose La. Darl DL1 .... 209 E5
Rose Lea. Wit Gil DH7 .... 35 B1
Rose St. 7 H le Sp DH4 .... 38 D8
Rose St. Trim TS29 .... 107 E4
Rose Terr. 6 Lang Pk DH7 .... 56 C6
Rose Terr. Mid in T DL12 .... 160 D8
Rose Terr. Pelton DH2 .... 19 E5
Rose Terr. Stanh DL13 .... 71 A3
Rosebank Cl. Sland SR2 .... 22 E8
Rosebay Ct. Darl DL3 .... 208 E3
Rosebay Rd. Brand DH7 .... 79 E4
Roseberry Cres. Crook DL15 .... 100 D4
Roseberry Cres. Thorn DH6 .... 83 C4
Roseberry Grange Municipal Golf
Course. W Pel DH2 .... 19 B6
Roseberry Rd. Trim TS29 .... 131 D8
Roseberry St. Stanl DH9 .... 18 D7
Roseberry Villas. Pelton DH2 .... 19 C5
Rosebery St. Darl DL3 .... 208 E3
Rosebery Terr. 4 Cons DH8 .... 14 F2
Rosebery Terr. 4 Shild DL4 .... 149 A2
Roseby Rd. Peter SR8 .... 85 F6
Rosedale. Spenny DL16 .... 103 E1
Rosedale Ave. Cons DH8 .... 14 D5
Rosedale Cl. Sedge TS21 .... 153 B7
Rosedale Cres. Darl DL3 .... 208 B4
Rosedale Cres. Shild DL4 .... 149 B1
Rosedale Rd. Belm DH1 .... 59 D4
Rosedale St. H le H DH5 .... 38 E1
Rosedale Terr. Peter SR8 .... 85 F7
Rosedale Terr. Will DL15 .... 102 A3
Roselea Ave. Ryhope SR2 .... 22 F7
Rosemary Ct. 7 Darl DL2 .... 224 C8
Rosemary La. Eas SR8 .... 63 B4
Rosemead Ave. Will DL15 .... 102 A3
Rosemount. Durham DH1 .... 58 D8
Rosemount Ct. Bish Au DL14 .... 148 D5
Rosemount Rd. Bish Au DL14 .... 148 D5
Rosewood. Chilt DL17 .... 150 E8
Rosewood Cl. Sacr DH7 .... 35 C3
Rosewood Gdns. C le S DH2 .... 20 B5
Rosewood Terr. Birt DH3 .... 9 B5
Roslin Terr. Hamst DL13 .... 123 B3
Roslyn St. Darl DL1 .... 224 A8
Ross. Ouston DH2 .... 9 A1
Ross St. 9 Seaham SR7 .... 41 D7
Ross Terr. 3 Ferry DL17 .... 129 A5
Ross Wlk. New Ay DL5 .... 171 F6
Ross Wlk. New Ay DL5 .... 171 F7
Rosslyn Ave. Ryhope SR2 .... 22 F7
Rosslyn Pl. Birt DH3 .... 9 D2
Rossmere. Spenny DL16 .... 103 E2

Toll Bar Rd. Sland SR2 22 E8
Toll House Rd. Durham DH1 57 F2
Tollgate Bglws. Ann Pl DH9 16 E5
Tollgate Fields. W Rain DH4 37 F1
Tollgate Garth. Darl DL1 209 F6
Tollgate Rd. H Mill NE39 4 F5
Tollgate Terr. Ann Pl DH9 16 E5
Tom Raine Ct. Darl DL1 209 A2
Tomlin St. Shild DL4 169 F8
Topaz St. Seaham SR7 41 A7
Torrance Dr. Darl DL1 209 E7
Torver Cl. Peter SR8 85 E6
Tow Law Cty Jun Mix & Inf Sch. Tow Law DL13 75 C2
Tow Law Ind Est. Tow Law DL13 75 B3
Tower Bank. M Law DH7 32 E8
Tower Ct. E Lane DH5 39 C1
Tower Hill. M St G DL2 225 F5
Tower Rd. Darl DL3 208 D3
Tower Rd. M Law DH7 & DH9 16 E1
Tower St. Eas SR8 63 F5
Town End. Mid in T DL12 160 E7
Town Farm Cl. Bish TS21 194 C7
Town Head. Egg DL12 162 C4
Town Head. Mid in T DL12 160 D8
Town Pasture La. Bar Cas DL12 201 D7
Towneley Ct. Stanl DH9 17 E5
Townend Ct. Hut Hen TS28 108 F5
Townley Fields. R Gill NE39 1 F2
Townley Rd. R Gill NE39 1 D2
Trafalgar St. Cons DH8 14 F2
Trafalgar St. Ferry DL17 129 C4
Trafalgar Terr. Darl DL3 208 E4
Trafford Cl. Darl DL1 209 E4
Travellers' Gn. New Ay DL5 171 E5
Treecone Cl. Silk SR3 22 A5
Treelands. Darl DL3 208 C1
Treen Cres. Murton SR7 40 D3
Trefoil Rd. Tanf L DH9 17 D8
Tregoney Ave. Murton SR7 40 D4
Trent Cres. Gr Lum DH3 37 B7
Trent Dale. Leadg DH8 15 D5
Trent Pl. Darl DL1 223 F6
Trent St. E Lane DH5 61 C8
Trevarren Dr. Sland SR2 22 F8
Trevelyan Coll. Durham DH1 80 C7
Trevelyan Pl. Crook DL15 100 C3
Trevelyan Pl. Peter SR8 85 B5
Trevithick Cl. 2 Darl DL1 209 B1
Trevone Sq. Murton SR7 40 D3
Trevor Green N. 5 New Ay DL5 171 E8
Trevor Wlk. 3 New Ay DL5 171 E8
Trident Rd. N Silk SR3 22 A7
Trimdon Grange Cty Inf Sch. Trim TS29 107 D3
Trimdon Jun Sch & Community Coll. Trim TS29 131 E8
Trimdon St Williams RC (Aided) Prim Sch. Trim TS29 131 E7
Trimdon Village Cty Inf Sch. Trim TS29 131 D8
Trinity Rd. Darl DL3 208 E2
Trool Ct. Silk SR3 22 A5
Troon Ave. Darl DL1 209 E6
Trotter Terr. Ryhope SR2 22 F6
Trotter Terr. Shot Co DH6 84 C6
Trout's La. Wit Gil DH1 57 D7
Trout's Lane Sch. Wit Gil DH1 57 E7
Troutbeck Cl. Spenny DL16 103 E2
Troutbeck Way. Peter SR8 85 E7
Trowsdale St. Ann Pl DH9 16 E5
Trueman Gr. 4 Darl DL3 209 A7
Truro Ave. Murton SR7 40 D4
Truro Cl. Darl DL1 209 E5
Tuart St. C le S DH3 20 C3
Tubwell Row. Darl DL1 208 F1
Tudhoe Colliery Jun & Inf Sch. Spenny DL16 104 B4
Tudhoe Grange Comp Sch. Spenny DL16 104 A1
Tudhoe Grange Comp Sch. Spenny DL16 104 A2
Tudhoe Ind Est. Spenny DL16 104 B4
Tudhoe La. Spenny DL16 104 A3
Tudhoe Moor Cty Inf Sch. Spenny DL16 104 B1
Tudhoe Moor. Spenny DL16 104 C1
Tudhoe St Charles's RC Sch. Spenny DL16 104 A2
Tudor Ct. Heigh DL5 170 E1
Tudor Ct. Shot Co DH6 84 D7
Tudor Dr. Tanf DH9 6 D3
Tudor Grange. Eas SR8 63 A3
Tudor Rd. C le S DH3 20 D5
Tudor Terr. Cons DH8 14 E3
Tummel Ct. Silk SR3 22 A6
Tunstall Ave. Bowb DH6 81 D1
Tunstall Bank. Ryhope SR2 & SR3 22 D7
Tunstall Gr. Bish Au DL14 147 F5
Tunstall Gr. Leadg DH8 15 D4
Tunstall Hope Rd. N Silk SR3 22 C8
Tunstall Rd. New Ay DL5 171 C6
Tunstall Terr. Darl DL2 224 B8
Tunstall Terr. N Silk SR2 22 B7
Tunstall Terr. Ryhope SR2 22 D7
Tunstall View. N Silk SR3 22 B8
Tunstall Village Gn. N Silk SR3 22 C7
Tunstall Village Rd. N Silk SR3 22 B7
Tunstall Villas. N Silk SR3 22 B7
Turnberry. Ouston DH2 8 F2
Turnberry Gr. Hartle TS27 111 C4
Turnbull Cres. Murton SR7 40 C3
Turner St. Cons DH8 14 D4
Turnpike Cl. Darl DL1 209 F6
Turnstone Dr. Wash NE38 9 F3
Tursdale Aged Mine Workers War Meml Homes. Cornf DH6 105 C3
Tuscan Cl. N Bran DH7 78 E8
Tutta Bridge Cotts. Gr Br DL12 219 A7
Tweddle Cres. B Rocks TS27 86 F2
Tweddle Terr. Bowb DH6 81 C1
Tweed Ave. Leadg DH8 15 D5
Tweed Cl. Pelton DH2 19 F8
Tweed Cl. Peter SR8 85 D5
Tweed Cl. Sland SR2 22 F8
Tweed Pl. Darl DL1 224 A6
Tweed Rd. Spenny DL16 104 B3
Tweed St. E Lane DH5 61 C8
Tweed Terr. Stanl DH9 17 F5
Twelfth Ave. C le S DH2 20 B4
Twelfth St. Peter SR8 85 F7
Twickenham Rise. Darl DL1 209 F4
Twinsburn Cl. Heigh DL5 170 D1
Twinsburn Rd. Heigh DL5 170 D1
Twizell La. W Pel DH9 18 F5
Tyne Ave. Leadg DH8 15 D5
Tyne Cres. Darl DL1 224 A6
Tyne Cres. Spenny DL16 103 F1
Tyne Rd E. Stanl DH9 17 F5
Tyne Rd. Stanl DH9 17 E5
Tyne St. Cons DH8 15 A2
Tyne St. E Lane DH5 61 C8
Tyne St. 5 Seaham SR7 41 D7
Tyne Terr. Eas SR8 63 D4
Tyne Wlk. Cound DL14 149 C8
Tynedale St. H le H DH5 38 E1
Tynedale Terr. Ann Pl DH9 17 A4
Tynedale Wlk. Shild DL4 170 B8
Tyzack St. Edmon DH7 35 B7

Ugly La. Kimble DH2 35 F4
Ullapool Cl. St on T TS21 195 F3
Ullathorne Rise. Start DL12 200 F5
Ullerdale Cl. Belm DH1 59 E4
Ullswater Ave. E Lane DH5 61 C8
Ullswater Ave. Even DL14 147 A1
Ullswater Cl. Spenny DL16 104 B1
Ullswater Cres. Blay NE21 2 B8
Ullswater Cres. Crook DL15 100 F2
Ullswater Rd. C le S DH2 20 B1
Ullswater Rd. Ferry DL17 128 F5
Ullswater Terr. S Hett DH6 61 E8
Ulnaby La. H Con DL2 206 F6
Union La. C le St DH2 & DH3 36 B7
Union La. Stanh DL13 71 B3
Union Pl. Darl DL1 209 B1
Union St. Bish Au DL14 148 C7
Union St. 3 Darl DL3 208 F2
Union St. H le H DH5 39 A4
Union St. Seaham SR7 41 D6
Union St. 2 Stanh DL13 71 A3
Unity Terr. Ann Pl DH9 17 B4
Unity Terr. Dipton DH9 16 E7
Unity Terr. Tant DH9 6 B2
Unshaw Moor Cty Jun & Inf Sch. Ush M DH7 56 F2
Unsworth Gdns. 7 Cons DH8 14 F2
Unsworth St. 6 Cons DH8 14 F2
Uphill Dr. Sacr DH7 35 D3
Uplands Rd. Darl DL3 208 E1
Uplands The. Birt DH3 9 D5
Upper Archer St. 1 Darl DL3 208 F2
Upper Chare. Peter SR8 85 D6
Upper Church St. Spenny DL16 104 B1
Upper Russell St. Darl DL1 209 A2
Upper Town. Wols DL13 97 F8
Upper Yoden Way. Peter SR8 85 E6
Upsall Dr. Darl DL1 & DL3 223 E8
Urpeth Terr. Beam DH9 19 B7
Urwin St. H le H DH5 39 B3
Ushaw Coll. Lang Pk DH7 56 D4
Ushaw Moor Jun Sch. Ush M DH7 57 A2
Ushaw Terr. Ush M DH7 56 F2
Ushaw Villas. Ush M DH7 56 F1
Usher Ave. Sherb DH6 59 F2

Vale St. E Lane DH5 61 B8
Vale View. Burnh DH7 33 E5
Valeside. Durham DH1 58 B2
Valley Cl. Tow Law DL13 75 B3
Valley Dene. Chopw NE17 4 B7
Valley Dr. Esh W DH7 55 C1
Valley Garth. Esh W DH7 55 C2
Valley Gdns. Cons DH8 14 C4
Valley Gr. Bish Au DL14 148 F5
Valley Gr. Lanch DH7 32 F3
Valley Rd. C le St DH2 19 E3
Valley St N. Darl DL1 209 A3
Valley Terr. How le W DL15 124 F7
Valley View. Ann Pl DH9 16 F5
Valley View. Birt DH3 9 B6
Valley View. Burnop NE16 5 F7
Valley View. Cons DH8 14 B5
Valley View. Cons DH8 31 C6
Valley View. H le H DH5 38 D1
Valley View. Leadg DH8 15 C3
Valley View. R Gill NE39 1 D2
Valley View. Sacr DH7 35 B2
Valley View. Sland B DH6 104 B6
Valley View. Thor DL13 99 B7
Valley View. Ush M DH7 57 B1
Van Mildert Cl. Peter SR8 85 B4
Van Mildert Coll. Durham DH1 80 B6
Van Mildert Rd. New Ay DL5 171 E6
Vancouver St. Darl DL3 208 E3
Vane Ct. Longn TS21 211 F5
Vane Rd. Bar Cas DL12 200 F6
Vane Rd. New Ay DL5 171 E7
Vane Road Jun & Inf Sch. New Ay DL5 171 F7
Vane St. Eas SR8 63 E4
Vane St. N Silk SR3 22 A7
Vane Terr. 7 Cockf DL13 166 C5
Vane Terr. Darl DL3 208 E2
Vane Terr. Seaham SR7 41 D8
Vart Rd. Bish Au DL14 148 B5
Vaughan St. Darl DL3 209 A7
Vaughan St. Shild DL4 148 E1
Vedra Cl. Wear DL13 66 D3
Verdun Terr. Cornf DL17 105 D1
Vere Rd. Bar Cas DL12 200 F6
Verity Rise. 1 Darl DL3 209 A7
Verner Cl. Hartle TS24 111 C5
Verner Rd. Hartle TS24 111 C5
Vernon Gdns. Darl DL1 209 B8
Viador. C le S DH3 20 C4
Vicarage Cl. How le W DL15 124 D7
Vicarage Cl. Pelton DH2 19 E7
Vicarage Cl. S Hett DH6 62 B6
Vicarage Ct. Heigh DL5 170 D1
Vicarage Dr. Trim TS29 107 E1
Vicarage Est. Wing TS28 108 E8
Vicarage Farm Cl. Escomb DL14 147 D8
Vicarage Flats. Brand DH7 79 B4
Vicarage Gdns. Will DL15 102 A3
Vicarage Rd. Cornf DL17 105 E1
Vicarage Rd. Darl DL1 209 B3
Vicarage Rd. N Silk SR3 22 A7
Vicarage Terr. Coxhoe DH6 106 A3
Vicarage Terr. Murton SR7 40 C2
Vicarage Terr. Nent CA9 42 A4
Vicars Cl. Thor Th TS21 175 D3
Viceroy St. Seaham SR7 41 D7
Vickers St. Bish Au DL14 148 B8
Victor St. C le S DH3 20 C3
Victor Terr. Bear DH7 57 B3
Victoria Ave. Bish Au DL14 148 C8
Victoria Ave. Brand DH7 79 C4
Victoria Ave. Crook DL15 100 F3
Victoria Cotts. Butter DL13 165 E8
Victoria Emb. Darl DL1 223 F8
Victoria Gdns. Spenny DL16 127 E7
Victoria La. Cound DL14 149 C8
Victoria Rd. Bar Cas DL12 201 A6
Victoria Rd. Darl DL1 208 F1
Victoria St. Cons DH8 14 E3
Victoria St. Crook DL15 100 E4
Victoria St. 14 Darl DL1 209 B1
Victoria St. Even DL14 167 D6
Victoria St. H le H DH5 39 A4
Victoria St. Lanch DH7 32 E4
Victoria St. Sacr DH7 35 C3
Victoria St. Seaham SR7 41 C7
Victoria St. Shild DL4 170 A8
Victoria St. Shot Co DH6 84 D6
Victoria St. Spenny DL16 127 E7
Victoria St. Will DL15 102 A4
Victoria Terr. Ann Pl DH9 16 F4
Victoria Terr. Beam DH9 19 A7
Victoria Terr. Chilt DL17 150 F8
Victoria Terr. Cockf DL13 166 D5
Victoria Terr. Coxhoe DH6 105 F3
Victoria Terr. 1 Durham DH1 58 B2
Victoria Terr. Hams NE17 4 B6
Victoria Terr. Mid in T DL12 160 D7
Victoria Terr. Murton SR7 40 D2
Victoria Terr. Pelton DH2 19 C6
Victoria Terr. R Gill NE39 1 C1
Victoria Terr. Stanh DL13 71 B2
Victoria Terr. Trim TS29 107 F5
Victory St E. H le H DH5 39 B4
Victory St W. H le H DH5 39 B4
View La. Stanl DH9 17 F7
View Tops. Beam DH9 18 F8
Viewforth Rd. Ryhope SR2 22 F5
Viewforth Villas. Durham DH1 58 A2
Vigo La. Birt DH3 20 D8
Vigodale. Birt DH3 9 E1
Villa Real Bglws. Cons DH8 15 B4
Villa Real Est. Cons DH8 15 A4
Villa Real Rd. Cons DH8 15 A4
Villa St. Spenny DL16 127 E7
Village Cl. New Ay DL5 150 E1
Village Ctr. Wash NE38 20 F8
Village The. Brance DH7 102 E8
Village The. Ca Eden TS27 85 D1
Village The. Ryhope SR2 23 A6
Villas The. Ann Pl DH9 16 E3
Villas The. Burnh DH7 33 D5
Villas The. Ferry DL17 128 E5
Villiers Cl. Chilt DL17 151 A8
Villiers Cl. Darl DL3 208 B2
Villiers Pl. C le S DH3 20 C4
Villiers Pl. 3 New Ay DL5 171 D8
Villiers St. Spenny DL16 127 F8
Vincent St. Eas SR8 63 E4
Vincent St. Seaham SR7 41 D6
Vincent Terr. Ann Pl DH9 17 A3
Vindomora Road. Ebch DH8 3 E4
Vindomora Villas. Ebch DH8 3 E4
Vine Pl. 6 H le Sp DH4 38 E8
Vine St. By Gr DL16 102 E1
Vine St. Darl DL3 208 E3
Vine St. Spenny DL16 103 F1
Viola Cres. Ouston DH2 8 F2
Viola Cres. Sacr DH7 35 D3
Violet Gr. Darl DL1 209 C2
Violet St. H le Sp DH4 38 D8
Violet Terr. Bourn DH4 21 D3
Viscount Rd. 4 N Silk SR3 22 A7
Vivian Cres. C le S DH2 20 C2
Voltigeur Dr. Hart TS27 111 A3
Vulcan St. Darl DL1 209 B4
Vyner St. Spenny DL16 127 E8
Vyners Cl. Spenny DL16 128 A6

Wackerfield. Hilton DL2 167 C2
Waddington St. 1 Bish Au DL14 148 B6
Waddington St. 2 Durham DH1 58 B2
Wadham Cl. Peter SR8 85 B5
Wadham Gr. Darl DL1 209 B6
Wagtail La. Crag DH9 18 A1
Wagtail La. Qua Ho DH9 17 F1
Wagtail Terr. Crag DH9 18 C2
Waine Cres. Bish Au DL14 148 B5
Wakenshaw Rd. Durham DH1 58 F3
Walcher Rd. New Ay DL5 171 D7
Walden Cl. Urpeth DH2 8 D2
Walden Terr. Fishb TS21 131 C4
Waldridge La. C le S DH2 20 A2
Waldridge La. C le St DH2 19 F2
Waldridge La. Wald DH2 35 E7
Waldridge Rd. C le S DH2 & DH3 20 B2
Waldridge Rd. C le St DH2 19 F2
Waldron St. Bish Au DL14 148 B8
Wales St. Darl DL3 209 A5
Walk The. Elwick TS27 134 C5
Walker Dr. Bish Au DL14 148 A4
Walker La. New Ay DL5 171 D5
Walker St. Bowb DH6 105 D8
Walker Terr. Ferry DL17 129 C5
Walker's La. Midd DL5 170 E7
Walkergate. 3 Durham DH1 58 C2
Walkworth La. Spenny DL16 104 A2
Wallace St. H le Sp DH4 38 D8
Wallas Rd. New Ay DL5 171 D6
Waller St. H le Sp DH5 38 E7
Wallflower Ave. Peter SR8 85 F7
Wallington Dr. Sedge TS21 153 A7
Wallish Walls Rd. Shot DH8 13 C1
Wallnook La. Lang Pk DH7 56 D7
Walmer Ave. Bish Au DL14 148 B6
Walpole Cl. Seaham SR7 40 F6
Walter St. Shild DL4 170 A7
Walter Terr. H le H DH5 39 B1
Waltham Cl. Darl DL3 208 B4
Walton Ave. Seaham SR7 40 F6
Walton Cl. Stanl DH9 18 A5
Walton Heath. Darl DL1 209 E6
Walton St. Darl DL1 224 B8
Walton Terr. Cons DH8 15 A4
Walton Terr. Cons DH8 30 A6
Walton Terr. Wing TS28 84 D1
Walton's Bldgs. 1 Ush M DH7 56 F2
Waltons Terr. N Bran DH7 78 F8
Walworth Cres. Darl DL3 208 C5
Walworth Rd. Ferry DL17 129 A7
Walworth Rd. Heigh DL2 190 A5
Walworth Rd. New Ay DL5 171 D4
Walworth Sch. New Ay DL5 171 B8
Wanlass Terr. Durham DH1 58 D2
Wansbeck Ave. Stanl DH9 17 F5
Wansbeck Cl. Pelton DH2 19 F7
Wansbeck Cl. Spenny DL16 103 E2
Wansbeck Ct. Peter SR8 85 C4
Wansbeck Gr. Leadg DH8 15 D5
Wansford Way. Whick NE16 2 F5
Wantage Rd. Belm DH1 59 D5
Warburton Cl. New Ay DL5 171 F7
Ward Ave. R Gill NE39 1 C2
Ward Terr. Wols DL13 98 A7
Warden Gr. H le Sp DH5 38 F7
Wardle St. Qua Ho DH9 17 E3
Ware St. Bar Cas DL12 201 A6
Wareham Way. Will DL15 101 F1
Waring Terr. Seaham SR7 40 F6
Wark St. C le S DH3 20 C2
Warkworth Ave. Bish Au DL14 148 A6
Warkworth Ave. Peter SR8 85 F8
Warkworth Cres. Seaham SR7 40 E7
Warkworth Dr. C le St DH2 36 A8
Warkworth Rd. Durham DH1 58 C7
Warkworth Way. 1 Darl DL1 209 C6
Warnbrook Ave. Murton SR7 40 D2
Warnbrook Cres. B Rocks TS27 86 F2
Warner Gr. 6 Darl DL3 209 A7
Warren Cl. Hartle TS24 111 F1
Warren Rd. Hartle TS24 111 F2
Warren Rd. New Ay DL5 171 D4
Warren St. Darl DL3 208 E3
Warren St. Peter SR8 86 A7
Warwick Ave. Cons DH8 30 A7
Warwick Cl. Spenny DL16 104 A2
Warwick Ct. Durham DH1 80 A7
Warwick Dr. H le Sp DH5 38 E7
Warwick Pl. Peter SR8 85 B7
Warwick Pl. Will DL15 102 A3
Warwick Rd. Bish Au DL14 148 A6
Warwick Road Sch. Bish Au DL14 148 A6
Warwick Sq. Darl DL3 208 B5
Warwick Terr. N Silk SR3 22 A8
Warwick Terr W. N Silk SR3 22 A8
Warwickshire Dr. Belm DH1 59 D2
Wasdale Cl. Peter SR8 85 E6
Washbrook Dr. Darl DL3 209 A7
Washington Ave. M St G DL2 226 B7
Washington Birtley Service Area. Birt DH3 & NE38 9 E3
Washington Cres. New Ay DL5 171 F8
Washington Highway. Pens DH4 & NE38 21 E8
Washington Highway. Wash DH4 & NE38 21 E8
Washington Hospl The. Wash NE38 20 E8
Washington Sq. Eas SR8 63 B3
Waskdale Cres. Blay NE21 2 B8
Waskerley Gr. Bish Au DL14 147 F5
Waskerley Pl. Wols DL13 97 F7
Waskerley Wlk. New Ay DL5 171 A7
Water Gap. Romald DL12 162 B1
Water House Rd. Esh W DL15 77 E4
Water La. Heigh DL5 170 D1
Water St. Sacr DH7 35 C3
Water View. M St G DL2 225 E8
Waterford Cl. E Rain DH5 38 D4
Watergate La. Crook DL15 100 F1
Watergate Rd. Cons DH8 29 F6
Waterloo Cl. Crook DL15 100 E4
Waterloo Terr. Shild DL4 148 E2
Waters End. Gain DL2 205 A6
Waterside. Darl DL3 208 C3
Watkin Cres. Murton SR7 40 C3
Watling Ave. Seaham SR7 40 F6
Watling Rd. Bish Au DL14 148 B4
Watling St. Leadg DH8 15 D4
Watling Street Bglws. Leadg DH8 15 C5
Watling Terr. Will DL15 101 E4
Watling Way. Lanch DH7 32 E3
Watson Cl. Seaham SR7 40 F6
Watson Cl. Wh Hi DH6 84 A3
Watson Cres. Wing TS29 108 B5
Watson Ct. Bar Cas DL12 201 A5
Watson Rd. New Ay DL5 171 C5
Watson St. Burnop NE16 6 B6
Watson St. Cons DH8 14 E4
Watson St. H Spen NE39 1 A5
Watson St. Spenny DL16 127 C5
Watson St. Stanl DH9 17 F8
Watson's Bldgs. Edmon DH7 35 B7
Watt St. Ferry DL17 128 E6
Watts St. Murton SR7 40 C3
Waveney Gdns. Stanl DH9 17 E4
Waveney Rd. Peter SR8 85 B4
Waverley Cl. Blay NE21 1 F8
Waverley Terr. Darl DL1 209 A1
Waverley Terr. Dipton DH9 5 E1
Waverley Terr. Shild DL4 149 A2
Wayland Terr. Darl DL3 208 D5
Wayside. Sland B DH6 104 B6
Wayside Ct. Bear DH7 57 B3
Wayside Rd. Darl DL1 209 B7
Wayside The. Hur on T DL2 224 C1
Wear Ave. Leadg DH8 15 D5
Wear Bank. Wols DL13 97 E5
Wear Chare. Bish Au DL14 126 C1
Wear Cres. Gr Lum DH3 37 B7
Wear Lodge. C le S DH3 20 C7
Wear Rd. By Gr DL16 102 E2
Wear Rd. Stanl DH9 17 F5
Wear St. C le S DH3 20 D2
Wear St. Cons DH8 15 A2
Wear St. Fence DH4 38 A7
Wear St. H le H DH5 39 A3
Wear St. 6 Seaham SR7 41 D7
Wear St. Spenny DL16 127 F8
Wear St. Tow Law DL13 75 C2
Wear Terr. Bish Au DL14 126 C1
Wear Terr. Stanh DL13 71 B2
Wear Terr. Wit le W DL14 124 D4
Wear View. By Gr DL16 102 E1
Wear View. Durham DH1 58 D2
Wear View. Frost DL13 96 B6
Wear View. Hunw DL15 125 E7
Wear View. Toro DL14 125 F2
Weardale Cres. Tow Law DL13 75 B3
Weardale Ct. How le W DL15 124 D7
Weardale Dr. Bish Au DL14 147 F4
Weardale Pk. Wh Hi DH6 84 A3
Weardale St. H le H DH5 38 E1
Weardale St. Spenny DL16 104 B1
Weardale Terr. Ann Pl DH9 17 A4
Weardale Terr. C le S DH3 20 D2
Weardale Wlk. Shild DL4 149 B1
Weare Gr. Still TS21 174 F3
Wearhead Mix Jun & Inf Sch. Wear DL13 66 D4
Wearside Dr. Durham DH1 58 D2
Weatherleyhill La. Satley DL13 & DH8 52 B6
Weaver's Way. Darl DL1 209 A2
Webb Ave. Murton SR7 40 C3
Webb Ave. Seaham SR7 40 F7
Webb Cl. New Ay DL5 171 C7
Webb Sq. Peter SR8 63 E1
Webster House. Durham DH1 58 F2
Wedgwood Rd. Seaham SR7 40 F6
Weeds. Westg DL13 68 B1
Weir St. Darl DL1 209 A2
Welbeck Ave. Darl DL1 209 E5
Welbeck St. Darl DL1 224 A8
Welbury Gr. New Ay DL5 171 F7
Welbury Way. New Ay DL5 171 D2
Weldon Terr. C le S DH3 20 D2
Welfare Cl. Eas SR8 63 E4
Welfare Cres. B Coll TS27 86 C3
Welfare Cres. S Hett DH6 62 B6
Welfare Rd. H le H DH5 39 A4
Welfare Terr. Coxhoe DH6 105 F4
Welford Rd. Cons DH8 30 C8
Well Bank. Billy R DL15 100 E8
Well Bank. L Con DL2 222 E8
Well Bank. New Ay DL5 171 F2
Well Bank. St J Ch DL13 67 A2
Well Chare. Cound DL14 149 B8
Well House Dr. New Ay DL5 150 C1
Well House Ride. New Ay DL5 150 D1
Welland Cl. Peter SR8 85 C4
Wellfield A. J. Dawson Sec Sch. Wing TS28 84 E1
Wellfield Comp Sch. Wing TS28 108 E8
Wellfield Rd. Murton SR7 40 B3
Wellfield Rd. R Gill NE39 1 C2
Wellfield Rd. Wing TS28 84 E1
Wellfield Rd N. Wing TS28 84 E1
Wellfield Rd S. Wing TS28 84 E1
Wellfield Terr. Ryhope SR2 22 E5
Wellfield Terr. Wing TS28 84 F1
Wellgarth. Even DL14 167 C6
Wellhope. Wash NE38 20 F8
Wellington Court Mews. 15 Darl DL1 208 F1
Wellington Dr. Grind TS22 155 D1
Wellington Rd. Bar Cas DL12 201 A7
Wellington St. H Pitt DH6 60 B5
Wells Cl. Darl DL1 209 E5
Wells Cres. Seaham SR7 40 F7
Wells Gr. Will DL15 101 F2
Welsh Terr. Ann Pl DH9 17 A3
Wensley Cl. Urpeth DH2 8 E1
Wensley Terr. Ferry DL17 129 C3

Ordnance Survey

STREET ATLASES

The Ordnance Survey Street Atlases provide unique and definitive mapping of entire counties

Street Atlases available

- Berkshire
- Bristol and Avon
- Buckinghamshire
- Cardiff, Swansea and Glamorgan
- Cheshire
- Derbyshire
- Durham

- Edinburgh
- East Essex
- West Essex
- Glasgow
- North Hampshire
- South Hampshire
- Hertfordshire
- East Kent
- West Kent
- Nottinghamshire

- Oxfordshire
- Staffordshire
- Surrey
- East Sussex
- West Sussex
- Tyne and Wear
- Warwickshire
- South Yorkshire
- West Yorkshire

The Street Atlases are revised and updated on a regular basis and new titles are added to the series. Each title is available in three formats and as from 1996 the atlases are produced in colour. All contain Ordnance Survey mapping except Surrey which is by Philip's.

The series is available from all good bookshops or by mail order direct from the publisher. However, the order form on the following pages may not reflect the complete range of titles available so it is advisable to check by telephone before placing your order. Payment can be made in the following ways:

By phone *Phone your order through on our special Credit Card Hotline on **01933 414000**. Speak to our customer service team during office hours (9am to 5pm) or leave a message on the answering machine, quoting T608N99 C, your full credit card number plus expiry date and your full name and address.*

By post *Simply fill out the order form (you may photocopy it) and send it to: Cash Sales Department, Reed Book Services, PO Box 5, Rushden, Northants, NN10 6YX.*

Ordnance Survey STREET ATLASES ORDER FORM

NEW COLOUR EDITIONS

T608N99 C	HARDBACK	SPIRAL	POCKET	£ Total
	Quantity @ £10.99 each	Quantity @ £8.99 each	Quantity @ £4.99 each	
BERKSHIRE	[ ] 0 540 06170 0	[ ] 0 540 06172 7	[ ] 0 540 06173 5	➤ [ ]
	Quantity @ £12.99 each	Quantity @ £9.99 each	Quantity @ £4.99 each	£ Total
DURHAM	[ ] 0 540 06365 7	[ ] 0 540 06366 5	[ ] 0 540 06367 3	➤ [ ]
HERTFORDSHIRE	[ ] 0 540 06174 3	[ ] 0 540 06175 1	[ ] 0 540 06176 X	➤ [ ]
TYNE AND WEAR	[ ] 0 540 06370 3	[ ] 0 540 06371 1	[ ] 0 540 06372 X	➤ [ ]
SOUTH YORKSHIRE	[ ] 0 540 06330 4	[ ] 0 540 06331 2	[ ] 0 540 06332 0	➤ [ ]
WEST YORKSHIRE	[ ] 0 540 06329 0	[ ] 0 540 06327 4	[ ] 0 540 06328 2	➤ [ ]

BLACK AND WHITE EDITIONS

T608N99 C	HARDBACK	SOFTBACK	POCKET	£ Total
	Quantity @ £12.99 each	Quantity @ £8.99 each	Quantity @ £4.99 each	
BERKSHIRE	[ ] 0 540 05992 7	[ ] 0 540 05993 5	[ ] 0 540 05994 3	➤ [ ]
BUCKINGHAMSHIRE	[ ] 0 540 05989 7	[ ] 0 540 05990 0	[ ] 0 540 05991 9	➤ [ ]
EAST ESSEX	[ ] 0 540 05848 3	[ ] 0 540 05866 1	[ ] 0 540 05850 5	➤ [ ]
WEST ESSEX	[ ] 0 540 05849 1	[ ] 0 540 05867 X	[ ] 0 540 05851 3	➤ [ ]
NORTH HAMPSHIRE	[ ] 0 540 05852 1	[ ] 0 540 05853 X	[ ] 0 540 05854 8	➤ [ ]
SOUTH HAMPSHIRE	[ ] 0 540 05855 6	[ ] 0 540 05856 4	[ ] 0 540 05857 2	➤ [ ]
HERTFORDSHIRE	[ ] 0 540 05995 1	[ ] 0 540 05996 X	[ ] 0 540 05997 8	➤ [ ]
EAST KENT	[ ] 0 540 06026 7	[ ] 0 540 06027 5	[ ] 0 540 06028 3	➤ [ ]
WEST KENT	[ ] 0 540 06029 1	[ ] 0 540 06031 3	[ ] 0 540 06030 5	➤ [ ]
NOTTINGHAMSHIRE	[ ] 0 540 05858 0	[ ] 0 540 05859 9	[ ] 0 540 05860 2	➤ [ ]
OXFORDSHIRE	[ ] 0 540 05986 2	[ ] 0 540 05987 0	[ ] 0 540 05988 9	➤ [ ]
EAST SUSSEX	[ ] 0 540 05875 0	[ ] 0 540 05874 2	[ ] 0 540 05873 4	➤ [ ]
WEST SUSSEX	[ ] 0 540 05876 9	[ ] 0 540 05877 7	[ ] 0 540 05878 5	➤ [ ]

See more titles overleaf

Ordnance Survey STREET ATLASES ORDER FORM

BLACK AND WHITE EDITIONS

T608N99 C	HARDBACK Quantity @ £10.99 each	SOFTBACK Quantity @ £8.99 each	POCKET Quantity @ £4.99 each	£ Total
SURREY	☐ 0 540 05983 8	☐ 0 540 05984 6	☐ 0 540 05985 4	➤ ☐
WARWICKSHIRE	☐ 0 540 05642 1			➤ ☐

BLACK AND WHITE EDITIONS

T608N99 C	HARDBACK Quantity @ £12.99 each	SOFTBACK Quantity @ £9.99 each	POCKET Quantity @ £4.99 each	£ Total
BRISTOL AND AVON	☐ 0 540 06140 9	☐ 0 540 06141 7	☐ 0 540 06142 5	➤ ☐
CARDIFF	☐ 0 540 06186 7	☐ 0 540 06187 5	☐ 0 540 06207 3	➤ ☐
CHESHIRE	☐ 0 540 06143 3	☐ 0 540 06144 1	☐ 0 540 06145 X	➤ ☐
DERBYSHIRE	☐ 0 540 06137 9	☐ 0 540 06138 7	☐ 0 540 06139 5	➤ ☐
EDINBURGH	☐ 0 540 06180 8	☐ 0 540 06181 6	☐ 0 540 06182 4	➤ ☐
GLASGOW	☐ 0 540 06183 2	☐ 0 540 06184 0	☐ 0 540 06185 9	➤ ☐
STAFFORDSHIRE	☐ 0 540 06134 4	☐ 0 540 06135 2	☐ 0 540 06136 0	➤ ☐

Name..

Address..

....

....Postcode

◆ Free postage and packing

◆ All available titles will normally be dispatched within 5 working days of receipt of order but please allow up to 28 days for delivery

☐ Please tick this box if you do not wish your name to be used by other carefully selected organisations that may wish to send you information about other products and services

Registered Office: Michelin House, 81 Fulham Road, London SW3 6RB.
Registered in England number: 1974080

I enclose a cheque / postal order, for a **total** of ☐

made payable to *Reed Book Services*, or please debit my

☐ Access ☐ American Express ☐ Visa

account by ☐

Account no ☐☐☐☐ ☐☐☐☐ ☐☐☐☐ ☐☐☐☐

Expiry date ☐☐ ☐☐

Signature..

Post to: Cash Sales Department, Reed Book Services, PO Box 5, Rushden, Northants, NN10 6YX

T608N99 C